Gender in the Ancient Near East

Gender in the Ancient Near East is a wide-ranging study through text and art that presents our current understanding of gender constructs in ancient Mesopotamia, Egypt, Anatolia, Cyprus, and the Levant, and incorporates current trends in gender theory.

Budin begins with definitions of sex and gender in modern society and scholarship before exploring ancient Near Eastern understandings of these concepts. Readers are then guided through sources in translation in order to understand how the denizens of the ancient Near East understood notions of femininity, masculinity, and other, with a final chapter considering how modern notions of hetero- and homosexuality apply to the ancient world. The volume also explores how these concepts are portrayed in ancient art and material culture through accompanying photographs and illustrations. The overview of both Near Eastern history and contemporary gender theory allows readers unfamiliar with the material easily to approach the subject and draw meaningful conclusions.

Gender in the Ancient Near East offers a comprehensive and engaging introduction to the subject for students of the ancient Near East and of gender in the ancient world. It is also of interest to those working in gender studies and queer studies.

Stephanie Lynn Budin is an ancient historian specializing in Greece and the Near East. She has published numerous books and articles on sex, gender, mythology, religion, and iconography, including *Freewomen, Patriarchal Authority, and the Accusation of Prostitution* (Routledge 2021) and *Artemis* (Routledge 2016).

Gender in the Ancient Near East

Stephanie Lynn Budin

LONDON AND NEW YORK

Cover image: Votive bed with an embracing couple, middle of the 2nd millennium BCE. Middle Elamite period (Iran). Discovery site: Susa. Paris, Louvre. Bas-relief, terracotta, Height: 0.1 m, Length: 0.06 m. Inv.: SB5888. Photographer: Hervé Lewandowski/Franck Raux © 2022. RMN-Grand Palais/Dist. Photo SCALA, Florence.

First published 2023
by Routledge
4 Park Square, Milton Park, Abingdon, Oxon OX14 4RN

and by Routledge
605 Third Avenue, New York, NY 10158

Routledge is an imprint of the Taylor & Francis Group, an informa business

© 2023 Stephanie Lynn Budin

The right of Stephanie Lynn Budin to be identified as author of this work has been asserted in accordance with sections 77 and 78 of the Copyright, Designs and Patents Act 1988.

All rights reserved. No part of this book may be reprinted or reproduced or utilised in any form or by any electronic, mechanical, or other means, now known or hereafter invented, including photocopying and recording, or in any information storage or retrieval system, without permission in writing from the publishers.

Trademark notice: Product or corporate names may be trademarks or registered trademarks, and are used only for identification and explanation without intent to infringe.

British Library Cataloguing-in-Publication Data
A catalogue record for this book is available from the British Library

Library of Congress Cataloging-in-Publication Data
Names: Budin, Stephanie Lynn, author.
Title: Gender in the ancient Near East / Stephanie Lynn Budin.
Description: Abingdon, Oxon; New York, NY: Routledge, 2023. | Includes bibliographical references and index.
Identifiers: LCCN 2022048614 (print) | LCCN 2022048615 (ebook) | ISBN 9780367331535 (hardback) | ISBN 9780367331542 (paperback) | ISBN 9780429318177 (ebook)
Subjects: LCSH: Women—History—To 500. | Women—Middle East—History. | Sex role—Middle East—History.
Classification: LCC HQ1137.M628 B83 2023 (print) | LCC HQ1137.M628 (ebook) | DDC 305.309394—dc23/eng/20221017
LC record available at https://lccn.loc.gov/2022048614
LC ebook record available at https://lccn.loc.gov/2022048615

ISBN: 978-0-367-33153-5 (hbk)
ISBN: 978-0-367-33154-2 (pbk)
ISBN: 978-0-429-31817-7 (ebk)

DOI: 10.4324/9780429318177

Typeset in Times New Roman
by Apex CoVantage, LLC

Printed in the United Kingdom
by Henry Ling Limited

Contents

List of Figures	vi
Chronologies	ix
Acknowledgments	xi
List of Maps	xii

1	Sex and Gender in Theory and Practice	1
2	Femininity	45
3	Masculinity	115
4	Gender Bending	175
5	Sexuality	247
	Bibliography	289
	Index	305

Figures

1.1	Rahotep and Nofret, Egyptian Museum, Cairo.	22
1.2	Figure of a Woman, Old Kingdom, Metropolitan Museum of Art 58.125.3.	22
1.3	Severed Penises Relief on Great War Temple of Ramesses III at Medinet Habu.	27
1.4	Iranian Kourotrophic Terracotta Plaque, Louvre Museum Sb 6582.	34
1.5	Ivory Plaque with Winged, Kourotrophic Goddess from Ugarit, Damascus Museum 3599.	35
1.6	Predynastic Ivory Kourotrophic Figurine, Ägyptisches Museum, Berlin, 14441.	35
1.7	Bronze Kourotrophic Figurine from Horoztepe, Museum of Anatolian Civilizations.	36
1.8	Early Bronze Age Jug from Pyrgos, Cyprus T.35/16+17, Limassol District Museum LM 1739/7.	38
2.1	Chalcolithic Cruciform Figurine from Yalia, Cyprus Museum, Nicosia, 1934/III-2/2.	47
2.2	Female Statuette from Lemba, Cyprus Museum, Nicosia, 1976/54.	48
2.3	Early Cypriot Plank Figurine, Cyprus Museum, Nicosia, 1963/IV-20/12.	48
2.4	Bomford Figurine, Cyprus, Ashmolean Museum AN1971.888.	49
2.5	Anthropomorphic Jar Handle from Kiš, Ashmolean Museum AN1925.230.	52
2.6	Type 1 Potency/Fertility Figurine, Egypt, Brooklyn Museum, 44.226.	56
2.7	Statuette of Wife of Merti, Old Kingdom, Metropolitan Museum of Art 26.2.3.	56
2.8	New Kingdom Wooden Statuette, Brooklyn Museum 54.29.	57
2.9	New Kingdom Ivory Figurine, Brooklyn Museum 40.126.2.	58
2.10	Funerary Wall Painting from the Tomb of Nebamun, British Museum EA 37986.	59
2.11	*Book of the Dead of Sesu*, Detail, British Museum EA 9941.1.	59
2.12	Stela of Qeh, British Museum EA191.	60
2.13	Diyala Female Terracotta Figurine, Oriental Institute A17892.	61

Figures vii

2.14	Nippur-Style Female Terracotta Figurine, MMA 59.41.21.	61
2.15	Silver and Gold Statuette from Hasanoğlan, Anatolia, Museum of Anatolian Civilizations, 13922.	62
2.16	Late Cypriot Bird Face Figurine, British Museum A 15.	62
2.17	Middle Bronze Age Terracotta Nude Female Figurine from Ebla, Syria, Aleppo Museum TM.92.P. 875+TM.94.P. 530.	63
2.18	Terracotta Plaque from Gezer, Israel, Ashmolean Museum 1912.621.	63
2.19	Gold Foil Dove "Goddess" from Grave Circle A, Shaft Grave III, Mycenae, Athens National Archaeological Museum 27.	64
2.20	Daidalic Terracotta of Anasyrma Female from Kato Syme Viannou, Crete, Herakleion Museum.	64
2.21	Cylinder Seal and Modern Impression from Ur III-Period Nippur, Oriental Institute 3346.	84
2.22	Old Babylonian Terracotta Plaque, Oriental Institute 9335.	85
2.23	Statue of Gudea of Lagaš, Metropolitan Museum of Art 59.2.	86
2.24	Cypriot Scenic Composition, Louvre AM 816.	92
2.25	Archaic Cypriot Terracotta Grinding Scene, Metropolitan Museum of Art 74.51.1643, Cesnola Collection.	93
2.26	Nubian Cemetery at Nuri.	94
2.27	Lunette of the Coronation Stela of King Aspelta, Egyptian Museum, Cairo, JE 48866.	95
2.28	Uqnitum Seal.	109
2.29	Composite Drawing of Seal Impression of Tar'am Agade (AFc1).	110
3.1	Narmer Palette, Egyptian Museum, Cairo, CG 14716.	125
3.2	Lion Hunt Stela, Baghdad Museum, 10113052.	127
3.3	Stele of the Vultures, Louvre Museum, AO 16 IO9, AO 50, AO 2246, AO 2348.	128
3.4	Neo-Assyrian Relief Showing Detail of the Battle of Til Tuba, British Museum, 124801.	137
3.5	Neo-Assyrian Relief Showing Aššurbanipal in Garden, British Museum, 124920.	137
3.6	King Tutankhamun in Chariot, Painted Chest, Egyptian Museum, Cairo.	138
3.7	Plan of Burial at Mari, Cyprus.	139
3.8	Statue of the God Min, Ashmolean Museum AN 1894.105e.	145
3.9	*Ša Rēši* Seals from the Reign of Adad-Nerari III.	161
3.10	Throne Dais of Šalmanezer III, Baghdad Museum.	162
3.11	Aššurnaṣirpal Relief, British Museum 124533.	163
3.12	Neo-Assyrian Relief of Sargon II with a *ša rēši*, Oriental Institute 872.	165
4.1	Early Dynastic Dedicatory Figurines from Tell Asmar, Oriental Institute D32373.	193
4.2	Akkadian Seal Depicting Ištar, Oriental Institute A27903.	203
4.3	Stela of Qeh, Bottom Detail, British Museum EA191.	210

viii *Figures*

4.4	Statue of Sobekneferu, Louvre E 27135.	217
4.5	Graffito of Hatshepsut and Senenmut from the Granite Quarries of Aswan at el-Mahatta.	219
4.6	Hatshepsut in the Chapelle Rouge at Karnak, Thebes.	220
4.7	Diorite Statue of Hatshepsut, Metropolitan Museum of Art 30.3.3.	221
4.8	Statue of Hatshepsut from Deir el-Bahri, Metropolitan Museum of Art 29.3.2.	221
4.9	Statue of Hatshepsut from Djeser-djeseru, Metropolitan Museum of Art 28.2.18.	222
4.10	Relief of Hatshepsut and Thutmosis III at the Chapelle Rouge at Karnak, Thebes.	223
4.11	Early Cypriot Anthropomorphic Terracotta Figurine, Glasgow Art Gallery and Museum.	234
4.12	Terracotta Figurine, possibly from Paphos, Berlin Museum Antiquarium T.C. 6683.	235
4.13	Early Cypriot White Painted Figurine from Ayia Paraskevi, Cyprus Museum, Nicosia, CS2028/I.	235
4.14	Middle Cypriot Red Figure Kourotrophos, Oriental Institute X.1611.	236
4.15	Middle Cypriot Terracotta Figurine, K. Severis Collection, Nicosia, 1539.	237
4.16	Middle Cypriot Dark Ware Figurine, Metropolitan Museum of Art 74.51.1537.	237
4.17	Late Cypriot Bird Face Figurine from Hala Sultan Teke, Larnaca District Museum 1021.	238
4.18	Statue of Ur-Nanše, National Museum of Damascus S 2071.	239
5.1	Scene from Mastaba of Niankhkhnum and Khnumhotep.	266

Chronologies

Egypt

3100–2686—Early Dynastic (Dynasties I–II)
2686–2181—Old Kingdom (Dynasties III–VI)
2180–2040—First Intermediate Period (Dynasties VII–XI)
2040–1730—Middle Kingdom (Dynasties XI–XIII)
1730–1550—Second Intermediate Period (Dynasties XIII–XVII; Hyksos Interlude)
1550–1080—New Kingdom (Dynasties XVIII–XX)
1080–664—Third Intermediate Period (Dynasties XXI–XXV)
664–525—Saïte Period (Dynasty XXVI)
525–332—Late Period (Dynasties XXVII–XXXI)

Mesopotamia

2900–2334—Early Dynastic
2334–2159—Akkadian Empire
2159–2112—Gutian Invasions; Reign of Gudea of Lagaš (c. 2150–2125)
2112–2004—Third Dynasty of Ur
2017–1792—Isin-Larsa Period
1813–1781—Old Assyrian Empire (Age of Samsî-Addu)
1792–1595—Old Babylonian Empire (Age of Hamurapi)
1595–1155—Kassite Era
1365–1031—Middle Assyrian Empire
934–612—Neo-Assyrian Empire
614–539—Neo-Babylonian Empire
550–331—Achaemenid Empire (Persia)
331–64 BCE—Hellenistic/Parthian

Cyprus

3800–3500—Early Chalcolithic
3500–2800—Middle Chalcolithic
2800–2300—Late Chalcolithic

x *Chronologies*

2500–2250—Philia Facies
2250–1900—Early Cypriot Bronze Age (EC)

    2250–2075—EC I
    2075–2000—EC II
    2000–1900—EC III

1900–1600—Middle Cypriot Bronze Age (MC)

    1900–1800—MC I
    1800–1725—MC II
    1725–1600—MC III

1600–1050—Late Cypriot Bronze Age (LC)

    1600–1450—LC I
    1450–1200—LC II
    1200–1050—LC III

1050–950—Cypro-Geometric I
950–900—Cypro-Geometric II
900–750—Cypro-Geometric III
750–600—Cypro-Archaic I
600–475—Cypro-Archaic II
475–400—Cypro-Classical I
400–300—Cypro-Classical II
300–50 BCE—Hellenistic

The Hittites

c. 1750—Age of the Assyrian trading colony at Karum Kaneš/Kültepe.
1650–1400—Old Kingdom
1400—c. 1200—New Kingdom

The Levant

4300–3300—Chalcolithic (Proto-Bronze Age)
3300–3050—Early Bronze Age (EBA) I
3050–2300—Early Bronze II–III
2300–2000—EB IV–Middle Bronze Age (MBA) I
2000–1750—MBA IIA
1750–1550—MBA IIB–C
1550–1400—Late Bronze Age (LBA) I
1400–1200—LBA II
1200–1000—Iron Age I
1000–586—Iron Age II
586–538—Babylonian Captivity (Israel-Palestine)
538–330—Persian Period
330–63—Hellenistic Period
63 BCE–640 CE—Roman/Byzantine Period

Acknowledgments

My heartfelt thanks go out to numerous people who helped in the writing of this book, either by sending me bibliographies, test-reading sections and chapters, providing photographs, or serving as very patient and (for the most part) tactful sounding boards. Eternal gratitude goes forth to Solange Ashby, Danielle Candelora, Shawna Dolansky, David Greenberg, Alison Acker Gruseke, Josué J. Justel, Marc Orriols-Llonch, Takayoshi Oshima, Ilan Peled, Thais Rocha da Silva, Elisa Roßberger, Janine Wende (digital librarian extraordinaire!), and Ilona Zsolnay. My thanks to the ANE and Egyptology "Libraries" that provided so many PDFs in an age of COVID-19 when the physical libraries were all shut down. It was a very interesting time to be writing a book. . . . Needless to say, all remaining errors and typos are my own.

Thanks to Amy Davis-Poynter at Routledge for inviting me to write this book and to Marcia Adams for helping get this project through to completion. You have both been very patient.

All due acknowledgement and gratitude go out to Agnès Garcia-Ventura and Saana Svärd for creating the Gender and Methodology in the Ancient Near East (GeMANE) series of symposia and publications. You are the mid-wives who are bringing forth gender studies in the ANE! Thank you!

My deepest appreciation to the Oriental Institute at the University of Chicago for making so many materials, both in text and image, so easily accessible. You are the model for an academic institution that generates, preserves, and disperses knowledge.

Finally, as ever, my most deeply felt gratitude goes to my husband Paul C. Butler for art, technical support, moral support, pretty much every possible kind of support, and lots of patience (a recurring theme in these acknowledgements). None of this would be possible without you.

Maps

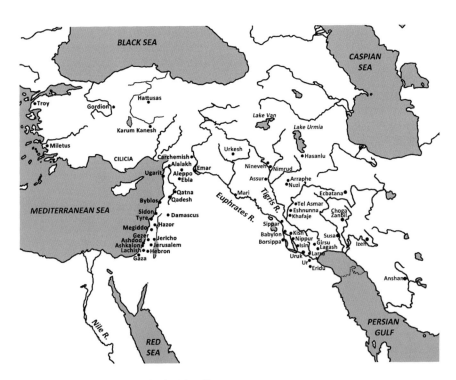

Map 1 Map depicting sites in the Near East.

Maps xiii

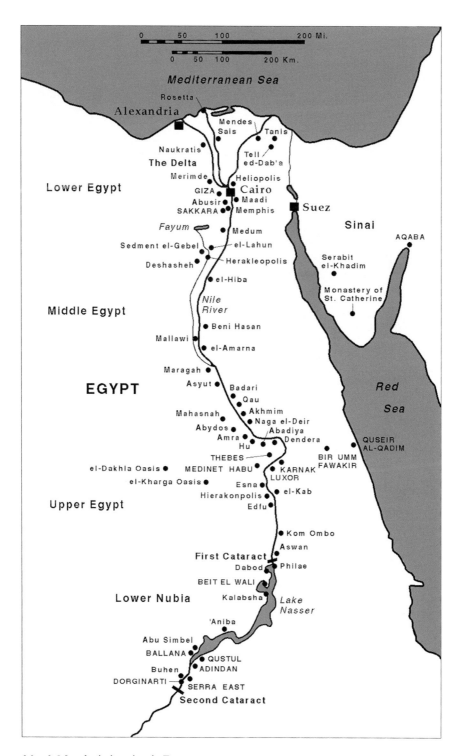

Map 2 Map depicting sites in Egypt.

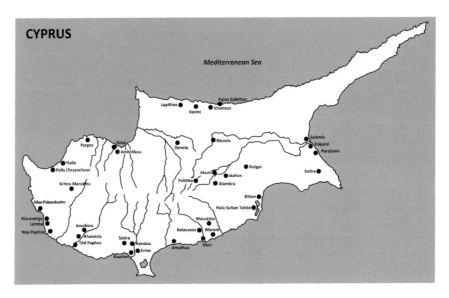

Map 3 Map depicting sites in Cyprus.

1 Sex and Gender in Theory and Practice

This is a book about gender in the ancient Near East, so a few definitions are in order. First: ancient Near East. This books considers the matter of gender in the regions of the eastern Mediterranean from the 3rd through the 1st millennia BCE. The areas covered include Mesopotamia, the Levant, Egypt, and to a lesser extent Anatolia and pre-Hellenic Cyprus (see maps in previous section).

Far more complicated is the definition of *gender*. Very basically, *gender is the beliefs held about individuals based on their sex*. These two concepts—gender and sex—have a complicated relationship in modern society and academia especially, so allow me this opportunity to discuss what they are and how they relate to each other.

Sex

"Sex" refers to which one of two roles an organism plays in those forms of reproduction that combine the genes of two organisms in the creation of the next generation—known as "sexual reproduction." Sexual reproduction involves the combination of two distinct cell types, both called gametes: One type (sperm) enters into the other (egg) to fertilize it. The egg then contains the combined genetic material of both parents to create the offspring. The organisms that produce sperm are called *male*, and the organisms that produce eggs are called *female*. This goes for humans, most vertebrates, and several species of plants. Basically, "sex" refers to gamete size and action.[1]

Sex, then, is a biological, reproductive designation. In many species, especially birds and mammals, this creation of distinct gametes also induces further anatomical differences between males and females, for in addition to creating eggs, females also spend some amount of time with the offspring residing in their bodies. For birds, this involves the anatomical ability to store eggs before laying them. For mammals—including humans—this involves incubating the offspring within a specialized organ (e.g. the uterus) for weeks or months before giving birth and supplying the offspring with milk, created by the mammary glands that give mammals their name. So there are anatomical differences between females and males based on the role played in reproduction: impregnatee or impregnator.

DOI: 10.4324/9780429318177-1

2 Sex and Gender in Theory and Practice

Finally, there are physiological differences that might emerge between males and females based on the need to attract mates and to defend offspring. This is especially visible in birds. Generally speaking, male birds are more colorful than females of the same species and have song-singing capabilities so as to attract a female mate for reproducing (many can also dance!). By contrast, female birds tend to be more drab the better to hide and to protect vulnerable offspring from predators.

Sex might practically be understood on two levels: genotype and phenotype— what is going on in the cells themselves (i.e. DNA) and how those traits visibly manifest in/on the body. The following is a quick explication of how these two categories function for humans specifically.

Genetics

As discussed previously, the cells that combine to form a new human are *sperm*, which contain 23 chromosomes (22 autosomes plus an X or Y chromosome) with minimal cytoplasm, and *eggs*, which contain 23 chromosomes (22 autosomes plus an X chromosome) and enough cytoplasm to sustain the new human until it can receive nutrients and gasses from the mother via the umbilical cord. The sperm penetrates the egg to fertilize it, meaning that the two sets of 23 chromosomes join to form a new human with the standard 46 chromosomes, assuming everything goes right (which is not always the case). Sperm are produced by males, who have X and Y chromosomes; eggs are produced by females, who have only X chromosomes.

It is first and foremost the X and Y chromosomes that code for whether a human will be female or male, although the genes on other chromosomes are also necessary for creating the full sexual phenotype. Furthermore, the genes on the X chromosome perform several functions other than just sex expression, including the formation of red blood cells and the regulation of blood clotting; regulation of copper levels in the body; and proper kidney, muscle, and nerve functions. Basically, a human cannot exist without at least one X chromosome.[2] By contrast, the tiny Y chromosome hardly has any genes at all, more than 95% of which code for the formation of the male phenotype.[3]

Two additional data are necessary to know. First, as noted, the human body cannot develop without an X chromosome. In the absence of a Y chromosome (and sometimes in the presence of one—see subsequently) the human body will develop as female.[4] There is no such thing as a sex-neutral human; it is a genetic impossibility. Second, a gene on the X chromosome called X Inactive-Specific Transcript (or XIST for short) turns off all but one X chromosome in every cell that has more than one. So, in an XX female, for example, only the genes from one of those Xs actually manifest, while the genes on the other X remain dormant.[5]

Phenotype

After fertilization, the human embryo begins in an *indifferent stage*, when the sex is not yet phenotypically expressed. In the fourth week of development, the embryo develops a "genital ridge" near the kidneys; in the seventh week, this

Sex and Gender in Theory and Practice 3

becomes the "bipotential gonad," which can form either testes or ovaries. If the embryo contains at least one X chromosome and no Y, two genes work together to form ovaries: the DAX1 gene on the X chromosome and WNT4 on chromosome 1. The ovaries then produce estrogen, which turns on other genes to form the female phenotype. If a Y chromosome is present, its gene called Sex-determining Region Y (a.k.a. SRY)—also called testis-determining factor (TDF)—turns the bipotential gonad into testes in the tenth week of pregnancy. These produce testosterone, which induces the formation of a male phenotype.[6] So, generally speaking, the combination of two X chromosomes (one from the mother, one from the father) yields a phenotypic female. The combination of X and Y (X from mom, Y from dad) yields a male.

At birth, there is not much by way of phenotypic difference between females and males other than the reproductive organs—females have labia, a clitoris, a vagina, and the internal organs of ovaries, fallopian tubes, and uterus, as well as mammary glands; males have a penis and testes. These are called primary sexual attributes. Once puberty starts changing human children into reproductive adults, secondary sexual attributes develop. Females develop breasts as the mammary glands mature; the ovaries start releasing eggs into a uterus that begins the approximately monthly build-up of lining that, if unused, discharges as the menses. For males, the testes start generating sperm that must itself discharge one way or another, and the voice deepens. Both sexes grow hair on the body, most males (and some females) grow hair on the face as well.

Other differences between females and males are mainly statistical. *In general*, based on population, males are slightly larger than females (although not to the same degree we see in mammals such as walruses or gorillas). But this is based on distinct population: Viking males might be slightly larger than Viking females, but Viking females are larger than ancient Greek males, and so on. In archaeological physical anthropology (the study of ancient human remains), bones can be sexed based on crania (the head), but local variations and tendencies must dominate the analysis. Basically, it is better to sex bones with pelvic structures, where differences between male and female are consistently pronounced. Likewise, males tend to be slightly stronger than comparable females, but this can also be swayed by lifestyle: A hard-working peasant woman probably has far more upper-body strength (and lower-body strength, for that matter) than a male white-collar worker plopped in front of a computer all day. The same can obviously also be said for a female tennis pro versus a male golfer . . .[7]

It is basically safe to say that the main biological differences between females and males are genetically in their X and Y chromosomes and physiologically in their reproductive organs and anatomy. Everything else is subject to population and lifestyle.

Is Sex Binary?

This is a question that comes up frequently in modern academia. It is predicated on two basic ideas: 1) not 100% of humans conform to the XX/XY = female/

4 *Sex and Gender in Theory and Practice*

male paradigm, and 2) there is no actual distinction between "biological" sex and "social" gender. We shall deal with the first issue here and take up the second after the discussion of gender.

The idea of non-binary sex[8] seems to have gotten its start in *popular* culture in 1993, when biologist Anne Fausto-Sterling published the article "The Five Sexes: Why Male and Female Are Not Enough" in *The Sciences*. Here she wrote about no fewer than three categories of humans who were not standard XX females or XY males but varieties of intersex. Thus, the "herm" (a true hermaphrodite with one testis and one ovary), the "merm" (with a testis and some aspects of the female genitalia), and the "ferm" (with ovaries and some aspects of male genitalia).[9] These, together with "true" males and females, would account for her five sexes. But perhaps even these were not enough,

> For biologically speaking, there are many gradations running from female to male; and depending on how one calls the shots, one can argue that along that spectrum lie at least five sexes—and perhaps even more. . . . Indeed, I would argue further that sex is a vast, infinitely malleable continuum that defies the constraints of even five categories.[10]

Although statistics were rather difficult to come by—this not being the sort of information one puts on a job application, say—Fausto-Sterling quoted John Money of Johns Hopkins University, a specialist in congenital organ defects (and world expert on hermaphroditism, as it was then called), saying that intersexed individuals may constitute up to 4% of lives births.[11] Four people out of every 100 are probably neither male nor female.

The academy went wild. Speaking for feminist theorists, Nancy Tuana, in her 1996 article "Fleshing Gender/Sexing the Body: Refiguring the Sex/Gender Distinction," declared,

> Calling us back to the "facts" of biology, Fausto-Sterling reminds us of intersexuality. She calls attention to the fact that intersexuals may constitute as many as 4 percent of births, yet their existence has been incredibly well erased by current medical practices and completely denied by Western legal systems.[12]

All new approaches emerged to uninscribe sex and gender from ancient depictions of humans. Thus in her 2005 article "The Gendered Sea: Iconography, Gender, and Mediterranean Prehistory" Lauren Talalay, an Aegean archaeologist, argued:

> What is clear from recent scholarship is that we can no longer think of these early images in simple sexual terms—figures may depict males, females, perhaps some kind of "third gender" hybrids, intentionally ambiguous representations, or even images that moved in and out of traditional sexual categories. Early Mediterranean taxonomies appear to have embraced multiple or ambiguous genders, a kind of general messiness that rubs against the grain of Western discourse.[13]

Sex and Gender in Theory and Practice 5

For art historian and specialist in prehistoric figurines Douglas Bailey:

> However, in light of what is now *uncontroversial* anthropological, sociological, and other social science research, the assumption that concepts such as male and female were static across time and space is unsupportable. Our error . . . has been to oversimplify the ways in which people thought about identity and indeed about what it meant to be human. . . . Their [figurines] use rests on the acceptance of a third assumption: that there was something that was conceived of as "female" and another thing understood as "male" in the European Neolithic. This assumption is also false. Having recognized that the majority of figurines have neither male nor female body parts, but are asexual, sexless, or perhaps most accurately "corporeal," it is less easy to accept that there were clear and stable Neolithic concepts of male and female.[14]

Archaeology merged with genetics merged with feminist theory to create whole new understandings of human biology:

> From such a standpoint, an individual's sex would not have to conform to a predetermined definition or result in specific behaviours; instead sex and sexuality are positioned upon a spectrum unbounded by prediscursive categories. . . . Taking the argument into the realms of the cellular, it has been argued that not even the usual genetic markers of sex are still accepted as indicating a clear biological distinction between the sexes. More and more evidence is summoned which shows that there are variations on the commonly accepted XX = female/XY = male paradigm, including XX males and XY females, and individuals with XXY, XXXY, and XXXXY who display male or hermaphroditic attributes. . . . Given this evidence, it is impossible to make a binary classification on the basis of the Y chromosome, since it cannot always explain an individual's set of sexual organs. . . . Individuals cannot be divided simply into binary groupings, because there are *so many variations* on this theme.[15]

Well, actually: No. In a follow-up article written with colleagues in 2000 (Blackless et al.), the authors began with a confession that in her 1993 article, "Fausto-Sterling cited a figure attributed to John Money that the frequency of intersexuality might be as high as 4% of live births, but Money responded that he never made any such claim."[16] So the figure is groundless.[17] Blackless et al. then intended to rectify the lack of statistics pertaining to the number of intersexed individuals in said article, where they came to the conclusion that intersexed individuals account for 1.728% of live births.[18] So, rather than 4 out of 100 being intersex, between 1 and 2 are. Fausto-Sterling supported this claim in her book-length study published the same year—*Sexing the Body*.

Again, the academy fell in love, and with it popular culture. In her review of the book, psychologist Celia Moore claimed

> Most people believe that there are only two sex categories. . . . Yet 17 out of every 1,000 people fail to meet our assumption that everyone is either male

6 *Sex and Gender in Theory and Practice*

or female. This is the approximate incidence of intersexuals: Individuals with XY chromosomes and female anatomy, XX chromosomes and male anatomy, or anatomy that is half male and half female.[19]

Again: No. The problem is that in the book and their article, Fausto-Sterling and colleagues brought together a host of categories of genetic irregularities pertaining to sex chromosomes and their expression on/in the human body of which only a tiny sub-category actually leads to a state of intersexuality. Once these non-intersex-leading irregularities were removed from the statistics, the percentage of intersex live births dropped to around 0.018.[20]

To give just a few examples: The mildest of these genetic anomalies are aneuploidies, where too few or too many chromosomes exist. Humans are diploids (chromosomes pair, such as the XX in females), so having only one is a monosomy, and having three or more is polysomy. These account for approximately half of all chromosomal anomalies in humans with a total frequency of 1 in 400 live births.[21] In terms of sex chromosomes, the only viable monosomy is Turner's syndrome, whereby a person has only one X chromosome with no pairing (X0). According to the World Health Organization, this occurs in some 1:3,000 live births, and those with the disorder are born phenotypically female.[22] These females tend to be shorter than their genetic make-up would otherwise suggest, and they may be subject to certain heart and kidney problems.[23] They are also infertile insofar as they cannot produce viable eggs. However, with egg donors and in vitro-fertilization, they can sustain pregnancy and give birth to viable offspring.[24] As noted in a study published in *The Lancet*, "A consistent feature documented in Turner's syndrome is the unambiguous identification with the female sex."[25]

On the polysomy side is Klinefelter syndrome, where males have one extra X chromosome (XXY).[26] This irregularity appears in c. 1:600 live births.[27] Other than slightly smaller testes than whatever counts as normal in puberty, the only other manifestation of Klinefelter syndrome is an increased rate of infertility. Otherwise, men with Klinefelter have normal secondary sexual characteristics and normal sexual function. Most cases go undetected unless a cause for infertility is sought.[28] Other polysomy sex irregularities are XXX females, XYY males, and males with XXXY or even XXXXY. XXX (1:1,000)[29] females tend to be taller and slimmer than average for their populations and may show some mental retardation. Otherwise, their phenotype expresses as female, and they are fertile.[30] XYY males (1:1,000)[31] are phenotypically male and, again, may show some signs of mental retardation. Otherwise, they tend to be taller than average, experience earlier puberty, have regular fertility, and are typically only diagnosed in searches for causes of behavioral problems.[32] As for cases of XXXY and XXXXY (as well as the previously mentioned XXX and XXY), recall that XIST turns off all but one of these extra X chromosomes. Provided the person reacts to testosterone, the phenotype is male.

There is also a smaller category of genetic variations that do have a phenotypic expression. However, the *external* manifestation appears to be "standard," and thus there is no sense that the individual implicated is outside of the binary order. Such is the case with complete androgen insensitivity syndrome (CAIS,

0.076:1,000),[33] an X-recessive disorder whereby the SRY gene translocates onto the X chromosome, causing XY individuals to develop as females.[34] Here, XY individuals do not respond to testosterone or other androgens *in utero* but do respond to estrogens and thus develop as females. At birth, they display a vagina and clitoris typical of XX females; at puberty they develop breasts.[35] It is usually only at puberty, if at all, that the condition is discovered when the individual does not menstruate.[36] More recently, the condition is discovered in athletes during regulatory testing.[37] In the absence of genetic testing, these individuals simply appear as typical females who neither menstruate nor reproduce. Individuals with CAIS self-identify as female.[38]

The flip side of CAIS is congenital adrenal hyperplasia (CAH, 0.0813:1,000[39]), an autosomal recessive condition that affects both males and females. People with CAH lack an enzyme that the adrenal glands need for proper hormone generation and wind up over-producing androgens such as testosterone.[40] Males with the condition may experience premature puberty with few other symptoms. The disorder is more severe in females. For early onset female CAH, also called adrenogenital syndrome (AGS, 1:5,000),[41] a cortisol deficiency combined with a compensatory increase in adrenocortical hormone (ACTH) *in utero* causes the female fetus's genitalia to malform, presenting as neither completely male nor female—thus a kind of hermaphrodite.[42] However, CAH/AGS also brings with it a host of health problems based on an inability to regulate the body's sodium levels properly. Infants with AGS develop dehydration, diarrhea, vomiting, and lack of appetite, among other health issues.[43] In antiquity, we might understand that such individuals had a high perinatal death rate, removing them from the general population and construction of sex/gender identity.[44]

True intersex/hermaphroditism is marked by the possession of one ovary and one testis. According to John Wiener:

> There is a great diversity of phenotypes and karyotypes among true hermaphrodites. The majority are 46, XX and phenotypically female, but the prevalence of these findings may have geographical differences. The phenotype is the result of interplay between hormonal products from both ovarian and testicular tissue. Testicular tissue is invariably present by definition, but the genetic signal for testicular development varies. Some cases have a Y chromosome in all cells whereas others have mosaicism[45] with the Y chromosome present in gonadal tissue only. SRY may be present in the absence of the Y chromosome via translocation or may be absent altogether. The presence of ovarian tissue in true hermaphrodites possessing the Y chromosome or SRY suggests that some gene products must be capable of blocking SRY from switching on testicular development in some gonads.[46]

Because such individuals are "corrected" at birth (usually to female, as this is the default sex of humans), it is difficult in modern times to determine how the phenotype will be expressed at puberty and into adulthood (although see Money et al. 1957 on this). The number of such individuals is also extremely low. According

8 *Sex and Gender in Theory and Practice*

to Blackless et al., there are no published statistics of individuals born with both testicular and ovarian tissue.[47] Nevertheless, they suggest that true hermaphrodites constitute 0.0117 per 1,000 live births worldwide, with strong geographic concentrations, such as southern Brazil and southern Africa.[48] Hermaphroditism tends to run in families.[49]

So there are *very* few humans who are hermaphroditic/intersex, that is, *both* female and male. There are no neuter humans because of the effect of the indispensable X chromosome that will automatically turn any body female without an intervening and fully functional Y chromosome "patch." And the most common "intersexing" genetics only manifest in the cells, not on the bodies.

This is critically important, because ancient peoples did not have access to the genetic information we do today; they did not know about DNA or Y chromosomes. Honestly, they didn't even know about the human egg until the 19th century CE. So when ancient peoples theorized on sex and sex identity (the body, not objects of desire), they did so purely on the basis of anatomy, with no ability to determine if said anatomy aligned with chromosomes. As Joanna Sofaer, physical anthropologist, put it, "past people did not see each other as genes but as bodies in the world."[50]

As we shall see, those bodies were very consistently sexed as binary: female and male.

Gender

The comparatively minor physiological differences between females and males (dimorphism) have nevertheless had resounding effects on the understanding of sexual difference and most certainly on relations between the sexes throughout world history. All world cultures have some notions of aspects of personality or intellect that are supposedly sex based. Males are more violent; females are more nurturing. Males are better at math; females have better verbal skills. Men cannot control their emotions/liquor/libidos; women cannot control their emotions/liquor/libidos. Et cetera. This is gender: the beliefs held about individuals based on their sex. These beliefs are unbelievably significant, for they—consciously or not—influence how individuals in a society learn to act and self-identify and how other members of that society expect each other to behave. The result is a constantly self-reinforcing process whereby males learn to act in a "masculine" fashion and females "feminine," strengthening the belief that males are innately masculine and females feminine, for whatever counts as "masculine" or "feminine" in that particular community. These aspects of behavior are taken as innate and justify relations between the sexes and their roles and positions within the overarching community.

These gendered differences are often explained and understood in light of reproductive difference, thus tethering gender to biology.[51] Females are more nurturing because they have to feed and care for the young, insofar as they, and not males, lactate and take primary responsibility for offspring even after birth. Males are more violent because they have to fight each other for mates (kind of

Sex and Gender in Theory and Practice   9

like buffalo), defend their families, and hunt for them while the women are home caring for the kids. Because males hunt they need better visual-spatial abilities; because women rear children they need better communication skills. Et cetera. It's all rationalization.

> Sexual reproduction does not *cause* gender practice, or even provide a template for it. There are many fields where strongly gendered behavior occurs which has not the slightest logical connection with sexual reproduction (football, shoe design, futures markets, lesbian sex, Handel oratorios, the appointment of bishops . . .).[52]

It is actually extremely difficult to determine if any behaviors are specifically feminine or masculine; it is the age-old question of nature vs. nurture. For example, it is/was commonly accepted that girls are more sociable than boys (perhaps a result of their assumed superior verbal abilities?), while boys are more violent than girls. A massive meta-analysis done in the 1970s revealed that:

> Any differences that exist in the "sociability" of the two sexes are more of kind than of degree. Boys are highly oriented toward a peer group and congregate in larger groups; girls associate in pairs or small groups of age-mates, and may be somewhat more oriented toward adults, although the evidence for this is weak.[53]

Whereas:

> The sex difference in aggression has been observed in all cultures in which the relevant behavior has been observed. Boys are more aggressive both physically and verbally. They show the attenuated (mock-fighting, aggressive fantasies) as well as the direct forms more frequently than girls. The sex difference is found as early as social play begins—at age 2 or 2½. Although the aggressiveness of both sexes declines with age, boys and men remain more aggressive through the college years.[54]

Over 30 years later, we have similar results:

> The gender similarities hypothesis states . . . that males and females are alike on most—but not all—psychological variables. Extensive evidence from meta-analyses of research on gender difference supports the gender similarities hypothesis. A few notable exceptions are some motor behaviors (e.g., throwing distance) and some aspects of sexuality, which show large gender differences. Aggression shows a gender difference that is moderate in magnitude.[55]

But even so, questions remain. Are boys more violent because of testosterone, or are they more violent because adults are more likely to assume that "boys will be

10 *Sex and Gender in Theory and Practice*

boys" and not scold them as severely when they fight as they might do to girls, who thus "learn better"? Are there more violent role models for boys than girls? Have girls become more aggressive in an age of Misty Knight, Buffy the Vampire Slayer, and Michelle Yeoh?

Because what counts as "feminine" or "masculine" varies considerably among cultures, classes, and ages, and because there is eternal debate as to how individuals learn (or not) and incorporate these gendered behaviors—to *perform* them, as it is commonly put—it is now understood that gender is *fluid*. There are considerable differences as to what constitutes feminine or masculine behavior the world over, again dependent on population, economic class, indigenous vs. immigrant vs. colonized status, and age—what is called *intersectionality*. However, there are also considerable differences in any individual's gendered performance based on particular circumstances. I act differently with my mother than I do with my boss than I do with my friends than I do with strangers. My "performance of self" is utterly mutable, and this includes how I might choose—consciously or not—to express my gender. So gender is not only fluid but fluid at all levels, in the human species at large down to the individual.

However, there are limits to such fluidity, insofar as my behavior, my performance, is restricted at least to some extent by the expectations of my society. As Connell and Pearse put it, "We make our own gender, but we are not free to make it however we like. Our gender practice is powerfully shaped by the gender order in which we find ourselves."[56] My desire to breach what is deemed "normal" or "acceptable" for my sex has external consequences. As a female, it is (now) generally deemed okay for me to wear pants; the only male alternative to pants is a kilt (and perhaps a tad difficult to explain as formal wear if the male wearing it is not ethnically Scottish). And yet no female politician can escape being judged on whether she wears a skirt (what length?) or a pantsuit (is she trying to deny her femininity?). Only recently can men have long hair (and they still cannot really wear barrettes). Writing on being a teenager in the United States in the 1960s, newspaper columnist Dave Barry recalls:

> In my late teens, I started to wear my hair longer—nothing extreme, pretty much the look favored by Moe of the Three Stooges—and when I was out in public, you'd have thought I was having unprotected sex with a llama right there on the sidewalk. People would laugh at me, or give me dirty looks and call me a hippie, or ask each other in a loud, self-amused voice—I can't tell you how many times I heard this hilarious question—"Is that a boy or a girl?" (Har! Good one!) Middle-aged guys in trucks would slow down next to me, roll down their windows, and scream "FAGGOT!"[57]

In December of 1993, Nebraska, United States, the transgender man Brandon Teena (formerly Teena Brandon) was gang raped and later murdered by locals who did not accept his adoption of male identity—a story dramatized in the movie *Boys Don't Cry*. There are limits to the fluidity of gender, although those limits themselves are fluid (e.g. hair length).

Fluid Sex/Gender(?)

As mentioned, there is currently a raging debate in academia as to whether sex is binary. One of the causes of this debate, as discussed, was that not all humans express the XX/XY = female/male paradigm. The other reason is that there is debate over whether biological sex exists at all or if it is simply a discursive (and oppressive) construct based on the long-standing notion of binary gender. That is: We think that there are males and females because for millennia we have chosen to divide populations into those with power (males) and those with less power (females). To quote one of the primary proponents of this debate—Judith Butler in her 1990 publication *Gender Trouble*:

> If the immutable character of sex is contested, perhaps this construct called "sex" is as culturally constructed as gender; indeed, perhaps it was always already gender, with the consequence that the distinction between sex and gender turns out to be no distinction at all. . . . As a result, gender is not to culture as sex is to nature; gender is also the discursive/cultural means by which "sexed nature" or "a natural sex" is produced and established as "prediscursive," prior to culture, a politically neutral surface *on which* culture acts. . . . Indeed, sex, by definition will be shown to have been gender all along.[58]

And followed up in her 1993 book *Bodies That Matter*:

> If gender is the social construction of sex, and if there is no access to this "sex" except by means of its construction, then it appears not only that sex is absorbed by gender, but that "sex" becomes something like a fiction, perhaps a fantasy, retroactively installed at a prelinguistic site to which there is no direct access.[59]

Obviously, this does not work from a reproductive standpoint (see previously). It also does not account for the fact that non-human species also have sex, usually binary, as well as plants, a fact that is never debated. Nevertheless, the debate as to whether there is any actual distinction between sex and gender continues. It mostly began in in the 1990s, when we started getting sloppy with our use of terminology. People in all disciplines, inside the academy or not, started to use *sex* and *gender* interchangeably.[60] Thus, as noted by Walker and Cook in 1998:

> The term *gender* began to be commonly used in the biomedical literature in the early 1970s by researchers interested in the relationship between a person's sex as indicated by his or her karyotype and the person's social identity. . . . However, much of the recent popularity of the term *gender* appears to reflect a lack of understanding of the significance of the sex/gender distinction. With increasing frequency, *gender* is being used to refer to an animal's biological identity (in other words, its sex).[61]

12 Sex and Gender in Theory and Practice

They go on to provide data on the "slippage" of these terms in the biomedical data from 1966–1997. Whereas from 1966–1974, only 3.39% of articles use *sex* and *gender* as synonyms, by 1990–1996, the percentage increased to 56.6.[62] Nowadays one hears about how doctors "assign a child's sex/gender at birth."[63] Not only does the doctor *not* assign a sex (which happened *in utero*), she cannot possibly assign a *gender* as she has no way of knowing how the child will develop in terms of personality and personal relationships, the core foundations of *gender*.

By the 1990s, two additional factors came to complicate the sex/gender dichotomy. One was the addition of sexual orientation such that it became a determining factor in the establishment of one's gender. Thus, "[o]verlaid on that set of binaries was taken, by the dominant culture, to be that of sexual orientation (when it was discussed at all) based on the sex (or is that the gender?) of the desired person."[64] Basically, the sex:biology/gender:culture axis became a grid trying to incorporate differences for hetero- and homosexuality. Needless to say, with so many inputs, binary forms appeared unsatisfactory.

A second complicating factor was a misunderstanding of the medical community's research on sexual dimorphism, especially throughout history, epitomized in the work of Thomas Laqueur in his 1992 book *Making Sex: Body and Gender from the Greeks to Freud*. Studies pertaining to how different, say, male and female brains or hormones are (in humans or otherwise), or male vs. female psychology, or how sexually dimorphic ancient philosophers such as Aristotle believed males and females to be, were translated by theorists into attestations that sex itself was not binary at the chromosomal (genetic) or genital (phenotypic) level but socially constructed via language. Thus, because scientists before and after the Age of Enlightenment understood genitals differently, then this must prove that genitalia are a social construction, not biological, the thinking goes. Likewise, because both males and females contain testosterone, have two legs (normally), and can display aggression, they cannot be seen as separate categories (in spite of the gametes they produce).[65]

By the time full-scale postmodernist third-wave feminism was hitting its stride, third-wave feminists were arguing for the complete collapse of the sex/gender dichotomy, with gender taking the lead. That is to say: Independent, biological, physical sex did not really exist, it was merely a projection of gender. Thus the quotations from Judith Butler previously. Butler was quickly followed by other third-wave feminists, such as Moira Gatens:

> Significantly, the sexed body can no longer be conceived as the unproblematic biological and factual base upon which gender is inscribed, but must in itself be recognized as constructed by discourses and practices that take the body both as their target and as their vehicle of expression. Power is not then reducible to what is imposed, from above, on naturally differentiated male and female bodies, but is also constitutive of those bodies, in so far as they are constituted as male and female.[66]

Such notions entered the realm of archaeology in 1991 with the publication of Jarl Nordbladh and Tim Yate's article "This Perfect Body, This Virgin Text: Between Sex and Gender in Archaeology." Here they argued:

> Archaeologists writing about gender have assumed sex is an unquestionable, biological fact, the background to history, the synchrony against which the diachrony is played out. The position sex-gender would thus be equivalent to that of nature-culture. But *biology is also a social and cultural construct*, and demonstrates that the binary framework of the categories male-female is itself not originary. More categories than two do exist . . . and may be the subject of cultural elaboration. In medicine this third category—strongly hidden in our own society—is called the class of abnormalities, into which are collected all those who do not directly fit the ideal sex stereotypes. . . . Modern medical science has developed several complicated methods for the determination of sex. Nevertheless, none of these gives a 100% division into separate classes. Several exceptions to the binary structure of sex have been noted.[67]
>
> The division between sex and gender is, therefore, no longer guaranteed by some external reality, a penis or a vagina: it is itself the abstraction of a cultural system brought about within an historical mode of the reality principle, determined by a third term that allows them to divide and separate, while at the same time binding these differences to those "external" discourses that are built up around them. . . . The notion of "males" and "females" outside of the symbolic system presupposes homogeneous subjects, "ideal" types that are anti-historical and indeed need entertain no relationship to history.[68]

Bringing the argument into the medical, Anne Fausto-Sterling argued that, "Our bodies are too complex to provide clear-cut answers about sexual difference. The more we look for a simple physical basis for 'sex,' the more it becomes clear that 'sex' is not a pure physical category."[69]

By the time Anne Minas Belmont was writing her 1993 work *Gender Basics: Feminist Perspectives on Women and Men*, she could actually complain (with bizarrely little understanding of past usages), "Thus the word 'sex' is coming to be restricted to biological, or genetic male/female differences, leaving its *official synonym*, 'gender,' free to drift toward meaning those differences that have social causes."[70] Likewise, Tuana cried, "Over a decade ago I argued that the distinction between sex and gender was pernicious and advocated that feminists refuse its polarization."[71] It was only a matter of time before the collapse entered the realm of ancient studies. And in the same vein, Laura Talalay argued that, "While these reductive definitions allow archaeologists to parse their research into tidy categories—sex is biologically determined, gender is socially constructed—the sex:gender paradigm is, in fact, no longer well supported."[72]

All of this discounts the physical reality of human (and other) bodies, which are material entities in a material world that reproduce sexually. As gender theorists

14 *Sex and Gender in Theory and Practice*

Raewyn Connell and Rebecca Pearse put it, "A large part of gender theory in the English-speaking metropole has become abstract, contemplative or analytical in style, or focuses entirely on cultural subversion."[73] Furthermore, as primatologist Frans de Waal has discussed, the discourse is both political and utterly inconsistent. As he notes in his book *Different: Gender through the Eyes of a Primatologist*:

> [W]hile we often keep biology at a distance in relation to gender, we positively embrace it when it comes to sexual orientation and transgender identity. Here we eagerly explore genetic differences and the role of hormones and the brain. The same American Psychological Association that calls gender a social construct defines sexual orientation as "one's enduring attraction to male partners, female partners, or both." Thus the usual emphasis on the role of the environment has been replaced by "enduring attraction." Sexual orientation and gender identity are considered an immutable part of the self. . . . This hate/love relationship is ideologically driven. Those who seek gender equality often find biology inconvenient. They believe that the easiest way to reach equality is by downplaying inborn sex difference. In contrast, in the fight against homophobia and transphobia biology is seen as a mighty ally. If we can prove a biological basis to homosexual conduct and transgender identity, this will silence those who claim them to be "unnatural" or "abnormal."[74]

In this book, sex and gender will be treated as separate entities. *Sex* is the biological category of an individual's role in reproduction (egg-maker or sperm-maker); *gender* is how the society expects an individual to act, behave, and perform based on that individual's sex.

Ancient Near Eastern Sex and Gender

Sex

To what extent did the ancients recognize our modern constructs of sex and gender? As will become apparent over the course of this book, the residents of the ancient Near East most assuredly recognized biological sex, and it was indeed binary—female and male. This comes across well in the study of early (late 4th–3rd millennia) Sumerian terms for humans. It should be noted here that, like modern English, but unlike the Semitic languages, the Sumerian language had no linguistic gender—no feminine "la mesa" but masculine "le voyage" or even neuter "das Buch."[75] Establishing the sex of any living thing, including humans, thus had to be done deliberately.

So, in the beginning, a human being was indicated by the unisex grapheme SAG: in the proto-cuneiform, pictographic script of the time an otherwise unmarked, hairless human head (variations shown):

Sex and Gender in Theory and Practice 15

On slightly later tablets the still unisex way of indicating a human being (often in a professional capacity) was to use the LU₂ sign,[76] basically the whole body:

To render a human (or any animal, for that matter) male the UŠ sign was used (also transcribed NITA OR NITAḪ), an ejaculating penis: ![sign]. To make a human or other animal female the SAL sign was used (also transcribed MUNUS), a vulva: ![sign].[77]

Thus, to indicate a human female, the signs used would be SAG.SAL.[78] The fact that "woman" equals "human with vulva" and "man" equals "human with penis" is probably the best argument in favor of binary sex as could be asked for.

To indicate a foreign, or even better: conquered, individual, early Sumerians used the sign KUR: ![sign] (basically, from the mountains). To indicate a woman of servant or slave status, then, the sign SAL.KUR was used, written ![sign], commonly transcribed GEME₂. A servant-class male was, of course, an UŠ.KUR, transcribed ARAD₂.

So, to begin, there were generic human beings, female and male human beings, and foreign/servile human females and males. Over time further terminology emerged that was both sex and status specific. For example, the ĜURUŠ, whose sign is a sledge with a litter that originally would have been pulled by an ox, except the ox was replaced by an apparently burly, young male field hand: ![sign]. The ĜURUŠ, then, is a youngish male either in or just before the physical prime of life and,

16 *Sex and Gender in Theory and Practice*

early on, one in the employ of another for brute physical labor. As we shall see, eventually the class signifier ("in the employ of another") fell by the wayside, and ĜURUŠ simply became the designation for "young man."[79]

Changes, of course, occur over time. The pictographic writing of early Mesopotamia was replaced by the wedge-impressions that gave cuneiform its name. In some instances the original image wasn't all that different:

In others, well . . .

By the middle of the 2nd millennium onwards, personal names were regularly prefixed with a determinative (signs that mark the category of a word, such as "personal name" or "type of wood"). A single, vertical wedge was mainly used before the names of males (, transliterated "DIŠ"), while that original SAL/MUNUS sign was often used before the names of females.[80] In some instances, especially in the cities of Nippur, Babylon, and Nuzi, a female name might be preceded by *both* determinatives: DIŠ.SAL. In all instances, this appears to result from cases where females were in roles usually filled by males, such as in the case of matronymics instead of the more common patronymics (but only for sons! For daughters, the SAL sign was used for mom) or when women were divorced and took on the role of head of household in legal and economic transactions.[81] No male bore both determinatives.

By the early 2nd millennium changes in the sex paradigms were afoot. This becomes apparent in two lexical lists dated to the Old Babylonian Period (c. 1800–1600): UGU-MU, a list of body parts and other data pertaining to humans, and Proto-LU$_2$, a list of human occupations. The first provides a list of what are literally five ages of humans, of which two refer specifically to males:

NAM-LU$_2$-TUR-ĜU$_{10}$	"My status as a young person (LU$_2$)"[82]
NAM-ĜURUŠ-(TUR)-ĜU$_{10}$	"My status as able-bodied (young) male"
NAM-KALAG-GA-ĜU$_{10}$	"My status as strong"
NAM-UR-SAĜ-ĜU$_{10}$	"My status as hero"
NAM-AB-BA-ĜU$_{10}$	"My status as male elder/'father'"[83]

The first, third, and fourth terms in this list are all sex/gender neutral: To be young, strong, and a hero can apply equally to males and females (maybe; see subsequently). As in English, children were simply children, with no specific need to denote sex (boy/girl). It is only at the height of physical prowess and the height of wisdom that the sexes are specified. For the former, we have our old friend the ĜURUŠ, possibly modified by the word for "young" (TUR). He is paralleled in the literature by the female KI-SIKIL—young/adolescent woman . Thus in the tale *Enlil and Ninlil* (ll. 10–11):

ᴰEN-LIL$_2$ ĜURUŠ TUR-BI NA-NAM

ᴰNIN-LIL$_2$ **KI-SIKIL** TUR-BI NA-NAM

Enlil was one of its young men,
Ninlil was one its young women.[84]

The strength of youth is contrasted with the strength of age, that is: wisdom. The fifth "Age of Man" is NAM-AB-BA-ĜU₁₀, which is literally one's "state" (NAM) of being a father (more accurately "paternal") AB-BA. Young men and old(er) men are literally and literarily contrasted. Thus, in the tale *Gilgameš and Agga* (ll 15–16):

ᵈGILGAMEŠ₂ EN KUL-ABA₄ᵏⁱ-A-KE₄ ᵈINANA-RA NIR-ĜAL₂-LA-E INIM **AB-BA** IRI-NA-KE₄ ŠAG₄-ŠE₃ NU-MU-NA-GID₂ 2-KAM-MA-ŠE₃ ᵈGILGAMEŠ₂ IGI ĜURUŠ IRIᵏⁱ-NA-ŠE₃ INIM BA-AN-ĜAR.

Gilgameš, the lord of Kulaba, placing his trust in Inana, did not take seriously the advice of his city's elders (AB-BA). Gilgameš presented the issue again, this time before the able-bodied men (ĜURUŠ) of his city.[85]

One of the ongoing signs that Gilgameš was a bit of an idiot is that he favored the advice of the young men over that of the city elders. It rarely ended well. . . . However, it should be noted that the only official bodies the king consulted were groups of males. Females are falling out of the public venue.

A similar tendency to start favoring males over females appears in Old Babylonian *Proto-Lu₂*. It is subtle. It is no statement of sexism or misogyny. Rather, unlike in the previous texts, males come to be the unmarked category, while females become marked. That is to say, masculine jobs, categories, and so on are simply listed as themselves, whereas females in those roles must be marked as specifically female.[86] And these are not categories easily understood as automatically pertaining to one sex or the other, like wet-nurse. Rather, *Proto-Lu₂* has such professions as:

KISAL LUḪ	Courtyard sweeper
ᵐᵘⁿᵘˢ KISAL LUḪ	Female courtyard sweeper
ENSI	Dream interpreter
ᵐᵘⁿᵘˢ ENSI	Female dream interpreter[87]

The same thing occurs in the roughly contemporary bilingual (Sumerian–Akkadian) lexical list LU₂-AZLAG₂ = *ašlāku*, wherein we find that the formerly sexless/genderless word LU₂ has acquired a masculine, or at least specifically *not* feminine, nature. Thus we have:

LU₂.KAŠKURUN₂.NA	Brewer
ᵐᵘⁿᵘˢkaškurun₂.na	Female Brewer
LU₂.GUB.BA	Frenetic
ᵐᵘⁿᵘˢGUB.BA	Female Frenetic[88]

This same tendency—whereby males are unmarked and females marked—continues throughout Mesopotamian history. Writing on (primarily 1st-millennium) omen texts, Virginie Muller observed that:

18   *Sex and Gender in Theory and Practice*

However, the protases [the 'if' clause] are usually concerned with men . . . and women appear in the protasis only in a few situations. The absence of women in protases can perhaps be explained if we take the term NA or LU₂/*awīlum* with the meaning "someone, anybody," in a neutral gender. Thus, texts specify MUNUS/*sinništu* only in particular situations, as do the therapeutic texts. These latter references make use of the generic term NA or LU₂/*awīlum* to describe pathologies, while the term MUNUS/*sinništu* makes its appearance only in cases related specifically to female genital problems.[89]

In other words, the word that used to mean "human" comes to mean "man as representative of human." That this "man" does not refer to both sexes is emphasized by the fact that a different term—MUNUS/*sinništu*—is used to refer to women specifically. Basically, women are becoming the second sex.

The Egyptians also understood biological sex to be binary, and they expressed the idea in similar ways.[90] Unlike the Sumerians, no Egyptian hieroglyphs exist which present the concept of an unsexed person—a human being (that original SAG sign). There are men, indicated by the sign A1[91] , which serves as both a determinative and a logogram for "man"=*z(j)*. The Egyptian term for "living person" (functionally "human")—*'nḫ*,

still uses the A1 sign as a determinative, functionally making "man" stand in for "human."

Females, by contrast, are indicated with the sign B1 . Either this sign or closely related variants were used to express biological aspects of being female. Thus the verb "to conceive" (*jwr*) was expressed as:

While "to give birth" (*msj*) reveals:

Additional variants exist for a pregnant woman (B2), a nursing woman (B5), and a woman holding a child (B6).

In addition to functioning as logograms and determinatives, the sexed hieroglyphs were combined with other signs to create gendered forms of neutral nouns. For example, the signs A1 and B1 contribute to the concept of "brother"—*sn*—and "sister"—*snt*:

As with cuneiform, personal names in hieroglyphs were marked by determinatives, symbols that give the category of words (e.g. human name, type of wood, etc.). The personal names of females are identified with the previously given B1 hieroglyph, while male names are marked with A1. The use of such sexing determinatives begins sporadically in the Old Kingdom and becomes increasingly common throughout Egyptian history.[92]

The sense of the sexually binary nature of humanity—and the universe in general—was very strong in Egypt,[93] such that, in order to express the concept of "everyone," both signs were used to express humanity fully. Thus the orthography for "people"—*rmṯ*—typically appears as

while "humanity"—*ḥnmmt*—is

and, of course, "everyone"—*ḥr-nb*—is

As observed by H.G. Fischer:

> The ... term *rmṯ* "people" may be followed solely by the male determinative, but that fact makes *the more usual addition* of the female determinative all the more significant. Thus the good opinion of women, as well as that of men, is sought in all sorts of moralistic statements, such as: "I never did what people dislike;" "I was one who did what all people praise;" "I was beloved of people;" "I never did (or said) what people contest."[94]

So, to make a term or concept pertaining to humans universalizing, the symbols for *both* men *and* women had to be included.

Not to be outdone by their northeastern neighbors, the Egyptians also expressed sexed concepts by way of hieroglyphs that represented human genitalia. For males, the symbols were D52 and D53— , [95]—while for females, the sign is N41— , a vagina, typically complemented with the linguistically feminizing –t (X1 =).[96] In the Old Kingdom the combination of these hieroglyphs were used to write *nk*—"to have sexual intercourse, to copulate" (D280): . However, starting in the Middle Kingdom, this glyph is replaced in this context with either D52 or D53. As Marc Orriols-Llonch notes, "From this, it can be

20 *Sex and Gender in Theory and Practice*

deduced that the sexual act evolves from being conceived in an egalitarian way to becoming a masculine act."⁹⁷

These hieroglyphs could allow for the sexing of deities. In Pyramid Text 359, §601b, we read the lines:

> i' ḥr n(i) nṯr.w m hi.w m ḥm.wt "I wash the face of the gods, even male and female"
> i' ḥr n(i) T. in nṯr.w m hi.w m ḥm.wt "The face of Teti is washed by the gods, even male, even female."⁹⁸

Here, the male deities are identified with either ⟨glyph⟩ or ⟨glyph⟩, while the goddesses appear with the symbol ⟨glyph⟩.⁹⁹ Just as with humans, the deities are sexed male and female.

These two categories of sexed hieroglyphs—full body and genitalia—combined to express the concept of "man/male"—*ṯзy*—and "woman/female/wife"—*ḥmt*.¹⁰⁰

Basically, "man" is the male one with a penis, "woman" is the female one with the vagina.

As with the Sumerians, statuses other than merely female or male appeared in the texts, and it would appear that, unlike their neighbors to the north, there was no particular need to sex these alternative categories. Thus, for example, the sign for "child" A17—⟨glyph⟩—can be either male or female, but is probably of a lower class than the child represented by A17a—⟨glyph⟩—neither of whom, of course, compare to a royal child, A18—⟨glyph⟩. So, for children at least, status trumps sex.

The Hebrew Bible also displays a binary approach to sex, displayed not least of all in its grammar, where nouns, adjectives, and verbs are gendered either masculine or feminine. More specifically, in its vocabulary, the Bible distinguishes between male and female on the one hand, man (adult, male human) and woman (adult, female human) on the other. As neatly summarized by Marc Brettler of the former:

> The two main sex terms in the Bible are *zakar* for male, and *neqebah* for female. They are used for both humans and domesticated animals (and nothing else). In rabbinic literature, *zakar* and *neqebah* may refer to grammatical gender, but we do not know how far back this usage extends. Almost all usages of *neqebah* are alongside *zakar*, and thus the two words form a clear polar contrast, in Genesis 6:19, where the animals *zakar* and *neqebah* are brought into Noah's ark, in Leviticus 3:1 where animal offerings, *zakar* and

Sex and Gender in Theory and Practice 21

neqebah, are prescribed, of Deuteronomy 4:16, where the making of images, *zakar* and *neqebah*, is prohibited. These cases highlight the fact that *zakar* and *neqebah* cover all sexual categories that the authors wish to recognize, namely they function as a minimal pair.[101]

Likewise, in Gen. 1: 27: "And God created man in his own image, in the image of God created he him; male and female created He them." (*We-yivrah Elohim et-haAdam betzalmo, betzelem Elohim bara oto:* **zakar** *we-***neqebah** *bara otam*).

By contrast, an adult human male is *'iš*, while an adult human female is *'iššah*. They also appear frequently together (at least as far as the *'iššah* is concerned—she shows up 781 times in contrast to the 2,198 examples of *'iš*), indicating that these, too, are an all-inclusive pair.[102] Animals, including humans, are male or female.

Gender

It is also clear that residents of the ancient Near East had their own concepts of gender, the social manifestation of sex, in all its mutability. If we turn back to our Egyptians, for example, depictions of males and females in art show tendencies that do not depend on biological sex. Four gender-based differences are apparent:

- From the Old Kingdom onward, males are painted with red skin, females with yellow(ish) skin.[103] The difference in skin color appears to relate to notions of whether one is understood to spend time inside versus outside of the home.[104] Egyptian females (and females in general in the Near East—see Chapter 2) were associated with domesticity, being linked to the house and household. As such, they were "paler" than their male counterparts who, presumably, spent more time outside in the sun and thus developed healthy tans.[105] We see the distinction clearly in the well-known 4th-Dynasty couple Rahotep and Nofret (see Figure 1.1).
- Women, especially of the elite classes (where ideology is more likely to trump reality), were more likely to be shown in passive poses, with feet together, arms either held to the body or shown embracing a husband.[106] Men were typically shown in more active poses, with one foot striding forward and one hand extended.
- Men were shown as being larger than females, and not merely by a matter of inches, as might be expected in reality. As shown by Ann Macy Roth, women in Old Kingdom mastaba chapels could be depicted as anywhere from 99–31% the size of their husbands. And while those husbands might be shown standing, seated, or engaged in some activity, only the women might be depicted kneeling by the husband.[107]
- Finally, while men keep their genitals discreetly hidden in their kilts, females often had both breasts and pubic triangle indicated through their clothing (Figure 1.2). Such sartorial distinctions are somewhat ironic: Women are simultaneously more and less dressed than men. It would appear that men (working outdoors in the hot sun?) were freer to strip in Egyptian society—at

22 *Sex and Gender in Theory and Practice*

Figure 1.1 Rahotep and Nofret, Egyptian Museum, Cairo.
Source: Jose Lucas/Alamy Stock Photo.

Figure 1.2 Figure of a Woman, Old Kingdom, Metropolitan Museum of Art 58.125.3.

least according to the rules of decorum[108] that governed Egyptian artistic representation throughout most of its exceptionally long history. By contrast, women are typically shown in clingy gowns, simultaneously covering and revealing the body underneath. Egyptian women (and females in general in the Near East—see Chapter 2) are more eroticized than men, with the appearance of their sexual attributes being both auspicious and a cause of daily joy.

Gendering also manifests in vocabularies. Returning to Mesopotamia, both Sumerian and Akkadian have words for the "state of being a woman" or "state of being a man." In Sumerian, these are NAM.MUNUS and NAM.NITAḪ; in Akkadian, they are *sinnišūtu(m)* and *zikrūtu(m)*.[109] Sumerian NAM refers to a state of being or fate; the Akkadian suffix *–ūtu* refers to a state of being or –ness quality. Thus, femaleness or the state of being male.

The concept of gender (as opposed to sex) also comes across especially well in references to being a "real" man or a "real" woman in the literature. Such references rarely apply to the object's anatomy (e.g. you are not a "real" man because you do not have a beard)[110] but because of the object's behavior. Thus, to return to our Sumerians, a series of "insult" dialogues in both the EMEGIR (standard) and EMESAL ("women's") dialects of Sumerian question the gender identity of the person being insulted, asking the questions:

U₃ ZE₄-E MUNUS-ME-EN
And you! Are you a (real) woman?[111]

Or

U₃ ZE₄-E LU₂-LU₇-ME-EN
And you, are you a (real) man?[112]

A sadly mostly abraded wisdom text from the Assyrian period—known simply as *The Assyrian Collection*—gives a tantalizing glimpse of displaced sex-gender in a marriage:

[a]-ḫ/mur-ru-ú
[a-n]a aššati-šu i-qab-bi
[at]-ti lu eṭ-lu
[a-na-k]u lu ar-da-tu
. . . a-na ĜURUŠ *at-tu-ru*
. . . l]u si-ni-šu
. . . zi-ka-ru[113]

An Amorite[114] (?) speaks to his wife:
You be the young man (*eṭlu*),
Let me be the young woman (*ardatu*).
. . . I became a young man (ĜURUŠ = *eṭlu*)
. . . may female
. . . male.

The clearest evidence that the peoples of the ancient Near East not only had gender constructions but that they, to a large extent, resembled modern gender

24   *Sex and Gender in Theory and Practice*

constructions comes across in the strong military imagery that was associated with males and how this was set in contrast to femininity. For example, the Hittite word *pišnātar* (LU₂-*nātar*) has the simultaneous meanings of masculinity/manhood/virility, courage, martial accomplishments, and male genitalia.[115] It is set in contrast to femininity/womanhood, especially emphasizing engendered characteristics, as in ritual text KUB 15.34 ii 17–19:

> LU₂-*ni* LU₂-*nātar tarḫuilatar* MUNUS-*ni* MUNUS-*nātar annitalwatar*
>
> Release to the man (LU₂) virility and bravery, to the woman (MUNUS) femininity and motherhood.

Already in the Sumerian literature we find manhood (NAM.NITAḪ) linked to the notion/place of battle, while femininity is related to beauty and sexuality. Thus in the list of the divine MES (attributes of civilization) that the goddess Inana stole from her uncle Enki, we read of:

> | NAM.UR.SAG | Status of the male soldier |
> | HILI NAM.MUNUS.E.NE | Attractiveness status of a woman |

The association between masculinity and militarism continues:
Gilgameš, Enkidu, and the Netherworld (l. 228 and 236):

> KI **NAM-NITAḪ**-A-KE₄ ME₃-A NU-UN-ŠUB KUR-RE IM-MA-AN-DAB₅
>
> He did not fall in battle on the field of **manhood**, but the netherworld has seized him.[116]

Likewise, in *The Instructions of Šurrupak* (ll. 65–72), we read of the enacting of martial masculinity on the field of manhood:

> Having reached the **field of manhood** (KI NAM-NITAḪ-KA), you should not
>   jump (?) with your hand.
> The warrior is unique, he alone is the equal of many;
> Utu is unique, he alone is the equal of many.
> With your life you should always be on the side of the warrior;
> with your life you should always be on the side of Utu.[117]

This engendering of male = martial not only goes back to the beginning of the 3rd millennium but goes back to the beginning of a child's life, present in the birth spells that greeted him or her before the umbilical cord was even cut. Thus a Sumerian birth incantation from the Fara Period declares:

> Incantation: The . . . bulls of Enlil go . . . into the holy stable of Enlil. The great midwife from Kullab came in order to inflict the incantation in the water, in the . . . chamber. **If it is female, let her bring out of it** [the chamber] **the**

Sex and Gender in Theory and Practice 25

spindle and the pin; if it is a male, let her bring out of it the throwing stick and the weapon. May Ningirima pronounce (?) the magic formula (and) may the blood like milk . . . like milk . . . the blood comes out. After it has come out, like the water of a ditch that fills the canal, like water entering a lake, it increases.[118]

A later, Ur III-period version of the same spell makes the same engendering reference:

> If it is a male, let him take a weapon, an axe, the force of his manliness. If it is a female, let the spindle and the pin be in her hand.[119]

As should be pretty evident at this point, masculine warrior status is matched by feminine textile work. In those Sumerian insult texts mentioned previously, one of the engendered insults levied by one woman against another in the text is that:

> NA-AĜ₂-MUNUS-E LA-BA-DI/DU₇ SIKI NU-UM-UN-DA-PEŠ₆-EᵍᵉˢBALA NU-MU-UN-DA-NU-NU!

> She is not fit for womanhood: She cannot pluck wool, she cannot operate a spindle![120]

Likewise, the *Sumerian Laws Handbook of Forms* reveals that:

> MA-NA SIKI EŠ₂-GAR₃ NAM-MUNUS AL-X ḪE-E

> The assigned work quota of womanhood is 20 shekels of wool.[121]

This contrast of weapon = male/spindle (et al.) = female does not merely continue through the life cycle throughout the Near East, it becomes a focus for the negotiation of gendered identity. Put simply, a man can be symbolically turned into a woman by removing his weapons and replacing them with the symbols of femininity, usually a spindle but also items such as mirrors or jewelry (such as the pin previously). Thus, in a Hittite prayer to Ištar of Nineveh, the speaker pleads:

> Take from (their) men masculinity, prowess, robust health, swords(?), battle axes, bows, arrows, and dagger! And bring them to Hatti! Place into their hands the spindle and mirror of a woman! Dress them as women![122]

Likewise, in the loyalty oath sworn by Hittite soldiers, we read the curse on those who fail, "Let them break the bows, arrows, weapons in their hands and let them put into their hands distaff and mirror!"[123]

The most detailed account we have of this changing of genders via possessed attribute is the Hittite "Paskuwatti's ritual to the goddess Uliliyassi against impotence" (see Chapter 5 for more on this). In this ritual, the female functionary Paskuwatti explicitly uses sympathetic magic to "cure" the man of femininity (l. 4):

26 *Sex and Gender in Theory and Practice*

I place a spindle and distaff in the patient's [hand], and he comes under the gates. When he steps forward through the gates, I take the spindle and distaff away from him. I give him a bow (and) [arro]w(s), and say (to him) all the while: "I have just taken femininity away from you and given you masculinity in return. You have cast off the (sexual) behavior expected [of women]; [you have taken] to yourself the behavior expected of men!"[124]

Returning to the milieu of battle and politics, (defeated) males could be verbally emasculated through name-calling and/or literally emasculated via castration, with no reference to mirrors or distaffs. In a mid-8th-century treaty signed between King Aššur-nerari V of Assyria and King Mati'-ilu of Arpad, there is a lengthy section describing the horrors to fall upon Mati'-ilu and his family should he be disloyal to Assyria. After sections pertaining to drought, starvation, the eating of babies, and the destruction of Arpad generally, the text continues with (r. v. 8–15):

If Mati'-ilu sins against this treaty with Aššur-nerari, king of Assyria, may Mati'-ilu become a *harīmtu*, **his soldiers women**, may they receive [a gift] in the square of their cities like any *harīmtu*, may one country push them to the next; may Mati'-ilu's (sex) life be that of a mule, his wives extremely old; **may Ištar, the goddess of men, the lady of women, take away their bow, bring them to shame**, and make them bitterly weep: "Woe, we have sinned against the treaty of Aššur-nerari, king of Assyria."[125]

The word *harīmtu* is usually translated as "prostitute," although in reality it refers to a woman with neither father nor husband. In this instance, then, the king is being transformed from the patriarch of a royal household into a woman with no (male) family or household. The soldiers are also being turned into women, both through the loss of their bows and through their own direct comparison with *harimātu*.[126]

Not to be outdone by their neighbors to the east, the biblical authors also feminized their rivals (often their neighbors to the east). Thus Jeremiah 50: 37:

A sword against her horses and against her chariots, and against all the foreign troops in her midst, so that they may become women!

And Nahum 3: 13:

Look at your troops:
They are women in your midst.

Similar feminization of male enemies appears in our records from ancient Egypt. The Kom el-Ahmar stele of the 13th-century King Merenptah refers to the Nine Bows (the traditional enemies of Egypt) as:

pḏ.wt psḏ.t hr-ḫꜣ.t=f mj ḫnr.yt

Nine Bows are before him [the king] like women of the harem.[127]

while a battle scene with Nubians from the Medinet Habu temple claims of the pharaoh that:

mꜣꜣ=f pḏ.tj.w mj ḥm.wt

He is looking at bowmen like women.[128]

Verbally calling one's enemies women was intensified by actually castrating defeated soldiers on the fields of battle and piling up their penises, as well as their hands and even tongues, as booty before the victorious monarch. Thus on the Great War Temple of Ramesses III at Medinet Habu the king is shown with a pile of severed penises displayed before him (Figure 1.3):

The inscription indicates that the Pharaoh received:

kp.w ḳrn.t nn r-ꜥ=sn ("hands and phalloi with foreskins beyond numbering")
  jr.n 1,000 s jr.n 3,000 kp jr.n 3,000 ḳrn.t ("1,000 men, 3,000 hands, 3,000 phalloi with foreskin"[129])[130]

The close association between males and weapons on the one hand and females and spindles (and mirrors and jewelry, etc.) on the other reveals two things about ancient Near Eastern gender. First, just as now, gender was a social construct

Figure 1.3 Severed Penises Relief on Great War Temple of Ramesses III at Medinet Habu.
Source: Photograph by Danielle Candelora. Used with kind permission.

28 *Sex and Gender in Theory and Practice*

that is mapped onto biological sex but was not one and the same with it. Biological males are engendered as masculine warriors, but that engendering can be reversed, turning them not only into women but, for the Assyrians, the most disenfranchised of women—*ḫarimātu* (from a patriarchal perspective, at least). Second, masculinity is pointedly contrasted with femininity. Emasculated males are not reduced to, say, eunuchs or slaves (symbolically; they are in reality), but they are symbolically turned into women. Male identity is at least in part predicated upon a contrast with femininity. And to become female is bad. As we shall see in later chapters, females were praised for taking on masculine attributes and gender, so by the end of the 2nd millennium, at least, sexism was clearly marked. As we saw, sexism emerged as a marker of Ancient Near East (ANE) societies.

Doing Gender (or at Least Writing About It)

As discussed previously, there is a tendency in modern academia (and elsewhere) to blur the boundaries between sex and gender, if not annihilate them entirely. Because of this, it becomes difficult to establish a methodology for the study of gender, especially in the ancient world. A few words on methodology are thus worthwhile here.

I recognize three separate if interacting elements: sex, gender, person. All humans are individuals, and what goes for the individual is not necessarily true for the community, and vice versa. An individual's sex is, of course, the role that s/he plays in reproduction. And gender is how both the person and her/his community *think* about sex beyond just the reproductive. The important word here is: *think*. To study gender, one must get at how people think, not what they actually are. As such, the best primary sources are those that reveal how people think, regardless of how realistic the text or image might be. For this reason, fiction is an ideal source of data when constructing gender paradigms (just as it is a really bad source when trying to understand actual people—I doubt we learn much about ancient sexuality by studying Šamḫat). This includes both general fiction and mythology, that is, how people thought about their engendered deities. While it is always important to remember that people are not deities (just because Athena was martial does not mean ancient Greek women were), numerous expressions of gender at large manifest in myth (Hesiod takes it for granted that no female deity will challenge Ouranos or Kronos for dominion over reality).

As discussed previously, there are *two* levels of gender manifestation—the individual and the societal. The person knows how s/he is supposed to "perform" her/his gender in society, and there are the expectations of society external to the person. When these get out of step with each other, trouble ensues. A woman who takes on the role of a man, or vice versa, does not necessarily indicate gender mutability: How the social matrix around her reacts is also relevant.

Who provides the data is of inestimable importance. In most instances in antiquity, data are provided by men, as they were the most common scribes and authors and artists. As such, we mostly hear a male voice in our texts and see art through male eyes. Granted, in our predominantly patriarchal societies, this means that we

Sex and Gender in Theory and Practice   29

get the dominant view of the world, including gender. But it must be remembered that what we are receiving is a biased view—what is desired, feared, assumed to be there without actually being there—rather than reality. For the record, thanks to psychology, this is all we ever actually get, ancient world or modern. But it is important to keep this fact in mind and not to confuse ideology and imagination with reality.

As ever, intersectionality is at issue. Gender is only one of several variables in a person's existence, including age, class, ethnicity, and so on, and what goes for an upper-class, young woman does not necessarily apply to a poor, old woman. Most non-fictional records from antiquity deal with the upper classes, and lower classes are seen from an elite perspective. So all studies of gender are multiply filtered, just as gender itself expresses in multiple fashion. The fact that some Egyptian queens could present themselves as male—Sobekneferu, Hatshepsut—does not mean that this option was available to women outside the palace.

Finally: There is no one single gender paradigm. There were many ways of "being a woman" or "being a man" in the ancient world, as now. Certain manifestations were certainly accepted as preferable or more representative than others, usually referred to in the modern literature as "hegemonic." For males, this might be the young, handsome, strong, martially–sexually adept, athletic jock; while for females it might be the young, beautiful, modest, supportive handmaiden. The king and queen will probably be portrayed that way, regardless of actual reality. But next to that jock is the brilliant nerd who founds an IT empire and becomes wealthy beyond belief (thus improving his reproductive success). Next to the handmaiden is Harley Quinn, who is probably far more sexually desirable to most of the men and women currently reading this paragraph. And don't get me started on Nubian queens! Stout, strong, aggressive, and kicking Roman ass, they dominate the entire concept of "hegemonic." Gender is most assuredly fluid.

Keeping such ideas in mind, let us take a look an example of ancient gender ideologies, where an important aspect of female life is viewed through the lens of (probably) male-authored myth and (probably) male-rendered art.

At the Interplay of Sex and Gender: Engendering Reproduction in the Ancient Near East

As might be expected, the best place to consider the interplay of sex and gender in the ANE (and probably anyplace else in human history) is in the realm of reproduction, where the biological fact of sexual reproduction runs headlong into the gendered matters of creation and childcare. Just like in modern times, it was women who got pregnant, gave birth, and (possibly) lactated, although it is not a given that any particular lactating woman fed a child, her own or otherwise. Thus: biological sex. However, unlike modern times, it was understood in the ANE that males (not females) were the source of new life and thus fertility. That is: Fertility was gendered masculine, *not* feminine. This is totally understandable considering that semen was evident since ancient times but the ovum was only discovered in 1827. Childcare was gendered female, regardless of the matter of lactation. Let us consider these aspects of reproduction in turn as a case study of gender as social construct in the ANE.

30 *Sex and Gender in Theory and Practice*

Fertility

As discussed at greater length in Chapter 3, fertility was gendered masculine in the ANE. Semen specifically was the source of all life, starting with the very creation of the universe, the rise of plant life and the animals dependent on those plants, and, of course, humans. Thus in Egypt we read of the origins of air (Shu) and moisture (Tefnut):

> I am this soul of Shu which is in the flame of the fiery blast which Atum kindled with his own hand. He created orgasm and fluid fell from his mouth. He spat me out as Shu together with Tefnut, who came forth after me.[131]

While in the Sumerian hymn *Enki and the World Order*, we read:

> After he had turned his gaze from there, after father Enki had lifted his eyes across the Euphrates, he stood up full of lust like a rampant bull, lifted his penis, ejaculated and filled the Euphrates with flowing water. . . . It brought barley, mottled barley indeed: the people will eat it.[132]

Creating Humans

So male seed/semen gave the "spark" of new life, but the female body was needed to mold that seed into a human being. This notion comes across strongly in two Mesopotamian myths featuring the god Enki—*Atrahasis* and *Enki and Ninmah*. In the former, dating to the Old Babylonian period (circa 1800 BCE), the deities decide to create humans to labor for them. Enki summons Nintu the womb goddess to create humanity, but the goddess counters that Enki must first provide her with purified clay. In this act, Enki infuses his "water," the Mesopotamian equivalent of semen, into the matter of creation. Furthermore, the god Geštu-e is slaughtered, and his blood is mixed with the clay, also infusing it with life. Thus, male liquids cause the inert clay to live. However, once the clay is properly invigorated, Nintu, either by herself or with the help of birth goddesses, forms the clay into human females and males who henceforth will reproduce themselves sexually:

> She pinched off fourteen pieces (of clay)
> (And set) seven pieces on the right, seven on the left,
> Between them she put down a mud brick.[133]
> She made use of a reed, opened it to cut the umbilical cord,
> Called up the wise and knowledgeable
> Womb-goddesses, seven and seven
> Seven created males,
> Seven created females,
> For the womb-goddess is creator of fate.[134]

Sex and Gender in Theory and Practice   31

The importance of the female's molding of the seed into a human comes across even more emphatically in the Sumerian tale of *Enki and Ninmah* ("Great Lady," a Mesopotamian mother goddess). Here, after having created humankind, these two deities get a bit tipsy while celebrating and devise a bet that no matter how bad a human the one can make, the other will find a place for it in society. Ninmah begins, creating humans who are blind, incontinent, paralyzed, or stupid. In every instance, wise Enki can find an employment for the disabled individual, even if it is merely "standing by the king." But when Enki must form a human himself, he creates:

> Umul (="My day is far off"): its head was afflicted, its place of . . . was afflicted, its eyes were afflicted, its neck was afflicted. It could hardly breathe, its ribs were shaky, its lungs were afflicted, its heart was afflicted, its bowels were afflicted. With its hand and its lolling head it could not put bread into its mouth; its spine and head were dislocated. The weak hips and the shaky feet could not carry (?) it on the field.[135]

Put simply, Enki created not the standard, adult human but an infant, possibly a fetus, for which no independent occupation might be found. Ninmah lost the bet, but the point was that a male alone could not form a human. He could, and did, provide the seed for the being, but a human could only be fully formed with the participation of a female.

Our limited Canaanite/Ugaritic repertoire offers a similar understanding of this paradigm. In the *Birth of the Gracious Gods* (*CAT* 1.23), the focus is on the father god El, whose phallic activities give rise to a pair of voracious deities who are born to young goddesses and suckle at the breasts of Athirat, the Canaanite mother goddess. Once again, we have the division of male as engenderer and female as bearer and nourisher.

> El's "hand" grows long as the sea,[136]
> El's "hand" is the ocean.
> . . .
> El charms the pair of maids.
> If the maiden pair cries out:
> "O husband! husband!
> Lowered is your scepter,
> Generous the "staff" in your hand."
> . . .
> He bows down to kiss their lips,
> Ah! their lips are sweet,
> Sweet as succulent fruit.
> In kissing, conception,
> In embracing, pregnant heat.
> The two travail and give birth

32   *Sex and Gender in Theory and Practice*

to the gods Dawn and Dusk.

. . .

Both travail and give birth,
Birth to the gracious gods.
Paired devourers of the day that bore them,
Who suck the teats of the Lady's breasts.[137]

Counterexamples come from both Israel and Egypt. In Israel, where our primary source is the Hebrew Bible, masculine monotheism worked against any gender complementarity in the divine realm. Unlike the creation myths from the rest of the ANE, neither version of the creation of humanity in Genesis has a female creatrix complementing the creator. Nevertheless, there are some data which suggest a feminine *aspect* to the god of the Jews. Genesis 1:27 may indicate a dual-sexed nature to the creator deity:

So God created humankind in his image,
In the image of God he created them;
Male and female he created them.[138]

This notion reflects what we saw in the creation of humanity in *Atrahasis*, where the birth goddesses made seven males and seven females, reflecting the sexes of the deities themselves and allowing for future sexual reproduction. Another passage cited for suggesting a feminine element in the Hebrew god is Genesis 49:25, wherein, among other blessings, Jacob blesses his sons:

By the God your father, who will help you,
By the Almighty who will bless you
With blessings of heaven above,
Blessings of the deep that lies beneath,
Blessings of the breasts and of the womb.[139]

The idea of God's assumption of female characteristics also plays out in the realm of reproduction, where God is credited with forming the fetus in the womb. Thus in Psalm 139 (ll. 13–14):

For it was you who formed my inward parts;
You knit me together in my mother's womb.
I praise you, for I am fearfully and wonderfully made.
Wonderful are your works.

Likewise, the LORD claims to the prophet Jeremiah (l. 5):

Before I formed you in the womb I knew you,
And before you were born I consecrated you.

Sex and Gender in Theory and Practice   33

The archaeological evidence combined with the close cognates between the ancient Israelite and Canaanite religions suggest that the ancient Israelites were originally polytheistic, with female goddesses such as Asherah (Ugaritic Athirat) complementing male gods such as El and Baal. Although these goddesses and "extraneous" gods were removed in the process of creating Israel's monotheism, the texts seem to indicate an original feminine presence, especially those involving reproduction.[140]

In Egypt, humans were understood to be modeled by the god Khnum, the potter deity. He moistened his clay with waters from the Nile, which was understood to be the male deity Hapy. As such, we see a continuation of the ANE motif that water is a masculine attribute that provides fertility. What is odd is that Khnum alone makes humans, without a female complement. For example, the Middle Kingdom *Admonitions of Ipuwer* laments that:

> Lo, women are barren, none conceive,
> Khnum does not fashion because of the state of the land.[141]

Likewise, in the New Kingdom *Tale of Two Brothers*:

> Pre-Harakhti said to Khnum: "Fashion a wife for Bata, that he not live alone!" Then Khnum made a companion for him who was more beautiful in body than any woman in the whole land, for (the fluid of) every god was in her.[142]

Nevertheless, when the deities themselves reproduced, it was done in standard heterosexual fashion. The paradigmatic union is that between Osiris and his sister/ spouse Isis, as recounted in Pyramid Text §§632–633:

> Your sister Isis comes to you rejoicing for love of you. You have placed her on your phallus and your seed issues into her, she being ready as Sothis, and Ḥar-Sopd has come forth from you as Horus who is in Sothis. It is well with you through him in his name of "Spirit who is in the *Dndrw*-bark"; and he protects you in his name of Horus, the son who protects his father.[143]

In general, then, reproductive fertility required both sexes. The roles were fixed: Males provided the fluid seed of life; females incubated, molded, and ultimately nourished that new life. But the masculine element was considered dominant in this process of creation: It was the male who created new life, which he then "gave" to the female. Thus, as Ann Macy Roth comments on Egypt:

> If we define fertility specifically as the act of creation itself, it can be argued that in ancient Egypt, women were not credited with creating new life. Instead, the creative role is attached exclusively to the male sex. This association can be seen clearly in the language, where the verb that we translate as "to conceive a child" is the same as the Egyptian verb used for "to receive" or

"to take." In the Egyptian view, the woman "receives" the child, already fully created, from the man. This view is stated explicitly in Akhenaton's Hymn to the Aton: praising the god as creator of human life, the hymn says that he has "placed seed in a woman and made the sperm into a person."[144]

Similar understandings for Iron Age Israel are expressed by Baruch Levine:

The womb provides the same nutrients to the embryo as the mother earth does to vegetation that grows in it. There is, however, no indication in the Hebrew Bible, as far as we can ascertain, that the female contributes a life essence, an egg, to the embryo; the role of the female is entirely that of nurturer. The seed is provided by the male, and it grows inside the womb.[145]

Childcare: The Kourotrophos

Outside of some mythological (read: fictional) references (see Chapter 3), *pregnancy* is gendered feminine. All images of pregnant individuals are female. The same goes for parturition, outside of some philosophical texts that claim that Sokrates was a midwife to the birth of ideas (a bit of creative license). So the biological aspects of child-bearing are never seen as anything other than feminine.

It is also interesting to note that *childcare* is also inevitably presented as feminine, even though there is no biological reason for this to be so. This is where the matter of sex turns into very socially constructed gender. Consider the gender implications of an image common to varying degrees throughout the area under consideration: the kourotrophos, the depiction of (inevitably) a woman with child (Figures 1.4, 1.5.1.6, 1.7).

Figure 1.4 Iranian Kourotrophic Terracotta Plaque, Louvre Museum Sb 6582.

Source: Drawing by Paul C. Butler. Used with kind permission.

Sex and Gender in Theory and Practice 35

Figure 1.5 Ivory Plaque with Winged, Kourotrophic Goddess from Ugarit, Damascus Museum 3599.

Source: Drawing by Paul C. Butler. Used with kind permission.

Figure 1.6 Predynastic Ivory Kourotrophic Figurine, Ägyptisches Museum, Berlin, 14441.

Source: Drawing by Paul C. Butler. Used with kind permission

Figure 1.7 Bronze Kourotrophic Figurine from Horoztepe, Museum of Anatolian Civilizations.

Source: Drawing by Paul C. Butler. Used with kind permission.

The kourotrophos is an ideal image with which to study ideas of sex, gender, and the female body in the archaeological context, for the image sits at the very nexus of biological sex and cultural gender. The kourotrophos, as the potentially lactating nourisher of an infant, stands between the biological birth mother and the culturally constructed caretaker, who need not be female but, somehow, always is.

If we create a continuum, with female physiology at one end and culture-specific socialization at the other, our starting point would be physical pregnancy and parturition. It is a 100% constant in human biology that it is the female of the species who receives sperm into her body where it may unite with an egg and fertilize it. That zygote, still within the female body, may then implant itself into the uterine wall and develop there. If all goes well in terms of fertility, the fetus incubates for approximately 9 months, at which point the infant is born, or at least removed from the female body. Birth from a female body is a constant factor in human life.

The next point on our continuum is lactation. With the obvious exceptions of those women who die in childbirth and those who, for whatever reason, do not lactate, most new mothers did feed their newborns via lactation for the first few weeks, months, or even years of life. In many instances, where the biological mother cannot or does not wish to breast-feed, a wet-nurse can be hired; antiquity provided few alternatives to breast milk for infants. Although not 100% of new mothers (or women, for that matter) lactate and feed children via nursing, 100% of lactation and nursing does come from women. Men cannot do it. It is a biological process exclusive to females. Therefore, one might argue that on strictly biological criteria, pregnancy, parturition, and lactation are exclusively female occupations.

At this point, our continuum leaves the biological and enters the cultural. As Kathleen Bolen put it:

> For conceptual clarity, two aspects of motherhood are often distinguished: biological mothering (the birth relation) and social mothering, although such divisions or categories must remain fluid and permeable. . . . There *is* a relevant undeniable biological "fact" in that females give birth. This reality contrasts with the changing ambiguity of parenting within ethnographic contexts and the growing acceptance of the construction of "biologically" based explanations. The conceptual distinction between mothering labor and birthing labor is important. Birthing labor, which *is* biological and culminates in giving birth, is undeniably female and remains universally in the realm of women. Raising, feeding, protecting, and caring for children commonly defines the activities of motherhood, and occur under a variety of conditions. Socially, all women are potentially mothers, yet often overlooked is the fact that these social functions are not limited to women, or even specific age groups.[146]

Once recovered from parturition, and even if the new mother does breast-feed (and this is not a given), there is no biological reason for the mother, or a female, to be the primary care giver of a newborn, *especially* if the child is fed by means other than human lactation.[147] A lactating mother may be present to feed the child, but otherwise that child can remain under the supervision of a grandparent, aunt/uncle, or older sibling, *inter alia*. If in times ancient and modern we associate childcare primarily with females, this is a cultural construct; it has little firm basis in biology other than the occasional need for breast-feeding at the hands (and breasts) of a lactating female.

> There is no evidence to show that female hormones or chromosomes make a difference in human maternalness, and there is substantial evidence that nonbiological mothers, children, and men can parent just as adequately as biological mothers and can feel just as nurturant.[148]

All associations between children and women after the cessation of breast-feeding (or, following Bolen, parturition) are entirely cultural. Although the frequency with which the "woman–child/children" dyad occurs in society might give the impression of a more universal (read: biological) basis for this, research by Nancy Chodorow and others has shown that this is in fact not the case.[149] Furthermore, Sherry Ortner has shown that a number of tendencies across cultures might account not only for the conceptual association of children with women but the concomitant identification of women with children.[150] This is in addition to modern tendencies to project the current "norm" onto antiquity, thus justifying and preserving the *status quo*.[151]

38 Sex and Gender in Theory and Practice

There is no biological reason for females to have the monopoly on childcare and thus kourotrophic iconography. Nevertheless, with the slight exception of a small, highly localized Egyptian outlier, the fact remains that in antiquity, the kourotrophos motif, *even when not showing nursing, even when shown in a familial context*, is exclusive to the female. Thus, for example, on an Early Cypriot double-spouted jug from a necropolis in Pyrgos, Cyprus[152] (Figure 1.8), we see a pair of females (with breasts) holding infants and apparently caring for a toddler at the foot of a chair in which sits a solitary male (with phallic bulge). Females are associated with children/childcare; males with nothing else to do are not. There can be no doubt that the kourotrophos—the anthropomorphic conceptualization of child-caretaking—is an engendered image, and that gender is feminine. It is wholly culturally constructed.

At this point, though, we must return to that original idea of fertility being a masculine trait: It was the father, not the mother, who actually created the new life. As such, the child is understood to belong to the father and his lineage, not to the mother('s). Just as in modern times a child will most likely receive the father's surname (in the European traditions exclusive of Spain and Iceland), so too in the ancient world, children belong the father's household and were part of

Figure 1.8 Early Bronze Age Jug from Pyrgos, Cyprus T.35/16+17, Limassol District Museum LM 1739/7.

Source: Used with kind permission of the Cypriot Department of Antiquities.

Sex and Gender in Theory and Practice 39

the father's ancestral cult, and, should the parents be divorced, the child would remain with the father in his household. Should the father die, the widow's only legal link to her husband's household (and claims thereupon) would be if she specifically bore a son. In the absence of male progeny, she would be sent home to her natal family.

Final Considerations

As noted previously, biological sex derives entirely from the way humans (et al.) reproduce, that is, by combining the genetic materials from two separate individuals of the species. As with many other animals and several species of plants, humans evolved to have two separate categories of individuals to play out this process: those who generate the penetrating gamete—sperm, and those who generate the penetrated gamete—eggs. Because we are mammals, this led to some additional layers of dimorphism, creating organs for the incubation of the fetus inside the body—the uterus, and milk generation—mammary glands/breasts.

And yet, on top of that basic reproductive biology, an entire way of *thinking* about those differences has emerged—gender, even when it comes to the process of reproduction itself. In the ancient world, fertility was gendered masculine; in modern times it is most assuredly gendered feminine. Pregnancy is still entirely gendered feminine, but males are now expected to take part in the parturition process, and fathers are increasingly being told by society in general to be more engaged in the up-bringing of their children—the "new" fatherhood. As I write this during the perturbations of the COVID-19 crisis, article after article about how women, but not men, are trying to juggle working from home while educating their children seem to indicate that we still have a rather long way to go with this one. Childcare is still gendered feminine.

Two final notes about the subject matter of this book. As noted at the beginning, this is a book about gender. *It is not a book about men and/or women* in the ancient Near East. It is about how their identities as men and as women (and as boys and as girls) were constructed and understood. Second, as you have probably already noticed, this book covers an incredible scope of space and time. Especially time. Things change over time, and what was true of 3rd-millennium Sumer does not necessarily pertain to the Neo-Assyrian Empire; what was true of 18th-Dynasty Egypt does not apply to *anything* else in Egyptian history, for the most part. I shall try to be as specific as possible in the pages that follow; please keep in mind that the data pertain to specific times and places without overly generalizing or universalizing.

Notes

1 Another way to think of it: "Gametes come in two varieties. Large ones are known as eggs, and individuals who produce them are known as females. Small, often mobile gametes are called sperm, and the individuals who make them are known as males" (de Waal 2022: 163).
2 Rodden Robinson 2010: 69.

40   *Sex and Gender in Theory and Practice*

3 WHO 2014. They also code for ear hair.
4 Wiener 1999: n.p.
5 Rodden Robinson 2010: 74–75.
6 WHO 2014; Rodden Robinson 2010: 69–71.
7 If Serena Williams got into a wrestling match with Tiger Woods, whom would you bet on?
8 The idea that there is no such thing as (human) sex at all goes back to Monique Wittig's essay "The Category of Sex," published in 1982, wherein the theorist contended that, "For there is no sex. There is but sex that is oppressed and sex that oppresses. It is oppression that creates sex and not the contrary." Her hypothesis was that the concept of "sex" was created by the dominant, oppressive members of society (males) to keep the oppressed members (females) in their place. It is social dominance, not biology. The pithy summary and retort of philosopher Kathleen Stock is worth quoting in full, "According to this so-called 'dominance' model of the sexes, it is as if, long ago, there was only a blooming, buzzing confusion of flesh, and perhaps also of sexual parts of different shapes. Then one day, a group of people came along and artificially moulded this proliferation into two categories for their own nefarious purposes, calling it 'natural': the dominant males and the dominated females. . . . [W]ho, exactly, was supposed to have started it? Did a random group of people start oppressing random others?" (2021: 69–70).
9 Fausto Sterling 1993: 21.
10 *Ibid.*
11 *Ibid.*
12 Tuana 1996: 64.
13 Talalay 2005: 146. See also Asher-Greve 2002:12; McCaffrey 2002: *passim*; Talalay 2000: 9.
14 Bailey 2013: 248. My emphasis.
15 Knapp and Meskell 1997: 186–187. My emphasis.
16 Blackless et al. 2000: 151.
17 It doesn't help that in her 2000 book *Sexing the Body*, Fausto-Sterling herself said of her 1993 article, "I'd intended to be provocative, but I had also been writing tongue in cheek, and so was surprised by the extent of the controversy the article unleashed" (Fausto-Sterling 2000: 78).
18 Blackless et al. 2000: 159.
19 Moore 2000: 554.
20 Sax 2002: 177.
21 WHO 2014.
22 WHO 2014; Rodden Robinson 2010: 76–77; Sax 2002: 176.
23 Rodden Robinson 2010: 77.
24 Sax 2002: 176.
25 See Sax 2002: 176.
26 WHO 2014; Rodden Robinson 2010: 76; Sax 2002: 176. Keep in mind that XIST deactivates the extra X.
27 WHO 2014.
28 Sax 2002: 176.
29 Rodden Robinson 2010: 76.
30 Sax 2002: 176.
31 WHO 2014.
32 Sax 2002: 176.
33 Live births per 1,000. Blackless et al. 2000: 153.
34 Wiener 1999: n.p.
35 WHO 2014.
36 Sax 2002: 175; Blackless et al. 2000: 153–154.

37 Fausto-Sterling 2000: 1–3.
38 WHO 2014, with citations.
39 Blackless et al. 2000: 156.
40 WHO 2014; Sax 2002: 175; U.S. Department of Health & Human Services website: "Congenital adrenal hyperplasia."
41 WHO 2014.
42 Wiener 1999: n.p.
43 U.S. Department of Health & Human Services website: "Congenital adrenal hyperplasia"; Wiener 1999: n.p.
44 Wiener 1999: n.p.
45 "Mosaicism" has nothing to do with tesserae. It is a genetic condition in which a single body contains cells with different genetic codes, typically the result of developmental aneuploidy. Sex chromosome mosaics are the most common in humans, whereby some cells of the body contain X0, others XXX or XXY. Rodden Robinson 2010: 232.
46 Wiener 1999: n.p.
47 Blackless et al. 2000: 157. See also WHO 2014, with additional references.
48 Blackless et al. 2000: 159; Wiener 1999: n.p.
49 Blackless et al. 2000: 159.
50 Sofaer 2013: 230.
51 Connell and Pearse 2015: 11.
52 Connell and Pearse 2015: 49. Emphasis in original.
53 Maccoby and Jacklin 1974: 349.
54 Maccoby and Jacklin 1974: 352.
55 Hyde 2005: 590.
56 Connell and Pearse 2015: 73.
57 Barry 1998: 115.
58 Butler 1990: 9–11.
59 Butler 1993: 5.
60 I see this all the time on official documents and questionnaires, asking me my age ("Old"), my race or ethnicity (where Portuguese-speaking Brazilians are "Hispanic" but Spaniards from Spain are not), and my gender. The options for that last one are never things like "Gracile Dyke" or "Butch Fairy" or even "*femme*," but male or female. I always want to cross out the word "gender" and replace it with "sex."
61 Walker and Cook 1998: 256.
62 *Ibid*: 259.
63 Asher-Greve 2018: 19 and 26. Money et al. 1957 *do* refer to such sex/gender assignments, but they are discussing hermaphrodites in the 1950s, when such biology was deemed "correctable." It is hardly the norm.
64 Masterson et al. 2015: 3.
65 See especially Asher-Greve 2018 on this. For a recent rebuttal of Laqueur, see King 2016.
66 Gatens 1996: 70.
67 Nordbladh and Yates 1991: 224. My emphasis.
68 *Ibid*: 233–234.
69 Fausto-Sterling 2000: 4.
70 Minas Belmont 1993: 4. My emphases.
71 Tuana 1996: 54.
72 Talalay 2005: 131.
73 Connell and Pearse 2015: 64.
74 De Waal 2022: 286–287, with citations. On a similar and more personal note, a former trans individual interviewed by Katie Herzog in her 2017 article "The Detransitioners: They Were Trans; Until They Weren't" observed that, "Everybody says that gender

Sex and Gender in Theory and Practice

is a social construct, but we also act like it's somehow an innate part of a person's identity." www.thestranger.com/features/2017/06/28/25252342/the-detransitioners-they-were-transgender-until-they-werent

75 Sumerian gender instead distinguishes between sentient/living and non-sentient/non-living, thus between a dog and a brick, much as with Japanese *iru* vs. *aru*.

76 Zsolnay 2018: 468.

77 Goodnick Westenholz and Zsolnay 2017: 13; Leick 1994: 92.

78 Goodnick Westenholz and Zsolnay 2017: 33, n. 13.

79 The reader is strongly encouraged to consult the chapter by Goodnick Westenholz and Zsolnay (2017) for more in-depth treatment of all these phenomena.

80 Brinkman 2007: 1.

81 Brinkman 2007; Abrahami 2011.

82 It is often the case with cuneiform that different signs can have the same phonetic value. To distinguish between these signs in transliteration, either subscript numbers are used, thus LU, LU_2, LU_3, LU_4, or accents are used for versions 2 and 3, and subscript numbers appear after that, thus LÚ (=LU_2), LÙ (=LU_3), LU_4. Both systems appear in this book equally.

83 Goodnik Westenholz and Zsolnay 2017: 26.

84 Text and translation from https://etcsl.orinst.ox.ac.uk/cgi-bin/etcsl.cgi?text=c.1.2.1& display=Crit&charenc=gcirc#

85 Text and translation from https://etcsl.orinst.ox.ac.uk/cgi-bin/etcsl.cgi?text=c.1.8.1.1 &display=Crit&charenc=gcirc#

86 This tendency may actually start to appear as early as the Early Dynastic period, when the KUR sign—ungendered—was understood to be a male captive/inferior, while the SAL element was added to KUR to indicate a female of that class. Thus, the male form is unmarked/standard, the female marked. Goodnick Westenholz and Zsolnay 2017: 15.

87 Goodnik Westenholz and Zsolnay 2017: 22.

88 Goodnik Westenholz and Zsolnay 2017: 23.

89 Muller 2016: 431.

90 On gender in Egyptian language and writing, see Allen 2001: 35–36.

91 These designations of hieroglyphic signs were devised by Alan Gardiner in his first organization of ancient Egyptian orthography.

92 David 2014: 58 and 65.

93 Roth 2005: 212. "For men to have existed, women must have been in existence from the very same moment; the two sexes were therefore regarded as of equal antiquity and equally essential to the existence and functioning of the created universe."

94 Fischer 2000: 46. My emphases.

95 I'm assuming you don't have to be told that these are penises.

96 Unlike Sumerian, but like the Semitic languages such as Akkadian, Egyptian language does have gender, with the feminine form—as with the Semitic languages—being marked by the phoneme –t. Allen 2001: 35.

97 Orriols-Llonch forthcoming.

98 Hays 2012: 375.

99 Orriols-Llonch forthcoming.

100 Much like the Greek *gynê*, the Egyptians had the same word for "woman" and "wife."

101 Brettler 2017: 199.

102 Ibid: 200.

103 The medium will have some bearing on the coloration of the individual depicted, so that a faience female might actually be blue, for example. Thus I specify *painted* colors here.

104 Roth 2005: 212.

105 Some women certainly worked in the fields, and male scribes worked indoors, so clearly we are looking at idealized gendered stereotypes, not reality, as is the case with gender studies inevitably.

Sex and Gender in Theory and Practice 43

106 Roth 2005: 212–213.
107 Roth 2006: *passim*.
108 "Decorum" in Egyptian art refers to how people can be portrayed doing what where and when.
109 Zsolnay 2018: 469. Old Babylonian made use of mimetion—that final –m, which fell off in later dialects. Thus the "(m)".
110 Although as we shall see in Chapter 3, the removal of a beard could function to emasculate a male rival.
111 Matuszak 2018: 264; Matuszak 2016: 230.
112 Matuszak 2018: 267.
113 Lambert 1996: 226.
114 Foster takes this as "blockhead" (Foster 1993: 337).
115 CHD "pišnatar".
116 Text and translation from https://etcsl.orinst.ox.ac.uk/cgi-bin/etcsl.cgi?text=c.1.8.1.4 &display=Crit&charenc=gcirc#
117 Text and translation from https://etcsl.orinst.ox.ac.uk/cgi-bin/etcsl.cgi?text=c.5.6.1& display=Crit&charenc=gcirc&lineid=c561.68#c561.68
118 Stol 2000: 60. As Ilona Zsolnay observed, "The ritual does not indicate that other genders (or sexes) were an option" (2018: 469 n. 43).
119 Stol 2000: 61.
120 Matuszak 2018: 263.
121 Matuszak 2018: 263.
122 Hoffner 1966: 331.
123 *Ibid*: 332.
124 Hoffner 1987: 277.
125 Text and translation from Parpola and Watanabe 1988, accessed via http://oracc. museum.upenn.edu/saao/saa02/corpus, adapted.
126 Budin 2021: 45–46.
127 Matić 2021: 116.
128 Ibid: 117.
129 This really does read like the word problem from hell . . .
130 Matić 2021: 124. See *idem*. 123–130 on the translation of "foreskin" for *ḳrn.t*.
131 Faulkner 2007: 1.73.
132 Black et al. 2004: 220–221.
133 A reference to the mud bricks upon which women in labor knelt or crouched during parturition in Mesopotamia and Egypt.
134 Dalley 1989: 16–17. Stol emphasizes that this passage is only preserved in two later Assyrian versions of the text discovered in Assurbanipal's library. Thus, they may be later additions to an earlier text and not part of the original conception of the origins of humanity (2000: 113–114).
135 ETCSL translation t.1.1.2, http://etcsl.orinst.ox.ac.uk/cgi-bin/etcsl.cgi?text=t.1.1.2#
136 On the euphemism "hand" for penis, see Paul 2002.
137 T.J. Lewis in Parker 1997: 210–213. The "Lady" is identified as Athirat in an earlier stanza.
138 All translations are NRSV.
139 On this "breast and womb" passage, see Smith 2002: 48–52.
140 On the archaeological evidence for "pre-Biblical" polytheism, see especially Keel and Uehlinger 1998. On the deities of ancient Israel, see Smith 2002.
141 Lichtheim 2006, Vol. I: 151.
142 Lichtheim 2006, Vol. II: 207.
143 Faulkner 2007: 120–121.
144 Roth 2000: 189.
145 Levine 2002: 341–342.
146 Bolen 1992: 49–50. Emphases in original.

44　*Sex and Gender in Theory and Practice*

147 The discovery of ancient Greek baby bottles with nipples shows that this was a possibility.
148 Chodorow 1978: 29.
149 *Ibid*: Chapter 2, with citations.
150 Ortner 1974: 77–78.
151 Bolen 1992: *passim*.
152 Limassol District Museum LM 1739/7.

2 Femininity

When one is reading, writing, and/or talking about feminine gender, one is dealing with how a given society perceives women and girls. In the ancient world, this is tricky because the vast majority of our sources were written by men, and generally an elite, reasonably well educated category of men at that. As a result, much of what we think we know about feminine gender in antiquity has the major stumbling block that what we actually get is a male conception of femininity without the input of females themselves.

This is almost certainly the case for fictional documents—myths, lyrics, epic literature—which nevertheless contain a wealth of information on how females were perceived in ancient societies (at least from that elite male perspective). Fortunately, a large number of "daily" documents are also preserved from Mesopotamia, the Levant, Anatolia, and Egypt, texts written on clay and pottery and thus preserved (inadvertently) for posterity. The vast majority of these were *also* written by males, of course. But two points must be kept in mind. On the one hand, at least *some* of the various letters, adoption contracts, last wills and testaments, bills of sale, leases, and inventories were written—or at least dictated by—females (writing itself was generally restricted to a small body of professional scribes). So we do get a female voice. On the other hand, the kinds of texts just mentioned are a bit more likely to deal with reality than the myths and lyrics. As such, they can serve as a foil for understanding the fictional accounts and provide another means of accessing how the ancients actually thought. The fact that a dying father expects the daughter he just turned into a son to marry and bear children (really: See Chapter 4) says a *lot* more about ANE gender constructs than, say, Aristophanes' account of the women of Athens dressing up as men to seize control of the government (*Ekklesiazousai*). Nevertheless, the bias of the male voice must be kept in mind.

Even more problematic is the bias of the modern mind and what modern-day scholars think femininity *should* have been. That is, we inflict our own notions of femininity onto the past. This is especially problematic in two key areas: fertility and sexuality.

DOI: 10.4324/9780429318177-2

46 *Femininity*

The Fertility Problem

As we saw in Chapter 1, the ancients associated fertility with males: It is a masculine attribute. This fact has had very little impact on the established scholarship. Browsing through even a 21st-century academic text on mythology or iconography, one will notice that most female deities are understood on some level to be mother goddesses, while any image with breasts, much less a pubic triangle, will be understood as a "fertility charm." Thus as one Assyriologist who was asked to give his impressions as an outsider of gender theory queried concerning the Mesopotamian goddess of war and sex Inana/Ištar:

> How did we ever come to believe that Inana has anything to do with fertility? Inana or Ištar is strongly associated with sex, war, and legitimate kingship— but hardly ever with fertility. In most traditions she has no children of her own—she has sex for pleasure. Thus, why fertility? A Google search turns up hundreds of pages saying that Inana/Ištar is the ancient Sumerian goddess of fertility—but to me she seems like the very opposite. Perhaps we may reconstruct this as the taming of Ištar. What were these Victorian men of the Church going to do with a wildly sexual goddess? How were they supposed to wrap their minds around such an anomaly? Is it possible that fertility was a concept that put her in a safe and recognizable place?[1]

From a textual/literary perspective, this fertility issue sprouts up whenever one deals with ANE goddesses (or their servants). Assyriology emerged out of Biblical studies, in an academic milieu steeped in Protestant Christianity. It was taken as a given that the pagan religions of the ANE, and especially those of the Canaanites, were sexual, orgiastic, and just generally morally bankrupt. Institutions such as sacred prostitution and child sacrifice abounded. In the scholarship, as adeptly put by Peggy Day:

> Disproportionately, it is the goddesses and their female cult functionaries and devotees who are made to shoulder the bulk of the blame for alleged moral depravities. When the proverbial bushes are beaten to see what deities lurk therein, "fertility" goddesses emerge from under every green leafy tree. And "fertility," when applied to goddesses and their votaries in mainstream scholarly practice, has carried the connotations of illicit sexual activity.[2] In addition, the overwhelming propensity for all goddesses to be labeled fertility goddesses reduces them to a single common denominator, thus obscuring their individuality and making them interchangeable, less threatening, and easier to trivialize.[3]

The excessive reliance on "fertility" also emerges in studies of the iconography: Female images are automatically assumed to be fertility amulets of some kind. Female images and figurines from the Mediterranean and Near East were/are typically categorized into two possibly overlapping categories—"Fertility Figurine"

Femininity 47

and less frequently "Concubine of the Dead" (placed in graves to provide sexual services to the deceased in the afterlife) (deceased that consist of men, women, and children, for the record). A third possibility was, of course, "sacred prostitute" (more on this subsequently).[4] This is the case whether the female icon in question is naked or clothed. So, for example, a quick survey of the Cypriot repertoire from the Chalcolithic through the end of the Bronze Age reveals nothing in the 20th-century scholarship but fertility figures. Jacqueline Karageorghis observed in her study of Cypriot Chalcolithic cruciform figurines (Figure 2.1) that:

> it is indisputable that the image of a strongly sexualized woman is promoted here. It is difficult to say whether this is the representation of a goddess of fertility or simply a magic image of the forces of fertility, but the main point is that the image of fertility is identified with woman.[5]

When writing about a larger version of these Chalcolithic images, the "Lemba Lady" (Figure 2.2), Veronica Tatton-Brown wrote that, "She must have been a fertility charm and may even represent a goddess."[6] The fact that the figurines in question are "sexualized" automatically leads to the assumption that they embody fertility, as though breasts and genitalia could have no other purpose or meaning. In the Metropolitan Museum of Art's catalogue of the Cesnola collection, it is written of the coroplastic Plank-shaped figurines (e.g. Figure 2.3) of the Early and Middle Cypriot Periods (2500–1600 BCE) that, "They do not represent divinities, but there is no doubt that they symbolize concepts of regeneration and fertility."[7]

Figure 2.1 Chalcolithic Cruciform Figurine from Yalia, Cyprus Museum, Nicosia, 1934/ III-2/2.

Source: Drawing by Paul C. Butler. Used with kind permission.

48 *Femininity*

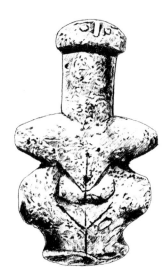

Figure 2.2 Female Statuette from Lemba, Cyprus Museum, Nicosia, 1976/54.
Source: Drawing by Paul C. Butler. Used with kind permission.

Figure 2.3 Early Cypriot Plank Figurine, Cyprus Museum, Nicosia, 1963/IV-20/12.
Source: Drawing by Paul C. Butler. Used with kind permission.

In his interpretation of the Late Cypriot III Bomford Figurine (Figure 2.4), H. Catling sees a divinity of Near Eastern derivation who, "in all likelihood . . . is the same goddess who was later to become the Paphian Aphrodite. In her Bronze Age manifestation, at least, she was doubtless a goddess of fecundity."[8] Once

Figure 2.4 Bomford Figurine, Cyprus, Ashmolean Museum AN1971.888.
Source: Drawing by Paul C. Butler. Used with kind permission.

again, the presence of the sexual attributes (breasts and genitalia) and the possible association with the later Greek goddess of sex leads to the hypothesis that the image in question must be a fertility image. In only a slight contrast to Catling, O. Masson, in his interpretation of this figurine, claimed that the image may in fact be Aphrodite or even Astarte but that ultimately such fertility goddesses would have assimilated and distributed attributes too diverse to allow for an identification with a single deity: "ce type de divinité féminine de la fécondité a dû donner lieu à des assimilations diverses."[9]

The figurines in question don't even have to be naked to be presented as fertility items: Images of females of all types are typically given the fertility analysis merely by fact of being female. Thus, in a 2020 science report in the *New York Times*, a collection of Phoenician female votive figurines discovered off the coast of Israel were presented by the researchers as:

> [T]hey accumulated over roughly 400 years, between the 7th and 3rd centuries B.C., in a series of votive offerings, as part of a cult devoted to seafaring and *fertility*. . . . These figurines, the majority of them, display attributes related to *fertility*, to *childbearing* and to *pregnancy*.[10]

Looking at the figurines, though, one sees no signs of fertility, childbearing, or pregnancy. They are not examples of the Phoenician *dea gravida*—distinctly pregnant. They are not pregnant, nursing, kourotrophic, or even eroticized. They are simply women in gowns. But *woman* is enough to equal "*fertility*." Likewise, a partial figurine discovered in Israel in March of 2021 consisted of the upper

50 *Femininity*

portion of a veiled woman shown from top of head (veil) to her hands clasped above the abdomen. The figurine was worn, but as she was veiled and no known figurines from the ANE are both veiled and nude, she was most likely dressed head to toe (much like the gowned figures in the previous paragraph). And still, the Israel Antiquities Authority reported in an article in the *Jerusalem Post* that, "The artifact depicts a stylized *bare-breasted* woman wearing a scarf with her hands folded under her chest. It probably served as an amulet for *fertility* and *protection for infants*, it said."[11] Woman = fertility is thus passed down from the academy to the general populace.

Much of this ideology stems from the Victorian Age and is typically pinned on the writings of James Frazer, specifically his massive compendium *The Golden Bough*. As Gwendolyn Leick noted in her work on Mesopotamian sex and eroticism:

> The literary texts are our main form of information on the cultural value of love and sensuality. When they were first translated, Sir James Frazer's *Golden Bough* had an enormous impact on the interpretation of these works. Every love-song, every hymn that mentioned Inanna and Dumuzi, as well as all the archaeological artefacts with sexual scenes, were automatically classified as being pertinent to a "Sacred Marriage" ritual, with the aim of perpetuating "fertility". This notion is still current among contemporary and eminent Assyriologists. But this simplifies the complexity of the subject far too much.[12]

Just as responsible for the "fertilization" of goddesses (and females generally) was the counterculture approach to feminism and the rise of feminist spirituality and the Goddess Movement in the 1970s and 80s. As noted by Gretchen Lemke-Santangelo in her book *Daughters of Aquarius*, hippies came late to feminism, starting only in the early to mid-1970s rather than the mid-1960s. Furthermore, and very importantly, the counterculture took a very different approach to feminism than what was emerging among the Second Wave feminists. Rather than viewing gender as a cultural construct that was at the root of women's oppression, "most hippie women adopted a feminism that affirmed and celebrated 'natural' or 'essential' female characteristics."[13] Furthermore, it was this branch of feminism that sought liberation and empowerment through the formation of a specifically women's or feminist spirituality. The combination of these two factors led to the creation of a religion (or series of religions) predicated on a quintessentially biologically essentialized Goddess approached and understood through spiritual and biological—rather than intellectual and falsifiable—avenues. As Marylyn Motherbear Scott (a hippie chick) put it:

> It was being on the land where the Mother Goddess began to speak most intimately to me, by being in nature, by knowing the passage of the seasons, by experiencing it full on. It wasn't book learning, it was experiential.[14]

Femininity 51

It was this cultural development that came to influence academia in the 1980s, most emphatically entering ancient Near Eastern studies with the 1983 publication of Samuel Noah Kramer and Diane Wolkstein's book *Inanna: Queen of Heaven and Earth: Her Stories and Hymns from Sumer*. While the original translations from the Sumerian were done by Kramer (one of the "fathers" of Sumerology), these tales were re-told and interpreted by Wolkstein, a folklorist and story-teller *deeply* entrenched in the feminist spirituality movement. Suddenly, Inana was a fertility goddess (e.g.):

> As Queen of the Land of Sumer, Inanna is responsible to and receives her power from the resources and fertility of the land. . . . The images presented in the first few lines (of *Inanna and Enki*)—shepherd, sheepfold, apple tree, young woman, and vulva—are all related to fertility.[15]

Within a decade, the fertility goddess problem had gotten so bad that by 1989 Biblical scholar Jo Anne Hackett could complain:

> I am of course pleased that Inanna and the others are of interest to those who are concerned with an alternative spirituality, but I have found, to my surprise, that they are often admired not because of their many sources of power and their multifaceted personalities, but rather because they are said to be "fertility goddesses."[16]

Fortunately, the pigeon-holing of all females—goddesses, mortals, figurines—into a single archetype is gradually leaving the various fields of inquiry. Thus while Inana/Ištar is still seen as a fertility goddess in all popular culture and far too much academic literature, less overtly erotic goddesses are now starting to be recognized as having their own unique—even non-feminine!—attributes. Thus, for the Ugaritic goddess Anat (on whom see more in Chapter 4), a late 20th-century text notes:

> The first readers of these [Ugaritic] texts tended to view her as yet another example of the ubiquitous "fertility-goddess," this time as the spouse of Baal. The narratives cited to demonstrate that Anat was a goddess of fertility are all, unfortunately, so broken as to be inconclusive about this role for her.[17]

Considering the fact that Anat possesses all of Ištar's martial attributes and none of her eroticism, and that she is a blood-thirsty battlemonger, this has rather convinced many in a more gender-savvy age that she is pretty much the *antithesis* of a fertility goddess—"inconclusive" is an understatement.

A similar process is now underway for (non-divine) female iconography from the ANE, although it is an exceptionally slow process. Efforts are now starting to push in the opposite direction, to see even nude female images as products of their time, place, and context and to provide more nuanced interpretations of their meanings. Thus, concerning one of the earliest versions of the nude female motif

52 *Femininity*

Figure 2.5 Anthropomorphic Jar Handle from Kiš, Ashmolean Museum AN1925.230.
Source: Drawing by Paul C. Butler. Used with kind permission.

in Mesopotamia, the so-called "Goddess" jar handles decorating funerary jars in the city of Kiš (Figure 2.5), a recent publication offers:

> Rather than a charm for fertility or a symbol of maternity or prostitution, the Nude Female who graced the handles of funerary jars in ancient Kiš and, later, surrounding territories was a *political* symbol. She was a marker of ethnic identity and unity, binding together the various classes, ages, and sexes of Kiš, defiant against the encroachment of foreign powers. The jar handles' femininity can be understood as the result of cross-cultural tendencies to associate females with containers, liquids, and the care of the dead. Over time, the anthropomorphism and feminization of the handles may have led them to be seen as simple manifestations of the goddess Inana, an erotic warrior goddess who recovered from death. The female body, even naked, might have a multitude of meanings. The Female and her body is not merely an object of male desire, but a multivalent symbol relevant to the political ideology of city-states.[18]

Likewise, in an OpEd in *Haaretz* on the matter of female figurines, we read:

> It is not just that we have no evidence that the nude female icon is associated with fertility; we have copious data that it does *not*. The figurines do not appear pregnant; they do not appear giving birth; they rarely appear with children (*especially* in the Levant); they do not appear lactating; they can

be *contrasted* with actual scenes of erotica, pregnancy, parturition, and lactation. Never mind the fact that ancient texts attribute fertility to males—NOT females—to begin with. But, the thinking goes, if one sub-category is depicted holding her breasts, what else can they possibly be? What else would a woman even care about?[19]

The Sex Problem

As we shall see, eroticism was an important aspect of feminine gender throughout the ancient Near East, a fact that tends to startle readers more accustomed to ancient Classical restrictions on and Judeo-Christian-Muslim condemnations of female sexuality. So the problem isn't so much that Near Eastern women were sexual but in how modern scholars have approached this issue. Assyriology especially emerged mainly among men working on Biblical studies in the Victorian era, meaning there were three interlocking ways that female eroticism was utterly daunting. As Niek Veldhuis observed previously regarding the (non-)fertility of Ištar, these were the people who had to find some way to rationalize and "tame" this Mesopotamian (and Egyptian) style of *joie de vivre*. There were two main ways to do this. One was to turn female sexuality (and anything that might be reminiscent of it) into fertility (see previously). The second was to remove all agency from females when it came to sex. The most common means of doing this was to turn female eroticism into prostitution. An utterly absurd number of terms and women in the ANE corpus are identified as prostitutes, either secular or, even more popular, sacred. Šamḫat in the *Epic of Gilgameš*, who has sex with Enkidu for seven straight days and nights (fourteen in some versions!) is typically presented as a "harlot." The titles of the vast majority of priestesses and cultic functionaries in Mesopotamia and the Levant (e.g. *qadištu, qedešâ*) are translated as "sacred prostitute," including the ones (*entu, naditu*) who are clearly sworn to celibacy. (No, I am not kidding). The ancient Egyptians also had multiple terms translated as prostitute, including a category of (wet-)nurses (*ḫnmt*).[20] All while there is not a *single* datum for the exchange of goods for sex in the entire Bronze Age textual corpus throughout the entire Near East. Let me repeat: There is not a single reference to the sale of sex from the entire Bronze Age. How, then, can we have so many potentially celibate prostitutes?

Mostly, it depends on definition. While in the 21st century we have agreed that a prostitute is a person who sells temporary access to his or her body for sexual purposes, another long-term definition was a woman, specifically, who socialized with men.[21] Any woman in the ancient records who engaged in social intercourse with men outside of her family might be understood as engaging in other kinds of intercourse as well, and thus the prostitute label was applied even in the absence of economic exchange. The more explicit the sexual intercourse (e.g. Šamḫat), the firmer the prostitute label. However, because deep down it was still understood in the 19th–21st centuries when these women (only women) were being defined as prostitutes that they provided sex in exchange for goods paid to them by men

54 *Femininity*

(specifically), their sexuality was seen to be controlled by men: Prostitutes do not have agency (at least according to the modern fantasy).

Between fertility and prostitution, female eroticism was constrained and put under a male yoke. Women and goddesses did not have sex because they enjoyed it but because they were providing their husbands with offspring or because a male clientele paid for it.

> You are allowed to be objectified by men and dress like a slut, but don't own your sluttiness. And do not, I repeat do not, share your own sexual fantasies with the world. Be what men want you to be.
>
> (Madonna, *Billboard* Woman of the Year 2016)

This is not how the ancients saw it. In the ancient Near East, women were understood to like sex, and their celebrations of eroticism formed a considerable portion of our corpus of ancient literature, even the parts written by men. The distractions of fertility and unbelievably prolific prostitution are merely that: distractions.

As ever, one must remain cognizant of the fact that we are dealing with over three millennia of history and numerous distinct societies and civilizations. What is true of 3rd-millennium Sumer is not necessarily the case for 2nd-millennium Anatolia or 1st-millennium Israel, much less any point in the history of Egypt. Nevertheless, certain traits do stand out as being gendered feminine in these ancient societies: eroticism, intermediary, nurturing, domesticity, and second sex.

Beauty and Eroticism

Females in the ANE were literally considered the "fairer" sex: Beauty was an aspect of feminine gender, and this beauty was understood to be erotic in nature. Rather than being responsible for fertility as men were, females—both mortal and divine—inspired sexual arousal and enjoyed the consequences thereof. Some texts even refer to sex as "that which pertains to women." Thus, on tablet BM 23631, a Sumerian hymn to Utu, the sun god, records what is apparently a very young Inana telling her brother (ll. 137–140):

> I am one who knows not that which is womanly (ÁG.MUNUS.E.NE)—men
> I am one who knows not *that which is womanly—copulating*
> I am one who knows not *that which is womanly—kissing*
> I am one who knows not copulating, I am one who knows not kissing.[22]

On tablet 1 of the Standard version of the *Gilgameš Epic*, the huntsman trying to thwart the wild man Enkidu sends the *ḫarīmtu* Šamḫat to seduce him, telling her (ll. 180–185):

> There he is Šamḫat! Bare your breasts,
> Spread your legs, let him take in your charms.

Femininity 55

Do not recoil but take in his scent;
He will see and approach you.
Spread your clothing so he may lie on you;
Do for the man the work of a woman![23]

Likewise, a curse from Anatolia reveals how the eroticism of women (along with motherhood) is as innately a part of femininity as fertility and warfare are of masculinity. Thus KUB XV 35 + I, ll. 51–58, (excerpted):

Then from the men take away masculinity (LÚ.NITA.tar), fertility, and health; take away weapons—bows, arrows, and daggers—and bring them to Hatti Land . . .

From the women take away motherhood, love, and sexuality and bring them to Hatti Land.[24]

The emphasis on the female as the primary erotic being also comes across in art: Depictions of nude females—often with emphasis on the pubic triangle and frequently adorned with copious jewelry—typify most ANE artistic repertoires. By contrast, naked[25] males appear only when shown as in real life, naked for the sake of work, being humiliated as a captive, in scenes of coitus, or, very occasionally, in scenes of orgy (such as the Turin Erotic Papyrus). The nude female, then, is not a representation of daily life (although those do appear, few and far between) but an idealized, symbolic image. Normally, of course, they are considered symbols of fertility (see previously).

Thus in ancient Egypt, from the 12th Dynasty through the New Kingdom on, we see a tradition of so-called fertility figurines that portray—in stone, faience, clay, wood, or ivory—an *en face* female with naturalistic proportions, all wearing jewelry, with a consistent emphasis on the pubic triangle (Figure 2.6). Some lie on a bed; some have a child either to the breast or to the side.[26] The elaborate jewelry, which may consist of necklaces/collars, bracelets, and hip girdles, indicates that the nudity is artistic rather than "daily." The presence of the bed as a full category (Geraldine Pinch's Type 6)[27] from the 18th and 19th Dynasties links the images with the realm of the erotic.

The emphasis on the pubic triangle was not reserved only for such figurines: Depictions of (elite) clothed women also had an emphasis on this sexual marker. The long robe that adorned elite women was rendered clingy and diaphanous (or, at least, rather see-through), such that the pubic triangle and navel, if not necessarily the breasts, were displayed. Thus, a wooden statuette from the 8th Dynasty (Old Kingdom) now in the Metropolitan Museum of Art (MMA; see Chapter 1, Figure 1.2) shows a woman in nearly imperceptible clothing. The lack of definition on the breasts, a clear line between the legs, and vulva make it clear that she is clothed. Nevertheless, the pubic triangle itself is visible. Just so the statuette of the wife of Merti, also in the MMA, from the 5th Dynasty (Figure 2.7). The exact same thing might be said for an 18th-Dynasty statuette now in the Brooklyn Museum (Figure 2.8).

56 *Femininity*

Figure 2.6 Type 1 Potency/Fertility Figurine, Egypt, Brooklyn Museum, 44.226.

Figure 2.7 Statuette of Wife of Merti, Old Kingdom, Metropolitan Museum of Art 26.2.3.

The eroticism of feminine nudity was especially prominent in depictions of adolescent females in New Kingdom Egypt, in multiple media. Thus an elaborately coiffed painted ivory statuette in the Brooklyn Museum (Figure 2.9) might be compared to the young female servants in a funerary wall painting from the tomb of Nebamun, now in the British Museum (Figure 2.10).

Femininity 57

Figure 2.8 New Kingdom Wooden Statuette, Brooklyn Museum 54.29.

It is worth noting that the male servants in the Nebamun scene are clothed, specifically in kilts that hide their genitalia. The girls wear elaborate wigs and jewelry (collars, bracelets) that emphasize their erotic appeal, while the boys are bald and functionally desexualized. This is a consistent fact in Egyptian art: While males might be shown naked in scenes of labor, they are never physically eroticized to the extent that females are. They are most typically shown wearing kilts that cover the genitalia. When they are shown naked in labor scenes, the penis is always flaccid, again de-emphasizing eroticism (although probably pretty naturalistic).[28] When male deities with erections are portrayed, it is often (although not exclusively) in the presence of a nude, erotic female (Figures 2.11 and 2.12)

58 *Femininity*

Figure 2.9 New Kingdom Ivory Figurine, Brooklyn Museum 40.126.2.

As Gay Robins theorized:

> [T]he effect on the heterosexual male of viewing the female body, especially the pubic region, is often sufficient to cause sexual arousal. Thus, as in many other cultures, it would seem that in ancient Egypt, a depiction of the external characteristics of the female pubic region was enough to encode a message of sexuality linked with fertility that referred not only to women but also to the aroused male.[29]

An even more extensive repertoire of an eroticized nude female appears throughout the ancient Near East with origins in central Mesopotamia. Although down to the mid-3rd millennium depictions of nude females were relatively common and often could appear side by side with nude males, at the end of the millennium, a new style emerged that became dominant throughout the duration of ANE history. Originally manifesting as crude jar handles in the Mesopotamian city of Kiš,

Femininity 59

Figure 2.10 Funerary Wall Painting from the Tomb of Nebamun, British Museum EA 37986. © The Trustees of the British Museum.

Figure 2.11 Book of the Dead of Sesu, Detail, British Museum EA 9941.1.

Source: Drawing by Paul C. Butler. Used with kind permission.

60 *Femininity*

Figure 2.12 Stela of Qeh, British Museum EA191. © The Trustees of the British Museum.

this new style consistently featured a nude, *en face* female typically decorated with jewelry (necklaces, earrings, bracelets) and rendered with an emphasized pubic triangle. When made as three-dimensional figurines, they were originally hand-made in terracotta with arms either reaching forward (Diyala region, Figure 2.13) or clutching the breasts (Aššur and Nippur, Figure 2.14)—they might also hold a disk/tambourine.[30] Beginning in the Akkadian period, they started to be mold-made, typically with the hands clasped upon the upper abdomen. This form became dominant in the Old Babylonian period, outnumbering all other mold-made images.[31]

This motif—the nude female with emphasized pubis, eroticized with jewelry, and often drawing attention to the breasts—continued as a popular motif throughout all the societies of the Near East. Quickly adopted in Anatolia and Syria, the icon spread south, east, and west, appearing as mold-made terracottas, in the glyptic iconography, as lead artefacts, carved into stone, molded as glass, embossed into gold, and rendered in the round in ivory and wood. The nude female was one of the most consistent, ubiquitous images of the ANE, making its way to Greece, Italy, and Spain. Figures 2.15–2.20 show a range from Anatolia to Greece. There is nothing even roughly comparable pertaining to males, and certainly not erotic/ized males.

Bath = Attraction of Male Gaze (Passive vs. Active)

The power of the nude female body to stimulate heterosexual male desire comes across most powerfully in bath scenes, endemic in ANE literature. What is of

Femininity 61

Figure 2.13 Diyala Female Terracotta Figurine, Oriental Institute A17892.
Source: Courtesy of the Oriental Institute of the University of Chicago.

Figure 2.14 Nippur-Style Female Terracotta Figurine, MMA 59.41.21.

62 *Femininity*

Figure 2.15 Silver and Gold Statuette from Hasanoğlan, Anatolia, Museum of Anatolian Civilizations, 13922.

Source: Drawing by Paul C. Butler. Used with kind permission.

Figure 2.16 Late Cypriot Bird Face Figurine, British Museum A 15.

Source: Drawing by Paul C. Butler. Used with kind permission.

Femininity 63

Figure 2.17 Middle Bronze Age Terracotta Nude Female Figurine from Ebla, Syria, Aleppo Museum TM.92.P. 875+TM.94.P. 530.

Source: Drawing by Paul C. Butler. Used with kind permission.

Figure 2.18 Terracotta Plaque from Gezer, Israel, Ashmolean Museum 1912.621.

Source: Drawing by Paul C. Butler. Used with kind permission.

64 *Femininity*

Figure 2.19 Gold Foil Dove "Goddess" from Grave Circle A, Shaft Grave III, Mycenae, Athens National Archaeological Museum 27.

Source: Drawing by Paul C. Butler. Used with kind permission.

Figure 2.20 Daidalic Terracotta of Anasyrma Female from Kato Syme Viannou, Crete, Herakleion Museum.

Source: Drawing by Paul C. Butler. Used with kind permission.

Femininity 65

particular interest is the interplay of active and passive in these scenes. In some narratives, it appears that the female deliberately disrobes in order to provoke an amorous response from a specific male, thus leading to coitus. In other instances, the scenario seems more accidental, the female more passive, but with the exact same results.

Thus, in the Sumerian tale of *Enlil and Ninlil*, Ninlil's mother Nunbaršegunu advises her daughter to avoid bathing in the visible location of the river, since so doing would invite the amorous gaze of Enlil. Apparently this sounded like a good idea to Ninlil, who proceeded to bathe in the river and visually aroused the young god in the process:

> At that time the maiden was advised by her own mother, Ninlil was advised by Nunbaršegunu: "The river is holy, woman! The river is holy—don't bathe in it! Ninlil, don't walk along the bank of the Idnunbirtum! His eye is bright, the lord's eye is bright, he will look at you! The Great Mountain, Father Enlil—his eye is bright, he will look at you! The shepherd who decides all destinies—his eye is bright, he will look at you! Straight away he will want to have intercourse, he will want to kiss! He will be happy to pour lusty semen into the womb, and then he will leave you to it!"
>
> She advised her from the heart, she gave wisdom to her. The river is holy; the woman bathed in the holy river. As Ninlil walked along the bank of the Idnunbirtum, his eye was bright, the lord's eye was bright, he looked at her. The Great Mountain, Father Enlil—his eye was bright, he looked at her. The shepherd who decides all destinies—his eye was bright, he looked at her. The king said to her, "I want to have sex with you!", but he could not make her let him. Enlil said to her, "I want to kiss you!", but he could not make her let him. "My vagina is small, it does not know pregnancy. My lips are young, they do not know kissing."[32]

They have sex; she gets pregnant, he has to skip town. Ninlil chases after Enlil to three separate towns. Each time the god attempts to hide by disguising himself; each time Ninlil sees through the disguise and has sex with the god yet again. She ends up bearing four children to her eventual spouse. Although Jerrold Cooper suggests that this is a story of rape, Leick has countered that Ninlil's seduction of Enlil was deliberate, emphasized by the fact that the goddess follows the god all over the land after he is banished for his unauthorized sex with the maiden.[33]

The motif of the woman who seduces the male by means of her bath-time nudity also appears in the Akkadian tale of *Nergal and Ereškigal*. Here, when the god Nergal must descend to the underworld to apologize for affronting the queen of the dead, he is sternly advised not to do "that which men and women do" if he sees Ereškigal nude when bathing. The god descends, and although he is careful not to eat, drink, sit, or any of the other acts that would imprison him in the Land of No Return, when the goddess attends to her toilette:

> She went to the bath
> And dressed herself in a fine dress

66   *Femininity*

And allowed him to catch a glimpse of her body
He [gave in to] his heart's [desire to do what men and women do].
The two embraced each other
And went passionately to bed.[34]

where they amorously engaged for six days and nights. At the end of the sixth day Nergal sneaked out of Ereškigal's house in history's first recorded "walk of shame" and escaped back to the realm of the living. When Ereškigal found out, she cried out:

Erra [Namtar], the lover of my delight—
I did not have enough delight with him before he left![35]

As Rivkah Harris noted, "Though Nergal may not have been able to resist Eresh-kigal's charms, he was sexually satisfied after six days. Ereshkigal obviously was not. . . . What may well be expressed here is the view that women have voracious appetites for sex, a not-uncommon view about women."[36]

That females could use their bath-time eroticism to weaken a foe with lust is the theme of a passage from the Hurrian *Song of Hedammu*. Here the Ištar-like goddess Šauška seduces her brother Teššub's enemy (§§11.2 and 16.2)

Now when Teššub finished speaking he went away. But Šauška went to the bath house. [The Queen of Nineveh] went there to wash herself. She washed herself. . . . She anointed herself with fine, perfumed oil. She adorned herself. And (qualities which arouse) love ran after her like puppies.

. . .
Šauška said to Hedammu: "Come up again. Come from the strong waters. . . ." Šauška holds out her naked members toward Hedammu. Hedammu sees the beautiful goddess, and his penis springs forth. His penis impregnates . . .[37]

The bathing motif appears as well in the Egyptian erotic literature. In the first stanza of the *Cairo Love Songs*, a female voice proclaims:

My god, my [lover . . .],
it is pleasant to go to the [canal]
. . .
and to bathe in your presence.
I shall let [you see . . .] my perfection
in a garment of royal linen, wet [and clinging].

Then I'll go into the water at your biding,
and I'll come out to you with a red fish
who will be happy in my fingers . . .
So come and look me over.[38]

In the Biblical story of David and Bathsheba, the sight of the nude female bathing caused David to lose all reason and commit the greatest sin of his reign (2 Samuel 11:2).

> One evening David got up from his bed and walked around on the roof of the palace. From the roof he saw a woman bathing. The woman was very beautiful, and David sent someone to find out about her. The man said, "She is Bathsheba, the daughter of Eliam and the wife of Uriah the Hittite." Then David sent messengers to get her. She came to him, and he slept with her.

Even in the absence of both bath motif and nudity, the idea of feminine beauty stoking masculine erotic desire is a long-standing motif in ANE literature.[39] When the Ugaritic goddess Athtart returns successful from the hunt, Baal becomes enflamed with desire at the site of her (*Athtart the Huntress*)

> [She had covered] her [body(?)] with a chemise of linen
> [Over] it she [placed] a coat of cypress-wooden mail.
> [And] her [beau]ty wore a sheen like the male stars,
> [a sp]lendour(?) like the female stars of Kuthan.
> [The] virgin(?)—Baal desired her,
> He wanted to possess her beauty . . .
> Before her face descended Almighty Baal.
> The awe struck (girl) was pleased(?),
> (that) he wanted to lo[ve her?] limbs(?).
> He began to throw his horns against the watchman.
> [And] Pidru [answ]ered him: Be careful, [o Baal]
> Do not waste [the . . .] of your [fl]esh against the watch[man!]
> Surely, you should give [. . .] for a prepared bed(?)!
> [If the desire] of Baal craves for [a living being],
> [of the lust of the Ri]der on the Clouds.[40]

Feminine Enjoyment

The fact that the erotic female seduces/entices the male does *not* mean that her own enjoyment of sex was secondary. In fact, it is the female enjoyment of sex that emphasizes the feminine nature of sexuality in the ANE. As we saw in the previous chapter, males enjoyed ejaculation (especially Enki). Narratives of their phallic exploits focus equally on matters of seduction/conquest (mainly Enki), fertilization (Enki, Atum, the Biblical patriarchs), and dealing with negative consequences (Enlil, Enki, Geb, Seth, Nergal, David. I know he's Greek, but Ouranos *really* comes to mind here). One rather gets the impression that ANE males don't enjoy sex as much as females—they are too busy trying to hightail it out of town. An illustrative contrast between feminine and masculine sexuality appears in the Mesopotamian *Disputation between Wood and Reed*. Here we see feminine

68 *Femininity*

adornment leading to enhanced beauty/eroticism and visual reception of the female leading to male arousal and fertility.

> The great earth (KI) made herself glorious, her body flourished with greenery.
> Wide earth put on silver and lapis lazuli ornaments,
> Adorned herself with diorite, chalcedony, cornelian, and diamonds.
> Sky (AN) covered the pasture with (irresistible) sex appeal, presented himself in majesty.
> The pure young woman showed herself to the pure Sky,
> The vast Sky copulated with the wide Earth,
> The seed of the heroes Wood and Reed he ejaculated into her womb.
> The Earth, the good cow, received the good seed of Sky into her womb.
> The Earth, for the happy birth of plants of life, presented herself.[41]

By contrast, the (admittedly male-authored) literature tends to focus on the female enjoyment of sex without references to issues of procreation (these are probably related concepts). *No* female in ancient history seems to have enjoyed sex more than Inana/Ištar. In a *pāru* hymn to the goddess we read (Von Soden 1991, rev., ll. 14–19):

> "Assemble to me the young men of your city"; exultation is the foundation for a city.
> "Let us go to the shadow of the city-wall!"; exultation is the foundation for a city.
> Seven (on) her chest, seven (on) her hips; exultation is the foundation for a city.
> Sixty and sixty satisfy themselves on her vulva; exultation is the foundation for a city
> The young men got tired, but Ištar did not tire; exultation is the foundation for a city
> "Enter, you men, into the excellent vulva!" exultation is the foundation for a city
> So the Maiden spoke; exultation is the foundation for a city[42]

In perhaps a more demure moment she converses with her bridegroom Dumuzi:

> "This vulva, . . ., like a horn, . . . a great wagon, this moored Boat of Heaven . . . . . . of mine, clothed in beauty like the new crescent moon, this waste land abandoned in the desert . . ., this field of ducks where my ducks sit, this high well-watered field of mine: my own vulva, the maiden's, a well-watered opened-up mound—who will be its ploughman? My vulva, the lady's, the moist and well-watered ground—who will put an ox there?"
> "Lady, the king shall plough it for you; Dumuzi the king shall plough it for you."
> "Plough my vulva, man of my heart!"[43]

Femininity 69

As Leick noted of this passage:

> It is hardly a coincidence that the description of the vulva in the text above captures the stages of sexual excitement in the woman. At the beginning her vulva resembles the narrow curve of the new moon until it opens "like a boat with its mooring ropes" (more likely to refer to the labia minora than pubic hair). Then there are several references to the transudation of the mucous membranes ("well-watered low land", "my vulva, a wet place") at which point she cries out for the "plough".[44]

But erotic bliss was not reserved exclusively for deities. Love songs with no reference to divinity also attest to the feminine enjoyment of sex. An Old Babylonian love song published by Joan Goodnick Westenholz reveals (ll. 2–15)

> The beating of your heart is joyful music
> Stir yourself and let me make love with you
> In your soft lap
> Of morning slumber
> Your caresses are sweet
> Growing luxuriantly is your fruit
> My bed of incense is *ballukku*-perfumed.
> O, by the crown of our head, the rings of our ears
> The mountains of our shoulders, and the charms of our chest
> The bracelet with date spadix charms of our waist
> Reach forth with your left hand and stroke our vulva
> Play with our breasts
> Enter, I have opened (my) thighs.[45]

The love songs from New Kingdom Egypt also display the female enjoyment of sexuality. From Papyrus Harris 500, Song Cycle III we read:

> Palm trees, heavy with dates,
>   Bend over my private garden
> Among such towering friends
>   Grow tall toward your private dream.
> Dear heart, it is I am your chiefest love,
>   First but from the ground of your caring,
> And I give back that love, am yours—
>   Take me and my gift of a garden.
>   . . .
> Heady with foreign blossoms,
>   Heavy with all sweet native flowers,
> A fountain plays in my garden,
>   Bubbles below the tall sun,
> For dipping your hand in

70 *Femininity*

> While easily we lie
> Waiting the cool of the northern seabreeze
>> That springs upriver at twilight.
> A charming spot to stroll,
>> Your hand covering mine;
> My body enjoys, relaxes, plays . . .
>> Oh, how my heart is high
> Matching the swing of our going—together,
>> Halves of a single love!
> The sound of your voice is sweet,
>> Full like the taste of date wine,
> And I, drunken girl in a tangle of flowers,
>> Live only, a captive, to hear it.
> But to have you here always, tall in my garden,
>> Devour you with my hungry eyes—
> Love, I'd be raised to pure spirit, translated,
>> Hovering over high earth!
> See me go! Light-hearted Walking on air!
>> Full of such love.[46]

Even the Bible, not exactly known for its focus on feminine pleasure in much of anything, least of all sex, nevertheless takes part in the Near Eastern tradition in the *Song of Songs*. Amidst masculine verses extolling the beauty of the "bride" (7:1–4)

> How beautiful your sandaled feet,
>> O prince's daughter!
> Your graceful legs are like jewels,
>> the work of an artist's hands.
> Your navel is a rounded goblet
>> that never lacks blended wine.
> Your waist is a mound of wheat
>> encircled by lilies.
> Your breasts are like two fawns,
>> like twin fawns of a gazelle.
> Your neck is like an ivory tower.

We also hear of the girl's love of her "bridegroom" and her desire for sex (e.g. 5: 2–6):

> I slept but my heart was awake.
>> Listen! My beloved is knocking:
> "Open to me, my sister, my darling,
>> my dove, my flawless one.
> My head is drenched with dew,

my hair with the dampness of the night."
I have taken off my robe—
    must I put it on again?
I have washed my feet—
    must I soil them again?
My beloved thrust his hand through the latch-opening;
    my heart began to pound for him.
I arose to open for my beloved,
    and my hands dripped with myrrh,
my fingers with flowing myrrh,
    on the handles of the bolt.
I opened for my beloved . . .

Adultery

The ancient Near East was a patriarchal place, and feminine desire always causes problems for the males who want to control female sexuality. Alongside the New Kingdom love songs and Mesopotamian hymns and the *Song of Songs* were tales (not to mention laws and court cases) pertaining to adultery. In the narrative literature, this adultery emerged through the agency of women. The tale of Joseph and Potiphar's Nameless Wife comes immediately to the western mind (Genesis 39). This Biblical narrative may have an ancestor in the Levanto-Anatolian orbit. A Hittite myth featuring deities with Canaanite names (Elkunirsa = El, and Ashertu = Ashera) shows what happened when the queen of the gods makes advances at the young buck Baal (§2):

> Elkunirsa looked at Baal and asked him, "Why have you come?" Baal said, "When I came into your house, Ashertu sent young women to me, saying, 'Come sleep with me.' I refused. Then she . . . me and spoke thus, 'Stay behind me and I shall stay behind you. Else I shall press you down with my word and stab you with my . . .' That is why I have come, my father. I did not come to you in the person of a messenger; I myself have come to you. Ashertu is rejecting you, her own husband. Although she is your wife, she keeps sending to me: 'Sleep with me.'"
>
> Elkunira replied to Baal, "Go threaten her, Ashertu, my wife, and humble her!"[47]

In the same genre is the Egyptian New Kingdom *Tale of Two Brothers*. Here the older brother Anubis lives with his wife in his house, and his younger brother Bata lives with them. One day when sent to fetch seed for planting in the fields, Bata comes across Anubis's wife in her chambers, having just finished adorning her hair. She approaches him, saying:

> "There is great manliness in you, for I have been observing your exertions daily." For it was her desire to know him sexually. She got up, seized him,

72   *Femininity*

and told him, "Come, let's spend for ourselves an hour in bed together. Such will be to your advantage, for I shall make fine clothes for you."[48]

Bata refused, and she accused him of attacking her, just as was the case for Joseph and Mrs. Potiphar and (in the Greek version of the tale) Hippolytos and Phaidra. Rather than ending up vizir (Joseph) or trampled by horses (Hippolytos), Bata wound up castrated.

One detail that is interesting to note is that Mrs. Anubis attempts to seduce Bata not with her own beauty but by offering to make him clothes ("Hey, Big Boy, wanna warp and weft?"). Another Egyptian narrative—*King Cheops and the Magicians*—this one dating to the Middle Kingdom, reveals a similar dynamic. Here the wife of the Chief Lector Webaoner became enamored of a man in the town. She had a servant bring the man a chest filled with clothing, and the two began an amorous affair which ended when Webaoner found out about it and fashioned a crocodile out of wax that became a real crocodile and ate the townsman when he went swimming. Again, it becomes increasingly clear why masculine tales of eroticism seldom play out as well as the feminine. Nevertheless, as Ann Macy Roth has discussed, these sartorial seductions are particularly interesting in that they are the only evidence for the exchange of goods for sex that exist for pre-Hellenistic Egypt. That is, they are the sum total of our evidence for ancient Egyptian prostitution, and in them it is the female who attempts to buy sexual access to the male, with textiles.[49] Again, it is the female who takes the sexual initiative.

As this section should somewhat indicate, there is, of course, a considerable gap between the social construct of feminine gender and the real, lived lives of ANE women. While the construct shows females reveling in their sexuality, the portrayals are often without pregnancy or the complications of marriage and relationships in a social matrix. They are fantasy. Real women were constrained in their sexual expression by such things as marriage and fertility (or the lack thereof). So while females were recognized as beautiful and desirable and desiring, actual human women could only act on this in a limited fashion in the real world. Female sex interfered with feminine gender.

Sex Goddesses

A final matter to consider in the relationship between sex and femininity is the fact that ancient pantheons have goddesses, but not gods, of sex: Inana, Ištar, Šauška, Hathor, Kypris, Aphrodite, Venus, and so on. Obviously this is simplifying a bit: All of these goddesses have multiple functions in their respective cultures, often including warfare, music, maternity, and queenship. But when we study ancient religions and mythologies, we inevitably come across at least one goddess who is presented as the goddess of sex, but never a god. Enki is not a "sex god"; remarkably, neither is Zeus. Baal might shtup a cow 70 times (*Baal Cycle*, fifth tablet, column V) and fall in lust with Athtart, but he's not a "god of sexuality." In that same text Father El receives his wife Athirat asking:

Femininity   73

"Does the 'hand'[50] of El the King excite you,
The love of the Bull arouse you?"[51]

But he's not a "god of sex" either. So, why sex goddesses but not gods? Is it them or us?

It's us.[52] It is important to recall that with the exception of the Greek pantheon, especially as presented in Hesiod's *Theogony*, ancient peoples rarely directly equated their deities with any specific concept. Deities were far more likely to be associated with specific places (e.g. Kypris is the goddess of Cyprus, Nekhbet is the goddess of Upper Egypt, Ereškigal is the goddess of the Underworld). Most deities started out as simply "Our God/ess" and acquired greater specificity only when confronted with other, similar deities. Otherwise, deities had a host of attributes, some of which may have been more striking to humans than others: Baal's associations with rain may or may not outweigh his associations with combat.

I believe that two factors are responsible for our recognition of certain goddesses as sex goddesses. One is the fact that most of us first start learning about ancient religions by learning Greek mythology.[53] And because Hesiod in his *Theogony* ties specific attributes to the various gods and goddesses, we come to think of them as, for example, Artemis the Hunting Goddess, Dionysus the God of Wine, Athena the War Goddess, as opposed to Ares the God of War, and so on. Even for the Greeks, though, this is a gross over-simplification, as becomes immediately apparent when one goes on to study the role of, say, Hestia or Hera in actual Greek religion. But it's a start, and it shapes people's way of thinking about ancient deities: NAME is God/dess of X. And so we come to label deities of different pantheons in the same way: Inana is the Goddess of Sex and War, Enki is the God of Fresh Water, Isis is the Mother Goddess of Magic and Healing, and Hannahanna is the Anatolian Birth Goddess.

It might instead be better to think of the deities of the various pantheons as themselves, with attributes and personalities, much like humans. Inana is herself— determined, erotic, violent, romantic, willful. Like Faith from *Buffy the Vampire Slayer*, or Helena from *Orphan Black*.

Second, we *expect* males to be sexual. It is not surprising when Zeus sticks it into anything with an orifice, or Enki impregnates his own daughter/granddaughter/himself. This is the modern take on masculine gender: that testosterone creates a strong sex drive, and that post-pubescent males think of sex once every six seconds. It does not stand out when gods are sexual, such that we think it a defining aspect of character: They're just being guys. When a female stands out as being erotic, however, we take note. If she is *very* sexual, we come to define her by this quality: She becomes a "goddess of sex." This is *especially* so if her sexuality is uncoupled from maternity, such that she cannot be conceived of as a "mother goddess" (although she probably will be somewhere anyway). Inana/Ištar is not a mother; neither is Hathor (who mainly babysits Horus), nor Šauška. Aphrodite may have children, but she is not an especially attentive mother (*Homeric Hymn to Aphrodite* V). So we call them "Goddesses of Sex," are flabbergasted when they combine this quality with violence and warfare, and eventually associate

74 *Femininity*

them with some kind of "sacred prostitute" functionaries or call them prostitutes themselves. Really, it's us: The ancients would not have thought to do that.

Why Feminine?

A final question is: Why it is the female who is associated with sex and beauty rather than the male. The ANE literature makes it clear that males enjoyed sex (sometimes a *lot*—see Enki). Works such as the *Song of Songs* and the Egyptian Love Songs have reciprocal expressions of desire for the beauty and love of both partners—the woman who expresses admiration and love of the male, just as the man sings of the beauty and desirability of the female. While Inana sings in praise of her vulva, Enki sings in admiration of his penis.

And yet it cannot be denied that there is an erotic imbalance in the portrayal of the sexes. Even clothed, the Egyptian woman highlights her pubic triangle, while Egyptian males keep their penises discreetly under wraps. The nude female is a longstanding icon in the ANE that reveals a symbolism to feminine nudity that does not appear with males. Our love lyrics reveal women and goddesses asking for someone to stroke and plough their vulvae; penis-wielders are rather independent—no male ever seems to call out for someone to stroke his dick.

Part of the explanation must of course be the androcentric, heteronormative nature of the sources. Most of our writings and art were probably written and rendered by male scribes and artists. The desire of the male for the female will thus outnumber expressions of female desire, and male expressions of homosexual desire were minimal and/or probably coded in ways that we no longer recognize. We are thus left with the female as the embodiment of eroticism.

Even so, it is likely that some aspects of the female voice are in fact present in our data. High-ranking Egyptian noblewomen had some control over their depictions in art, so there was volition in the portrayal of their pubic triangles. Images of the nude female—plentiful as they were—were used by females as well as males (e.g. they show up in the graves of males, females, and children) and thus had meaning for both sexes.

As Jerrold Cooper has discussed, it is likely that at least some aspects of the Mesopotamian repertoire of erotic lyrics derive from the woman's voice. As he has noted,

> We have no information about Sumerian women's secular songs or poetry, nor would we expect to, given the nature of our sources. . . . [But] [t]he odds are very good that if the Sumerian love songs are in a women's voice, there could have been an actual genre of women's love and wedding songs that served as their model.[54]

That is to say, the songs hymned to Inana and Dumuzi may derive from a women's oral tradition of erotic poetry, here deemed especially important because of the sex of the goddess so honored.[55] Furthermore, in contrast to the roughly

Femininity 75

penetrative, fertility-oriented expressions of male sexuality, Cooper notes that the love songs present the female experience of sexuality as sensual, fully corporal (as opposed to merely genital), and utterly devoid of the resultant fertility (=pregnancy).[56] For these reasons, it is likely that the Sumerian love songs do indeed present a feminine experience of sexuality.[57] Likewise, Gwendolyn Leick has suggested that the Sumerian Royal Love Songs originated in the competitive context of the polygynous royal household, where the king's wives were in competition for their lord's affections.

> Polygyny fosters sexual competition to win the favours of the "master", and expertise in erotic matters is an important factor. . . . Some of the love-songs, especially when they are directed at the king, could be understood as a manifestation of seduction through poetic artifice. Others, such as those which are set in the form of a dialogue between lovers, are a stylistic variation of the same scenario. . . . We know that royal wives "composed", or at least commissioned, literary compositions. . . . I would like to believe that they represent the "true" voice of Sumerian women.[58]

In other words, it would seem that women also recognize eroticism as feminine. This is not masculine objectification of the female, with women merely internalizing the conventions of their patriarchal, heteronormative matrix.

The more holistic nature of female sexuality seems not to be the answer either. Just as the male experience is focused in the penis, so, too, in the ANE is feminine desire primarily focused on the vulva. As noted by Ilona Zsolnay, "Derrières, penises, and bosoms are far less the subject of erotic verse than vaginas."[59]

Two biological data appear to be significant for this aspect of engendering. One is the simple fact that women are capable of having a *lot* more sex than males. The potential for multiple orgasms and the lack of need to stop and rest between acts of coitus (in males, the flaccid state) mean that females can be more continuously sexually active than males, with a much greater potential for orgasm. Consider Inana in that *pāru* hymn previously, wearing out all the young men of the city. However, second is the fact that human females take longer to reach orgasm than males and that women are somewhat less likely to be guaranteed an orgasm in (genital) sex. There is a greater possibility that women require more sex for sexual satisfaction. After six days and nights, Ereškigal did not yet have her fill of Nergal.

The greater female potential and desire for sex plays out throughout the simian–hominid realm. Female capuchin monkeys solicit marathon sex from males to the point of utterly exhausting their mates:

> They go through these poke-and-run charades the whole day until the male drops dead, or nearly so. During every copulation, both sexes whistle, chirp, and squeal excitedly. Males, however, are sometimes reluctant to the point of seeming indifferent. Or perhaps we should turn this around and say that the female's fire burns hotter than the male's, who has trouble keeping up.[60]

76 *Femininity*

Closer to our own species (don't even get me *started* on bonobos!), Frans de Waal has observed of chimpanzee libido that:

> The initiative among adolescents lies more with the female. She wants everything she can get and demands so much of the male that sometimes he cannot satisfy her. When he has reached this point he may briefly place a finger in the vagina of the presenting female. Usually he will avoid her.[61]

When the Sexual Revolution hit the United States and mixed with the emergent counterculture (a.k.a. hippie) movement, both sexes discovered that the male fantasy of limitless sex had very real biological limits,

> In sexual games, once the double standard was removed, women discovered that they often more than held their own with men, whose fantasies of endless women clashed with the reality of spent male potency. Women laughed and moved on to the next guy.[62]

Quite simply, when it comes to biology:

> All in all, it's time to abandon the myth that males have a stronger sex drive and are more promiscuous than females. We let this myth seep into biology during Victorian times, when it was enthusiastically embraced as normal and natural. We bent reality to meet our moral standards. This myth is still standard fare in biology textbooks, but support for it has never been overwhelming. Contradictory evidence for female sexuality has been accumulating with regard to both our own species and others. Female sexuality seems as proactive and enterprising as that of males, even if for different evolutionary reasons.[63]

Finally, back in the ANE, there is the fact that it was understood that female beauty stimulated the male to sexual arousal that led to sexual intercourse that brought about fertility that resulted in life. Quote A.M. Roth, "[W]omen seem to have had a dual role: they aroused the man and stimulated his creative act with their beauty and sexual attractiveness, and then they nourished the life that his creative power produced."[64] Males may have been understood as the sources of fertility in the ancient world, but they key to that fertility was female beauty. Feminine eroticism was the source of life.

Intermediary

In the so-called "Baal Cycle" from Ugarit (CAT 1.1–1.6) the storm god Baal, having just defeated his rival, the sea god Yamm, decides that it is time for him to have his own house (read: temple). Problem: To do so requires the approval of the head of the pantheon, the sky god El (read: alpha male). To request El's approval, Baal does not approach the elder deity himself but instead goes through a three-part diplomatic maneuver whereby he first gets the support of the goddess

Femininity 77

Anat, his best friend, who turns out not to be the most diplomatically savvy deity in the pantheon: Having explained his lack of a proper house, Anat replies (CAT 1.3, Column V, ll. 1–4):

> I will drag him [El] like a lamb to the ground;
> I will make his gray hair run with blood,
> The gray hair of his beard with gore,
> Unless he gives Baal a house like the gods',
> And a house like that of Athirat's sons!

She makes the same threat to El directly, at which point it becomes pretty clear that Baal needs to find a more tactful intercessor. Thus he and Anat go to Kothar-wa-Ḥasis, the artisan god, and ask him to make a gift to bring to Athirat (CAT 1.4, Column I, ll. 20–22):

> Produce, please, a gift for Lady Athirat of the Sea,
> A present for the Creatrix of the deities.

Gift in hand, they approach the goddess as she does her laundry (CAT 1.4, Column III, ll. 25–36):

> Just when mighty Baal arrives,
> Adolescent Anat arrives,
> They entreat Lady Athirat of the Sea,
> Beseech the Creatrix of the deities.
> And Lady Athirat of the Sea answers:
> "Why do you entreat Lady Athirat of the Sea?
> Why do you beseech the Creatrix of the deities?
> Have you entreated Bull El the Beneficent,
> Or beseeched the Creator of creatures?"
> And Adolescent Anat answers:
> "Let us entreat Lady Athirat of the Sea,
> Let us beseech the Creatrix of the deities,
> [. . .] we will entreat him."

Having received the gift, Athirat agrees to help Baal and Anat. She approaches El while he feasts (CAT 1.4, Column IV, ll. 31–51, excerpted):

> She comes to the mountain of El and enters
> The tent of the king, the Father of Years.
> At the feet of El she bows down and falls,
> Prostrates herself and honors him.
> There El perceives her,
> He breaks into a smile and laughs
> . . .

78 *Femininity*

"Why has Lady Athirat of the Sea arrived?
Why has the Creatrix of the deities come?
Are you very hungry, having traveled.
Or are you very thirsty, having journeyed?

. . .

Or does the 'hand' of El the King excite you,
The love of the Bull arouse you?"
And Lady Athirat of the Sea answers:
"Your decree, O El, is wise,
You are wise for eternity,
A victorious life is your decree.
Our king is Mightiest Baal,
Our ruler with none above him.

. . .

In lament he cries to Bull El, his Father,
To El, the King who created him.
He cries to Athirat and her sons, the goddess and the band of her brood:
'For Baal has no house like the gods,
No court like Athirat's sons . . .'"

El, won over, agrees to the new construction (CAT 1.4, Column V, ll. 1–5):

"Let a house be built for Baal like the gods,
A court, like Athirat's sons."
And Lady Athirat of the Sea answers:
"You are great, O El, so very wise;
The gray hair of your beard instructs you,
Your soft beard down to your chest."[65]

It must be noted from the outset that Baal has his own messengers, the gods
Gapn and Ugar, whom he first sends to Anat. Likewise, Lady Athirat has her
own manservant, Qudšu-wa-Amraru (remarkably, no such servant is known for
Anat . . .). Nevertheless, neither makes use of these male servitors or messengers
for the highly diplomatic mission of approaching El. Nor does Baal ever seem to
conceive of speaking with El directly to make his request, even after defeating a
rather powerful foe such as Yamm. When negotiating status between two powerful males, it is the females who function as intermediaries. Anat explains to Baal
how best to approach Athirat ("Give her a gift"), and Athirat herself cajoles El
with flattery (and perhaps her own erotic appeal—"Does the hand of El the King
excite you?"). In the end, Baal gets what he wants.

In his analysis of this section of the *Baal Cycle*, Neal Walls sees this series of
exchanges as highly gender dependent:

[T]he role of Anat as Baal's messenger or intermediary is connected to her identity as a female. In fact, Baal uses only female intermediaries, Anat and Athirat,

Femininity 79

rather than his lackeys Gupan and Ugar when he desires El's acquiescence to his claim of divine kingship. This fact illustrates the importance and necessary subtlety of the mission to El, since only important deities were importuned. Moreover, the gender of the intermediaries is probably essential as they mediate between the two antagonistic males working out their new relationship.[66]

This narrative displays another aspect of feminine gender in the ANE: the feminine role as intermediary, intercessor, and "connective tissue." Such intercession could take numerous forms; in the literature it is often between two males of close rank,[67] while in religious praxis it is between the distinctly separate ranks of mortals and deities.

In the *Epic of Gilgameš*, three females stand out as performing this role of intercessor. First is Gilgameš's own mother Ninsun. When her impetuous son decides to go off and slay the Monster of the Cedar Forest Humbaba, she offers a lengthy prayer on his behalf to the solar deity Šamaš, frequently, it should be noted, by invoking Šamaš'a own wife Aya:

> [Ninsun] climbed the staircase and went up onto the roof.
> On the roof she set up a censer to Šamaš.
> Scattering incense she lifted her arms in appeal to the Sun God:
> "Why did you afflict my son Gilgameš with so restless a spirit?
> . . .
> During the days of his journey there and back,
> Until he reaches the Forest of Cedar,
> Until he slays ferocious Humbaba,
> And annihilated from the land the evil thing you abhor,
> Each day when you travel the circuit of the earth,
> May Aya the Bride unfearing remind you:
> 'Entrust him to the care of the watches of the night!'
> . . .
> May Aya the Bride unfearing remind you:
> 'The day Gilgameš and Enkidu encounter Humbaba,
> O Šamaš, rouse against Humbaba the mighty gale winds . . .
> Let rise thirteen winds and Humbaba's face darken,
> Let the weapons of Gilgameš then reach Humbaba!'
> After your very own fires are kindled,
> At that time, O Šamaš, turn your face to the supplicant!
> Your fleet-footed mules shall bear your onwards.
> A restful seat, a bed for the night shall be what awaits you.
> The gods, your brothers, shall bring food to delight you,
> Aya the Bride shall wipe your face dry with the fringe of her garment."[68]

So here we see a double feminine intercession. Ninsun invokes Šamaš by invoking his own wife Aya to protect Gilgameš. The dynamic is Gilgameš–Ninsun–Aya–Šamaš.[69]

80   *Femininity*

Later, after the death of Enkidu, Gilgameš goes to find Ut-Napištum—Mesopotamian Noah—to find out how he managed to acquire eternal life. Ut-Napištum explains the irreproducible conditions of the Great Flood, and, in crotchety old-man fashion, tells the young whippersnapper to get off his lawn and go home. It is the old man's wife who intercedes on behalf of the young hero. First, when Gilgameš falls asleep (insisting that he's not at all tired), Mrs. Ut-Napištum:

> Said his wife to him, to Ut-Napištum the Distant:
> "Touch the man and make him wake up!
> The way he came he shall go back in well-being,
> By the gate he came forth he shall return to his land."[70]

Later, when Gilgameš prepares to leave in failure, Mrs. Ut-Napištum once again puts in a good word for him with her husband:

> Said his wife to him, to Ut-Napishtum the Distant:
> "Gilgameš came here by toil and by travail,
> What have you given for his homeward journey?"[71]

As discussed by Rivkah Harris:

> [S]he speaks and acts on behalf of Gilgamesh. Hers is an intercessory role, a not-uncommon feminine and maternal role in Mesopotamian literary texts. She beseeches her husband not to let Gilgamesh die when he falls asleep. . . . It is she who, mindful of society's rules of hospitality and sensitive to his enormous efforts, sees to it that he does not leave empty-handed.[72]

In this instance, the dynamic is Ut-Napištum–Mrs. Ut-Napištum–Gilgameš. In the first dynamic, Ninsun, herself a goddess, serves as intermediary between a deity (Šamaš and Aya) and a mortal. In the latter case, a mortal female intercedes between two males who are both powerful in their own, separate ways. The final female serving an important intermediary function in the *Gilgameš* narrative—Šamḫat—will be discussed subsequently.

Hieros Gamos

The role of female deities as intermediaries between males of different ranks appears not only in literary accounts but in the ideologies of religious praxis in Mesopotamia. Starting in the late 3rd millennium, kings of Ur might suggest that their (sexual) relationships with Inana specifically induced the powerful goddess to support and intercede for them in life and in the council of the deities. Starting in the 2nd millennium, and definitely into the 1st, the dynamic changed such that the female spouses of powerful male deities interceded on behalf of the king, often within the context of a *hieros gamos*, wherein the deities (or their

Femininity 81

cult images) were understood to have sex. One of the desired outcomes of these exchanges was the gods' consequent good will to the king.

An example of the earliest dynamic appears in the hymn *Šulgi* X. Here, among other lyrics, we read Inana's words:

> "I shall decree a good fate for him! I shall treat Šulgi, the good shepherd, tenderly! I shall decree a good fate for him! I shall treat him tenderly in his . . .! I shall decree the shepherdship of all the lands as his destiny! (ll. 36–41)
>
> In battle I shall be the one who goes before you. In combat I shall carry your weapon like a personal attendant. In the assembly I shall be your advocate. On campaign I shall be your encouragement. (ll. 49–51)
>
> An has determined this for you, and may he never alter it! May Enlil, the decreer of fates, never change it!" Thus Inana treated him tenderly. (ll. 71–73)[73]

As Beate Pongratz-Leisten interprets these lines:

> The blessing lists in detail the duties assumed by Inanna on behalf of the king. These are: (1) protecting him in his role as a warrior defending the cosmic order and (2) performing her role as agent in interceding for him in the assembly of the gods, (3) the role of Ištar as divine messenger bringing him the decisions of the great gods Anu and Enlil is illuminated by lines 71–72.[74]

By the mid-2nd millennium, a renegotiation of power starts to appear. While Ištar is still a powerful and dominant deity, her rapport with male deities in the pantheon starts to take on greater importance vis-à-vis her blessings for the king. Thus, in a hymn to the goddess by the Old Babylonian king Ammi-ditāna (AO 4479), we read (ll. 45–56):

> From Anum, her bridegroom, she has demanded for him
> A long life forever.
> Many years of life to Ammiditana
> Ištar has granted and given.
>
> By her command she has made bow down
> At his feet the four corners of the earth,
> And all the orb of the earth
> She has bound to his yoke.
>
> Her heart's desire, the song of her praise,
> Is fitting for his mouth, Ea has obeyed her command.
> "I have heard her eulogy" (said Ea), and he was delighted with it.
> "May her king live" (he said), "may she love him forever!"[75]

While Ištar is a dominant deity and queen of the pantheon, she shares her rulership with An, and it is to him, and further on Ea, to whom she turns to request long

82 *Femininity*

life and power for Ammi-ditāna. So we see a mix of the goddess providing for her favored king independently, as with Šulgi, and her turning to male deities to provide this service for her.

By the 1st millennium, the "transfer of power" is mostly complete, such that goddesses are depicted approaching their spouses to request favors for the king. Typically, these requests occur in the context of a *hieros gamos*, wherein the request for blessing occurs as an aspect of the deities' pillow talk. As early as the reign of Esarhaddon we see the king invoking the goddess Nanaya of Uruk (a manifestation of Ištar) to intercede with her husband Nabû on behalf of the king. Thus, "O Nanaya of Uruk, the superior lady, when you happily dwell in your cella, may you speak a favorable word for me, Esarhaddon, king of Assyria, before Nabû, your spouse" (Esarhaddon Uruk C: 16–17).[76] Later, it is the consort Tašmetu who serves as intermediary between Nabû and the king. Their "bedding" ritual was the subject of numerous letters among the kings, priests, and temple officials, including one from the reign of King Aššurbanipal, of which the colophon reads:

> Tašmetu, the great Lady, your beloved spouse, who intercedes for me daily before you in the sweet bed, who never ceases demanding that you protect my life. The one who trusts in you will not come to shame, O Nabû![77]

This trend continues into the Neo-Babylonian period. Not only did King Nabonidus invoke Aya as an intermediary before her husband Šamaš in Sippar (see previously, n. 69), so too did he call on the lunar goddess Nikkal to intercede on his behalf with her own husband Sîn (Nabonidus 1 ii 38–39): "May Nikkal, the mother of the great gods, speak favorably on my behalf before Sîn, her beloved."[78]

As Martti Nissinen observed of these dynamics:

> As regards the gender matrix involving divine male–female gender, it is interesting to note how it mirrors the human male–female gender matrix of the patriarchal society. The gender differentiation is clearly based on a hierarchical ladder, on which the female deity occupies the step below the male deity. . . . While subordinate to her divine spouse, "in front of" whom (*ina pān*) the goddess speaks on behalf of the king, she has in the capacity of intercessor a role that makes her the central figure and the influential party of the divine love ritual: what the goddess says, the god performs.[79]

Furthermore:

> The intercession on behalf of the king and country appears to be a central function in these rituals, in which the goddess plays the key role. Traditio-historically, one is tempted to see a continuation between the goddess who intercedes for the king with her beloved, and Mary, the Holy Mother of God, who pleads with her Son for mankind.[80]

Femininity 83

Lamma

So, yes, if you were a king, it was possible to get some rather high-ranking goddesses to intervene on your behalf with some rather high-ranking gods. Then there was everyone else. Fortunately, the Mesopotamians were kind enough to realize that even poor folk needed the occasional intermediary with the deities, and thus the religion provided both personal deities (something like a guardian angel) and intervening goddesses. The former were both male and female. The latter were exclusively female and were known as ^dLamma. While best known as common characters in the glyptic iconography, they also appear in royal inscriptions, where their protective/intermediary role is explicit. Thus, from the Old Babylonian period, we read the bilingual year names from the reign of Ammi-ditāna:[81]

> Year in which Ammi-ditāna the king made and adorned with reddish gold and precious stones powerful naked **protective deities** (DINGIR-LAMMA DINGIR-LAMMA), who pray for his life, and brought them to Inanna the great lady of Kiš who raises the head of her king.
>
> Year in which Ammi-ditāna the king made and adorned with reddish gold and precious stones powerful naked **protective deities** (^dLA-MA), who pray for his life, and brought them to Inanna the great lady of Kiš who lifts up his kingship.

By contrast, in the Sumerian *Lament for the City of Unug*, it is made clear that the city comes to ruin when

> Its good UDUG deities went away, its LAMMA deities ran off. Its LAMMA deity (said) "Hide in the open country" and they took foreign paths. The city's patron god turned against it and its shepherd abandoned it. Its guardian spirit, though not an enemy, was exiled (?) to a foreign place. Thus all its most important gods evacuated Unug, they kept away from it.

But in the end, things will get better:

> If An looks kindly upon that man and at the well-built city, the place of determining fate, proclaim "Man and city! Life and well-being!" for him. Let praise ring out. Let him be made surpassing above all, to his right or left. Tireless LAMMA deity, take hold of his head, pronounce his fate in charitable words—by the command of An and Enlil it will remain unaltered for a long time.[82]

As Julia Asher-Greve described her role in Mesopotamian religion:

> The paramount character of Lamma . . . is that of good, kind, beneficent and sometimes eloquent divine "chaperone" who loves the truth, listens to prayers, guides speech and tongue, and *mediates between high-ranking*

84 *Femininity*

> *deities and mortals*; she is the deity of good fortune, *advocate and intercessor for her protégé*.[83]

The Lamma goddess is most apparent in the glyptic iconography, where she appears in presentation scenes mediating between a worshipper and a high-ranking deity as early as the 3rd millennium BCE. Thus, on this seal from Ur III-period Nippur (Figure 2.21), a Lamma goddess with a simple horned miter leads a female worshipper by the wrist to an enthroned goddess with a more elaborate horned miter. The Lamma deity is literally physically intermediary between the worshipper and the deity.

Over time there are variations in this basic motif, often involving whether the goddess stands before or behind the mortal she presents to the deity and how many horns she bears on her head. But her role as intermediary between mortal and deity lasts throughout Mesopotamian history.

The attentive reader probably noticed that in the year names of Ammi-ditāna up there, the king refers to the Lamma statues as naked. They are never portrayed as such in the glyptic. However, the combination of (female) nudity and intervening (female) may play out in an alternative medium: terracotta. Starting in the Akkadian Dynasty (2334–2230 BCE) mold-made terracotta plaques come to be produced and distributed throughout Mesopotamia. By far (very far) the most common item so produced was an *en face* nude female, typically portrayed with her hands clasped upon her upper abdomen (e.g. Figure 2.22).

Figure 2.21 Cylinder Seal and Modern Impression from Ur III-Period Nippur, Oriental Institute 3346.

Source: Courtesy of the Oriental Institute of the University of Chicago.

Femininity 85

Figure 2.22 Old Babylonian Terracotta Plaque, Oriental Institute 9335.
Source: Photograph taken by Elisa Roßberger. Used with kind permission.

This clasped-hands gesture was the most common pose of anthropomorphic statues in the preceding Early Dynastic corpus, as one might see from a random collection of male and female (clothed) dedicatory figurines from Tell Asmar (see Figure 4.1), as well as numerous depictions of deities. Such a gesture also pertains to royalty, especially in religious contexts, as with King Gudea of Lagaš (Figure 2.23). In her study of this latter king's iconography, Claudia Suter said of his clearly preferred pose:

> Because statues of human beings with their hands held on the chest are dedicated in temples, they are usually interpreted as representations of worshippers, and their gesture as one of prayer. The various narrative contexts in which the gesture is encountered, however, speak against this thesis, not least because it does not befit deities. The figures exhibiting this gesture are neither agents nor beneficiaries of the depicted events. Considering that we do most of our activities with our hands, this accords with the mere notion that hands resting on the chest are inactive. That the arms do not simply hang down may imply that attentiveness was involved rather than mere passivity. If it was a symbolic gesture, it must have denoted the attentive attendance of an event.[84]

What these nude female terracotta plaques might have represented, then, was an amalgam of two contemporary iconographies. On the one hand, they appear to be

86 *Femininity*

Figure 2.23 Statue of Gudea of Lagaš, Metropolitan Museum of Art 59.2. Harris Brisbane Dick Fund.

a mold-made variation of the terracotta nude females that begin to appear in the late 3rd millennium (see previously) whose elaborate jewelry and iconography suggest divine images. On the other hand, they display the posture of polite attention that typifies statues and figurines that represent mortal interaction with the deities, an interaction intensified by the use of *en face* posture that strengthens the connection between object and viewer. As such, it is possible that these objects served as conduits between mortal owners and divine recipients of prayers. They are, in their own way, a plebian manifestation of the intervening Lamma.[85]

Death

The intervening qualities of goddesses did not apply only to life. As one might expect, such functions were critically important to the Egyptians in death as well. As early as the Old Kingdom (reign of King Teti), goddesses, especially Nut, the Sky Goddess, were presented as the body of the coffin who held the body of the deceased within herself as within a womb. By the New Kingdom, this ideology had expanded such that the "coffin goddess" served as an intermediary between the deceased and the realm of the deities. Thus, as explicitly rendered on one of the coffins of King Merenptah (fl. 1213–1203 BCE), it is, atypically, the goddess Neith who serves as coffin womb and intermediary for the pharaoh:

> "I am your mother, who nurses your beauty,
> I am pregnant with you in the morning,
> and I deliver you as Re in the evening.
>
> I carry you, you being on my back,
> I elevate your mummy, my arms under you,
> I continually take your beauty into myself.

Femininity 87

When you enter me, I embrace your image,
I am the coffin that shelters your mysterious form

. . .

I cause the four noble women to come to you,
that they may make light for you on all your ways,
that they may repel your enemies for you every day
and drive away the rebel, the evil one, for you.
I place you on his back,
he will not escape you,
you will not be disgusted by him, ever.

I bring you the two kites
with their sistra and necklaces;
they will bind the headcloth around your head
and beat for you on the two copper gongs.
I cause you to hear the mourning of Isis,
the cries of the great king maker,
as she cries for you, her arms on her knee,
before your body on the bier.
I cause Nephthys to mourn for you,
wailing at the top of her voice.
I place (for you) the two sisters at (your) head and (your) feet

I bring you Shu with his august *ba*,
that he may endure on your right side,
going up and down in your body
and in and out of your nostrils.
I bring you Geb to look after you;
I cause him to say to you 'my eldest son!' and to say regarding you, 'my
office belongs to him!'

. . .

I call your mother Nut to you,
and Tefnut on your left side,
that they may throw their arms around you
and recognize their son in you.
I cause your mother to spread herself over you,
and I cause her to take you into herself as 'She Who Takes the Great One
into Herself.'

I bring you Horus, that he may worship you,
I set you upright and let him speak to you.
He brings you your enemies as prisoners
and annihilates them beneath you, forever.

To me, to me, my son with hidden name,
Osiris, king of the gods!
May you grant that the Osiris King (beloved of Amun, *ba* of Re),
the son of Re (Merenptah, satisfied with *maat*) remain

88   *Femininity*

in the following of the Great God,
while the gods of the netherworld are the protection of his body
and lay low his enemies."[86]

Such treatment was not reserved exclusively for royalty. A depiction on the wall of the deceased Thothemheb, who lived during the reign of the 19th-Dynasty Pharaoh Ramses II, in Thebes, shows the man with the "Goddess of the West" (= death = Hathor) and her promise to present him to numerous deities of the afterlife:

To speak of Hathor chief of Thebes,
the eye of the sun that dwells in . . .:
"Welcome, Thothemheb, you of sincere heart,
You cool one, [silent of] Karnak,
safe mouth from Thebes!
My heart (is) mixed with your essence.
I made . . . for your mummy
and a place sanctified for your body.
I shall report you to the Great God
to say welcome to you.
I shall command you to the Harachte,
so that he may place you among his worshipers.
I shall hand you over to the lord of Hermupolis,
so that he may keep your bread as a sacrifice.
I shall command you to . . .
so that he . . .
I shall [transfer] you to the Sokar and the Henu barge,
so that you enter the *iif* sanctuary.
I shall commit you to Nefertem
so that you can go around the walls with him.
I shall entrust you to the 'Salvation awakens'(?),
[so that he [places] you among his] promised ones(?)
I'll command you to the Penpen
so that he may gather your offerings.
I shall command you to . . .
. . . [like] you were on earth.
may he praise you a million times."[87]

Marriage

Females passed between houses in patrilocal marriage, and this was rather consistent in ANE marriages. In some cases, as in Mesopotamia, the bride not only relinquished her natal home but also the cult of her father's ancestors so as to worship those of her husband. As such, she got a new house, a new family, and to a certain extent even new gods. This inevitably gave females a liminal position within the household: In her natal home, she was destined to leave; in her new home, she was an outsider. Once a bride produced a son, she was considered to be relatively well entrenched in her husband's household, as she could claim a blood tie to the family. However, should the husband die before generating a son, it was far more likely that the (young?) bride would be sent back to her own family for the arrangement of a new marriage. Should the husband die later in life, even after the birth of numerous children, the wife was expected to leave the household should she remarry, abandoning all the property of her former husband's household. Patrilinear families with their property thus formed relatively stable anchors in the community in which females were passed around through marriage. The stress and alienation this placed on young women was recognized, even for a goddess such as Inana:

> Verily, your father is a stranger only.
> Verily, your mother is a stranger only.
> His mother you will respect as if she were your mother
> His father you will respect as if he were your father.[88]

On the flip side, though, this also means that females functioned as the intrafamilial links that bound a society together, especially as wives maintained relations with both natal and marital families. For example, as we see in a letter from the workmen's village of Deir el-Medina, a father assures his daughter that, should her husband leave her, he (her father) will continue to care for her and provide her a place to live:

> The workman Hor-em-wia says to the lady Tenet-djseseret, his daughter: "You are my good daughter. If the workman Baki throws you out of the house, I will act. As for the house, it belongs to the Pharaoh; but you will dwell in the portico in my storehouse, because I am the one who built it, and no one in the land will throw you out of there!"[89]

More visible in the textual record, of course, are all those princesses who traveled from palace to palace to forge alliances between powerful kings and queens. Notable in this respect was the marriage between the Pharaoh Ramesses II to a daughter of King Hattušili III and Queen Puduḫepa of Hatti. Although the Egyptian wrote to both sovereigns, it would appear that it was actually Puduḫepa who was principally in charge of the very long-term nuptial arrangements. First and foremost, it was critical that the Hittite princess receive the status of chief consort of the pharaoh: That is, she was to be his primary wife and queen of Egypt. As Puduḫepa insisted:

> As for the daughter that I shall give my brother. . . .[90] I want to make her superior [to all the other daughters of the Great Kings]; no [one should be able] to find another beside her. Should I compare [the daughter that] I shall someday

90   *Femininity*

give to my brother to the [daughter of the king of Assyria of t]he d[augh]ter of the king of Zulabi?[91]

The pharaoh consented. Even so, life, that thing that happens when you are making other plans, intervened and delayed the nuptials, a matter which Ramesses brought up repeatedly with Puduḫepa, who held her own in their encounters (ÄHK 105 = KUB XXI 38):

HIM: My sister, you promised to give me your daughter! That's what you wrote. But you've withheld her and are angry with me. Why have you not now given her to me?

HER: I have indeed withheld my daughter, and you will certainly approve, not disapprove of my doing so. I cannot give my daughter to you right now because, as you know well, the storehouse of Hatti has been burnt. Anything that did survive Urhi-Tešub [a pretender to the Hittite throne] handed over to the Great God. . . . Does my brother possess nothing at all? Only the son of the Sun-god, the son of the Storm-god, and the Sea have nothing? Do YOU have nothing? Yet, my brother, you seek to enrich yourself at MY expense! That is worthy of neither your reputation nor your status![92]

Eventually the princess made it to Egypt, was married, and took the name Maat-Hor-Neferure as the consort-queen of Ramesses. Apparently, he was delighted with the arrangement, writing to both Hattušili and Puduḫepa (ÄHK 51):

Wonderful! Wonderful is this situation about which my brother has written to me. The Sun God, the Storm God, the Gods of the Land of Egypt, the Gods of the Land of Hatti have granted that our two great countries will be united forever![93]

Princesses were living political connective tissue. As Trevor Bryce neatly summed it up, "[P]rincesses, particularly from the highest-ranking mothers, were from their birth potential marriage-alliance material."[94]

Telephone, Telegraph, Tell a Woman

"The typical primate society is at heart a female kinship network run by older matriarchs."[95]

Less showy than their royal counterparts, such intrafamilial connections were equally relevant to the social networks of smaller, village-based communities, where exogamy was the norm. As Carol Meyers discusses in the context of early Iron Age Israelite society:

Because most settlements were small, it would have been common to obtain brides from a nearby village or town. This had the pragmatic function of creating alliances among neighboring settlements and contributing to the web of kinship in which households were situated. These inter-settlement alliances, coinciding in ancient Israel with clans, typically help maintain peace among contiguous settlements and increase the likelihood that related households help each other in difficult times. Because women typically retain their natal affiliations, they are positioned to maintain connections with households and thus lineages in nearby settlements.[96]

Furthermore, women formed what would today be called mutual support groups within their communities. This is because much of women's daily labor, predominantly food processing and textile production, took place in social groupings that allowed for chit-chat and gossip. This is archaeologically manifest in the location of tools such as ovens and grain-grinders and loom weights.

For example, an extensive study of the placement of cooking ovens undertaken by Aubrey Baadsgaard, who registered 235 ovens from 18 Iron I–Iron II (1150–586 BCE) sites in Israel, revealed that close to half of these were located *outside* of closed domestic units (i.e. houses). Thus, while 55.2% were purely domestic, 20.7% were in open courtyards, 10.2% were in open areas, 4.9% were in public buildings, and 2.5% were located in streets.[97] Furthermore, the more public the oven, the larger its size. Domestic (private) ovens were on average 55 cm in diameter, while those in public buildings were 60 cm, those in streets or open spaces 61 cm, and those in courtyards some 63 cm in diameter.[98] Clearly, the more open the location, the greater the body of women making use of the resource. The location of these larger ovens in open-access locations seems to indicate that they were not reserved for single households but rather served as common apparatus for multiple families, thus serving as loci of gathering and communication among the womenfolk. In her final analysis, Baadsgaard concluded:

> [T]he evidence clearly indicated that ovens were not located in defined or secluded women's spaces, but rather in highly accessible areas near entryways and courtyards that would facilitate visitation and cooperation among women as part of completing domestic tasks. Variation in oven location suggests that women could arrange the spaces used for domestic activities to accommodate such cooperative networks.[99]

It is likely that is was specifically the "small-scale" nature of such domestic labor that made these women's networks feasible. Men were also primarily involved in food production, of course, but the gender-based division of labor typically saw older adolescent and adult males working in the fields, which were divided along family or clan lines. As such, males worked alongside other males within their *own* kin groups. Females, by contrast, worked with females from within the greater community. This, combined with marriage practices that caused women to form links between households, leads to Meyer's conclusion that: "Indeed, not only because of their group labor but also because of their marital and consanguineal

92 *Femininity*

ties, women were better positioned than men to mediate such relations."[100] And it was not merely in Israel where this was the case but any society based on a close-knit, working-class economy. Thus we find the letter (ostracon) from Deir el-Medina:

> Said by Isis to (her) sister[101] Nebu-em-nu, in life, prosperity and health.
> Please pay attention and weave for me this shawl very, very quickly, before (the god) Amenophis comes, because I am completely naked. Make one [for my] backside because I am naked![102]

Even ancient Cyprus, where we often lack a written record, provides evidence for such communal labor among women over the course of millennia.

The first terracotta (Figure 2.24) dating from the Early Cypriot Bronze Age (2250–2000 BCE) shows a group of women working together around a trough or large basin. The one to the far left carries a child, while the one to the far right holds a water jug, both indicative of female sex.[103] While the four women right and center give the impression of women working at the local basin—perhaps washing, perhaps preparing comestibles—the woman with her hands engaged with the baby also provides a sense of comradery: the women gathering together to chat while dealing with the daily chores. The second image (Figure 2.25) dates some two millennia later, to Archaic Cyprus (750–500 BCE). Here we see two women engaged in grain production, one with a winnowing basket while the other grinds the grain. The evidence truly suggests that women's labor was generally (conceived of as) communal as opposed to done in isolation. The image of women working while secluded in the household interior has become rather dated.

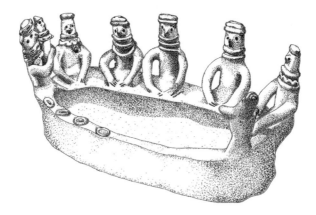

Figure 2.24 Cypriot Scenic Composition, Louvre AM 816.

Source: Drawing by Giulia Albertazzi.

Figure 2.25 Archaic Cypriot Terracotta Grinding Scene, Metropolitan Museum of Art 74.51.1643, Cesnola Collection.

Connecting the King to the Past and the Future—Nubia

The importance of royal women as a dynastic "binding element" becomes especially apparent in Nubia, particularly in the better known Napatan period (8th–4th centuries BCE), when the Kingdom of Kush used the Egyptian language and writing system (hieroglyphs). When Kush took over Egypt during the 25th Dynasty (747–656 BCE) following the conquests of King Kashta and his successor King Piye, the new dynasts adopted aspects of the culture of their Egyptian "hosts." One cultural aspect that resonated between *both* cultures was the necessity of a feminine element in an otherwise male monarchy. For the Egyptians, this generally manifested in the need for a consort queen who served as the embodiment of Egypt itself, symbolically manifest in the "Two Goddesses"—Nekhbet and Wadjet of Upper and Lower Egypt, respectively—and the royal Isis who accompanied and supported the king in his manifestation as earthly Horus.[104]

For the Nubians, the role of women in the royal dynasty was more significant and more practical. To begin, it is possible that the Kushite Dynasty practiced at least to some degree avuncular succession, whereby legitimate heirs to the throne were not the sons of the reigning king but rather the son(s) of the king's sister(s). Potentially counter-intuitive in a patriarchal structure, this system guarantees that a successor is a blood relative of the reigning king. As a male, one can never be 100% certain that one's child is one's own: The child who came out of the woman who came out of the same womb as the king was absolutely, no question about it, the king's blood relative.

The probability for such succession practices appears in the importance of women designated *śnt njśwt*—"Sister of the God (=King)." This title shows up in dynastic lineages wherein new kings display their legitimacy for the throne and where, significantly, these women might also be identified as *mwt*—"mother"— of the (previous) king. The *combination* of these titles and the importance of the women who bore them can be seen in the burial patterns surrounding the pyramid of King Taharqa at the Nubian cemetery at Nuri (Figure 2.26). The king's tomb was surrounded by those of numerous female relatives of various ranks. Those close to the king—and presumably of high status—belonged to women who bore both designations: "Mother of a King"/"Sister of a King":[105]

94 *Femininity*

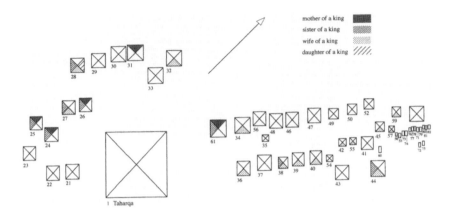

Figure 2.26 Nubian Cemetery at Nuri.

Source: From Lohwasser 2021: 67.

Thus we find in Tomb 24 Queen Nasala, daughter of King Atlanersa, sister-wife of King Senkamaisken, and mother of Kings Anlamani and Aspelta (on whom see subsequently). In Tomb 26 we find the daughter of King Aspelta—Queen Amanitakaye, sister-wife of King Amtalqa and mother of King Malenqen.[106]

The role of the mother who is also the king's sister also manifests clearly in royal lineages, for example, the inscription on the "Election Stele" of King Aspelta (c. 600–580), who traced his lineage (and thus legitimacy) back to the originator of the Napatan Dynasty King Alara. In the text, the god Amun-Re extolls the new king of Egypt, claiming (ll. 19–21):

> Then this god, Amun-Rê, lord of the Thrones of Two-lands, said:
> "His father was my son, the Son-of-Rê, . . ., justified;
> and his mother is king's sister, king's mother, mistress of Kush,
> the Daughter of Rê, . . ., may she live forever,
> whose mother (again) was king's sister,
> divine adoratrix of Amun-Rê, king of the gods of Dominion (Thebes), . . ., justified;
> whose mother (again) was king's sister . . ., justified;
> whose mother (again) was king's sister . . ., justified;
> whose mother (again) was king's sister . . ., justified;
> whose mother (again) was king's sister . . ., justified;
> whose mother (again) was king's sister, mistress of Kush, . . ., justified;
> It is he who is your lord."[107]

As discussed by Angelika Lohwasser:

> Aspelta's genealogy documents his "pure" lineage by noting that seven generations of his female ancestors were *snt njswt*; they all belonged to that group of

women who bequeath the right to the throne, substantiating the legitimacy of his selection. Aspelta thus belonged to the pool of *snw njswt* [sons of the god], and, moreover, his association extended back through time over seven generations.[108]

The importance of Aspelta's mother Nasala, the king's sister, is also highlighted by the fact that it is her speech which initiates the text of the Election Stele (ll. 1–5):

> Utterance by the king's sister, the king's mother, mistress of Kush [Nasala]:
> "I am come to you, Amun-Rê, lord of the Thrones of Two-lands,
> the great god, who is in front of his harem, whose name is known,
> who gives bravery <to> him who is loyal to him,
> establish your son whom you love, [Aspelta], may he live forever,
> in the highest office of Rê, that he may be great(er) in it than all gods.
> Make numerous his years of life on <earth> like Aton of Napata.
> Give him all life and dominion from you, all health from you all happiness from you, and appearing on the throne of Horus forever."[109]

Only after her invocation and prayer does the god (!) Amun-Re speak to his "son," followed by a blessing offered by the goddess (!) Mut.

A third reference to the importance of the king's sister/king's mother appears on the lunette that toped King Aspelta's election stele (Figure 2.27):

Figure 2.27 Lunette of the Coronation Stela of King Aspelta, Egyptian Museum, Cairo, JE 48866.

Source: From Lohwasser 2021: 63.

96 *Femininity*

Here King Aspelta appears kneeling before the god Amun-Re, who places his hand upon the new sovereign's head. Facing these divinities is Nasala herself—king's sister, king's mother—wearing the double shawl worn by Nubian women[110] and holding up two sistra indicative of her priestly function.

The new king must have been young enough not to have been married yet, as scenes of royal investiture typically involve *two* women: the king's mother and the king's wife. The former, as here, plays the sistra in holy celebration, while the latter pours a libation of water or milk—a distinctly Nubian role for women.[111] Nevertheless, be they one or (more typically) two, no scene of kingly investiture ever occurred without the presence of the royal women.[112] For Lohwasser, their presence of was of critical importance not only for the legitimation of the new king (for which only the mother was necessary) but for their symbolic role linking the king to the past and *future* of the dynasty. To quote Lohwasser:

> Mother and wife of the king also function as two genealogical transformers. His wife, through her fertility, guaranteed the continuity of rulership; she also insured the continuation of the family of the actual king. Through the medium of his wife, the king could influence the future. She connected him with his descendants. His mother provides the link to the past, his contact with earlier generations, serving as an interface between the king and the genealogical network of his family. She is his link to the past while his wife is his link to the future. In this system, the king, anchored to the present, is connected to the historical succession of rulership by these women as the exponents of queenship.[113]

Nubian queens thus served as elements of connectivity. It was through their bodies that, potentially, dynastic lineage and legitimacy were transferred down the ages and reigns. Thus the new king was not so much the son as the nephew of the previous king (excluding those instances when brothers inherited from each other after an untimely death), born of the king's sister, womb-mate of the reigning sovereign. More esoterically, the royal women served as conduits through time, binding the king to his ancestors on his mother's side and his descendants through his wife.

Nurturing

As discussed already in the previous chapter, fertility in the ANE was a masculine attribute. New life was formed via male "seed" and was passed along to the female for incubation and nurturing/nourishing. Speaking for Egypt in a way that actually summarizes all of the ANE on this matter, Ann Macy Roth wrote:

> The male role in sexual reproduction was seen as the actual creation of new life, which was then implanted in the female. Fundamentally, children were viewed as extensions of their father's life force; the mother's role in their nature was decidedly secondary. Instead, women seem to have had a dual

role: they aroused the man, stimulated his creative act with their beauty and sexual attractiveness, and then they nourished the life that his creative power produced.[114]

Or, as in the Hittite saying:

LÚ-*ni* LÚ-*natar tarhuilatar*
SAL-*ni* SAL-*natar annitalwatar*.
To the man virility and potency
To the woman femininity and motherhood.[115]

The female's role in childcare, as presented in the image of the kourotrophos, was discussed in Chapter 1. From the more biologically based aspects of childcare duties, the feminine attribute of nurturance extended out into far more culturally based ideologies. Thus, in the Old Kingdom Pyramid texts, we read in Utterance 406, §707:

Bring me the milk of Isis, the flood of Nephthys, the overspill of the lake, the surge of the sea, life, prosperity, health, happiness, bread, beer, clothing, and food that I might live thereby.[116]

The reference to the "milk of Isis" summons other references to beneficial liquids, all leading to a list of benefits necessary to live a good life: health, beer, clothing, and so on. The life-sustaining power of (divine) milk leads to every other good thing life and good fortune might provide. This continuum between feeding at one end leading to other life-sustaining services appears on the far more mundane level of the 18th Dynasty *Instructions of Any*, where the father instructs his son (7.17–8.1):

Double the food your mother gave you,
Support her as she supported you;
She had a heavy load in you,
But she did not abandon you.
When you were born after your months,
She was yet yoked <to you>,
Her breast in your mouth for three years.
As you grew and your excrement disgusted,
She was not disgusted, saying: "What shall I do!"
She sent you to school,
And you were taught to write,
She kept watching over you daily,
With bread and beer in her house.[117]

Clearly there was a notion in the ancient world that milk led eventually and inevitably to beer . . .

98   *Femininity*

The idea of "female = nourisher" was in fact so strong that goddesses who were otherwise in no way, shape, or form associated with maternity could neverthe-less be presented as nurturing, lactating divine protectors. We especially see this in Mesopotamia, where in the Neo-Assyrian Period prophecies express a kourotrophic relationship between Ištar and the royal family. Thus, in an address to King Aššurbanipal:

> You were a little one, Aššurbanipal, when I left you to the Queen of Nineveh, you were an infant, Aššurbanipal, when you sat on the knee of the Queen of Nineveh. Her four teats are placed in your mouth, two you suck, two you milk to your face.[118]

Likewise: "The goddess Ištar of Arbela speaks as follows: 'I am your great mid-wife, I am your good wet-nurse'."[119] Ištar, the goddess free from maternity and child-care, is nevertheless portrayed as both theoretical mother and symbolic nurse maid.

The role of the female as nurturer did not end with childcare. The acts of pro-viding physical and emotional well-being to others of any age (nowadays referred to as "emotional labor") were distinctly gendered feminine throughout the ANE, although, as we shall see, those "others" tended to be men.

No female expressed this fact so well as the *harīmtu*[120] Šamhat from the *Epic of Gilgameš*. After luring Enkidu away from his animal companions via marathon sex, she introduced him to the world of humans by clothing him, introducing him to the gods, and teaching him to eat and drink like a man (Tablet II):

> "Come, I shall lead you to Uruk the Town Square,
> To the sacred temple, the home of Anu!
> Enkidu, arise, let me take you
> To the temple Eanna, the home of Anu
> Where men are engaged in labors of skill;
> You, too, like a man, will find a place for yourself."
> Her words he heard, her speech found favor:
> The counsel of the woman struck home in his heart.
> She stripped and clothed him in part of her garment,
> The other part she put on herself.
> By the hand she took him, like a god she led him
> To the shepherds' camp, the site of the sheep-pen . . .
> Bread they set before him,
> Ale they set before him
> Enkidu did not eat the bread, but looked askance,
> How to eat bread Enkidu did not know,
> How to drink ale he had never been shown.
> The *harīmtu* opened her mouth,
> Saying to Enkidu,
> "Eat the bread, Enkidu, essential to life,

Drink the ale, the lot of the land!"

. . .

The barber groomed his body so hairy,
Anointed with oil he turned into a man.
He put on a garment, became like a warrior,
He took up his weapon to do battle with lions.[121]

In short, Šamḫat was an ersatz mother to Enkidu, with all Oedipal connotations.

The combination of female as provider both of food and sex also appears in the Anatolian myth of *Illuyanka*. Here, a divine serpent defeats the Storm God. Rallying support, the Storm God summons the other deities of the pantheon, and it is the goddess Inara who effectively comes to his aid by holding a feast (nourishment) and by seducing an ally (sex) (§§4–10):

> Then the Storm God invoked all the gods, "Come together to me." So Inara prepared a feast.
>
> She prepared everything on a grand scale: storage vessels full of wine, storage vessels of *marnuwan* beer and *walhi* drink. In the vessels she prepared abundant refreshment.
>
> Then Inara went to the town of Ziggaratta and found a mortal named Hupasiya.
>
> Inara spoke to him thus, "I am about to do such-and-such a thing. You join with me."
>
> Hupasiya responded thus to Inara, "If I may sleep with you, then I will come and perform your heart's desire." So he slept with her.
>
> Then Inara led Hupasiya off and concealed him. Inara dressed herself up and called the serpent up from its hole, saying, "I am preparing a feast. Come eat and drink."
>
> The serpent and his offspring came up, and they ate and drank. They drank up every vessel, so that they became drunk.[122]

The image of a goddess soothing an adult god throwing the divine equivalent of a temper tantrum appears in the Hattic myth *The Disappearance of Telipinu*. "Disappearance" tales were common in Anatolian mythology, where a deity would storm off (literally in the case of the Storm God), sulk, and the song would relate the loss of fertility to the land, animals, and people that resulted from the absence. Thus they lost various storm deities, solar deities, and even the goddess of childbirth herself, Ḫannaḫanna. In this particular version, the storm deity Telipinu went into a rage. Kamrusepa, the goddess of magic, intervened to remove the anger from the sulky god (§§16, 18, and 23):

> Kamrusepa saw him and moved for herself with the eagle's wing. She stopped it, namely, his anger. She stopped it, the wrath. She stopped sin; she stopped sullenness. . . . "And I have made a burning back and forth over Telipinu, on one side and on the other. And I have taken from Telipinu, from his body, his

100 *Femininity*

evil; I have taken his sin; I have taken his anger; I have taken his wrath; I have taken his pique; I have taken his sullenness. . . . I have taken evil from Telipinu's body. I have taken his anger; I have taken wrath. I have taken his sin; I have taken sullenness. I have taken the evil tongue; I have taken the evil path."[123]

Emotional labor.

There can be no doubt that the nurturing aspect of femininity was the most essentialized, biologically-based aspect of feminine gender, emerging from women's roles as mothers. Even though many of the things eventually provided by females extended well beyond the realm of *in utero* nourishment and breast milk (e.g. beer), the psychological link between nourishing mother and emotionally–physically providing female remained well intact. Such is no doubt the basis of the guilt trip proffered by a son to his mother in an Old Babylonian letter sent by Iddin-Sîn (away at boarding school) to his mother Zinû, which reads in part:

> The son of Adad-iddinnam, whose father is a servant of my father, has *two* new garments to wear, but you keep getting upset over just *one* garment for me. While you gave birth to me, his mother got him by adoption, but you do not love me in the way his mother loves him![124]

A lack of maternal love leads to a lack of sufficient clothing and emotionally ruffled feathers in need of soothing.

Domestic

When studying ancient economics, one comes across a number of remarkably similar, apparently self-contradictory data when it comes to the gendering of occupations. As Cécile Michel observed when studying the archives of the Old Assyrian trading settlement at Karum Kaneš (modern Kültepe in Turkey):

> The inventory of professionals attested in Old Assyrian sources includes men specialized in weaving and finishing textiles, but no feminine profession linked to textile production is mentioned. We know very well, of course, that Aššur women spent much of their lifetime producing textiles for the international trade with Anatolia, and that they were paid in return for their production. They are, however, not referred to as weavers in the texts![125]

Henry George Fischer made a similar observation when looking at religious titles and functions in Old Kingdom Egypt. After listing the numerous roles women fulfilled in the cults of various deities, he concluded:

> In short, women played an essential role in the temple rituals—particularly those of Hathor and Neith—even though they are not known to have held any

Femininity 101

administrative posts in this connection, or to have held the title of *ḥry-ḥbt* "lector priest."[126]

Why is it that women working in a particular industry are not recognized in the contemporary records as working in that particular industry? Even when, as is quite clear from the records at Karum Kaneš, they make money from their work and thus would qualify as what we would call "professional employment"? The reason is that in the ANE, females were associated with *domesticity*. Females were linked to the household so thoroughly that not only were their professions generally extensions of domestic tasks as understood, but there was a cognitive dissonance involved with their extra-domestic occupations: Women's "work" did not qualify as a "job."

To be perfectly clear: Women worked, and women had jobs. They appear in our earliest personnel lists. But the masculine-gendered nature of professionalism (see Chapter 3) appears in the diachronic changes, statistics, and categorizing practices of the ANE as pertain to women vs. men.

The kinds of professions (by which I mean non-domestic-labor-for-the-family) women took part in varied considerably over the three-millennium history of the ANE. For example, in Old Kingdom Egypt, women could not only be singers, dancers, weavers, and doctors, they could also be *overseers* of singers, dancers, weavers, and doctors, as well as professional mourners, cultic officials, and assistants to female royalty.[127] However, they were never scribes and thus did not take part in the governmental bureaucracy.[128] By the Middle Kingdom, professional women were removed from positions of authority—no more female overseers. This in spite of the fact that women are attested in this period as being not only scribes but also official "sealers" (*sḏꞽw.tyt*), a title typically pertaining to male officials in the governmental bureaucracy from "state treasurer" to minor officials.[129] However, as William Ward observes, the females in these more "white collar" professions did so in the contexts of noble households, *not* the state apparatus. On the one hand, women were demonstrating higher levels of professional education; on the other, they were removed from positions of authority. Such fluctuations were not the case for men, who consistently filled all professional levels (slave through king) throughout ANE history, class and talent permitting.

Likewise, women consistently had fewer extra-domestic jobs than did men. In Iron Age Israel, the presence of stamp seals and seal impression with women's names indicates that women engaged in extra-domestic trade and were, as Carol Meyers put it, "businesswomen." However, of the more than 1,200 such seals and sealings known, only about 3% bear women's names.[130] Businesswomen were clearly in the minority. An analysis of recorded business transactions in early Old Babylonian Sippar reveals that women were active parties in 32% of the sales contracts and 30% of the lease transactions; by the late Old Babylonian period, these numbers drop to 8% and 22%, respectively.[131] Females are always in the (extreme) minority in the professional world, and their numbers fluctuate in a way that is not the case for males.

102 *Femininity*

Furthermore, as noted, women's work was seldom considered a "job" in the way that men's work was. A good case in point comes from those previously-mentioned archives pertaining to Karum Kaneš, that trading town in eastern Anatolia where Old Assyrian merchants would come to trade for the textiles woven by their families (typically female) back home in Mesopotamia. As Cécile Michel observed in her extensive studies of these documents, the vast majority of professional titles in both Aššur in Mesopotamia and Kaneš in Anatolia pertains *exclusively* to males: officials such as, *inter alia*, the *hamuštum*,[132] *šiprum* (messenger), *ṭubšarrum* (scribe), *itinnum* (brick-maker), *nappāhum* (metallurgist), *naggārum* (carpenter), *šasinnum* (boyer), *parkullum* (seal engraver), *pahhārum* (potter), and *aškāpum* (leather-worker). *Even the professions that deal with the creation of textiles—ušpārum* (weaver) and *ašlākum* (fuller)—tasks normally gendered feminine in the ANE, when seen in a professional capacity, are considered to be in the domain of men.

A few final things to keep in mind. Like all pre-/non-industrial economies, the vast majority of people living in the ANE were farmers or pastoralists; at least 90–95% of the population at any given time was occupied in the production of food. Much of the economy was home centered (the word "economy" comes from the Greek *oikonomikos*, literally meaning "regulation of the household"). Families produced their own food, their own textiles for clothing, and often many of their own tools and household items. Surplus was generated for barter and, at larger scales, for longer-distance trade. Certain occupations involved a greater degree of specialization, either because more specialized tools were involved (e.g. iron smelting) or more training was required (e.g. scribe). But, for the most part, the economy was mainly centered on the household, and females were major contributors to that local and extra-local economy just as men were. So: Women worked just as much as men, at least in the non-elite classes.

However, once work leaves the household and enters into the public sphere, there are suddenly far, far fewer females in the documentation. What extra-domestic professions women do engage in tend to reflect a sub-section of domestic tasks, and women form only a small percentage of supervisors or high-ranking bureaucrats. Often those supervisors and high-ranking bureaucrats work within the domain of female royalty or nobility—thus, for example, female scribes work for the queen.[133]

As with the rest of this book, what we are looking at here is not reality but *gender*—the *social construction* of sex-based difference. The absence of women in these sources, and where they appear when they do, pertains only partially to what women actually did and partially to how the mostly male scribes who recorded them thought about them.

On that note, first and foremost, females were understood to be wives and mothers. Their primary functions were to marry; to bear children for their husbands and care for them (the children) (and the husbands); and to manage the household, especially in the areas of food production (i.e. cooking) and textile manufacture (i.e. sewing). The importance of textile manufacture was so important in the conception of femininity that spindles routinely functioned as symbolic of femininity

Femininity 103

in the ANE, as discussed in Chapter 1. The contrast between the female "house-wife" and male "breadwinner"—to use utterly modern terminology—is well summarized in a line from the 18th Dynasty Egyptian *Instructions of Any*:

> A woman is asked about her husband,
> A man is asked about his rank.[134]

This dynamic in Egypt, observed Gay Robins, not only manifested in such public discourses as funerary texts but even in the use of various hairstyles. For men, there was great variety in coiffure types, ranging from elaborate wigs of various lengths for the elite to the plain hair of various colors for more servile classes (the poor had to settle for encroaching grey and male-pattern baldness) to fully shaven as a mark of purity, especially for priests. By contrast, there were somewhat fewer options for females, with the distinction between elite and servant being less marked than was the case for males.[135] The cause for this distinction?

> The identity and status of elite men depended mainly on their position in the government bureaucracy; on their monuments, men constructed their identity textually by listing all their titles of office. In other words, men looked outside the home to fulfill their ambitions, their concerns being centered on the social structure of government order and control. Women, by contrast, had few official titles. Instead, their identities on monuments were constructed in terms of their kinship to a man: *mwt.f* "his mother," *ḥmt.f* "his wife," *sꜣt.f* "his daughter," or *snt.f* "his female relative." These kindship terms were often followed by the most common title given to women, *nbt pr* "mistress of the house," signifying a married woman and denoting her main sphere of activity.[136]

Or, to put it simply, "A woman is asked about her husband; a man is asked about his rank."

Perhaps no greater hymn to the domesticity of woman exists than the end of the Book of Proverbs in the Hebrew Bible, the "words of Lemuel, King of Massa, with which his mother admonished him." After a few requisite passages on what it takes to be a good man (see Chapter 3), Lemuel's mother describes the ideal wife (ll. 10–27, excerpted):

> What a rare find is a capable wife!
>   She is worth far more than rubies.
> Her husband has full confidence in her
>   and lacks nothing of value.
>   . . .
> She selects wool and flax
>   and works with eager hands.
> She is like the merchant ships,
>   bringing her food from afar.

104   *Femininity*

> She gets up while it is still night;
>> she provides food for her family
>> and portions for her female servants.
> She considers a field and buys it;
>> out of her earnings she plants a vineyard.
> She sets about her work vigorously;
>> her arms are strong for her tasks.
> She sees that her trading is profitable,
>> and her lamp does not go out at night.
> In her hand she holds the distaff
>> and grasps the spindle with her fingers.
> She opens her arms to the poor
>> and extends her hands to the needy.
> When it snows, she has no fear for her household;
>> for all of them are clothed in scarlet.
> She makes coverings for her bed;
>> she is clothed in fine linen and purple.
> . . .
> She makes linen garments and sells them,
>> and supplies the merchants with sashes.
> . . .
> She watches over the affairs of her household
>> and does not eat the bread of idleness.

The tie to the house was sufficiently strong that class need not even be a mitigating factor. Or, for that matter, mortality. In the Ugaritic *Baal Cycle* when the deities Baal and Anat go to visit the queen of the pantheon Athirat (CAT 1.4, Colum II, ll. 3–11):

> She takes her spindle in her hand,
> A mighty spindle in her right hand.
> She conveys her garment in the sea,
> Her two robes in the rivers,
> Her robes, the covering of her skin.
> She sets a pit on the fire,
> A pot on top of the coals.
> All the while she is servile before Bull El the Beneficent,
> Deferential to the Creator of Creatures.[137]

Basically, the queen of the gods is doing textile work while doing her laundry, all while remaining subservient to her husband (see subsequently: "Second Sex"). Likewise, in the Hurrian *Song of Hedammu*, fragment 6, when the gods are threatened with being reduced to labor: "Even Teššub, Kummiya's heroic king, will himself grasp the plow. Even Šauška and Ḫebat will themselves grind at the millstones."[138] If the deities are reduced to peasantry, the male Teššub will work outside in the fields, while the goddessfolk will be grinding flour indoors (but, per the women's networks discussed previously, at least together).[139]

When (mortal) women do perform extra-domestic work, the jobs tend to reflect a particular *sub-section* of housework. To run a house, a woman must perform numerous tasks, including food processing from horticulture through baking and brewing; textile work at most if not all levels; child-care; probably a considerable amount of healing activities, including the knowledge and maintenance of a pharmacopeia; making tools, toys, and possibly her own pottery; household repairs; caring for the animals; getting surplus products to some kind of market; and, when necessary, defense against intruders. In addition, ethnographic evidence also suggests that women helped with the harvest.[140] In short, even a "housewife" does a *lot* of jobs around the house. When she leaves the house, she is typically associated with only a few of these, usually textiles, cooking, and occupations associated with her bodily functions.

Consider, for example, the texts from Karum Kaneš discussed previously. All extra-domestic jobs were recorded as belonging to males, even those occupations that involved the making of textiles: *ušpārum* (weaver) and *ašlākum* (fuller). The only professional title that accrued to both men and women was *sābium/ sābītum*—inn-keeper/barkeep.[141] It seems that females as well as males were acceptable as managers of hospitality services and purveyors of beer, that is, a home away from home. Official job titles that pertained to women were *šabsūtum* (midwife), *ēmiqtum* (nurse/healer), and *mušēniqtum* (wet-nurse), occupations that were "natural" extensions from typical household duties.

A similar dynamic appears in Egypt: Extra-domestic professions for women tend to reflect household duties. In addition to such jobs as midwife (*'in't*) and wet-nurse (*mn't*) are weaver, bread-baker, beer-brewer, singer, dancer, and, of course, *irit-šni*—hairstylist. However, as Fischer notes for the Old Kingdom at least, only men bear the professional title "baker" (*rtḥ*).[142] Furthermore, while women might serve as "overseer of the house of weavers," so might men, and it is generally men who work as overseers or managers, even in the case of female-oriented occupations such as performer.[143] Come the Middle Kingdom, women lost the position of "overseer" in any capacity.[144]

And so we see in the ancient world a phenomenon not entirely atypical of even modern times. Certain tasks are generally gender specific, especially those that are biologically based (and here I am thinking very specifically of wet-nurse). Other tasks are gender based only insofar as they adhere to the division of men:professional:public/women:domestic:private. Males plough the fields outdoors while women grind the grain indoors. Men go out to Anatolia to sell textiles while women stay home in Aššur to make those textiles. If it is a task done at home, it is in the domain of women—such as bread baking; when it becomes an extra-domestic "profession," it is suddenly in the domain of men. And if the job involves any degree of authority—supervisor, manager—that role typically goes to males, even if the people being supervised are females in a feminine profession. All this leads to the observation of Annette Depla:

106 *Femininity*

According to the writings analysed above, a woman's place was centred in the home. Men were not comfortable with the idea of women wielding power outside the domestic domain and the didactic literature presented here suggests that steps were taken to circumscribe a woman's power outside the house. The procreation and rearing of children were the wife's prime duty.[145]

What this leads to is the fact that women were, as Simone de Beauvoir rightly noted, the second sex.

Second Sex

The ancient Near East was a patriarchal society, meaning that males had more power and authority at all levels of society than did women at comparable levels. What this means in terms of gender construction is that we hear about women, goddesses, and the construction of feminine gender primarily via a male voice. Basically, for the most part, we see femininity as men saw it. Obviously, this will skew things a bit. As in modern times, it causes us to see females not as autonomous, individual entities but as the sex-in-relation-to-males.

We see this in our own society as well. In his spoof on the standard American horror film *Cabin in the Woods*, Joss Whedon divided females into two categories, the Whore (she who had sex with males) and the Virgin (she who has not yet had sex with males). It was, of course, mandatory for the Whore to die first; the Virgin could live, but only so long as she suffered. A century ago the Cambridge-School Classicist Jane Ellen Harrison argued that the "Ancients" (all of them) worshipped a singular goddess in double form: Maid and Mother. Later the poet Robert Graves, in his *White Goddess*, added the third: Crone. While embraced by modern, matricentric pagan religions, this is nevertheless simply another manifestation of woman-in-terms-of-man: Maiden—she who has not had sex with a male; Mother—she who has had sex and born a child with a male; Crone—she who is too old for sex with a male. Female = gender-in-relation-to-a-male (and whether she has had sex with one).[146] And these are coming from the more *feminist* sides of the current community.

This tendency to see females-in-relation-to-males manifests in the ANE (and elsewhere in the ancient world), where females often appear as someone's daughter, wife, or mother. Granted, males *also* appear as members of a family: They are sons, husbands, and fathers as well. *However*, unlike most females, males often take their sense of identity not from ties to members of their families but from their role in society: king, priest, scribe, canal-supervisor, potter. While some women may do this, it is far more common for them to be known as daughters, wives, and mothers, and much of the power they possess in society often comes from these roles (see subsequently). Thus, women are more defined by men than men are defined by women.

A woman is asked about her husband,
A man is asked about his rank.

By hearing much about the construction of femininity via the male voice, we are also presented with a paradigm that favors the subordination of females to males and the praise of a femininity that can be controlled (even though it can't, as the males also complain). This appears in all societies under consideration.

In the Anatolian narrative *The Sun God, the Cow, and the Fisherman*, the Fisherman brings home an abandoned child and orders his wife to pretend to go into labor so that they might claim the child as their own. She obeys her husband, leading to the interjection in the narrative:

> An ideal woman's mind is clever. She has cut herself off from commanding others. She is dependent on the authority of the god. She stands in woman's subordination and she does not disobey her husband.[147]

A pair of Sumerian proverbs reveals the double standard involved in raising sons and daughters. According to the first, "A mother is able to discipline her daughter but not her son." Apparently boys will be boys. The second reads, "A rebellious male may be permitted a reconciliation. A rebellious female will be dragged in the mud." Because boys will be boys, indiscretions or lapses of judgement on the part of males are eventually forgivable and do not cause permanent damage for either the son or the family. By contrast, the daughter who acts out causes *permanent* damage to herself and her household. She must be controlled.[148]

The Old Kingdom *Instruction of Ptahhotep* reveals how a man (specifically) might maintain a happy household with his wife, noting her beneficial features and the absolute necessity of keeping her in her place (i.e. subordinate to him):

> If you are excellent, you shall establish your household,
> And love your wife according to her standard;
> Fill her belly, clothe her back,
> Perfume is a prescription for her limbs.
> Make her happy as long as you live!
> She is a field, good for her lord.
> You shall not pass judgement on her.
> *Remove her from power, suppress her*;
> Her eye when she sees (anything) is her storm wind.
> This is how to make her endure in your house.
> You shall retain her. A female
> Who is in her own hands is like rain:
> She is sought for, and she has flown away.[149]

And who can ever forget the Biblical dictate of Genesis 3:16 to Eve, "Yet your desire shall be for your husband, and he shall rule over you."

Ancient (and modern) presentations of feminine gender are skewed. Often the femininity we see is seen through the lens of male priorities and paranoias. This may cause females to appear more erotic, more domestic, more or less nurturing than they "should" be. Females are far more like to be understood in-relation-to,

108 *Femininity*

and ideals and recommendations for proper behavior typically involve whatever is most convenient for men. Even goddesses can be extolled for doing the laundry and being submissive to a husband.

But this is not exclusively the case.

Women's Voice

The ancient Near East was a patriarchal society, meaning that males had more power and authority at all levels of society than did women at comparable levels. However, this does not mean that females had no power or authority. And females did exist at all levels of society, from queen right down to slave. Although subject to (and often object of) a patriarchal milieu, women had far more authority than many modern audiences would understand. We are not talking about the victims of a Taliban regime here. Women above the slave class had economic rights, conducted business, ran households and extra-domestic industries, engaged in legal disputes and served as witnesses, occasionally were educated and literate (not always easy considering the writing systems involved; trust me!), and were often the equals of males in the religious apparatus of their respective societies (more so in Mesopotamia and Syria than the Levant or Egypt). More affluent women had buying power and spent their money (what we would call money) on statues, tombs, seals, and art in which they had considerable say in design and decoration. Women wrote.

So we are not totally at a loss as to what women thought of themselves or other females, and the males they had to deal with. We can, even if only occasionally, see how they chose to represent themselves to the world. Sometimes they followed the stereotypes created by a masculine voice, other times not.

Thus, at one end of the social spectrum, we see an old woman from the New Kingdom site of Deir el-Medina representing herself in a lawsuit against her own sons for failing to take care of her (Ashmolean 1945.97:2.1–7).

> As for me, I am a free person of the land of Pharaoh. I brought up these eight servants of yours, and I gave them household goods—everything which one usually does for people like them. Now look, I have grown old. Now look, they are not looking after me in my turn. As for every one of them who has given me a hand, I will bequeath him my property, (but) for everyone who has not helped me, I will not bequeath him my property.[150]

In defiance of her role as dutiful wife and loving mother, but perhaps clinging to some stereotype of the wise elder, a woman attempts to disinherit her sons. (Unfortunately it seems that Sumerian proverb about not being able to discipline sons was accurate: She lost the suit.)[151]

At the other end of the social spectrum, the Hurrian city of Urkeš (modern Tell Mozan) was once ruled by King Tupkiš and his consort wife Uqnitum. Eight separate seals were used by this queen: One gives her the title "Queen"

Femininity 109

Figure 2.28 Uqnitum Seal.
Source: Drawing from Marilyn Kelly-Buccellati and the Institute for Mesopotamian Area Studies.

(NIN), another the title "Wife of Tupkiš" (DAM TUPIKIŠ), the others merely referring to her as "Wife" (DAM).[152] The seal that refers to the queen by her longest title—Wife of Tupkiš—shows the royal family in a domestic setting (Figure 2.28). If we orient the inscription to the sealing's left, sitting directly to the right of the inscription is the queen seated upon a stool and holding a child with a raised hand upon her lap. Above the child's hand and just before his face is a star. To the right of the seated pair is an older, standing child who faces the last figure in the composition: the king himself seated upon a stool. The standing child has his hand upon the king's knee, probably indicating that this child is the crown prince. The king holds up a cup to his family. Behind him is the inscription, underneath which is a ram with its head towards the king. The king is certainly the main focus of the composition, as all characters, even the ram, face him. Nevertheless, the king faces his wife, offering the queen a certain reflected equality with her spouse.

As the queen consort, but *not* the only wife of the king, Uqnitum had a vested interest in displaying the fact that she was the mother of the heir apparent. Here she shows herself to be the king's equal, sitting head to head (isocephaly) with him in an intimate, domestic setting. As excavator Marilyn Kelly-Buccellati discussed the iconography:

> The main concern expressed in the Uqnitum seal iconography and seal inscriptions is that she be viewed as the most important woman in the court of Tupkish. To communicate this, she is shown in one of her seals seated opposite him. Furthermore she is depicted at the same height and surrounded by her children. The fact that she is also seated and is the same size as her husband indicates a level of consequence for her as queen and mother of the future generation of rulers, rarely seen in Mesopotamian art. Following on

110 *Femininity*

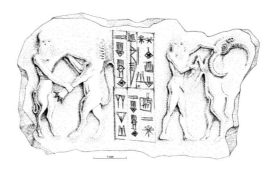

Figure 2.29 Composite Drawing of Seal Impression of Tar'am Agade (AFc1).

Source: From Buccellati and Kelly-Buccellati 2002: 14.

this but no less prominently she intends to establish a connection between the king, her young son and the succession to the throne.[153]

By contrast, the queen and royal consort of the next generation—Queen Tar'am-Agade—was the daughter of Naram-Sîn of Akkad, a lineage of sufficient importance that the queen apparently felt no need to portray herself as a mother in her iconography but instead took status from her father. Her seal (Figure 2.29) shows a combat scenes, and her inscription reads: "(Of) Naram-Sîn, the king of Akkad, Tar'am-Agade, his daughter."[154]

Eschewing scenes of maternity, nurturing, and domesticity, Tar'am-Agade chose to represent herself with scenes of violence and dominance. Rather than wife and mommy, she presented herself in the lineage of an emperor—"Who's my Daddy? The *King*, that's who!"

There is only so far that actual, flesh-and-blood females might be expected to perform (according to) their gender.

Notes

1 Veldhuis 2018: 455.
2 See subsequently on this.
3 Day 1991: 141.
4 Asher-Greve and Sweeney 2006: 151.
5 Karageorghis 1992: 19.
6 Tatton-Brown 1997: 48.
7 Karageorghis 2000: 19.
8 Catling 1971: 29.
9 Masson 1973: 115–116. See also Budin 2002: 315–316.
10 www.nytimes.com/2020/09/01/science/archaeology-phoenician-israel-shavei-zion.html. My emphases.
11 www.jpost.com/archaeology/biblical-fertility-amulet-found-in-the-negev-661413. My emphases.
12 Leick 1994: 5–6.

Femininity 111

13 Lemke-Santangelo 2009: 158.
14 Ibid: 161.
15 Wolkstein in Wolkstein and Kramer 1983: 146.
16 Hackett 1989: 67. This answers Veldhuis's question at the top of this chapter.
17 Handy 1994: 103.
18 Budin 2019: 196.
19 www.haaretz.com/archaeology/archaeology-has-a-problem-with-females-and-figurines-1.10012823?lts=1626727710920
20 Orriols-Llonch forthcoming; Dieleman 1998: 11–12; Eyre 1984: 96, who notes that, "actual evidence for prostitution in the New Kingdom is slight."
21 Budin 2021: Chapter One.
22 Kramer 1985: 127. Leick's (1994: 85) translation reads:

> What concerns women, (namely) men, I do not know
> What concerns women, (namely) love-making, I do not know
> What concerns women, (namely) kissing, I do not know.

23 George 1999: 7, adapted.
24 Wegner 1981:59, my translation from the German.
25 I am here deliberately contrasting the notions of "nude" and "naked," following the theories of Sir Kenneth Clark. For him, to be naked merely means not to be dressed— it is a natural state. By contrast, to be nude is artistic, a deliberate rendering (Clark 1959: 3).
26 See recently Budin 2011: Chapter 2, with citations.
27 Pinch 1983: 406–407.
28 Robins 1996: 34–35.
29 Robins 1996: 39.
30 Dales 1960.
31 Moorey 2001: 77, with citations.
32 Translation from http://etcsl.orinst.ox.ac.uk/cgi-bin/etcsl.cgi. She may have gotten this line from Inana, previously.
33 Leick 1994: Chapter 4. Philip Jones is even more emphatic in his interpretation that Ninlil is a wholly passive victim in this narrative. "Enlil rapes Ninlil. Banished from Nippur for his crime, he thrice seduces her by deceit" (Jones 2003: 299).
34 Dalley 1989: 171.
35 Ibid: 172.
36 Harris 2000: 136.
37 Hoffner 1998: 54–55, excerpted and slightly adapted.
38 Simpson 1972: 309–310.
39 Leick 1994: 49.
40 Translation by Dijkstra 1994: 116–118, adapted.
41 Leick 1994: 18; van Dijk 1964: 45.
42 Von Soden and Oelsner 1991: 341.
43 https://etcsl.orinst.ox.ac.uk/cgi-bin/etcsl.cgi?text=t.4.08.16#, ll. 18–34
44 Leick 1994: 91–92.
45 Goodnick Westenholz 1987: 423.
46 Foster 1974: 36–37, excerpted.
47 Hoffner 1998: 91.
48 Simpson 1972: 95, adapted.
49 Roth 2005: 214.
50 On the euphemism "hand" for penis, see Paul 2002.
51 *Baal Cycle* Tablet 4, column IV. Smith in Parker 1997: 128.
52 It usually is.
53 And, in the case of Egyptian mythology, learned about it *through* the Greco-Roman sources, such as Plutarch's *De Iside et Osiride*.

112   *Femininity*

54 Cooper 1997: 89, excerpted.

55 Wiggermann 2010: 412.

56 Cooper 1997: 95.

57 For much more on the Inana-Dumuzi love songs, see Sefati 1998.

58 Leick 1994: 112–113, excerpted. For additional data on women as the composers of Sumerian and Akkadian literature among other genres of writing, see Lion 2011.

59 Zsolnay 2014: 283.

60 De Waal 2022: 165.

61 De Waal 2007: 156.

62 Rorabaugh 2015: 117.

63 De Waal 2022: 173.

64 Roth 2005: 213.

65 All translations Smith in Parker 1997.

66 Walls 1992: 180.

67 This function of females is not restricted to humans. In his study of chimpanzee politics, Frans de Waal observed that, "If neither [male] was prepared to make the first conciliatory move—by looking at the other, holding out a hand, panting in a friendly way, or simply going up to his opponent—the two would continue to sit tensely opposite each other, and it was frequently a third party who helped them out of the impasse. This third party was always one of the adult females" (2007: 107).

68 George 1999: 24–25, excerpted and slightly adapted.

69 Centuries later, royalty continued to invoke Aya as an intermediary to Šamaš. In an inscription accompanying the rebuilding of Šamaš's temple in Sippar—the Ebab-bar—the Neo-Babylonian king Nabonidus wrote, "May Aya, the great bride who dwells in the bedroom, constantly make your face shine, may she every day speak favorably on my behalf to you!" (Pongratz-Leisten 2008: 62–63; Nissinen 2001: 106, with citations).

70 George 1999: 96.

71 Ibid: 98.

72 Harris 2000: 124.

73 https://etcsl.orinst.ox.ac.uk/cgi-bin/etcsl.cgi?text=t.2.4.2.24&charenc=j#

74 Pongratz-Leisten 2008: 57.

75 Translation by Marin Worthington, www.soas.ac.uk/baplar/recordings/ammi-ditnas-hymn-to-itar-read-by-doris-prechel.html

76 Nissinen 2001: 110–111, n. 131.

77 Pongratz-Leisten 2008: 65; Nissinen 2001: 97–98.

78 Nissinen 2001: 110–111, n. 131.

79 Nissinen 2001: 113, excerpted.

80 Ibid: 129.

81 https://cdli.ox.ac.uk/wiki/doku.php?id=ammiditana, MCS 2 50, VAT 679, and BA 6.3.

82 https://etcsl.orinst.ox.ac.uk/cgi-bin/etcsl.cgi?text=t.2.2.5&charenc=j#

83 Asher-Greve and Westenholz 2013: 193–194, excerpted. My emphases.

84 Suter 2000: 261–262.

85 The lack of horns argues against the identification of this nude female as a deity. However, the hand-made terracotta figurines which first appear in the 3rd millennium are also without horns, and it appears that horns became a *consistent* aspect of divine iconography only at the end of the millennium. It is possible, then, that their divinity was recognized even in the absence of the horned miter.

86 Assmann 2005: 165–169, excerpted.

87 Assmann 1978: 35–36, my translation from the German.

88 Leick 1994: 78; Jacobsen 1987: 21.

89 McDowell 1999: 42, #17.

Femininity 113

90 A term of respect and recognition of equal status. Not a familial relation.
91 Meier 2000: 171–172.
92 Bryce 2003: 114–115, excerpted and slightly adapted.
93 Ibid: 116.
94 Ibid: 115.
95 De Waal 2022: 6.
96 Meyers 2013: 142.
97 Baadsgaard 2008: 29, with additional, much smaller percentages to equal 100%.
98 Ibid.
99 Ibid: 42.
100 Meyers 2003: 426.
101 Again, a term of endearment, not necessarily a familial title.
102 McDowell 1999: 41, #15 B.
103 Budin 2011, 2019.
104 Troy 1986.
105 Lohwasser 2001: 67.
106 Dunham and Macadam 1949: 142 and 144.
107 FHN 1998, Vol. I: 240–241.
108 Lohwasser 2001: 65–66.
109 FHN 1998, Vol. I: 232–233.
110 Lohwasser 2021: 65.
111 Ibid: 66. On Nubian women and libation, see: Ashby 2019.
112 Lohwasser 2021: 67.
113 Lohwasser 2001: 72.
114 Roth 2005: 213.
115 Puhvel 2002: 548–549.
116 Faulkner 2007.
117 Lichtheim 2006, Vol II: 141.
118 Stol 2000: 191–192.
119 *Ibid*.
120 This word is typically mistranslated as "prostitute, harlot" in most modern transla-
     tions. That is not, in fact, the definition of *ḫarīmtu*. The word designated a woman
     who is not under patriarchal authority, insofar as she has neither father nor husband
     and is not dedicated to a deity. As such, she has a degree of sexual liberty not available
     to "normal" Mesopotamian females, and thus, as with Šamḫat here, was available to
     have sexual relations with a strange man on request. Request, not payment.
121 George 1999: 12–14, excerpted and slightly adapted.
122 Hoffner 1998: 11–12, adapted.
123 Ibid: 16–17, excerpted and adapted.
124 Couto-Ferreira 2016: 28.
125 Michel 2016: 200.
126 Fischer 2000: 25.
127 Fischer 1989: 14–24.
128 *Ibid*: 24.
129 Ward 1989: 35–37.
130 Meyers 2013: 173.
131 De Graef 2018: 135.
132 See Michel 2020: 62 on this non-translatable title.
133 For a monograph-length study of this in 1st-millennium Mesopotamia, see Svärd
     2012.
134 Lichtheim 2006, Vol II: 140.
135 Robins 1999: 66.
136 Ibid: 66–67. On the title *Nbt Pr* see Li 2017: 28–30.

114 *Femininity*

137 Smith in Parker 1997: 122.
138 Hoffner 1998: 52.
139 Tasks that were gendered feminine in the mortal sphere were also gendered feminine in the divine realm and generally done or at least presided over by goddesses. Thus, in Mesopotamia, for example, weaving was the domain of the goddess Uttu; the goddess Ninkasi was the patron of beer; healing was the responsibility of Gula; and a few, frequently syncretized, goddesses presided over midwifery—Nintu, Belet-ilī, Aruru, Mami. Yes, the Mesopotamians had a mother goddess named Mami. In this way, the tasks of women (weaving, brewing, etc.) had divine counterparts, meaning that women's work was just as religiously sanctioned as that of men. This contrasts with Biblical culture. In the Hebrew Bible, God is the "founder" of the fields of law, politics, and religious ritual—occupations reserved *exclusively* for males. Women's work (weaving, brewing, etc.) has no divine patron or counterpart. Tikva Frymer-Kensky sees this as an opportunity for mortal women to receive a boost in status by taking claim for these cultural artefacts and thus an improvement over the pagan model: "The very importance of humans in the field of the biblical philosophy of culture creates a flight from the human and a reemergence of females to do some of the work of the ancient goddesses" (1992: 117). By contrast, I argue that removing the divine counterparts of women's work leaves women *merely* doing mortal labor while men do "God's work." This can only have a detrimental impact on women's status.
140 Ebeling 2016
141 Michel 2016: 197–198. On the *sābītum*, see Langlois 2016.
142 Fischer 2000: 21.
143 Ibid: 19–20.
144 Li 2017: 31; Ward 1989: 37.
145 Depla 1994: 48.
146 On the Cambridge School in this creation of the Goddess Movement, see Hutton 2019: Chapter 14.
147 Hoffner 1998: 87.
148 Harris 2000: 72.
149 Depla 1994: 32. My emphasis.
150 Sweeney 2016: 248.
151 *Ibid.*
152 Buccellati and Kelly-Buccellati 1995–1996: 14–20.
153 Kelly-Buccellati 2010: 189. See also Kelly-Buccellati 1998: 44.
154 Buccellati and Kelly-Buccellati 2002: 13.

3 Masculinity

Males focus on sex and power.

(Frans de Waal, *Chimpanzee Politics*)

Theorizing Masculinity

Discussing masculinity in the 21st century comes with a lot of baggage. This comes from the fact that while men might be the first sex in our long-standing patriarchies, masculinity is definitely the second gender. We did not start studying or theorizing males until after we had already put femininity through its paces, after decades of first-wave feminism, women's studies, second-wave feminism, gender studies, postmodernism, third-wave feminism, and the rise of queer theory. By this point, a number of (subconscious) rules had become well entrenched in the study of gender. For example, because feminism existed at least in part to lead to women's liberation, it became politically inconvenient to speak of biological essentialism—the idea that any difference between males and females or their roles in society was predicated on physiology. If that were to be the case, then there would always be a go-to reason for why females could not be equal to males (and, of course, would default to being subordinate to them).[1] So, in the nature-vs.-nurture debate, we embraced nurture and refused to recognize nature.

An extreme of this was and is the theory of gender performance, espoused most famously by Judith Butler. As discussed in Chapter 1, according to this ideology, there is no such thing as biological sex to begin with, merely a socially constructed, fluid gender which is performed according to the dictates of the society in which it is construed. So masculinity, like femininity, is a performance.

Next came the work of Raewyn Connell, who theorized that there are actually multiple masculinities. Whatever any given society deems the "ideal man" is an expression of *hegemonic masculinity*. But in addition to this hegemonic version are numerous other expressions of masculinity—subordinated, complicit, and marginal, all with their own variations—each of which exists as a legitimate, if not ideal, form of maleness. Hegemonic masculinity itself must constantly be renegotiated, both in terms of its construction and who in society actually wields

DOI: 10.4324/9780429318177-3

116 *Masculinity*

it: basically, who the alpha male is and why. Often this is done by contrasting one's masculinity with that of subordinated and marginal males, those who do not live up to the hegemonic ideal (although they are still men). So as the dominant males in a community fight it out—violently or otherwise—to see who has the biggest hegemony, complicit males bask in a kind of reflected glory, being like hegemonic males but without having to fight quite so hard. In a kind of counter-culture, marginal men revel in their own type of masculine identity. An effemi-nate homosexual male may not "live up" to the "standard" of a quintessentially hegemonic male like Arnold Schwarzenegger (muscle-bound, A-list movie star, former governor of California) or Damien Mander (former mercenary soldier and founder of the International Anti-Poaching Foundation), but when the cast of "Queer Eye for the Straight Guy" help a complicit male to improve his social standing and sex life with their greater understanding of social mores and fashion, then they are most assuredly demonstrating their greater cultural and social capi-tal. So: multiple ways of being a man, multiple masculinities. All of which are, of course, performed.

The matter of constant renegotiation of status brings up an important issue in the study of masculinity, and that is the absolutely chronic need to *prove* one's masculinity. As we shall see in the following, as far back as we can go in the his-torical record (and even past that), we have evidence that masculinity has always been understood as contingent, something that must be achieved and that must constantly be reproven.

This doesn't really happen to females, certainly not to the same extent. Females, of course, have their own ideals as expressed by their own societies, often involv-ing adequate levels of beauty, however construed, and success as mothers and, potentially, wives. But this is rarely presented as adequate *femininity* per se. We might think of the historically brief period in the United States in the 1950s exam-ined by Betty Friedan in her *Feminine Mystique*. At this time, women were under considerable social pressure to be, specifically, *feminine*, an identity composed of total dedication to husband, children, and home, an identity that was supposed to lead to happiness and sexual fulfillment. An identity, Friedan discovered, created by war-traumatized males fantasizing about their own construct of the "ideal" woman and inflicted incessantly upon popular culture (all the magazine editors and TV moguls were male). At this (again: brief) time, women were indeed con-cerned with being adequately feminine. It tended to make them miserable, and by the 1970s, most were getting over this construction and finding new ways to be female, most of which were and are far more exhausting. But there was seldom a concern throughout history of being a "real woman" such as there was for being a "real man." There is no feminine counterpart to "Real Men Don't Eat Quiche." The closest one might come is the song by Aretha Franklin, "(You Make Me Feel Like) A Natural Woman." But the unanswered question remains: As opposed to what?[2]

The problem with masculinity and its variously performed multiples is that there is at least one clearly defined opposite to masculinity: femininity. For women, there is no clearly defined, terrifying other. History has a long record of praising women who behave (within certain parameters) like men, showing the supposedly masculine traits of rationality, self-control, courage, and self-sacrifice. If a woman is inadequately feminine, does that mean she is masculine? Is that bad? If not masculine, then what? Females don't have to worry overmuch about falling out of their category. By contrast, for males, there is a clearly, chronically well-articulated alternative to being a "real" man—being a woman (a.k.a. a sissy, a pussy, etc.). Nothing can be worse for a male, it would seem, than being female. And so masculinity must constantly be renegotiated and emphatically performed so as not to fall into this other, lesser category of being.

This fear, the fear of becoming female for not being adequately male, is a core attribute of masculinity. And this is why theory needed Connell's notions of multiple masculinities. No, not every man can be Arnold Schwarzenegger, but just because you aren't built like a house and speak with an Austrian accent doesn't mean that you aren't a "real" man.

And so the modern academy—including ANE studies—speaks in certain extremely well-worn refrains when it comes to discussing masculinity, all of which involve "performance" (not sexual) (although that can be part of it) and "multiple" masculinities, at the head of which is "hegemonic." Thus in her study of 2 Samuel 10:1–5, Hilary Lipka writes:

> In order to understand Hanun's intent in cutting beards and baring buttocks, and the response that this act inspired in both the emissaries and David, we must consider the ancient Israelite construction of masculinity, focusing on what attributes are associated with the hegemonic masculine ideal that permeated many biblical texts. We will then consider situations in which men are depicted as having their performance of hegemonic masculinity undermined through various circumstances or actions, and the relationship between shame and performance of alternative constructions of masculinity in some of these texts.[3]

When confronting the notion of the masculinity of Neo-Assyrian kings, Omar N'Shea notes,

> Much has been written about the meaning of Neo-Assyrian kingship to the Assyrians themselves, but scholarship has, as yet, not attempted to ascertain the degree to which Neo-Assyrian kingship relied on the construction and performance of ideal, hegemonic masculinity for its exercise of rule.[4]

In the introduction her book *Being a Man: Negotiating Ancient Constructs of Masculinity* Ilona Zsolnay writes:

> Several of the investigations confirm that the maintenance of patriarchal power was very much a preoccupation of the societies of Mesopotamia, Israel, Anatolia, and Persia. Its legitimation and normalization justified the masculine authority of gods, kings, and fathers. Yet, as this power was rooted

118   *Masculinity*

in the proper performance of culturally defined and mutable hegemonic masculinities, it was tenuous. These studies demonstrate that the threats to their performance were great and varied depending on the culture, medium, and characteristics which were thought to define them.[5]

One clear benefit of Connell's work is that in considering multiple forms of masculinity, it does focus on what was the most populous category of males in the ANE: human beings with penises who would probably go on to sire children. That is, to one extent or another, heterosexuals. Again, in the 21st century, yet another, additional bit of baggage that comes with studying masculinity is the fact that the majority of scholars working on this field have lost either interest or belief in heterosexual, biological men. As noted, masculinity studies came onto the scene considerably later than women's/feminist studies, when those fields of inquiry were already moving towards gender and queer studies. By the time men arrived, there was already extensive debate as to whether "Man," as a sex, actually existed (and, for that matter, "Woman") or if it were merely a performance of socially inscribed masculinity. Likewise, heterosexuality—termed "heteronormativity" in modern scholarship, generally with a sneer of disdain—is eschewed in favor of more queer lines of inquiry. As such, rather than studying masculinity as construed, lived, and understood by the residents of the ANE, modern scholars focus more energies on third gender and queering. These are absolutely important, interesting, and relevant topics. It simply means that there can be a dearth of scholarship on regular guys.

Obviously, this varies according to discipline. There are copious materials on masculinity in the Bible of every possible manifestation—from straight, hegemonic males to an array of homosexual constructs.[6] By contrast, the study of masculinity in Egyptology tends far more towards the postmodern. For example, a now-standard work on ancient Egyptian gender is Carolyn Graves-Brown's *Sex and Gender in Ancient Egypt: "Don Your Wig for a Joyful Hour"* (2008). The essays that deal specifically with men/masculinity are Thomas A. Dowson's "Queering Sex and Gender in Ancient Egypt," with the case study of the 5th-Dynasty males Niankhkhnum and Khnumhotep, who are most assuredly lovers; Greg Reeder's "Queer Egyptologies of Niankhkhnum and Khnumhotep," which is a study of the 5th-Dynasty males Niankhkhnum and Khnumhotep, who are most assuredly lovers; and R.B. Parkinson's "Boasting About Hardness: Constructions of Middle Kingdom Masculinity," which begins with a look at the debate about the 5th-Dynasty males Niankhkhnum and Khnumhotep, who may be lovers, stating:

I also consider how far the way in which men were portrayed can be considered erotic, and the manner in which some Middle Kingdom poems suggest that representations of masculinity were cultural constructs that were probably seen by the ancient actors to be potentially fluid, unstable and contingent. I suggest that these contingent constructs can offer the potential for a "queer" gaze, taking "queer" as "*whatever* is at odds with the normal, the legitimate, the dominant."[7]

Masculinity 119

In short, in an 11-chapter book considered a standard for gender studies in Egyptology, the queer approach to masculinity is dominant and almost exclusionary. Again, this is not to say that such approaches are not important, necessary, and fruitful. The problem resides in the fact that it becomes difficult to find scholarship on more standard types of masculinity: the normal, the legitimate, the dominant (or at least hegemonic).[8]

"Be a Man!"

The extent to which these various modern theories are relevant to the ancient world is debatable. As noted in Chapter 1, that the residents of the ANE had a concept of gender distinct from sex was apparent in the fact that a person could be disassociated from his masculinity or her femininity. Thus, "And you! Are you a real woman?"[9] and, "And you, are you a real man?"[10] But this issue appears far more frequently for males, suggesting that masculinity was in fact a quality that had to be continuously reestablished and earned. Or lost.

Fortunately, we have numerous texts from the ANE that spell out quite clearly what was necessary "to be a man." Thus the Old Assyrian King Samsî-Addu rebuked his lollygagging son Yasmah-Addu at Mari with, "Are you a baby? Don't you have hair on your chin? Even today, even though you are a mature adult you have not set up your household!"[11] A 20th-Dynasty personal letter from Deir el-Medina to the scribe Nekhemmut reads, "You are not a man since you are unable to make your wives pregnant like your fellow men."[12] From Karum Kaneš in Anatolia, we read in a letter from a Mesopotamian merchant, "Amurili should know how to show respect! He should not always be thinking of food and drink! He should be a man!"[13] And In 2 Kings 2: 2–3, the dying King David instructs his son Solomon, "'I am about to go the way of all the earth,' he said. 'So be strong, act like a man, and observe what the LORD your God requires.'"[14]

These quotations give a sense of what it was "to be a man" (i.e. masculine) in the ANE: martial competence ("be strong"); fertility; self-control; and social acumen, especially regarding professional conduct (in this particular instance: king). These help us to address the applicability of current theories to the issue of ancient masculinity. For example, it is simply not possible to "perform" fertility: One is fertile or one is not; it's not like faking an orgasm. So the idea that gender is merely a performance clearly must be rethought. While a scribe might have very different opportunities to express the ideal of martial competence than does a king or a soldier, all three are nevertheless considered "real" men through cultivation of the other characteristics: fertility; self-control; polite, professional conduct (plus, there is no reason the scribe would not accompany the army to battle, and we have records that scribes most assuredly did so). There does not appear to be a different set of desiderata for different categories of masculine men. If the king is the hegemonic male, that probably has a lot more to do with his socio-economic status than his "performance" of masculinity. When it comes to masculinity, one size did fit all, regardless of how often one had occasion to wear the suit.

120   *Masculinity*

Regarding the necessity of proving one's masculinity, of "being a man," another important factor must be kept in mind. In modern times, the clear-cut "Other" of a manly man is a woman, the feminine (and those non-hegemonic males who are closer to the feminine side of the gender continuum). This was not entirely the case in the ANE. Often it took the intervention of an extremely powerful deity (e.g. Ištar) to turn men into women.

> If Mati'-ilu sins against this treaty with Aššur-nerari, king of Assyria, may Mati'-ilu become a *ḫarīmtu*, his soldiers women . . . may Ištar, the goddess of men, the lady of women, take away their bow, bring them to shame.[15]

> To turn a man into a woman and a woman into a man are yours, Inana.[16]

So while the "threat" of femininity was certainly there, there were other, more threatening Others. Specifically, the threat of (still) being a *child*. The attributes of masculine gender don't pertain to males per se but specifically to grown men ("Man" = adult male human). Boys are not expected to be soldiers (they may fight, but not with the discipline and purpose of soldiers). Boys are not expected to be fertile (leave that for your wedding night). Boys don't have jobs and don't deal with politics. Boys have not yet developed proper self-control, because they are not yet men. And unlike the threat of being turned into a woman by Ištar, the panicky ambiguity of whether one has actually passed over the threshold into manhood was very, very real.

> Why do you stay in town like a feeble old man?
> How can you stay at home like a lisping child?
> Are we to eat women's bread, like one who has never marched on the battlefield?[17]

Again, this is not as problematic for females: Females have biology. Females mark their transition into womanhood with blood: menarche, defloration, parturition.[18] Once one is a mother, one is a woman, and in the ancient world, motherhood was the destiny of most women. Fewer coming-of-age rituals were thus necessary for females, even if in modern times we complement the biological with more social débutante balls, sweet sixteens, and quinceañeras.[19] From the works of Arnold Van Gennep and Pierre Videl-Naquet's *Black Hunter* on, there has been an academic focus on rituals that allow males to make a palpable transition from boy to man, from the world of mom and other women to the world of martial, political, self-controlled fathers. Samsî-Addu will tell his son to leave the women's quarters, get onto the plain of battle, and be a man. Basically, telling someone to "Be a man" was the equivalent of saying "Grow up." This probably goes a long way to explaining why very early on in Sumerian orthography there developed a distinction between a man (NITA) and a young man (ĝURUŠ) (see Chapter 1).

Finally, I would suggest that we do consider biology in our understanding of what constitutes masculinity, not necessarily in terms of hormones (although that

Masculinity 121

probably plays a part) but in terms of ethology and evolution. There are simply certain continuua with masculinity. Rather than calls to Foucault, Butler, and Connell, perhaps we might consider the story of Yeroen, his friend Luit, and Nikkie, male chimpanzees at the Arnhem Zoo in the Netherlands. Yeroen, the oldest, was also the alpha male, meaning that he received the most status in the group and had the greatest sexual access to the females and thus better opportunities for reproduction (although this often actually translated as being the male the other chimps were most careful to trick when having sex with each other). One summer Luit challenged Yeroen for alpha status, helped in his endeavor by Nikkie, who harassed the females whenever they tried to come to Yeroen's defense (in chimpanzee politics, the support of the females is a critical aspect of alpha status). Once Luit won—established himself as the dominant, hegemonic male—he proved an excellent alpha, resolving conflicts within the group, suppressing bullying, and maintaining the peace. But Yeroen was not to be outdone. No longer the strongest of the males, he formed an alliance with the young, strong, but somewhat dim Nikkie. In their alliance, Yeroen helped Nikkie to overthrow Luit and become group leader—a position Nikkie could only maintain with Yeroen's help. Thus, not by brawn but by politics, Yeroen once again achieved high status in the group, the chimpanzee equivalent of a retired Japanese emperor. Nevertheless, Luit continued to jockey for position, with an ongoing give and take between him and Nikkie. One night, Yeroen and Nikkie ganged up on Luit and killed him, biting off his scrotum. In the end, Yeroen proved the true alpha: When he could no longer "rule" by force, he ruled by forming careful alliances and setting up a "puppet" alpha. Two types of strategy, one goal: power.[20]

Males in the ANE cannot be said to behave that differently.

What follows are aspects of ANE masculinity divided into three general categories. The first consists of violence and fertility—those things that were understood to be distinctly masculine in the ANE. Men were the soldiers, kings flaunted their warrior and hunter status, and it was males, not females, who created new life (see a bit more on this in Chapter 1). The second category is professionalism; basically, males had jobs. Women also had jobs, of course, especially in cottage-based industries such as weaving, but also as doctors, midwives, real estate prospectors, and so on.[21] But this was seldom *presented* as typical in ANE societies, where the norm for females remained "Occupation: Housewife." By contrast, men were expected to have jobs: king, bureaucrat, soldier, manager, farmer, inspector, musician, physician, scribe, and so on. Males were expected to have an official role in society in addition to their role in the household. Males were extra-domestic.

The third category are those things that make one a specifically *good* man, that is, things that are not innate but that must be embodied, displayed, performed in order to qualify as a good example of masculinity (i.e. a grown-up). This is most especially self-control, what the Greeks would call *sophrosynê*. The wisdom literature is replete with fathers telling sons to show self-control, both physically and socially, so as to be good men. By contrast, the male-authored literature displays frequent concern that females do not/will not embody this ideal, leading to conflict and potential poverty. As such, self-control might be gendered as masculine, at least from a masculine perspective.

122 *Masculinity*

Violence

> "Had women ever marshalled troops?" (*Instruction of King Amenemhet to his son Sesostris*).
>
> > "Will women now be hunting?" (*Aqhat Epic*).

The past 5,000+ years of chronic warfare, violence, brutality, and carnage are pretty much a guy thing.

> If there is one aspect of social life that is gender-biased, it is physical violence. Males are overwhelmingly its source. This is universally true for humans (look up the homicide statistics of any nation), and it applies equally to most other primates. Not that female primates never turn violent, but they are more often on the receiving end. Males are victims, too, but generally at the hands of their own sex. Male brutality relates either to dominance and territoriality, when it is aimed at other males, or to sexual relations, when it targets females.[22]

This is not to say that females neither cause nor fight in wars: They do. But even though the literary tradition is filled to the brim with male authors claiming that wars are started because of women (e.g. Homer, Herodotos), the less literary (e.g. Thucydides) usually situate such conflicts in the realms of politics, which tend to be male dominated. And while women have been joining the men-folk on the front lines since time immemorial, those who fight as soldiers often show up disguised as males, amazons notwithstanding.[23] So the almost universal practice in the ANE of associating masculine gender with weapons—especially those (axe, stick, arrow, etc.) given to baby boys in contrast to the spindles given to baby girls (see Chapter 1)—pertains to this significant and highlighted aspect of masculine gender.

The idea that man = warrior is clearly expressed in the opening tablets of the Standard Version of the *Epic of Gilgameš*, attributed to the scribe Sîn-leqi-unninni. While the scribe does begin by praising the great king in terms of his wisdom, travel, and building activities, when giving the first glimpse of the king of Uruk, he recounts how Gilgameš was (Tablet 1, 29–35):

> Surpassing all other kings, heroic in stature,
> Brave scion of Uruk, wild bull on the rampage!
> Going at the fore he was the vanguard.
> Going at the rear, one his comrades could trust!
> A mighty bank, protecting his warriors
> A violent flood-wave, smashing a stone wall!
> Wild bull of Lugalbanda, Gilgameš, perfect in strength.[24]

As the scribe goes on to note, "He has no equal when his weapons are brandished."[25]

All fine and well: A king needs to be martial to protect his people. However, the king's friend Enkidu must *also* become a warrior and hunter to achieve manhood. Having been tamed by Šamḫat and taught to eat bread and drink beer—the way of humankind—next (Tablet 2):

Masculinity   123

The barber groomed his body so hairy,
Anointed with oil he turned into a man (*awīlu*).
He put on a garment, became like a warrior,
He took up his weapon, to do battle with lions.
When at night the shepherds lay sleeping,
He struck down wolves, he chased off lions.[26]

Perhaps just as importantly, once Enkidu and Gilgameš become best friends (after a fight, of course), Enkidu is recognized by the populace of Uruk as an ally and even protector of the king because (Table 3, ll. 8–10):

He is tested in battle and tried in combat,
He shall guard his friend and keep safe his companion,
Enkidu shall bring him safe home to his wives.[27]

Actually, technically, neither Enkidu nor Gilgameš were tested in battle or tried in combat. Enkidu faced off against lions and wolves. Gilgameš played war games with his own citizens. The description of king and hero is cast in terms of combat and violence, even when these elements do not belong to the biography of the individual in question.[28] Both Gilgameš and Enkidu are heroes—are "real" men—purely on spec. Neither man had yet proven his manhood on the field of battle, which is the main reason Gilgameš felt it imperative to go slay Humbaba in an effort to assert his masculinity (Tablet 2, Old Babylonian version ll. 184–187):

I shall conquer him in the Forest of Cedar:
Let the land learn Uruk's offshoot is mighty!
Let me start out, I will cut down the cedar,
I shall establish for ever a name eternal![29]

This plan is presented for approval to both the elders and "the young men of Uruk-the-Sheepfold, the young men of Uruk who understand combat." The elders at least try to talk him out of it. . . . Males in the *Epic* are presented as martial beings. Gilgameš is the great king, the Shepherd of Uruk, who first manifests as a belligerent male, a trusty warrior. Enkidu becomes a human through sex but a male through adoption of warrior and hunter status. Both seek eternal reputation through the slaying of a monster, and on this matter they consult males identified through their own relationship to combat.

Baal Cycle

This idea that a male becomes a "real" man through violence also plays out in the Ugaritic *Baal Cycle* (*CAT* 1.1–1.6). Although the precise organization of the tablets remains open to debate, Mark S. Smith has suggested the following order of events (extreme summary): Yamm (the Sea) calls out Baal and challenges him to combat. El and Athirat—the heads of the pantheon—approve the combat. Baal

124 *Masculinity*

gets weapons from Kothat-wa-Hasis (smith god) and with these defeats Yamm. Baal is proclaimed victor and king and celebrates with a victory feast. He then requests a "house" (temple) from El. Once established in his house, Baal is then challenged by a new adversary—Môt (Death). They fight; Baal loses. Môt brags of this before Baal's friend Anat; Anat wipes the floor with Môt. With the help of Anat and Šapaš (the Sun), Baal returns, faces Môt in combat again, and ultimately triumphs.

Baal both creates his place in the world and maintains it through violence. His place in the pantheon is established with his conquest of Yamm. Not only does this allow him to establish a "household" for himself—a marker of male adulthood—but he celebrates this *rite du passage* with what Smith notes is an ultramasculine victory fête (*CAT* 1.3, Column 1, 8–17)

> He stood, served, and offered him drink,
> Put a cup in his hand,
> A goblet in both hands;
> A large, imposing vessel,
> A rhyton for mighty men;
> A holy cup women may not see,
> A goblet Athirat may not eye.
> A thousand jars he drew of wine,
> A myriad he mixed in his mixture.[30]

To quote Smith:

> [T]he vessel for drinking is "a huge vessel" . . ., one perhaps for "mighty men," *mt šmm*. Clearly this vessel is not for women: it is called "a holy cup (that) women may not see//a goblet (that) Athirat may not eye." In other words, this drinking puts males at the center of the activity and excludes women; not even the goddess Athirat is supposed to lay her eyes on it. The mention of the goddess in this manner seems to be a sort of superlative, gendered delimitation: no female, human or divine, is to look upon this vessel of male drinking. In this context, this vessel marks the domain of males at the center of this drinking feast. The polarity of gendered expression here evokes a boundary: men at the center, women at the periphery or in subservience.[31]

The narrative repeats, replacing Yamm with Môt. Again, Baal needs the help of other members of the pantheon to overcome his opponent, this time Anat rather than the weapons of Kothar-wa-Ḥasis. In fact, the final combat appears to be fought without weapons at all, a more primal form of fighting (1.6, Column 6, 16–22):

> They eyed each other like fighters:
> Môt was fierce, Baal was fierce.
> They gored each other like wild bulls:
> Môt was fierce, Baal was fierce.

They bit each other like serpents:
Môt was fierce, Baal was fierce.
They dragged each other like runners:
Môt fell, Baal fell.[32]

Like Gilgameš, the young male Baal achieves manhood in his community by way of violence, fighting and overcoming both the Sea and Death itself. This allows him to establish his own household (for a god: a temple) and to celebrate in the hyper-masculine context of the warrior's feast.

The Early Iconography of Kingship

Narmer Palette

The origins of kingship in both Egypt and Mesopotamia are iconographically depicted as powerful men killing things, often, but not necessarily, other men. Thus, an object seen as a critical piece of transitional iconography in the establishment of Egyptian kingship is the Narmer Palette (Figure 3.1), a slate cosmetic palette brought to light at the dawn of the 20th century along with other Nagada III and Early Dynastic artifacts in a cache deposited under the floor of a temple of Horus at Hierakonpolis.[33] The "verso" side of the palette (technically the back, but bearing what appears to modern eyes to be the primary image) shows the image of the king wearing the white crown of Upper Egypt and a kilt with a bull's tail. In this right arm he holds aloft a mace which he is apparently using to smite the kneeling man before him, whom he holds by the forelock with his left hand. Behind the king is a much smaller sandal-bearer. Above the kneeling enemy and facing the king is a falcon with one claw and one human arm; the latter he uses to lead a personified "land" sign by a rope attached the "land's" nose. From the land six papyrus stalks

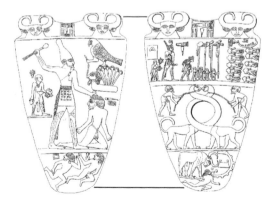

Figure 3.1 Narmer Palette, Egyptian Museum, Cairo, CG 14716.
Source: Drawing from Kemp 2006: 84, fig. 27.

126 *Masculinity*

bloom. Above this middle register are two bovine heads (Hathor or Bat?) on either side of the *serekh* that contain the hieroglyphs of a catfish and chisel, traditionally read as "Nar.mer." In the bottom register are two nude, dead/sprawled males with coiffures similar to that of the man being maced in the main register. These would appear to be additional dead enemies.

The recto side of the palette has three registers below the top edge with identical bovine heads and *serekh*. The uppermost register shows the king wearing the Red Crown of Lower Egypt. He is flanked by two diminutive attendants and preceded by four standards each held by a tiny standard bearer. All face towards the right, where there are ten nude, decapitated bodies with the heads placed between the feet—clearly the result of post-mortem ritual violence. The middle register shows two Mesopotamian-inspired long-necked lions with necks entwined. Each one is held on a leash by a small, bearded attendant. The bottom register shows the king in the form of a bull butting a fortified enclosure, all above the sprawled body of a nude male.[34] For John Baines, "The two principal scenes might be read serially as a military victory indicated by the decapitated corpses, followed by the ritual execution of the enemy leader."[35]

There is debate as to whether this artifact represents an historical encounter. The traditional interpretation is that it shows the victory of the king of Upper Egypt over the land and king of the Delta. However, more recent evidence argues that the "Two Lands" of Egypt were already sufficiently united at this point that the portrayal of a "final confrontation" is highly unlikely. Furthermore, while the motif of the Egyptian king smiting the dickens out of foreigners remained a constant in Egyptian royal iconography, internal rebellions were not. As such, Baines has suggested that the palette portrays a "ritual affirmation of conquest, not a real event."[36] By contrast, Ellen Morris has argued that the scenes might refer not to the grand unification of North and South but to a skirmish with a Delta "kinglet, perhaps in a battle that was pivotal in establishing [Narmer's] uncontested control of the Delta."[37]

What all interpretations of the palette recognize is the firm establishment of the image of the martial king in Narmer's iconographic program. Toby Wilkinson sees this piece as transitional from an age when royal power was represented in the form of specific wild animals (such as catfish!) dominating others (hunting violence) to an iconography of an anthropomorphic king dominating and killing human enemies (martial violence):

> [T]he king is shown in human form (although wearing a bull's tail) as a huge, towering figure, smiting his enemy with a mace. This, the quintessential icon of Egyptian Kingship, with its origins far back in the early Predynastic Period, was to become the primary symbol of royal power from the reign of Narmer onwards. The Narmer Palette is thus a striking amalgam of earlier and later conventions of royal iconography.[38]

For Morris, "it is clear that the idea of the king as a fighter and punisher . . . was to emerge as a central tenet in the ideology of Early Dynastic kingship," thus exemplifying the role of the king as "the crusher of rebels and the expander of the ordered state."[39]

Lion Hunt Stele

From Mesopotamia comes the late 4th-millennium basalt sculpture depicting a male killing a lion (Figure 3.2). The work appears to consist of two non-divided registers. In both is depicted a single man with a beard and headband, belt and kilt, and a quasi "chignon" hairstyle. As both males are portrayed identically, it might be supposed that they are both the same man, shown in two separate phases of the lion-killing process. Such an idea is borne out by the two depictions. In the lower register the man uses bow and arrow (long-range weapons) to shoot two visibly wounded lions. In the upper register, the man stabs a single lion with a spear (short-range weapon). To create a narrative of the events portrayed, we might suppose, reading bottom to top, that this man first faces off against a pride from a distance, then finishes off the final lion with a spear.

The garb worn by the male is typical of the LÚ.GAL ("Big Man") or king in early Mesopotamian iconography—rounded beard, headband, chignon, skirt.[40]

Figure 3.2 Lion Hunt Stela, Baghdad Museum, 10113052. Osama Shukir Muhammed Amin, Wikimedia Commons.

128 *Masculinity*

This conquest of lions shows the king in his role as "defender of the sheepfold-city," much as was Gilgameš of Uruk (see previously). Rather than a depiction of the king as defeater of foreign enemies, we have here the king as defeater of the forces of chaos and external threat. Violence harnessed to overcome violence.

Stele of the Vultures

Getting back to the theme of defeating foreign enemies, though, is the Stele of the Vultures (Figure 3.3). This sculpture dates to c. 2500–2450 BCE and was discovered at the site of Telloh in Iraq in 1880.[41] Dedicated to Ningirsu, the city god of Lagaš, it commemorates the victory of King Eannatum of Lagaš over the city of Umma. Both sides of the monument highlight martial victory. On the obverse we see the god Ningirsu himself in what must be the aftermath of the battle/war. He holds in his left hand a dominated Anzu bird, beneath which is a net filled with naked, captive male prisoners. Ningirsu bashes one of them on the head with the

Figure 3.3 Stele of the Vultures, Louvre Museum, AO 16 IO9, AO 50, AO 2246, AO 2348.

Source: Drawing by Elizabeth Simpson, figure 3 (obverse) and figure 8 (reverse), in Winter 1985.

Figure 3.3 (Continued)

mace that he wields in his right hand. Prisoners of war are soundly defeated by the city deity. Behind Ningirsu is the upper head of a goddess revealing a horned miter and the upper tips of maces. While such iconography is normally reserved for Ištar in the Akkadian Period, it has been argued instead that here we have a depiction of Ningiru's mother Ninhursag. Below this register we see Ningirsu again, this time riding a chariot, with Ninhursag facing him from the right.

The reverse of the stele as preserved shows four registers. At the top is the king with chignon and headband and wearing a tunic that reveals the right arm and upper chest. Behind him to the left is a row of soldiers in phalanx formation, holding before them rectangular shields with several rows of spears poking forward. Beneath their feet, and before the king to the right of the register, are naked, fallen, and bound prisoners. The register beneath this also reveals a group of soldiers with shields and spears to the left. Before these soldiers in the center of the composition is the king in identical garb and coiffure, this time wielding a

130 *Masculinity*

spear (? the tip is not preserved) above his head as he rides in a chariot. The third register as preserved shows just the foot and skirt-tip of the seated king (?) looking leftwards to a libation in the center of the composition, while to the left are a "stack" of naked, bound, apparently dead enemies. All that remains of the final, bottom register is a long spear aimed at a bald head facing left.

What we have depicted, then, are two separate males. On the obverse the male is bare-chested with an elaborate beard and is clearly an order of magnitude larger than the enemies he holds in his net (and, for that matter, mom). While it is impossible to see if he wears the horned miter emblematic of divinity by the late 3rd millennium, the fact that he appears in-scene with a female who does also argues in favor of the interpretation that he is a god, specifically the city god Ningirsu as named in the inscription. By contrast, the central, highlighted male on the reverse shows a beardless, tunic-clad male with a helmet but no horned headdress (although he does still bear the emblematic chignon coiffure). He is depicted larger than the other men in the scene, but only minimally so; one might see the size more related to a being in the foreground as opposed to distant infantry. Either on foot or in chariot, he consistently appears at the head of a regiment—the war leader. The accompanying inscription identifies the man as "Eannatum, LÚ.GAL of Lagaš."

The inscription itself relates the history of the conflict between Lagaš and Umma, which takes a decided turning point when Eannatum is created by Ningirsu, Warrior of Enlil (column 4, ll 9–12),

> [The god Ni]n[ĝir]su [imp]lanted the
> [semen] for E-[a]natum in the [wom]b[42]

He is nursed by Ninhursag and made king. After trying to resolve the dispute over the territory of Gu'eden through diplomatic means, the war begins. Eannatum is wounded, but ultimately is victorious.

> Oh E-anatum . . . you will slay there. Their myriad corpses will reach the base of heaven. [In] Ĝiš[a] (Um[ma]) . . . [his people] will raise a hand against him, and he will be killed within Ĝiš[a] (Umma) (itself).
> He fought with him. A person shot an arrow at E-anatum. He was shot through(?) by the arrow and had difficulty moving.[43]

The Gu-edin territory is returned to Lagaš and Ningirsu ("Eannatum restored to the god Ningirsu's control his beloved field, the Gu'Eden") under a treaty that invokes Enlil, Ninhursag, Enki, Sîn, Utu, and Ninki. Eannatum then goes on to list other rulers he defeated in combat, all commemorated by the erection of a stele.

Both the text and the imagery highlight the martial prowess of both the king himself and that of the city god Ningirsu. In point of fact, the inscriptions makes it clear that Eannatum was functioning as the agent of the god from the beginning. As such, as with Egypt, the martial violence manifest in the king is not a random, chaotic violence (always bad) but a means towards the re-establishment of divine order. To quote the Blues Brothers, "We're on a mission from God."

Masculinity   131

Kings and Violence

From the beginning, then, the violence of the king was a force for good. This martial violence is inevitably portrayed as a means of defending one's kingdom from the onslaught of enemies. Because it is a controlled, divinely sanctioned use of force to maintain cosmic order, it is a source of bragging rights for kings, and ultimately a, if not the, foundation for masculine identity in royalty.

The extreme importance of martial ability in the establishment of (royal) masculinity comes across well in the annals of the Hittite King Mursili, especially as this monarch must defend himself against accusations of being a child rather than a king. Having mounted the throne after the unexpected death of his brother Arnuwanda, the king recalls how (*Ten-Year Annals*, AM 16–21):

> When my brother Arnuwanda became a god [died], the enemy lands who had not yet made war, these enemy lands also made war. And the neighboring enemy lands spoke as follows: "His father, who was king of the Land of Hatti and a Hero-King, held sway over the enemy lands. And he became a god. But his son who sat upon his father's throne and was previously a great warrior fell ill, and he also became a god. Yet he who has recently sat upon his father's throne is a child. He will not preserve the Land of Hatti and the territory of the Hatti lands."[44]

And likewise (*Comprehensive Annals*, AM 18–21):

> You are a child; you know nothing and instill no fear in me. Your land is now in ruins, and your infantry and chariotry are few. Against your infantry I have many infantry; against your chariotry I have many chariotry. Your father had many infantry and chariotry. But you, who are a child, how can you match him?[45]

According to Trevor Bryce, King Mursili was probably in his early 20s when he assumed kingship: not a "child" at all. The references to his "childishness" were thus an attack on his ability to be king, cast specifically with reference to his inability to be a successful warrior. Here again we see the inverse of masculinity being portrayed not as femininity but as being a child. To be a "real" man, a true king, Mursili had to prove his mettle through combat. Which he did quite successfully.

It is thus hardly surprising that this aspect of masculine royalty is taken up repeatedly in the praise of historic kings. In Mesopotamia, this is especially so for the second king of the 3rd Dynasty of Ur—Šulgi. And it is perhaps also not surprising that this king specifically chose to associate himself with an earlier martial king in his hymns of self-praise, to wit: Gilgameš. In a hymn that Jacob Klein calls "Šulgi and Gilgameš: Two Brother-Peers," (*Šulgi O*) he claims that:

> In this meeting, the two protagonists speak to each other, man to man, in a state of perfect awakening in order to enhance mutually their fame and

132 *Masculinity*

glory. The remaining portion of the hymn seems to contain lengthy dialogue between Šulgi and Gilgameš, in which the divine brothers alternate in singing each other's praise and glory.[46]

(*Šulgi O*, ll. 28–84, excerpted):

On the day when the destiny of the Land was determined, when the seed of all living beings was originally brought forth, when the king appeared radiantly to his comrade—on that day, Gilgameš, the lord of Kulaba, conversed with Šulgi, the good shepherd of Sumer, at his shining feet. So that their praise would be sung forever, so that it be would handed down to distant days, so that it should not be forgotten in remote years, they looked (?) at each other favorably in their mighty heroism. Šulgi, the good shepherd of Sumer, praised his brother and friend, Lord Gilgameš, in his might, and declared to him in his heroism: "Mighty in battle, destroyer of cities, smiting them in combat! Siege-weapon skilled with the slingstone against the holy wall! You brought forth your weapons against the house of Kiš. You captured dead its seven heroes. You trampled underfoot the head of the king of Kiš, En-me-barage-si. . . . You brought the kingship from Kiš to Unug." Thus he eulogised him who was born . . . in Kulaba. . . . (Gilgameš speaks:) "Like . . ., falsely (?) . . ., you trampled underfoot . . ., . . . as if in a mighty clamp. You gathered its . . . like swallows rising into the air. You entered with them into the presence of Enlil in the shrine of Nibru. Even those . . . who escaped from the . . ., wail bitterly . . . a copper (?) statue fashioned (?) in Urim, . . . the seven gods, stationed beside, wielding battle-axes. Fearsome (?) hero . . ., king of Sumer, you stand firm in your strength (?)."[47]

In *Šulgi B*, the king vaunts both his skill as a warrior and his prowess as a hunter (ll. 21–76):[48]

When I sprang up, muscular as a cheetah, galloping like a thoroughbred ass at full gallop, the favor of An brought me joy; to my delight Enlil spoke favorably about me, and they gave me the scepter because of my righteousness. I place my foot on the neck of the foreign lands; the fame of my weapons is established as far as the south, and my victory is established in the highlands. When I set off for battle and strife to a place that Enlil has commanded me, I go ahead of the main body of my troops and I clear the terrain for my scouts. I have a positive passion for weapons. Not only do I carry lance and spear, I also know how to handle slingstones with a sling. The clay bullets, the treacherous pellets that I shoot, fly around like a violent rainstorm. In my rage I do not let them miss. I sow fear and confusion in the foreign land. I look to my brother and friend, youthful Utu, as a source of divine encouragement. I, Šulgi, converse with him whenever he rises over there; he is the god who keeps a good eye on my battles. The youth Utu, beloved in the mountains, is the protective deity of my weapons; by his words I am strengthened and

Masculinity 133

made pugnacious (?). In those battles, where weapon clashes on weapon, Utu shines on me. Thus I broke the weapons of the highlands over my knees, and in the south placed a yoke on the neck of Elam. I make the populations of the rebel lands—how could they still resist my weapons?—scatter like seed-grain over Sumer and Akkad.

I stride forward in majesty, trampling endlessly through the esparto grass and thickets, capturing elephant after elephant, creatures of the plain; and I put an end to the heroic roaring in the plains of the different lions, the dragons of the plains, wherever it approaches from and wherever it is going. I do not go after them with a net, nor do I lie in wait for them in a hide; it comes to a confrontation of strength and weapons. I do not hurl a weapon; when I plunge a bitter-pointed lance into their throats, I do not flinch at their roar. I am not one to retreat to my hiding-place but, as when one warrior kills another warrior, I do everything swiftly on the open plain. In the desert where the paths peter out, I reduce the roar at the lair to silence. In the sheepfold and the cattle-pen, where heads are laid to rest (?), I put the shepherd tribesmen at ease. Let no one ever at any time say about me, "Could he really subdue them all on his own?" The number of lions that I have dispatched with my weapons is limitless; their total is unknown.

In summary (ll. 81–94):

I am Šulgi, **god of young manliness**, the foremost of the troops. (ᵈŠUL-GI DIĜIR NAM-ĜURUŠ-A SAĜ-KAL ERIN₂-NA-ME-EN). When I stretch the bowstring on the bow, when I fit a perfect arrow to it, I shoot the bow's arrow with the full strength of my arms.[49]

It is important to note that Šulgi's self-praise consisted of much more than martial prowess. In his hymns he vaunts his wisdom; his education; his ability to read, write, and compose; his skill on various musical instruments; his lovely singing voice; his ability to make everyone happy by his mere presence. He absolutely would have been diagnosed with a narcissism complex in modern times, assuming he wrote these hymns himself (only Old Babylonian copies remain,[50] and it is entirely possible that they were composed to laud an idealized former statesman in later centuries). Nevertheless, being a victorious warrior is an ongoing critical aspect of his presentation as a good ruler.

The Egyptian king was responsible for maintaining Ma'at—cosmic order; as such, it was less in line with Egyptian royal propaganda to dwell on the need for violence: It would suggest that the king was not quite doing his job. Nevertheless, *realpolitik* being what it is, even the king must occasionally resort to violence and instruct his heirs to do the same. Thus the Intermediate Period author of *The Teaching for Merikare* could tell the future king:

But I lived, and while I existed the barbarians were as though in the walls of a fortress; [my troops] broke open. . . . I caused the Delta to smite them,

134   *Masculinity*

I carried off their people, I took away that cattle, until the detestation of the Asiatics was against Egypt. Do not worry about him, for the Asiatic is a crocodile on his riverbank; he snatches a lonely serf, but he will never rob in the vicinity of a populous town.[51]

Even so, the ideal was that restraint was preferable, especially when dealing with one's own subjects:

Do justice, that you may live long upon the earth. Calm the weeper, do not oppress the widow, do not oust a man from his father's property, do not degrade magnates from their seats. Beware of punishing wrongfully: do not kill, for it will not profit you, but punish with beatings and with imprisonment for thus this land will be set in order excepting only the rebel who has conspired.[52]

A similar sentiment was offered by the Middle Kingdom King Ammenemes to his son Sesostris I. Here the kings declares:

Men dwelt in peace through what I had done, talking of me, for everything that I commanded was in good order. I have curbed lions, I have carried off crocodiles, I have crushed the people of Wawat, I have carried off the Medjay, I have made the Asiatics slink like dogs.[53]

In contrast to these wise, violent when necessary kings, we might consider our less-than-a-real-man ruler of the Syrian city of Mari—Yasmah-Addu—installed as prince by his father, the Old Assyrian King Samsî-Addu. Clearly not living up to the model set by his more martial brother Išme-Dagan, Yasmah-Addu is reproached (yet again) by his father:

Here, your brother has won a victory. But you, over there, you are lying about amongst the women. It is now on you, when you arrive with the armies at Qatna, to show that you are a real man! Just as your brother has acquired great glory, so you too, with this expedition to Qatna, acquire great glory![54]

This contrast between masculine martial valor and "lying about amongst the women" or femininity in general is well expressed in the Biblical materials. Here we see a clear division of war-time labors between males and females. It was for the men to fight in defense of the land, most especially the kings once there were kings (an institution desired to provide defense against the Philistines especially: 1 Samuel 8), and it was for women to sing the praises of victorious warriors, to denigrate the fallen enemy, and to lament the dead. Thus in 2 Samuel 1:19–25:

Your glory, O Israel, is slain on your high places!
How the mighty have fallen!
Tell it not in Gath,

> publish it not in the streets of Ashkelon,
> *lest the daughters of the Philistines rejoice,*
> *lest the daughters of the uncircumcised exult.*
>
> . . .
>
> *You daughters of Israel, weep over Saul,*
> who clothed you luxuriously in scarlet,
> who put ornaments of gold on your apparel.
> How the mighty have fallen
> in the midst of the battle!

Per this "division of labor," there could be no greater shame for the warrior than to be killed by a female. To be clear, this is not a case of a male warrior facing off against a female warrior, as would be the case with Ugaritic Anat or Mesopotamian Ištar (on their martial personae, see Chapter 4). Females are pointedly non-martial in the Hebrew Bible, and those very few occasions where a woman does kill a male (warrior) are given a feminine twist. Thus when the judge Deborah rejoiced at the death of the enemy Sisera at the hands of the woman Jael, she sang (Judges 5: 24–27):

> Most blessed of women be Jael,
> the wife of Heber the Kenite,
> of tent-dwelling women most blessed.
> He asked for water and she gave him milk;
> she brought him curds in a noble's bowl.
> She sent her hand to the tent peg
> and her right hand to the workmen's mallet;
> she struck Sisera;
> she crushed his head;
> she shattered and pierced his temple.
> Between her feet
> he sank, he fell, he lay still;
> between her feet
> he sank, he fell;
> where he sank,
> there he fell—dead.

Sisera entered the tent of what he believed to be an ally: the wife of a clansman allied to his own kingdom. Thus, he enters an interior, domestic, feminine space. He requests water, that is, food preparation services from the woman in her own space. She gives him milk—a beverage that would actually exacerbate his dehydration and make him weaker.[55] When he lets his guard down (it's only a woman here), she kills him with a tent peg, a part of the ersatz domestic structure that is feminine space. If a woman kills a soldier, it will be in the most feminine way possible.

136 *Masculinity*

A similar situation pertains to the death of Abimelech, although with somewhat less direct intention on the part of the female in question (Judges 9: 52–55):

> And Abimelech came to the tower and fought against it and drew near to the door of the tower to burn it with fire. And a certain woman threw an upper millstone on Abimelech's head and crushed his skull. Then he called quickly to the young man his armor-bearer and said to him, "Draw your sword and kill me, *lest they say of me, 'A woman killed him.'*" And his young man thrust him through, and he died. And when the men of Israel saw that Abimelech was dead, everyone departed to his home.

To be a warrior, then, is to be masculine in a way that is pointedly contrasted with femininity. We might recall the various curses and insults from Chapter 1 that called on the deities to turn warriors into women and replace bows with spindles.

Reality

Interesting fact: For all their boasting of glorious victories in war and claims to martial prowess, kings were generally pretty careful not to fight themselves. This is another one of those places where theory differs considerably from reality. As Bryce mused in his discussion of the Hittite army:

> But while many Hittite kings were no doubt well trained in the arts of war, they almost certainly directed most of their military operations from a vantage-point safely removed from the thick of battle, or if ever participating in the battle itself, well protected by their bodyguards. . . . Hittite pragmatism would surely have seen to it that His Majesty was not too closely exposed to the hazards of war. For all his military prowess, the possibility that a well-directed enemy shaft, or a lucky sword thrust, could in an instant plunge the whole kingdom into crisis was an unacceptable risk. In all Hittite history, and in spite of the fact that many kings spent part of almost every year of their lives on the battlefield, there was not one king, as far as we know, who died on the battlefield.[56]

A similar dynamic might be appreciated in the Neo-Assyrian wall reliefs that record the death of the Elamite King Teumman during the reign of King Aššurbanipal. In the relief narrative of the Battle of Til-Tuba (Figure 3.4), one sees a chaotic field of battle in which the Elamite king and his son Tammaritu are killed by Assyrian soldiers wielding axes and maces (symbols of royal authority for official executions, according to Julien Reade).[57] Their heads are cut off.

Contrast this with the relief wherein we see King Aššurbanipal himself with the head of his former nemesis (Figure 3.5): The king is enjoying a sip in the palace garden accompanied by his wife, her servants, and attendants fanning the pair. The head of Teumman dangles from a nearby tree branch. The king may be a victor, but he is not a warrior.

Masculinity 137

Figure 3.4 Neo-Assyrian Relief Showing Detail of the Battle of Til Tuba, British Museum, 124801.

Source: © The Trustees of the British Museum.

Figure 3.5 Neo-Assyrian Relief Showing Aššurbanipal in Garden, British Museum, 124920.

Source: © The Trustees of the British Museum.

We might also consider the depictions of the world-famous King "Tut" Tutankhamun, who appears in his tomb in august warrior guise (Figure 3.6). When studying the mummified, physical remains of this young pharaoh, however, it was determined that he had a host of physical ailments, especially foot and leg problems, as well as malaria, that would have completely barred him from taking part in such martial activities. The king was not a soldier. He was merely portrayed as such.

This is not to argue that *no* kings took part in actual battle; some must have. It is merely to point out that the relationship between violence and masculinity

138 *Masculinity*

Figure 3.6 King Tutankhamun in Chariot, Painted Chest, Egyptian Museum, Cairo.
Source: Science History Images/Alamy Stock Photo.

at the hegemonic level may have been far more propaganda than real. It was the ideal that counted.

Below the hegemonic level, the ancients realized that violence was not necessarily a good thing. One might say it is a double-edged sword. One might say that it is an aspect of toxic masculinity. As we shall see, fathers with a scribal bent tended to advise their sons to avoid it in social settings (e.g. "Don't pick a fight with a drunk.") As such, what was lauded in the ancient sources is not so much violence *per se* as *martial potential* in time of need. Males are expected to be good soldiers, which includes discipline and self-control (or, at least, should). The king justifies his kingship at least in part by his ability to wield violence (at least theoretically) in the maintenance of divine cosmic order. The male subject must be ready to fight on the "field of masculinity" (KI NAM-NITAḪ-KA) at a moment's notice. Thus, among numerous bits of advice for being a good man in ancient Sumer, the *Instructions of Šuruppag* (ll. 68–72) do offer a tip of the stylus to martial endeavors:

> Having reached the field of manhood (KI NAM-NITAḪ-KA), you should not jump (?) with your hand. The warrior is unique, he alone is the equal of many; Utu is unique, he alone is the equal of many. With your life you should always be on the side of the warrior; with your life you should always be on the side of Utu.[58]

Of course, not everyone might be so thrilled to pitch in when *officium vocat*. The (admittedly somewhat humorous) 20th-Dynasty Egyptian Papyrus Lansing,

Masculinity 139

in which we see the benefits of being a scribe laid out in contrast to other, lesser professions, has this to say about being a soldier:

> Come, let me tell you the woes of the soldier, and how many are his superiors: the general, the troop-commander, the officer who leads, the standard-bearer, the lieutenant, the scribe, the commander of fifty, and the garrison-captain.... He is called up to Syria. He may not rest. There are no clothes, no sandals. The weapons of war are assembled at the fortress of Sile. His march is uphill through mountains. He drinks water every third day; it is smelly and tastes of salt. His body is ravaged by illness. The enemy comes, surrounds him with missiles, and life recedes from him. He is told: "Quick, forward, valiant soldier! Win for yourself a good name!" He does not know what he is about. His body is weak, his legs fail him. When victory is won, the captives are handed over to his majesty to be taken to Egypt.... He dies on the edge of the desert, and there is none to perpetuate his name. He suffers in death as in life.[59]

Even so, in much of the ancient world, being a soldier/warrior was a mark of status for many males, and it is what ultimately distinguished them from boys one the one side and women on the other. A fine archaeological display of such martial masculinity, especially in its contrast with maternal femininity, appears in a Cypro-Archaic I (c. 650 BCE) tomb from the village of Mari on the southern coast of Cyprus, discovered in 1991 (See Figure 3.7). As discussed by the excavator Maria Hadjicosti:

> Mari Tomb 1 is a rare example of a case in which the ages and sexes of the occupants have clearly been established.... Results of the analysis provide

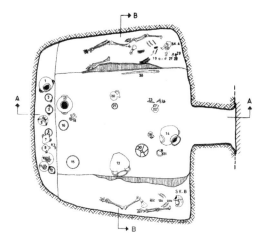

Figure 3.7 Plan of Burial at Mari, Cyprus.
Source: From Hadjicosti 2002: 136.

140 *Masculinity*

information that the occupants of the tomb consist of "a robust male (Individual A) of at least 26 years of age with osteoarthritis, a gracile adult female (Individual B) of short stature (approximately 155.7 cm. in height), and a 4–5 year old child (Individual C)." The child was identified among the remains of the female skeleton upon the examination of the bones, while the position of the two adult individuals was clearly defined during the excavation.[60]

The rock-cut chamber tomb had three benches along its walls. The male remains were laid out upon the northern bench, the female and toddler bones upon the southern bench, while grave goods, mostly pottery vessels, were upon the shorter western bench opposite the tomb entrance and dromos. As Hadjicosti remarked, the quality of the grave goods did not give the impression of a royal or even exceptionally wealthy tomb, comparatively speaking.[61] Concerning these offerings, the larger ceramic vessels, especially those pertaining to food storage, were closer to the female, while all metal artifacts were closer to, or even upon the bench with, the male. These metal objects consisted of: a well-intact iron long sword, a bronze bowl, an iron knife, and a fragmentary bronze fibula. Such metal artifacts had come to light in different combinations in affluent burials throughout Cyprus, all leading to their interpretation as indicating a warrior identity. Thus, a long sword came to light together with chariot accessories and horse's gear in Salamis, with a helmet and scepter in Tamassos, and with a bronze bowl in Nicosia. Bronze fibulae were found together with horse's gear and a dagger at Kouklia-*Alonia*, an iron knife and bronze bowl in Idalion, and an iron knife at Aghios Athanasios.[62] With all four items in combination in Mari Tomb 1, it is evident that the buriers of the couple strove to highlight the male's martial identity.

This male, decked out in accoutrements of battle and status, might be contrasted with his female companion, who was associated with items pertaining to domesticity and motherhood. Again to quote the excavator:

The deposition of the child near her right side accentuates of the woman's role as mother, suggesting that motherhood in the Cypro-Archaic I period constitutes the primary role of women in the family and in society at large. In addition, the placement of the large amphorae representing food containers and the vessels containing pebbles, perhaps a substitute for food, close to her side of the chamber, accentuates her dominant role in the household.[63]

Not a royal or necessarily elite burial but still manifesting a gendered divide: The male is the soldier/warrior, the female is the mother and housewife.

In the end, it might be reasonable to think of masculine violence as the counterpoint to feminine eroticism. It is not necessarily that males are violent so much as violence is sexed masculine, that males are expected to have the potential for violence that may be called upon in specific circumstances (although hopefully not as often as females are called upon to be erotic!). But as we saw in the previous chapter in the section "Adultery," feminine eroticism has its limits that are

Masculinity   141

more or less (depending on context, but especially in marriage) strictly enforced. So is masculine violence.

But Is It a Penis?

In her essay on the homoerotic gaze in Neo-Assyrian monumental iconography, "Men Looking at Men: The Homoerotics of Power in the State Arts of Assyria," Julia Assante wrote:

> Of all the weapons in the arsenals of antiquity the bow and arrow, when employed, graphically imitate the penile passage from a state of highly focused tension to one of release, penetration and, in the social terms of ancient Mesopotamia, conquest.[64]

When I asked my husband what he thought about the arrow as phallic signifier, he was quite definitive in his response: Men do not want any phallic signifier that is detachable—heck no! This is perhaps indicative of a long-standing debate on the symbolic significance of weapons in general, and the bow and arrows combination specifically: Are they understood to be phallic in ANE iconography and psychology?

There can be no doubt that, *in general*, in the context of the ANE, bows and arrows were understood to be symbols of masculinity. This comes across perhaps the most strongly in texts from Anatolia, where the über-masculine bow is contrasted with the consummately feminine spindle (and occasionally mirror). In a Hittite prayer to Ištar of Nineveh, the practitioner pleads:

> Take from (their) men masculinity, prowess, robust health, swords(?), battle axes, bows, arrows, and dagger! And bring them to Hatti! Place in their hands the spindle and mirror of a woman! Dress them as women![65]

Likewise, in the loyalty oath sworn by Hittite soldiers, we read the curse on those who fail, "Let them break the bows, arrows, weapons in their hands and let them put in their hands distaff and mirror!"[66]

Perhaps the most emphatic extant reference to the masculine nature of the bow and arrow in Hittite ideology is present in a Hittite incantation against impotence known as *Paskuwatti's ritual to the goddess Uliliyassi* (see also Chapter 5). The ultimate purpose of this ritual is to take away a man's femininity and replace it with masculinity. In this ritual, the female functionary Paskuwatti uses sympathetic magic to "cure" the man of "effeminacy" (l. 4):

> I place a spindle and distaff in the patient's [hand], and he comes under the gates. When he steps forward through the gates, I take the spindle and distaff away from him. I give him a bow (and) [arro]w(s), and say (to him) all the while: "I have just taken femininity away from you and given you masculinity in return."[67]

142   *Masculinity*

In other ANE contexts, especially the Biblical, the bow and arrow have more of a military association than anything specifically masculine *per se*, although as men were the exclusive warriors (Jael notwithstanding) this military reference placed the objects within masculine symbolism. In 2 Samuel 1:22, we read of Jonathan's bow as a parallel to Saul's sword. In Hosea 1:5, the LORD claims that he will "break the bow of Israel in the valley of Jezreel," thus depriving Israel of military victory. In 2 Kings 13:15–19, the drawing of the bow and the striking of arrows represent King Joash's victories over Aram.

A rather interesting quasi-counter-example comes from Ugarit, where it is the gender-bending goddess Anat who uses a bow in battle. Thus in the *Baal Cycle*, Anat first appears (CAT 1.3, Column II, 13–16):

> Knee-deep she gleans in warrior blood
> Neck-deep in the gore of soldiers
> With a club she drives away captives,
> With her bow (string) the foe.[68]

In the Mesopotamian *Tale of Anzu*, Ninurta's arrows are the most significant weapon discussed in the fight against the Anzu bird. And in the *Enuma Eliš*, it is the arrow from Marduk's bow that finally defeats Tiamat (Tablet IV):

> Face to face they came, Tiamat and Marduk, sage of the gods.
> They engaged in combat, they closed for battle.
> . . .
> And he forced in the *imhullu*-wind so that she could not close her lips,
> Fierce winds distended her belly
> . . .
> He shot an arrow which pierced her belly,
> Split her down the middle and slit her heart,
> Vanquished her and extinguished her life.[69]

As Jerrold Cooper discusses Marduk's ultimate success against the divine matriarch (when all his older predecessors had failed):

> Although he too was armed with spells, he also had, unlike his predecessors, a battle chariot and real weapons, especially his bow. And it is with these weapons, not with spells, that he slew Tiamat. Real men, men who are more than a match for the woman Tiamat, the text seems to tell us, use real weapons in battle, and the field, as we know from Sumerian texts, was the ki nam-nita, the "locus of masculinity."[70]

So there is most assuredly a symbolic connection between bows and arrows and warfare, and a connection between warfare and masculinity. But is it a penis? One must recall that goddesses were also capable of using bows and arrows. While Anat's use of the bow certainly seems to underline her

Masculinity 143

masculine gender, there is far less to suggest that Egyptian Neith was seen as a gender bender herself. Even so, from as early as the late 4th millennium, the goddess was symbolized by a pair of crossed arrows, apparently accompanying the depiction of a beetle. Come the 1st Dynasty, her cult symbol was a tied pair of bows, and she was later known as the Mistress of the Bow and Ruler of Arrows.[71] There would appear to be a clear connection with combat but not masculinity.

The notion that anything that is longer than it is wide and that gets inserted somewhere is a penis is utterly Freudian. And while Freud was correct in many of his theories, he was not infallible.[72] While there are very clear symbolic links between the bow and arrow and militarism and masculinity coming from the ANE repertoire, there is no need to apply potentially anachronistic notions of direct phallic imagery.

Even so, some more explicit texts from Hittite Anatolia do seem to suggest a reverse symbolism: It is not that the bow/arrow is a penis, but rather the "penis" simultaneously serves as a symbol of militarism and fertility. In the *Propitiation Ritual for the King's Sister Ziplandawiya* (CTH 443.A §8"), King Tudhaliya I (or II) the king is blessed:

> We brought the statues to exactly their place. They lined them up on another rock. The container of dough where the honey was poured, she sets it on the rock. She breaks up 3 thick breads. She libates wine. She speak as follows, "As this rock is everlasting, may the lord, his wife, and his children likewise be everlasting. Let his weapon be pointing forth (TUKUL-*šu parā neanza*)." They offer a *tūruppa*-bread with wine.[73]

Likewise, the *Daily Prayer to Telipinu* has as a blessing:

> Keep giving to them male children, female children, grandchildren, and great-grandchildren. Keep giving them assent and obedience. Keep giving them flourishing of grain, grapes, cattle, sheep, and people. Keep giving them the powerful divine weapon of a man pointed straight ahead (LÚ-*aš tarḫūilin parā neyantan* ᵈ·ᵍⁱˢTUKUL-*in*).[74]

The weapon (TUKUL), clearly both divine and wooden in the second example, is directly linked with the male subject in both texts and appears alongside references to fertility and abundance. Rather than warfare, that weapon sticking out straight ahead is associated with progeny (children and grandchildren), the flourishing of animals and plant life, and longevity. As Mary Backvarova put it, "The reference to the king's 'weapon pointing forth' has an obvious double meaning, as weapon and vigorous phallus producing progeny."[75]

So, the bow and arrow need not be a penis, but in some cases the penis is a "weapon" that produces life instead of death. Perhaps this makes it easier to understand how fertility in the ancient world was understood to be a masculine concept.

144 *Masculinity*

Fertility

> Today let my penis be praised!
>
> (*Enki and Ninmah*, l. 134)

It is convenient to study the phenomenon of male fertility in three separate if overlapping categories. The first is cosmogony, whereby reality itself or aspects of the natural world are brought into existence by the (phallic) actions of a god. As we shall see, in this aspect, males might function completely alone, with no need for female contribution or assistance. The second is the phenomenon of male pregnancy, where male deities are so fertile as to take on the female role of incubator. The third is reproductive fertility, whereby either divine or human generations are bought forth, including the creation of humanity itself. This last category was already discussed briefly in Chapter 1; here we consider the first two.

Cosmogony

Male sexuality is the dominant force for fertility in ANE mythologies—it is associated with baseline creation, either of reality itself or of the natural phenomena that make up the world. Typically, this creativity is expressed in phallic and fluid-based imagery, whereby male orgasm brings forth a fluid that either engenders reality *in toto* or fertilizes a pre-existing world. The primary example of creation emerging from ejaculation comes from the Heliopolitan cosmogony of ancient Egypt. The Old Kingdom (c. 2700–2200 BCE) Pyramid Texts relate how the primordial god Atum emerged upon the *benben* stone from the watery chaos called *Nun*. In a moment of either loneliness or arousal, he masturbated and ejaculated the deities Shu (air) and Tefnut (moisture):

> Atum evolved growing ithyphallic, in Heliopolis. He put his penis in his grasp that he might make orgasm with it, and the two siblings were born—Shu and Tefnut.[76]

This narrative is repeated in the New Kingdom (c. 1550–1100 BCE) Papyrus Bremner-Rhind, where an additional detail notes that rather than emerging from Atum's penis, the twins were born from his mouth,[77] possibly suggesting a kind of auto-fellatio on the part of Atum. This aspect is presented in the Middle Kingdom Coffin Texts, where the god Shu claims:

> I am this soul of Shu which is in the flame of the fiery blast which Atum kindled with his own hand. He created orgasm and fluid fell from his mouth. He spat me out as Shu together with Tefnut, who came forth after me.[78]

Upon their "birth," the male and female Shu and Tefnut begin the process of sexual reproduction, engendering the deities Nut (sky) and Geb (earth). These grandchildren of Atum themselves engage in sexual reproduction so extensively that their father Shu must eventually separate their bodies so that their children might be born.

In a perhaps somewhat comical portrayal of the motif of the female who arouses male sexual desire and thus fertility (see Chapter 2), in the Papyrus Jumilhac version of *The Contendings of Horus and Seth*, we read:

> When Seth saw Isis in this place, he transformed himself into a bull in order to run after her; but she disguised herself by assuming the appearance of a dog with a knife at the end of its tail. Next she began to run before him, and Seth was not able to overtake her. Then he scattered his seed on the ground and the goddess said, "It is an abomination to have scattered (your seed), O Bull." His seed sprouted on the Gebel into plants.[79]

Phallic fertility is also emphasized in the Egyptian iconography. Several male deities are presented as ithyphallic as a manifestation of their role in creation, self-regeneration, and/or resurrection.[80] Thus one might consider a portrayal of the previously mentioned familial unit of Shu, Nut, and Geb (Figure 2.11). Here Geb holds his erect phallus in a manner reminiscent of Atum while gazing above at his sexual partner Nut. Another common image is that of the ithyphallic god Min, whose cult originated in Coptos during the Early Dynastic period. Originally portrayed alone and, once again, masturbatory (Figure 3.8), he also appeared in New Kingdom iconography gazing upon the foreign goddess Qedešet (image 2.12, to the left). Qedešet bears a strong resemblance to Egyptian potency/fertility

Figure 3.8 Statue of the God Min, Ashmolean Museum AN 1894.105e.

Source: Drawing by Paul C. Butler. Used with kind permission.

146   *Masculinity*

figurines, small terracotta items used to enhance physical or magical potency in Middle and New Kingdom Egypt.[81] The pairing of Min with Qedešet may thus be related to her ability to spark and/or intensify the god's erection.

Two other deities often depicted with an erect phallus were Amun and Osiris. Amun appears to have acquired his ithyphallic tendencies through syncretism with both Min and Atum. Osiris is specifically shown with erect phallus when in the *duat*, the underworld, where his ithyphallic rendering is representative of his resurrection. The erect penis is not only a sign of life but of new life.[82]

In Mesopotamia, the masculine nature of fertility is expressed in the exploits of some exceptionally creative deities, most notably the god of fresh water, Enki. Enki was remarkable for his phallic fertility, giving rise to rivers and with them vegetal, animal, and human/divine abundance. This is most explicitly presented in the Sumerian hymn *Enki and the World Order*. In lines 250–265, we read:

> After he had turned his gaze from there, after father Enki had lifted his eyes across the Euphrates, he stood up full of lust like a rampant bull, lifted his penis, ejaculated and filled the Euphrates with flowing water. . . . The Tigris . . . at his side like a rampant bull. By lifting his penis, he brought a bridal gift. The Tigris rejoiced in its heart like a great wild bull, when it was born. . . . It brought water, flowing water indeed: its wine will be sweet. It brought barley, mottled barley indeed: the people will eat it. It filled the E-kur, the house of Enlil, with all sorts of things.[83]

Additional passages in the hymn refer to Enki's control over fertility, although with less phallic language. Lines 18–30 note Enki's control over vegetal fertility, lines 32–37 note that Enki makes young men and women sexually appealing and amorous, lines 52–60 and 326–334 establish the god's ability to spark fertility in herd animals and the produce of the fields, and lines 193–205 even attribute to the god the birth of mortal kings. This association between masculinity and earthly bounty also appears in the high god Enlil. At the end of the Sumerian tale *Enlil and Ninlil*, the poet calls Enlil, "Lord who makes flax grow, lord who makes barley grow, you are lord of heaven, lord plenty, lord of the earth!"[84]

The cosmogony presented in the book of Genesis is distinct insofar as the deity conceptualized by the biblical redactors was transcendent and thus, although decidedly male, could not be discussed as having a penis or creating the world in any embodied fashion. Nevertheless, elements of both creation accounts (Genesis 1 and 2) reflect aspects of the Egyptian and Mesopotamian narratives. In addition to the male-as-creator paradigm, Genesis 1 portrays a primordial state of watery chaos—the *tohu-wa-bohu*—that is equivalent to the Egyptian *Nun*. Just as Atum emerged from this *Nun* upon the *benben* stone, so too did Elôhîm command (Genesis 1:6), "Let there be a dome in the midst of the waters, and let it separate the waters from the waters."[85] In properly disembodied fashion, Elôhîm then calls reality into being through the force of his word rather than through the force of his phallus. The account of Genesis 2:

Masculinity 147

4–76 more closely reflects the kind of creation and male fertility we see in the Mesopotamian accounts:

> In that day the LORD God made the earth and the heavens, when no plant of the field was yet in the earth and no herb of the field had yet sprung up—for the LORD God had not caused it to rain upon the earth, and there was no one to till the ground; but a stream would rise from the earth, and water the whole face of the ground.

In this account, earth already exists but is understood to be lifeless. The process of making a living, useful earth is tied to the presence of a stream rising, comparable to the life-giving waters ejaculated by Enki, and the eventual downfall of fertilizing rains, comparable to those of Adad in *Atrahasis* (see subsequently). Creation is still predicated upon a male's fluids.

Not all of the ANE corpora preserve creation accounts; they are notably absent from the extant Anatolian and Ugaritic/Canaanite texts. Nevertheless, even these mythic cycles present evidence of the male-as-fertilizer paradigm, notably in tales of what happens when a fertility deity is absent. When the Hittite Rain/Storm god Telipinu disappeared:

> Telipinu too went away and removed grain, animal fecundity, luxuriance, growth, and abundance to the steppe, to the meadow. . . . Therefore barley and wheat no longer ripen. Cattle, sheep, and humans no longer become pregnant. And those (already pregnant) cannot give birth. The mountains and trees dried up, so that the shoots do not come (forth). The pastures and springs dried up, so that famine broke out in the land. Humans and gods are dying of hunger.[86]

A similar situation emerges when Baal, the Ugaritic rain/storm god, was vanquished by Môt ("Death") in the Ugaritic *Baal Cycle*. While the god is dead, El dreams how: "Parched are the furrows of the fields," but when he returns, "The heavens rain oil, the wadis run with honey."[87] Perhaps the most famous ANE account of a god's absence leading to famine appears in the 2nd-millennium Akkadian tale of *Atrahasis* (the Mesopotamian Noah). When the gods wish to destroy humankind, they attempt to starve them to death by withholding the powers of the rain god Adad, once again linking notions of fluid fertility and earthly abundance with a male deity.

Finally, even kings can be mediators of earthly fertility in the ANE corpora, especially as regards the loss of fertility when the rightful king is slain. In the Ugaritic *Epic of Aqhat*, soon after the hero Aqhat dies (CAT 19 column 1, ll. 38–46):

> Now Danel, man of Rapiu
> Adjures the clouds in the awful heat,
> "Let the clouds make rain in the summer,
> The dew lay dew on the grapes."
> Seven years Baal is absent,

148 *Masculinity*

Eight, the Rider of Clouds.
No dew, no downpour,
No swirling of the deeps,
No welcome voice of Baal.[88]

With the death of Prince Aqhat, the land experienced a drought, cast in terms of the absence of the rain god Baal.

Even the Hebrew Bible presents accounts of the loss of fertility when the rightful king dies. In 2 Samuel 1:21, when King Saul of Israel has been slain along with his heir Jonathan, David sings the lament:

You mountains of Gilboa,
Let there be no dew or rain upon you,
Nor bounteous fields!
For there the shield of the mighty was defiled
The shield of Saul, anointed with oil no more.

Male Pregnancy

Perhaps the ultimate representation of male fertility comes from those narratives where male deities get pregnant, as occurs in myths from Egypt, Mesopotamia, and Anatolia. The New Kingdom Egyptian tale *The Contendings of Horus and Seth* relates how Seth's attempts to rape Horus were reversed by Isis, leading to Seth's impregnation:

At evening time, bed was prepared for them, and they both lay down. But during the night Seth caused his phallus to become stiff and inserted it between Horus's thighs. Then Horus placed his hands between his thighs and received Seth's semen. Horus went to tell his mother Isis: "Help me, Isis, my mother, come and see what Seth has done to me." And he opened his hand and let her see Seth's semen. She let out a loud shriek, seized her copper knife, and cut off his hands. . . . Then she fetched some fragrant ointment and applied it to Horus's phallus. She caused it to become stiff and inserted it into a pot, and he caused his semen to flow down into it.

Isis at morning time went carrying the semen of Horus to the garden of Seth and said to Seth's gardener: "What sort of vegetable is it that Seth eats here in your company?" So, the gardener told her: "He doesn't eat any vegetable here in my company except lettuce." And Isis added the semen of Horus onto it. Seth returned according to his daily habit and ate the lettuce, which he regularly ate. Thereupon he became pregnant with the semen of Horus.[89]

Seth becomes aware of his pregnancy in court, where he was attempting to wrest kingship from Horus in part based on his perceived "domination" of the younger god. Upon the discovery of Horus's semen in his uncle, the judge Re caused the semen to emerge from Seth's head in the form of a solar disk, which Re then took for himself.

In the Sumerian tale *Enki and Ninhursag*, Enki eats a large quantity of his own semen that the mother goddess Ninhursag had placed in a variety of plants. Enki gets sick from this, as he becomes impregnated with plant deities which he cannot remove from his body. The deities call for Ninhursag, who functions as a surrogate birth canal for Enki:

> Ninhursaĝa laid Enki in her vulva,
> [placed cool hands . . .]
> "My brother, what part of you hurts you?"
> "My brainpan hurts me!"
> She gave birth to Abu out of it.
> "My brother, what part of you hurts you?"
> "The top of my hair hurts me!"
> She gave birth to Ninsikila out of it.[90]

In the Anatolian *Song of Kumarbi*, the god Kumarbi becomes pregnant after biting off the genitals of the sky-god Anu, whom he is attempting to overthrow.

> Kumarbi bit Anu's loins, and his "manhood" united with Kumarbi's insides like bronze. When Kumarbi had swallowed the "manhood" of Anu, he rejoiced and laughed out loud. Anu turned around and spoke to Kumarbi: "Are you rejoicing within yourself because you have swallowed my manhood?
> "Stop rejoicing within yourself! I have placed inside you a burden. First, I have impregnated you with the noble Storm God. Second, I have impregnated you with the irresistible Aranzah River. Third, I have impregnated you with the noble Tasmisu. And two additional terrible gods I have placed inside you as burdens. In the future you will end up striking the boulders of Mount Tassa with your head!"[91]

There is no evidence that the fertilizing activities performed by the gods in the process of creation were problematic for them. Quite to the contrary, Atum and Enki seem to have enjoyed themselves immensely. This changes when fertility goes from cosmogonic to reproductive, and the gods discover that they literally do not have the equipment necessary to give birth. This is somewhat less problematic for Egyptian Seth, whose discomfort comes more from the fact that he was at least symbolically raped by Horus. For Enki and Kumarbi, though, they discover that once pregnant, they are incapable of removing their offspring from their bodies. Kumarbi must give birth upon the ultra-feminine *harnau* birthing-stool,[92] while Enki must enlist the help of the mother goddess Ninhursag to remove his multiple offspring from his body.

El/YHWH is presented as less anthropomorphized in the Hebrew Bible than his counterparts to the north, east, and south. While he himself does not become pregnant, he is credited with *forming* the fetus in the mother's womb. We see this in

150   *Masculinity*

Jeremiah 1:5, where God claims, "Before I formed you in the womb I knew you." Likewise in Psalm 139, the psalmist sings:

> For you created my inmost being;
> you knit me together in my mother's womb.

So, again, the deity of the Hebrew Bible is less anatomically involved in the process of fertility/reproduction (no penis, no pregnancy) but shown as active in the formation of the child in the womb—just not his own.

In the end, it is clear that that people of the ANE understood that this concept of male pregnancy was exclusively in the domain of the divine/literary. For normal men, the obvious understanding, as presented by the prophet Jeremiah (30:6), was:

> Ask now and see: Can a man bear a child? Then why do I see every man with his hands on his loins like a woman in labor? Why has every face turned pale?

Professionalism

Atrahasis (Tablet 1)

> When the gods instead of man
> Did the work, bore the loads,
> The gods' work was too great,
> The work too hard, the trouble too much . . .
> The Anunnaki of the sky
> Made the Igigi bear the workload.
> The gods had to dig out canals,
> Had to clear channels, the lifelines of the land . . .
> For 3,600 years they bore the excess,
> Hard work, night and day.
> They groaned and blamed each other,
> Grumbled over the masses of excavated soil:
> "Let us confront . . . the chamberlain,
> And get him to relieve us of our hard work!
> Come, let us carry Enlil,
> The counsellor of the gods, the warrior, from his dwelling!"[93]

It is the dawn of time, humans have not even be created yet, and the gods already have jobs. For the Igigi, it is canal-digging and brute-force labor; for the Anunnaki: management. Enlil is a warrior and counsellor, assisted by his vizier Nusku.

Genesis 4: 1–2

Now the man knew his wife Eve, and she conceived and bore Cain, saying "I have produced a man with the help of the LORD." Next she bore his brother Abel. Now Abel was a keeper of sheep, and Cain a tiller of the ground.

Masculinity 151

Two generations into the existence of humanity and we already have farmers and shepherds. Cain went on to found a city named for his son Enoch, suggesting a bit of city planning and architecture at a time when we would at best be expecting hunters and gatherers.

Men have jobs. Or perhaps just as accurately, professionalism is an aspect of masculinity. Jobs exist almost as soon as there are anthropomorphic beings, and it is typically the males in the various societies of the ANE—mortal and divine—who are recorded in our documents as having professions. And, as noted in Chapter 2, the "professional" quality of occupations stands out for men even when they take part in industries that in a more domestic context would typically accrue to women.

Thus in the Middle Kingdom *Satire on the Trades*, when a father explains to his son why he should be a scribe, he observes of the weaver:

> The weaver inside the weaving house is more wretched than a woman. His knees are drawn up against his belly. He cannot breathe the air. If he wastes a single day without weaving, he is beaten with 50 whip lashes. He has to give food to the doorkeeper to allow him to come out to the daylight.[94]

Textile-work may be feminine, but having a job is masculine.

The rest of this didactic, possibly humorous, narrative bears this out. The father—Dua-Khety—is rather thorough in his descriptions to his son Pepy. In convincing the boy to become a good scribe, he relates the woes of, in order: the carpenter, the jeweler, the barber, the reed-cutter, the potter, the bricklayer, the vintner/farmer, the field hand, the weaver, the fletcher, the messenger, the furnace-tender, the cobbler, the launderer, the fowler, and the fisherman. Presumably the family is not upper-class enough for jobs in upper management. Even so, every profession presented is understood in terms of a male subject: neither the weaver nor even the launderer is ever understood to be female, a fact consistent with the non-fictional documents from the Middle Kingdom.[95] The same is true for a 19th-Dynasty school texts in the Lansing Papyrus. Here the author ridicules the washerman, the potter, the cobbler, the temple custodian, the merchant (and concomitant tax-collector), sailor, carpenter, field hand, and scribe. Only that last one is a desirable profession. Every single one of them is male.

Less literary are the lists of employees at Deir el-Medina who worked on the royal tombs of the Valley of the Kings in New Kingdom Egypt. This was a village where artisans lived with their families, thus a population of men, women, and children. Nevertheless, all the jobs, at least those officially listed, belonged to men. Thus on the verso of an ostracon dating to the second year of King Merenptah (?), we read of:

> Those who will be brought to the settlement of the Necropolis as craftsmen:
> 2 draughtsmen
> 2 chisel-bearers
> 2 plasterers
> 2 craftsmen of the *kha*-tool
> 2 coppersmiths to make the tools of the gang of Pharaoh

152 *Masculinity*

> 2 sandal-makers
> 10 supply staff
>
> . . .
>
> 1 bearer
> 2 officers
> 2 guardians
> 2 war-Hor (???)

And this Great Place of Pharaoh will be furnished with them.[96]

The preponderance of "male" professions appears in the scribal lists of Mesopotamia. Because of the ungendered nature of the Sumerian language, it is not entirely possible to determine the gender of professional titles in the earlier lists. However, once bilingual texts became the norm, it becomes possible to determine the gender of professional titles in the Akkadian equivalents. Furthermore, by this point, it becomes more common to add the SAL determinative to the LU$_2$ sign to indicate female sex, even in the Sumerian (see Chapter 1). Thus we might consider the Old Babylonian list LU$_2$-AZLAG$_2$ A. In this list of over 500 terms pertaining to humans, mostly professional titles, only five are marked with the SAL determinative, each one following the (unmarked thus) masculine equivalent (ll. 21–30):[97]

LU$_2$ ^{kaš}KURUN$_2$-NA	*sa$_3$-bu-u$_2$*	beer brewer
SAL LU$_2$ ^{kaš}KURUN$_2$-NA	*sa$_3$-bi-i-tum*	female beer brewer
LU$_2$ GUB-BA	*mu-uḫ$_2$-ḫu-um*	frenetic
SAL LU$_2$ GUB-BA	*mu-ḫu-⌈tum⌉*	female frenetic
LU$_2$ TILLA$_2$	*wa-ṣu$_2$-⌈u$_2$⌉*	one gone out
⌈SAL⌉ LU$_2$ TILLA$_2$	*wa-ṣi-i-⌈tum⌉*	female one gone out
LU$_2$-ĜEŠ-GI-SAĜ-KEŠ$_2$	*na-aq-⌈mu⌉*	cultic performer
SAL LU$_2$-ĜEŠ-GI-SAĜ-KEŠ$_2$	*na-qi$_4$-im-⌈tum*	female cultic performer
LU$_2$-NI$_2$-SU-UB-BA	*za-ab-bu-u$_2$*	ecstatic
⌈SAL⌉ LU$_2$-NI$_2$-SU-UB-BA	*za-ba-a-tum*	female ecstatic

As discussed in the previous chapter, beer-brewer was one of the few occupations traditionally held by women, possibly because food-production was already seen as feminine (although see previously: textiles). Otherwise, trades open to males *and* females are rather limited: various categories of cultic workers (prophets, performers), and those who "go out." It may be worth noting here that traditionally in the modern scholarship the term *waṣītum*, but *not waṣû*, is taken as "tramp, slut, whore."[98]

Having a profession is a masculine attribute. It is consistent over time and is seen to go back to the dawn of time. Men consistently function in the same domains, from high governmental, bureaucratic posts through middle management to craftsman to laborer. They always form the vast majority of professionals in the documents, and they are far more likely to be considered professionals in the documents, even when doing "women's" work. Males are thought of as having professions, and, as with anything pertaining to gender, it's how people think of it that matters.

Self-Control

> A talker is a mischief-maker.
>
> (*The Teaching for Merikare*)

The genre of "wisdom literature" in the ANE mainly consists of fathers (fictional or otherwise) giving advice to their sons (ditto) about how to be "good" men. These texts come from the upper echelons of society, having been written by kings, upper-level bureaucrats, and scribes—all male. It is perhaps not surprising, then, that much of this good advice is similar in most respects, be it from Mesopotamia, Egypt, Ugarit, or Judah. In what follows, I have focused on those texts that do *not* pertain to royalty, as what is good for a king rarely translates to the rest of society.[99]

From Mesopotamia, the *Instructions of Šuruppag* are the advice of Šuruppag, son of Ubara-Tutu, to his own son Ziudsuru. Ziudsuru, known in Akkadian texts as Ut-Napištim, is the Sumerian Noah, the survivor of the Great Flood, and thus lays claim to considerable antiquity. So, too, does the text: The *Instructions of Šuruppag* in their Sumerian form date back at least to Early Dynastic (3rd millennium) Abu Ṣalabikh, and the text became part of the scribal curriculum in Old Babylonian Nippur.[100] An Akkadian translation goes back at least to the Middle Assyrian period.[101] The Akkadian-language *Counsels of Wisdom*, by contrast, are a bit latter: Lambert dates them to the Kassite era (1600–1200 BCE), possibly being as old as the preceding Old Babylonian Period.[102]

The *Instruction of Šimâ Milkī*[103] comes from a tablet found in Ugarit, although written in Akkadian rather than Ugaritic. The text, especially with its reference to Enlil-Banda, is clearly intended to be associated with Mesopotamia and its wisdom tradition. Nevertheless, there is no evidence for the name *Šimâ Milkī* yet known from Mesopotamia, and the only other comparable text—a distant copy (?)—was found in Hattuša in Anatolia.[104]

From Egypt, the *Maxims of Ptahhotep* date to the early Middle Kingdom, with at least one later edition written in the New Kingdom.[105] The *Teaching for the Vizier Kagemni*, what is extant of it, comes from the same papyrus as the earlier version of *Ptahhotep* and thus also dates to the Middle Kingdom.[106] Later in date is the *Instruction of Any*, which appears to date to the 18th Dynasty, with the only known fully surviving manuscript being pBoulaq 4 in the Cairo Museum, dating to the 21st or 22nd Dynasties. Unlike the earlier instructions, it is middle class in its approach, meant for the average man rather than nobility.[107] Dating to the Ramesside Period (19th Dynasty) is the *Instruction of Amenemope*, again with extant manuscripts deriving from later eras.[108] This text also shows a slight divergence

154 *Masculinity*

from the earlier wisdom texts directed at high-end bureaucrats. As observed by Miriam Lichtheim:

> The shift of emphasis, away from action and success, and toward contemplation and endurance, leads to an overall regrouping of values and a redefinition of the ideal man. As early as *Ptahhotep*, the ideal man lacks all martial values; he was a man of peace who strove for advancement and was generous with his wealth. The new ideal man is content with a humble position and a minimal amount of material possessions. His chief characteristic is modesty. He is self-controlled, quiet, and kind towards people.[109]

The *Instruction of Amenemope* is credited with being an influence on the Biblical *Book of Proverbs*, especially books 22 and 23. It is likely, then, that these verses of advice from the Hebrew Bible have origins as early as the late Late Bronze Age. Nevertheless, their insistence that "the fear of the LORD is the beginning of wisdom" shows a focus on divinity that is not as tangible in the Egyptian materials, and with a monotheism not present elsewhere in the ANE. As is typical of this genre, *Proverbs* is primarily presented as the advice of a father to a son, mostly the wisdom of King Solomon to an unnamed son. However, later passages are attributed to Agur, son of Jakeh of Massa, and the *mother* of King Lemuel of Massa. This is the only female voice in the ancient wisdom literature.

Dominant themes that emerge in the literary genre are: Don't be arrogant; be generous, not greedy; and most of all: Be quiet.[110] Every so often a father might advise his son not to get into a fight, strongly suggesting that the masculine association with violence was ideally tempered in real life.[111] What follows is a concatenation of pan-ANE recommendations passed from "father" to "son" in the construction of a self-conscious, commonly held form of ideal masculinity.

Don't Be Arrogant

Do not be arrogant because of your knowledge, but confer with the ignorant man as with the learned. . . . Good speech is more hidden than malachite, yet it is found in the possession of female slaves at the millstones.

(Maxims of Ptahhotep 1)[112]

If you are lowly and serve a wealthy man, let all your conduct be good before god. When his former poverty is known to you, do not be arrogant against him because of what you know about his former state.

(Maxims of Ptahhotep 10)[113]

Yet do not be proud by virtue of your strength among your contemporaries. Take care not to be opprobrious.

(Teaching for the Vizier Kagemni 2.3)[114]

Masculinity 155

The garrulous man fills (?) his bread bag; the haughty one brings an empty
bag and can fill his empty mouth only with boasting.

(Instructions of Šuruppag, 106–108)[115]

[. . .] the lowly, take pity on him.
Do not despise the miserable and [. . .]
Do not wrinkle up your nose haughtily at them.
One's god will be angry with him for that,
It is displeasing to Šamaš, he will requite him with evil.

(Counsels of Wisdom, 56)[116]

When arrogance comes, then comes disgrace; but with humility comes wisdom.

(Proverbs 11:2)

Arrogance yields nothing but strife!

(Proverbs 13: 10)

Be Generous, Not Greedy

Beware of an act of avarice; it is a bad and incurable disease. Intimacy is
made impossible by it; it alienates fathers and mothers and maternal brothers,
it drives wife and husband apart, it is a gatherer of all that is evil and a bag
of all that is hateful.

(Maxims of Ptahhotep 19)[117]

Do not be greedy for a cubit of land,
Nor encroach on the boundaries of a widow.

(Instruction of Amenemope, Chapter 6)[118]

Do not set your heart on wealth . . .
Do not strain to seek increase,
What you have, let it suffice you.
If riches come to you by theft,
They will not stay the night with you.

(Instruction of Amenemope, Chapter 7)[119]

Do not covet the treasures of the ruler.

(Instruction of Šimâ Milkī, 26)[120]

Do not eat bread while another stands by without extending your hand to him.

(Instruction of Any)[121]

Give food to eat, beer to drink,
Present what is asked for, provide for an honor.
One's god will be happy with him for that.

156   *Masculinity*

It is pleasing to Šamaš, he will requite him with favor.
Do good deeds and be helpful all the days of your life.

(*Counsels of Wisdom*, 61)[122]

Do not pounce on a widow when you find her in the fields
And then fail to be patient with her reply.
Do not refuse your oil jar to a stranger,
Double it before your brothers.
God prefers him who honors the poor
To him who worships the wealthy.

(*Instruction of Amenemope*, Chapter 28)[123]

A generous person will prosper; whoever refreshes others will be refreshed.
People curse the one who hoards grain, but they pray God's blessing on the
one who is willing to sell.

(*Proverbs* 11:25–26)

A generous man is blessed, for he gives of his bread to the poor.

(*Proverbs* 22: 9)

Don't Be Violent

You should not loiter about where there is a quarrel; you should not let the
quarrel make you a witness. You should not let (?) yourself . . . in a quarrel.
You should not cause a quarrel; . . . the gate of the palace. . . . Stand aside
from a quarrel, . . . you should not take (?) another road.

(*Instruction of Šuruppag*, 22–27)[124]

Do not speak rudely to a brawler; when you are attacked hold yourself back:
You will find this good when your relations are friendly.

(*Instruction of Any*)[125]

Do not enter into a crowd if you find it in an uproar and about to come to
blows. Don't pass anywhere nearby, keep away from their tumult, lest you
be brought before the court when an inquiry is made. Stay away from hostile
people, keep your heart quiet among fighters.

(*Instruction of Any*)[126]

Do not inspire terror in men, for God is also repelled. . . . Plan to live in peace,
and what men give will come of its own accord.

(*Maxims of Ptahhotep* 6, excerpted)[127]

Be Quiet

You should not speak improperly; later it will lay a trap for you.

(*Instructions of Šuruppag*, 42–43)[128]

If you find a disputant arguing, one having authority and superior to you, bend down your arms and bow your back . . . he will be dubbed an ignoramus when your self-control has matched his prolixity.

(Maxims of Ptahhotep 2)[129]

In a quarrel, do not speak: Your silence will serve you well.
(Instruction of Any)[130]

A man may be ruined by his tongue; beware and you will do well
(Instruction of Any)[131]

Great respect is given to the quiet man.
(Maxims of Ptahhotep 9)[132]

Hold your tongue, watch what you say.
A man's pride: the great value on your lips.
Insolence and insult should be abhorrent to you.
Speak nothing slanderous, no untrue report.
(Counsels of Wisdom, 26)[133]

Cling to the silent, then you find life,
Your being will prosper upon earth.
(Instruction of Amenemope, Chapter 5)[134]

The crocodile that makes no sound,
Dread of it is ancient.
Do not empty your belly to everyone,
And thus destroy respect of you;
Broadcast not your words to others,
Nor join with one who bares his heart.
Better is one whose speech is in his belly
Than he who tells it to cause harm.
(Instruction of Amenemope, Chapter 21)[135]

Hold your tongue as you pass thought the bustling street, say nothing derogatory of people. A friend has nothing to say of one not a friend.
(Instruction of Šimâ Milkī, 21–23)[136]

He who guards his tongue preserves his life; he who opens wide his lips, it is his ruin.

(Proverbs 13: 3)

And, of course:

158 *Masculinity*

Even a fool, if he keeps silent, is deemed wise; intelligent, if he seals his lips.

(*Proverbs* 17: 28)

And most importantly:

You should not pass judgment when you drink beer.

(*Instructions of Šuruppag*, 126)[137]

Don't indulge in beer lest you utter evil speech.

(*Instructions of Any*)[138]

The Good Man (Be Honest, Don't Consume Too Much, Be Contented, Be Generous, Be Kind)

The submissive man prospers, the moderate man is praised, the tent is open for the silent man, and the place of the contented man is wide.

(*Teaching for the Vizier Kagemni* 1.1)[139]

Suppress your desires, control your mouth; so will your counsel be heard among the magistrates. . . . Be patient when you speak, and you will say distinguished things; then will the magistrates who shall hear say, "How good is his utterance!"

(*Maxims of Ptahhotep* 44)[140]

As for him whose heart obeys his belly, he puts dislike of himself in the place of love; his heart is sad and his body unanointed. Joyous are the hearts of those whom god has given, but he who obeys his belly has an enemy.

(*Maxims of Ptahhotep* 14)[141]

If you sit with a crowd, abstain from the food you desire, for controlling your desire is only for a brief moment: Gluttony is despicable, and one points one's finger at it.

(*Teaching for the Vizier Kagemni* 1.5)[142]

Son, do not frequent public houses,
Excessive drinking, gluttony bloat the body.

(*Instruction of Šimâ Milkī*, 17–18)[143]

Beware of robbing a wretch,
Of attacking a cripple;
Don't stretch out your hand to touch an old man,
Nor mouth off to an elder.

(*Instruction of Amenemope*, Chapter 2)[144]

Do not laugh at a blind man,
Nor tease a dwarf,
Nor cause hardship for the lame.
Don't tease a man who is in the hand of the god,
Nor be angry with him for his failings.
(*Instruction of Amenemope*, Chapter 25)[145]

Do not cheat a man through pen on scroll,
The god abhors it;
Do not bear witness with false words,
So as to brush aside a man by your tongue.
Do not assess a man who has nothing,
And thus falsify your pen.
If you find a large debt against a poor man,
Make it into three parts;
Forgive two, let one stand,
You will find it a path of life.
(*Instruction of Amenemope*, Chapter 13)[146]

The Bad Man

Who insults can hurt only the skin; greedy eyes (?), however, can kill. The liar, shouting, tears up his garments. Insults bring (?) advice to the wicked. To speak arrogantly is like an abscess: An herb that makes the stomach sick.
(*Instructions of Šuruppag*, 134–142)[147]

There are six things the LORD hates,
seven that are detestable to him:
haughty eyes, a lying tongue,
hands that shed innocent blood,
a heart that devises wicked schemes,
feet that are quick to rush into evil,
a false witness who pours out lies
and a person who stirs up conflict in the community.
(*Proverbs* 6: 16–19)

Like a coating of silver dross on earthenware
are fervent lips with an evil heart.
Enemies disguise themselves with their lips,
but in their hearts they harbor deceit.
Though their speech is charming, do not believe them,
for seven abominations fill their hearts.

160 *Masculinity*

Their malice may be concealed by deception,
but their wickedness will be exposed in the assembly.

(Proverbs 26: 23–26)

There are those who curse their fathers
and do not bless their mothers;
those who are pure in their own eyes
and yet are not cleansed of their filth;
those whose eyes are ever so haughty,
whose glances are so disdainful;
those whose teeth are swords
and whose jaws are set with knives
to devour the poor from the earth
and the needy from among mankind.

(Proverbs 30:11–14)

Eunuchs

No study of gender in the ancient Near East would be complete without a section on eunuchs. The problem is that the evidence for eunuchs is ambiguous at best, and the greater probability is that there was no such creature in the ANE before the rise of the Achaemenids, outside the scope of this study.

Rather, the evidence for eunuchs in Mesopotamia (and extending out from there to Anatolia and Ugarit) depends on two somewhat related data. The first is the term LÚ. SAG/*ša rēši* (Sumerian/Akkadian)[148] in the Mesopotamian corpus. The second is the presence of beardless males in scenes of royalty in the Middle to Neo-Assyrian Empires.

These two data are related because in the glyptic iconography of this period court functionaries identified as LÚ.SAG/*ša rēši* on their seals are shown as beardless in the accompanying iconography. In a study of eleven such seals dating to the reign of Adad-Nerari III (Figure 3.9), Zoltán Niederreiter noted that all of these seals were of exceptionally high quality, attesting to the general prestige of the owners. Ten of the eleven seals bore inscriptions marking their owners as a LÚ. SAG, either of the king or a local governor. In these ten seals, the LÚ.SAG is shown beardless and standing in the presence of a deity.

Iconographically, then, it appears that the LÚ.SAG/*ša rēši* is to be understood as beardless.

Furthermore, LÚ.SAG/*ša rēši*—which means "of the head"—is presented in direct opposition to those court functionaries in the Neo-Assyrian Empire who were categorized as *ša ziqni*—those "of the beard."[150] For example, in King Esarhaddon's Succession Treaty (SAA 02, 006), the pairing of the *ša ziqni* and the *ša rēši* appears five times, each in a list that reveals opposed pairings to indicate the concept of "everyone." Thus:

(ll. 73–82): If you hear any improper, unsuitable or unseemly word concerning the exercise of kingship which is unseemly and evil against Aššurbanipal,

Masculinity 161

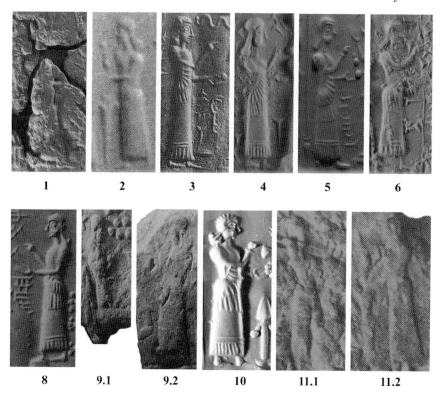

Figure 3.9 Ša Rēši Seals from the Reign of Adad-Nerari III. From Niederreiter 2015: 131. [149]
Source: Used with kind permission of the author.

the great crown prince designate, either from the mouth of his brothers, his uncles, his cousins, his family, members of his father's line; or from the mouth of magnates and governors, **or from the mouth of the bearded (and) the ša rēšis** (*lu ina pî* LÚ *šá ziqni* LÚ.SAG.MEŠ), or from the mouth of the scholars or from the mouth of any human being at all, you shall not conceal it but come and report it to Aššurbanipal, the great crown prince designate.[151]

Or ll. 162–166:

If an Assyrian or a vassal of Assyria, or **a bearded (courtier) (or) a ša rēši** (*lû* LÚ *šá ziqni lû* LÚ.SAG), or a citizen of Assyria or a citizen of any other country, or any living being at all besieges Aššurbanipal, the great crown prince designate, in country or in town, and carries out rebellion and insurrection.[152]

These two verbal categories—*ša ziqni* and *ša rēši*—are replicated in the royal iconography, where the king (always bearded) appears in context with bearded and

162 *Masculinity*

clean-shaven attendants. Thus, on the throne dais of King Šalmanezer III (Figure 3.10), we see the crowned king holding a staff and bow. Behind him is a beardless courtier holding the king's parasol, himself followed by two additional beardless courtiers armed with bows and swords. These three are followed by a bearded courtier with staff, bow, arrows, and sword.

Likewise, a wall relief depicting Aššurnaṣirpal after a successful bull hunt (Figure 3.11) shows the crowned king shaded by one beardless attendant followed by two others bearing bows, arrows, and swords. Facing these are a beardless flyswatter, two additional courtiers (one bearded), and bearded musicians.

Two additional texts have offered support of the identification of the *ša rēši* as a eunuch in light of the bearded-beardless dyad. One is the text of an oracle given to King Aššurbanipal just before his accession to the throne, when the goddess Mulissu predicted for him dominion (ABRT 26,4):

> [*ma*]- ⌈*a*⌉ *a-di ina muḫḫi* (UGU) *mārē* (DUMU.MEŠ) *šá šá ziqnī* (SU₆.MEŠ) *ina muḫḫi* (UGU) *ḫalpete ša rēšī* (ˡúSAG.MEŠ)
>
> Over the sons of bearded men, over the successors of *ša rēši*s.[153]

Bearded functionaries have sons (DUMU.MEŠ), whereas "head" men have successors (*ḫalpete*), but, presumably, not sons.

The second text comes from a *sagallu* incantation (CT 23.10, 13–14) wherein is offered the spell/curse:

> Spell: "You flashed like the stars, be extinguished like embers. May your roots dry out, your trunk wither!
> Like a *ša rēši* who does not beget, may your semen dry up!
> (*kīma*(GIN₇) *šu-ut re-e-ši la a-li-di ni-il-ka li-bal*)"[154]

The logic is that the *ša rēši* is a male, a court functionary, who does not have a beard and who does not have sons because his semen has "dried up." Both of

Figure 3.10 Throne Dais of Šalmanezer III, Baghdad Museum. Osama Shukir Muhammed Amin, Wikimedia Commons.

Figure 3.11 Aššurnaṣirpal Relief, British Museum 124533. © The Trustees of the British Museum.

these facts have been attributed to the supposition that he is a eunuch: that he has neither beard nor progeny because he has been castrated.

Of this there is no evidence. As Ilan Peled noted in his 2016 work on *Masculinities and Third Gender*, there is no actual reference to the process of castration of the LÚ.SAG/*ša rēši* in the Mesopotamian corpus (which is also why there tends to be a debate as to whether this castration took place via the cutting off/out of the testicles or merely by way of crushing the testicles).[155] In this we might see an echo of the *harīmtu* debate, where prostitutes were identified in the absence of any reference to payment for sex. In point of fact, all references to castration in the Mesopotamian corpus involve circular reasoning: The terminology taken to refer to castration is actually *ša rēši*. This comes across most clearly in a pair of Middle Assyrian Laws, §§15 and 20, both dealing with sexual infractions. In the first, if a man catches his wife in adultery:

MAL §15, 51–57

If the husband of the woman kills his wife,
he shall also kill the man (= the adulterer);
If he cuts off the nose of his wife,
he shall turn the man into (a/the) *ša rēšēn*[156]
(*a'īla* (LÚ) **a-na ša re-še-en ú-tar)**,
and they will completely mutilate his face;
And if [he releases] his wife,
[he shall] (also) re[lease] the man.[157]

The second law pertains to male homosexuality:[158]

MAL §20, 93–97

If a man penetrates his fellow man,
(and) they indict him,

164   *Masculinity*

(and) they prove him (= his guilt):
they shall penetrate him;
they shall turn him into (a/the) *ša rēšēn.*
(***a-na ša re-še-en ú-tar-ru-uš***)[159]

In both instances, it is assumed that the expression *a-na ša re-še-en ú-tar* means "to turn into a *ša rēši*" = to castrate.[160] An identical translation/interpretation comes from the Levantine city of Ugarit. Here, in a letter describing the delivery of goods, we read (RS 17.144, ll. 10–19):

No[w], as [m]y brother wrote concerning a *ša rēši* and a mul[e], and concerning a horse: I herewith sen[d] to my brother one mare and one boy. **May they make him a *ša rēši* there (*aš-ra-nu-ma a-na* LÚ-SAG *ut-tim*). That boy is** very good-looking![161]

So, we know that the *ša rēši* was castrated because he was turned into . . . a *ša rēši*. Obviously, there are methodological problems here.

This is exacerbated by the fact that once the idea that the *ša rēši* is a eunuch takes hold, other data are tweaked to support the supposed meaning. For example, from the Middle Assyrian period comes a set of three cylinder seals belonging to two courtiers of Kassite Babylonia. The first two belong to "Kidin-Marduk son of Ša-ilimma-damqa, *ša rēši* of Burnaburiaš, king of the world."[162] The first seal shows Kidin-Marduk kneeling before an enthroned male, probably the king. *Both* males are bearded, revealing that this *ša rēši* was, in fact, bearded. The third seal belongs to "Adad-ušabši son of Kidin-Marduk, the *ša rēši* of Burnaburiaš."[163] In addition to being bearded, Kidin-Marduk had a son.[164] Both arguments used in favor of the idea that the *ša rēši* is a eunuch—beardlessness and lack of progeny—do not apply here. The rationale offered is that the meaning of *ša rēši* only changed to mean "eunuch" exclusively in the Neo-Assyrian period.[165]

However, a document from the Neo-Babylonian period refers to another *ša rēši* who fathered offspring, apparently one who followed in his footsteps. In CT 56.610, we read the dedication wherein, "Mušēzib-Nabû the slave, whom Mušēzib-Bēl, *ša rēši* of the king, **son of Nabûaḫḫē-šullim the *ša rēši*,** gave to Šamaš."[166] So: after the period when the *ša rēši* came to be understood as a eunuch. In such instances, it is typical to argue that these sons must be adopted, with no supporting evidence other than the presumed state of the *ša rēši*'s testicles.[167] Even if the sons were adopted, the rationale still makes little sense. As Stephanie Dalley put it, "In cases when a LÚ SAG adopts a son, it is hard to understand why this is allowed, if the purpose of castration was to ensure that family loyalties could not supersede loyalty to the king."[168]

Additional problems come to the fore when considering the iconography. Both Martti Nissinen and Omar N'Shea have argued that our beardless courtiers appear as distinctively eunuchoid in the Neo-Assyrian reliefs. Specifically, they have "soft, rounded bodies [that] stand in distinction to those of the king, with his lush beard, well defined musculature, direct gaze, and . . . significantly taller body."[169] The taller body is simply to be expected: The king is the king. Other than the elaborate beard, though, there are no clear distinctions between the king and the beardless courtier. If we look at the side-by-side depiction of Sargon II and one such "eunuch" (Figure 3.12), we see that the "eunuch" has the same full shoulders as does the king and the same musculature of the forearms. They even wear similar jewelry and carry the same weapons. The only difference is the beard. And because the depictions are so stereotyped (all bearded courtiers look the same, all beardless courtiers look the same), it is impossible to hazard a guess as to what the bearded courtiers' faces would have looked like if shaven. That is: Are the rounded facial features of the beardless courtiers intended as eunuchoid/feminine, or are they simply how faces were understood to look under the beard? As we only have the two categories for males, is it possible that the artists simply based clean-shaven faces off of how they rendered female faces, such as the queen?

For many of these reasons, in the past 20 years, opposition has grown against the definition of LÚ.SAG/*ša rēši* as "eunuch."[170] Alternative theories have been put forth. For example, regarding the Middle Assyrian Law penalties §§15 and 20, Stephanie Dalley has suggested that rather than translating "LÚ *a-na ša re-še-en ú-tar*" (15), "*a-na ša re-še-en ú-tar-ru-uš*" (20) as "turn him **into** a *ša rēši*/eunuch/castrate," instead to take the expression as "turn him **over to** the *ša rēšen* (for punishment)." That is: hand over the perpetrator to the king's officials for punishment.[171] This would align better with the general ethos of the Middle Assyrian punishments: If the wife is merely disfigured (her nose cut off), it would be surprising to have the male both disfigured *and* castrated (an act that might reasonably be expected to result in death).

An alternative hypothesis was suggested by Luis Siddall. Taking as a starting point that the *ša rēši* might be contrasted with the *ša ziqni*, and thus that the *ša rēši* is beardless, Siddall suggests that part of the punishment in both cases involves the perpetrator having his beard cut off.[172] This does assume that the contrast between *ša rēši* and the *ša ziqni* existed in Middle Assyrian times and

Figure 3.12 Neo-Assyrian Relief of Sargon II with a *ša rēši*, Oriental Institute 872.
Source: Courtesy of the Oriental Institute of the University of Chicago.

166   *Masculinity*

that the functionary designated *ša rēši* was understood to be beardless at this point (see previously: Kidin-Marduk). However, there are in fact biblical parallels for such a punishment/humiliation. In 2 Samuel 10: 4–5 (and almost identically in 1 Chronicles 19: 4–5), we read how emissaries of David were received less than diplomatically by Hanun in Jericho:

2 Samuel 10: 4–5:

So Hanun seized David's envoys, shaved off half of each man's beard, cut off their garments at the buttocks, and sent them away.[173] When David was told about this, he sent messengers to meet the men, for they were greatly humiliated. The king said, "Stay at Jericho until your beards have grown, and then come back."

For Hilary Lipka:

One effective means of undermining masculine performance in biblical texts was by destroying, altering, or otherwise tampering with biological markers that served as attributes of masculine identity. . . . Whether half the beards were shaven or all the beards, the psychological effect on the men must have been virtually the same. The removal of a man's facial hair was seen as a means of depriving him of one of the essential attributes of hegemonic masculinity, and thus taking away his masculine identity, since the beard was one of the primary ways that a man was differentiated from women and boys. Removing or tampering with a man's beard thus resulted in an undermining of his ability to perform this construct.[174]

With regard to Middle Assyrian Law §15, such a removal of the beard would also prevent the man from hiding his facial disfigurement.

Another set of texts pertaining to the *ša rēši* that has come under debate is a palace decree from the reign of Tukulti-Ninurta I (fl. 1240) that was replicated in the reign of Tiglath-Pileser I (fl. 1100). This difficult text declares:

Tukulti-Ninurta (Palace Decree no. 8,50–51):

ki-i ma-zi-iz pa-ni.MEŠ *i-ḫi-ru-ú-ni **lu-ú šá rēš** (SAG) **šarri** (LUGAL) lu-ú ma-zi-iz pa-ni ša la-a mar-ru-ru-ni i-qa-bi-ú ša ša-nu-ut-[te-š]u a-na ma-zi-iz pa-nu-ut-te id-du-nu-uš*

This is typically taken as:

Royal court attendants of dedicatees of the palace personnel who have access to the palace shall not enter the palace without an inspection; if he is not (properly) castrated, they shall turn him into a (castrated) court attendant for a second time.[175]

Masculinity 167

Peled instead translates:

> When they inspect the courtiers, they shall declare whether a *ša rēši* of the king or a courtier is not *checked*. For a second time, they shall give him for "courtier-ship".[176]

Tiglath-pileser I (Palace Decree no. 20,98):

> *šúm-ma la-a mar-ru-ur ša ša-nu-ut-te-šu a-na ma-zi-iz pa-nu-ut-te ú-ta[r-r]u-šu*
>
> If he is not *checked*, for a second time they shall tu[r]n him for "courtier-ship".[177]

The suggestion, originally proposed by Leo Oppenheim, is that before these courtiers—*šá rēš* (SAG) *šarri* (LUGAL)—can be admitted to the palace ("harem" is often assumed), they must be inspected to assure that they are fully castrated. If not, they must be sent back to be castrated a second time.[178]

"So, wait," I hear you males of the masculine persuasion thinking. "You're telling me that some poor guy gets his balls *crushed*, like, with a rock or a brick or a hammer or something? *Then*, if he recovers from that, they do an inspection to make sure his balls are totally crushed, and if they aren't, they crush his balls *again???* And then, if he recovers from *that*, they give this guy weapons and tell him to go stand next to the king? Are you kidding me?"

Sometimes the academic solution defies logic.

So, at the current moment, there is no evidence that the LÚ.SAG/*ša rēši* has been castrated, merely that a *ša rēši* has been *ša rēši*ed. They are contrasted with courtiers with beards, including the fact that the *ša ziqni* is succeeded by his sons, whereas the *ša rēši* is succeeded by his successors. The idea that he has no sons at all is contradicted in the textual record, where in both the glyptic and the tablets there is reference to the sons of a *ša rēši*, with no evidence that these sons were adopted. Only the *sagallu* incantation indicated that a *ša rēši* has dried up semen and does not sire children. This is not much to go on. Basically, in order to argue that a *ša rēši* is a eunuch, one pretty much has to start with the idea that a *ša rēši* is a eunuch and work backwards.

Because so much pertaining to this topic is, ultimately, quite speculative, I shall offer here some speculation of my own. The courtiers of the Neo-Assyrian Empire were divided into two categories, the *ša ziqni* and the *ša rēši*. The former could be succeeded by their sons, suggesting that their functions/positions were inheritable, as was common in the ancient and not-so-ancient world. By contrast, the *ša rēši* took on a host of functions—including military commander and governor—that were not inheritable. Such functions may have been seen as far too important to trust to the hazards of biological reproduction. A fine military leader such as Samsî-Addu could still sire a son like Yasmah-Addu. Instead of these court positions being inheritable by questionable/un-tested sons, the functions of the *ša rēši* could only be held by those qualified to hold them, possibly through examinations.

168   *Masculinity*

Should they fail these, they must be tested a second time ("When they inspect the courtiers, they shall declare whether a *ša rēši* of the king or a courtier is not *checked*. For a second time, they shall give him for "courtier-ship").[179]

As represented in the Neo-Assyrian wall reliefs, the king is often surrounded by beardless officials, these often armed with a bow.[180] It is assumed that these are eunuchs who are permitted to be close to the king insofar as, being without family (castrated), their complete loyalty is to the king and empire: They are not a threat.[181] Or, possibly, following the theories of Irene Winter and Luis Siddall, the clean-shaven aspect of the courtiers highlights the lush, abundant beard of the king.[182] The fact that the king appears in contexts of military victory flanked by apparent *ša rēši*s (in contrast to bearded courtiers?) is hardly surprising considering how often high-ranking *ša rēši*s served as military commanders and generals-in-chief. In requests for omens from the solar god Šamaš, we see:

- Should Esarhaddon, king of] Assyria, send Ša-Nabû-šû, GAL.LÚ.SAG.MEŠ (*ša rēši*), [and the army] at his disposal [to take the road, and] to go to capture the city Amul? (SAA 04 063)
- Will the LÚ.GAL.SAG (*ša rēši*) of Esarhaddon, ki]ng of Assyria, and [his] troop[s and army who] have gone against him, [drive Mugallu and his troops away] from the w[all of . . ., and will he] aban[don the w]all? (SAA 04 003)
- Should Nabû-šarru-uṣur, LÚ.GAL.SAG (*ša rēši*), and the men, horses, and army [of] Aššurbanipal, king of Assyria, which are at [his disposal, go to recover the fort]resses of Assyria which the Manneans conq[uered? (SAA 04 267)[183]

These "eunuchs" were clearly formidable warriors, as we see in the annals of King Šamši-Adad V (A.O. 103.1):

> On my second campaign I issued orders and sent Mutarris-Aššur, the LÚ.GAL. SAG.MEŠ (*ša rēši*), one clever and experienced in battle, a sensible man, with my troops and camp to the land Nairi. He marched as far as the sea of the west. He overcame (and) defeated 300 cities of Sarsina, son of Meqdiara, (and) eleven fortified cities together with 200 cities of Ušpina. He carried off from them booty, property, possessions, their gods, their sons, (and) their daughters. He razed, destroyed, (and) burned their cities. On his return he defeated the people of the land Sunbu. He received tribute of teams of horses from all the kings of the land Nairi.[184]

This in itself might lend an interesting interpretation to the matter of beardlessness. Beards are impractical in battle: They can be grasped and used to restrain the enemy. As Plutarch recorded of Alexander the Great, "Don't you know that in battle there is nothing handier to grasp than a beard?" (Plutarch, *Regum et Imperatorum Apophthegmata* 27). Perhaps beardlessness is a marker of a man who actually fights, a warrior in deed rather than imagery. Again, this is just speculation. And if that chief warrior—the king—still sports a beard, let us recall the other speculation, that beards belong to those members of court who could inherit their position. The king most assuredly would want to advertise his close familiar relationship to his predecessor . . .

One thing that scholars who write on the LÚ.SAG/*ša rēši* seem to agree on is that he was absolutely gendered masculine and that he was of very high status in the Neo-Assyrian period.[185] In addition to his frequent occupation as general-in-chief of the army, *ša rēši*s also served as governors of important cities such as the capital city Kalhu, Aššur, Arraphe, Rasappa, Rimusu, and Nasibina, as well as serving as the palace herald.[186] In terms of the relief art, Jacob Wright and Michael Chan have observed that:

> Iconographically, the close spatial proximity between eunuchs and the king represents their unmediated access to the crown: in palace reliefs, eunuchs consistently stand nearest to the king. . . . These images reflect their function as a concrete extension of the royal arms, as the king's right-hand men and trusted courtiers.[187]

Not only could the *ša rēši* stand nearest the king: He could, in a pinch, *become* the king, as was the case with the king's *ša rēši* Sin-šumu-lēšir in the 620s (a period of considerable chaos for Assyria, to be sure).[188]

In the end, the matter is still up for debate. The general current consensus is that the *ša rēši* is in fact a eunuch and that he is most assuredly gendered masculine. For Omar N'Shea:

> That a eunuch could rule the imperial core and periphery implied that castrates were perceived as male, rather than third gender, and that biological perfection was not at all times necessary for the construction of elite masculinities. . . . [R]oyal masculinity was not always dependent on a lack of a lack, and biological potency and a beard were not always required.[189]

I, personally, do not think that the evidence that the *ša rēši* is a eunuch is entirely compelling, so it is difficult to determine exactly how he contributed to Mesopotamian constructions of masculinity. At best, we might debate how masculinity related to beards in 1st-millennium Mesopotamia (and the Levant). The data from Anatolia are too dependent on those from Mesopotamian to furnish independent evidence for castration, and the data from the Hebrew Bible (the Biblical *sārîs*) too dependent on the Persian institution to be meaningful for the periods under consideration here. The Egyptians didn't even have eunuchs (or individuals taken to be eunuchs, Potiphar notwithstanding), so, again, there is little to contribute from that perspective.

Rather, I think the issue of the LÚ.SAG/*ša rēši* is similar to that of the *ḫarīmtu*: Sexed topics get blown out of proportion in ANE studies. In the absence of any evidence for sex for pay in Mesopotamia, we still managed to translate the word *ḫarīmtu* as "prostitute." In fact, we managed to translate several words as some kind of prostitute, even words clearly referring to celibate cult functionaries (e.g. the *nadītu*). For the *ša rēši*, we began with a man without a beard and notions of

170 *Masculinity*

eunuchs from other, comparable cultures, most notably Persia.[190] In proper orientalist fashion, we assumed that we should also have such an exotic creature in the land demonized by the Bible, and we managed to work castration ("to be *ša rēšied*") into the picture, providing us with our desired eunuchs.

Notes

1 Between physiology and the biblical story of Adam and Eve, I'd have to give the edge to Adam when it comes to rationalizing the oppression of women.
2 Cher?
3 Lipka 2017: 176–177.
4 N'Shea 2018: 316.
5 Zsolnay 2017: 9.
6 See especially the relevant essays in Zsolnay 2017; Nissinen 1998; and Kirova 2020 as a few examples.
7 Parkinson 2008: 116, quoting Halperin 1990, like everyone else. Emphasis in original.
8 Granted, "normal, straight" males have been the primary, overwhelming subject of pretty much all historiography up to the end of the 20th century, so it is easy to argue that it's been done. I certainly seldom bothered looking at males or masculinity before writing this book, a few previous articles on fertility notwithstanding. But by ignoring non-queer males, we tacitly confirm their normativity, their position as the "standard" against which everything else is compared, is the inevitable Other. Normal males have to get onto the couch, get into the grid like everyone else and become an *object* of inquiry, not the presumed *subject*.
9 Matuszak 2018: 264; Matuszak 2016: 230.
10 Matuszak 2018: 267.
11 *Documents épistolaires du palais de Mari*, Tome I, #35 [I 61]. My translation from the French.
12 Robins 1993: 77–78.
13 Michel 2001: N. 354.
14 Needless to say, Marc Brettler's analysis of this passage reads: "'Be[ing] strong' is a main component of such a man, and the expression of the verse may even be understood as 'Perform your proper role as a hegemonic man (and not a woman or child) by being strong, and eliminating the various enemies of the royal house'" Brettler 2017: 201.
15 Text and translation from Parpola and Watanabe 1988, accessed via http://oracc. museum.upenn.edu/saao/saa02/corpus, adapted.
16 https://etcsl.orinst.ox.ac.uk/cgi-bin/etcsl.cgi?text=t.4.07.3&display=Crit&charenc= j&lineid=t4073.p13#t4073.p13
17 *Erra Epic*, translation by Dalley 1989: 287.
18 King 1983.
19 And often forgo the motherhood. And possibly even the defloration.
20 De Waal 2007: Chapter Two and Epilogue.
21 For much, much more on this see Lion and Michel 2016.
22 De Waal 2022: 174–175.
23 See especially Wheelwright 1989 on this. Or, if you prefer: Mulan.
24 George 1999: 2.
25 Ibid: 3.
26 George 1999: 14. Text taken from the Standard Version (ll. 59–60) with lacuna filled by Old Babylonian version (ll. 106–111).
27 George 1999: 23.

Masculinity 171

28 As noted by Mark S. Smith, "[T]he story of Gilgamesh also stands apart as the *adventures* of two heroes *rather than combat*." Smith 2014: 4–5 (see also pg. 53), my emphases.
29 George 1999: 20.
30 Smith 2014: 176.
31 Ibid: 178, slightly excerpted.
32 Ibid: 166.
33 Morris 2013: 37; Fairservis 1991: 1.
34 Baines 1995: 116–117.
35 Ibid: 117.
36 Ibid.
37 Morris 2013: 50.
38 Wilkinson 2000: 28.
39 Morris 2013: 49–50, excerpted.
40 Couturaud 2021: 110.
41 Ibid: 112; Winter 1985: 13.
42 Frayne 1998: 129.
43 Ibid: 131.
44 Bryce 1998: 208
45 Ibid.
46 Klein 1981: 10.
47 https://etcsl.orinst.ox.ac.uk/cgi-bin/etcsl.cgi?text=t.2.4.2.15#
48 https://etcsl.orinst.ox.ac.uk/cgi-bin/etcsl.cgi?text=t.2.4.2.02#
49 https://etcsl.orinst.ox.ac.uk/cgi-bin/etcsl.cgi?text=t.2.4.2.02#
50 Klein 1981: 8.
51 Faulkner in Simpson 1973: 188.
52 Ibid: 183.
53 Ibid: 196.
54 *Documents épistolaires du palais de Mari*, Tome II, #452 [I 69+]. See also Harris 2000: 23.
55 Really, don't drink milk when you're thirsty.
56 Bryce 2002: 109.
57 Reade in Curtis and Reade 1995: 77.
58 https://etcsl.orinst.ox.ac.uk/cgi-bin/etcsl.cgi?text=t.5.6.1#
59 Simpson 1973: 172, excerpted. One might recall the line in Monty Python's Flying Circus when Eric Idle claims he wants to leave the army. When asked why, he responds. "It's dangerous!"
60 Hadjicosti 2002: 134.
61 Ibid: 136.
62 Ibid: 139–140, with references.
63 Ibid: 14–141. See Chapter 2 for more on this topic.
64 Assante 2017: 61.
65 Hoffner 1966: 331.
66 Ibid: 332.
67 Hoffner 1987: 277.
68 Smith in Parker 1997: 107. For more on this goddess, see Chapter 4.
69 Dalley 1989: 253.
70 Cooper 2017: 115.
71 Lesko 1999: 46.
72 For example, anything he ever said about women, ever.
73 Bachvarova 2017: 90.
74 Ibid.

172 *Masculinity*

75 Ibid.
76 Allen 2003: 7.
77 Meskell and Joyce 2003: 95.
78 Faulkner 2007: 1.73.
79 Hollis 1990: 174. Neal Walls (2001: 105–106) has a nice discussion of this passage in relation to male performance anxiety.
80 Roth 2000: 198.
81 Budin 2011: 126–135.
82 Robins 2008.
83 Black et al. 2004: 220–221.
84 Translation from http://etcsl.orinst.ox.ac.uk/cgi-bin/etcsl.cgi?text=t.1.2.1&charenc=j#
85 All translations NRSV.
86 Hoffner 1998: 15.
87 Smith in Parker 1997: 158–159.
88 Parker in Parker 1997: 66–67.
89 Simpson 1972: 120.
90 Jacobsen 1987: 202–203, with several more lines of aches, pains, and births.
91 Hoffner 1998: 42–43.
92 Puhvel 2002.
93 Dalley 1989: 9–10, excerpted.
94 Simpson in Simpson 1973: 333.
95 Ward 1989: 35.
96 McDowell 1999: 229.
97 http://oracc.museum.upenn.edu/dcclt/corpus
98 Budin 2021: 33.
99 *Proverbs* is the exception. Assuming you think it was actually written by Solomon. I have some doubts.
100 Black et al. 2004: 284.
101 Lambert 1996: 92.
102 Ibid: 97.
103 Formerly known as *Šube-Awilim*.
104 Foster 1993: 332.
105 Faulkner in Simpson 1973: 159.
106 Simpson in Simpson 1973: 177.
107 Lichtheim 2006, Vol. II: 135.
108 Ibid: 147.
109 Ibid: 146.
110 One might argue that in modern times the opposite of all this wisdom is known as "toxic masculinity."
111 Other themes that run through most of the texts are more practical in nature: Don't commit adultery, don't stand surety for anyone, work hard.
112 Faulkner in Simpson 1973: 161.
113 Ibid: 163.
114 Simpson in Simpson 1973: 178.
115 https://etcsl.orinst.ox.ac.uk/cgi-bin/etcsl.cgi?text=t.5.6.1#
116 Foster 1993: 329
117 Faulkner in Simpson 1973: 166–67.
118 Lichtheim 2006, Vol. II: 151.
119 Ibid: 152.
120 Foster 1993: 333.
121 Lichtheim 2006, Vol. II: 141.
122 Foster 1993: 329.
123 Lichtheim 2006, Vol. II: 161.

Masculinity 173

124 https://etcsl.orinst.ox.ac.uk/cgi-bin/etcsl.cgi?text=t.5.6.1#
125 Lichtheim 2006, Vol. II: 140.
126 Ibid: 142.
127 Faulkner in Simpson 1973: 162.
128 https://etcsl.orinst.ox.ac.uk/cgi-bin/etcsl.cgi?text=t.5.6.1#
129 Faulkner in Simpson 1973: 161.
130 Lichtheim 2006, Vol. II: 137.
131 Ibid: 140.
132 Faulkner in Simpson 1973: 163.
133 Foster 1993: 328.
134 Lichtheim 2006, Vol. II: 151.
135 Ibid: 159.
136 Foster 1993: 333.
137 https://etcsl.orinst.ox.ac.uk/cgi-bin/etcsl.cgi?text=t.5.6.1#
138 Lichtheim 2006, Vol. II: 137.
139 Simpson in Simpson 1973: 177.
140 Faulkner in Simpson 1973: 175.
141 Ibid: 165.
142 Simpson in Simpson 1973: 178.
143 Foster 1993: 333.
144 Lichtheim 2006, Vol. II: 150.
145 Ibid: 160.
146 Ibid: 155–156.
147 https://etcsl.orinst.ox.ac.uk/cgi-bin/etcsl.cgi?text=t.5.6.1#
148 For the equation of these terms, see Peled 2016: 208.
149 Niederreiter 2015: 131, Fig. 3.
150 Groß and Pirngruber 2014: 169; Grayson 1995: 92.
151 http://oracc.museum.upenn.edu/saao/corpus
152 Ibid.
153 Peled 2016: 224; Groß and Pirngruber 2014: 169.
154 Peled 2016: 225; Dalley 2001: 203; Grayson 1995: 91.
155 Peled 2016: 207.
156 The term appears in the dual in Middle Assyrian corpora.
157 Peled 2016: 212; see also Dalley 2001: 200 and Grayson 1995: 91.
158 See full discussion of this text in Chapter 5.
159 Peled 2016: 213–214; see also Grayson 1995: 91.
160 Grayson 1995: 91.
161 Peled 2016: 220. Peled takes the first use of *ša rēši* as "eunuch."
162 Collon 1987: 58–59, #s 239–240.
163 Ibid, #241.
164 Siddall 2007: 226; Dalley 2001: 200.
165 Dalley, Siddall, etc.
166 Peled 2016: 225. On other sons of *ša rēši*s, see Dalley 2001: 204.
167 Peled 2016: 226; Siddall 2007: 232.
168 Dalley 2001: 205. On nepotism among *ša rēši*s, see Groß and Pirngruber 2014: 165.
169 N'Shea 2016: 215.
170 See especially Dalley 2001; Siddall 2007; and Groß and Pirngruber 2014.
171 Dalley 2001: 200–201.
172 Siddall 2007: 228.
173 At least he didn't kick them into a bottomless pit screaming "This is Sparta!"
174 Lipka 2017: 182.
175 Siddall 2007: 228.
176 Peled 2016: 215.

174 *Masculinity*

177 Peled 2016: 215. On the expression *mazzāz pāni*, see Groß and Pirngruber 2014.
178 Peled 2016: 215–216 (including reference to Oppenheim); Barjamovic 2011: 59; Siddall 2007: 228–229.
179 Dalley 2001: 201.
180 Assante 2017: 72.
181 N'Shea 2016: 218–219.
182 Siddall 2007: 236. On kings and beards, see Winter 1997: 370–371.
183 http://oracc.museum.upenn.edu/saao/corpus. On MANY other high-ranking functions of *ša rēši*s in the Neo-Assyrian corpus, see Groß and Pirngruber 2014: 166–168.
184 RIME 3: 184: A.O. 103.1
185 Siddall 2007: 225–226.
186 Grayson 1995: Appendix A.
187 Wright and Chan 2012: 107.
188 N'Shea 2016: 219; Peled 2016: 231; Barjamovic 2011: 59, n. 64; Siddall 2007: 236–237.
189 N'Shea 2016: 219.
190 Grayson 1995: 86–91.

4 Gender Bending

Gender is fluid, meaning that people do not always act in ways that conform to (their societies' notions of proper behavior for) their sex (or, for that matter, class, age, ethnicity, etc.). In the ancient Near East, where sex was understood to be binary (female and male), this most often manifested as one sex adopting in some capacity the attributes of the other sex. This could be in terms of dress, titles, or legal capacities, *inter alia*. The result of this was that the gender-bending individual acquired some prerogatives that normally accrued (exclusively) to the other sex. Thus, for example, in Egypt some royal women who became king adopted the attributes of male sex—Sobekneferu and Hatshepsut. In Bronze Age Syria, a woman could be made both mother and father of the household, thus giving her certain rights over the household property, while daughters could be turned into sons—*ana martūti epešu*—with concomitant economic rights.

A major stumbling block in the study of gender-bending is determining what actually constitutes "bending." To recognize gender-bending roles and activities, I must first know what constitutes "feminine" or "masculine" behavior for the society in question rather than imposing my own notions, or my own society's notions, onto the culture in question.[1] That is, can an individual from one culture (e.g. 21st-century CE New York) understand the gender constructs of another (e.g. 21st-century BCE Uruk)?

For example, in his 1987 article "Goddesses in the Pantheon: A Reflection of Women in Society?" W.G. Lambert opined of Nisaba, the goddess of grain and scribal activity, that, "Neither activity was especially appropriate for a lady. In Sumerian society female scribes were very rare, and grain is sexually neutral."[2] Regarding the goddess Inana:

> Inanna, "Mistress of Heaven" as the name was understood by the Sumerians, the Babylonian Ištar, was goddess of love and war. The latter aspect was inappropriate for women in Sumerian society, and no tradition of Amazons is known there. Sexual love, on the other hand, a theme continued in the Greek Aphrodite and the Roman Venus, was appropriate for a goddess in that prostitutes in ancient society were normally female.[3]

DOI: 10.4324/9780429318177-4

176   *Gender Bending*

So, it is "inappropriate" for female deities to be accountants and warriors because women simply don't do these things (unless one considers the running of the household economy, which women throughout world history have done, and the role of women in family businesses, as especially clear in the epistolary archives from Karum Kaneš/Kültepe,[4] and the domestic production of bread and beer, generally in the hands of females,[5] and the presence world over of female warrior deities—Neith, Hathor/Sekhmet, Aštart, Athene, Bellona, Ma, the Morrigan, Freyja, Durga, Kali, Amaterasu-o-mikami, not to mention the archaeologically attested existence of human female warriors such as among the Sarmatians and Vikings, most notable recently in burial Bj.581 from Birka, Sweden).[6] It is "appropriate," however, for a goddess to be associated with love because women are whores.[7] There is clearly no small amount of bias here.[8]

The previous few chapters have provided some grounds for determining what attributes were associated with masculinity and femininity, and so we can work with those here. So much for *gender*. What is also relevant here is what, exactly, constitutes *bending*.

Trans, Trans, Trans . . .

There is much talk of "Trans in Antiquity" these days, such that it gets easy to forget that "trans-" is a prefix requiring an actual noun or adjective.[9] In the study of ancient gender bending, it helps to think in terms of three specific categories: transvestite, transgender, and transsexual. A *transvestite* is a person who wears the clothing and other bodily adornments of a person of the opposite sex—thus a man who dresses as a woman or a woman who dresses as a man. A *transgender* individual is a person of one sex who adopts the clothing and behavioral patterns of a person of the other sex, possibly even socially identifying as a person of that opposite sex (e.g. a woman who dresses as a man, behaves like a man, adopts a male name, and presents herself as male in social contexts). In modern times, when personal views become available, transgender individuals often claim that they are a person of one sex born into the body of the opposite sex. A *transsexual* is a person who medically alters her/himself to become physiologically a person of the opposite sex, usually through a combination of surgery and hormone therapy.

The ancients simply didn't have our science and technology, so there were no transsexuals by this definition in the ancient world. As we have already seen, the closest they came to such surgical changes were castrated eunuchs, and eunuchs self-identified, and were identified in society, as male/masculine (see Chapter 3).

What we are left dealing with in antiquity, then, are transvestites and transgender people. As we shall see, there were a few Mesopotamian male cult functionaries who may have worn women's clothing (at least on one side of the body) during rituals, while a single condemnation of cross-dressing in the Hebrew Bible suggests that it may have been a matter of concern at some point. But it turns out that the evidence for such a practice in Mesopotamia is minimal and ambiguous.

Gender Bending 177

The evidence for transvestitism from Egypt is mainly bound up in the persons of Sobekneferu and Hatshepsut, who were extraordinary cases, to put it mildly.

So we are left with transgender, people who take on the gender identity of the opposite sex. With this, a few things must be understood from the outset. First: Deities are not people. The presence of a gender-bending deity says little to nothing about the people who worship that deity. Ištar may be a warrior goddess, but this reveals nothing about women in Babylon.

Second: We have no data whatsoever that indicate that being transgender was an individual choice that a person made in order to express/live what she or he felt to be her/his "true" or "actual" sex. This is mainly because we have so few personal data of that kind about *anything* from the ancient Near East. How people felt about their bodies, their identities, their sexualities is not the kind of information left to us in the records, assuming such musings were ever put into writing in the first place (and if we don't have it from Egypt of all places, then it probably didn't exist). So the individual commoner flouting gender conventions is not something that can be addressed in modern scholarship: We just don't have the data. There may have been the ancient equivalents of Gentleman Jack, Mary Mead, George Sand, and Ziggy Stardust (who was technically aiming for androgynous), but we cannot access them.

Third: What we do have is evidence that people flouted gender roles and conventions for public reasons, such as political roles and economic prerogatives. So gender bending took place for social reasons, even if we have no data about how people felt about this.

Fourth: We have no evidence of any individual adopting *fully* the gender of the opposite sex. The ancient Near East provides no evidence for people such as the Albanian *virgjinéshē*, women who, upon taking a vow of virginity, are (mostly) identified as males in their communities, where they dress and act as males, often take on a male name, and can take part in male-exclusive activities such as smoking, joining the army, and serving political functions.[10] Again, all evidence for transgendered identity and behavior from the ANE were public, *social* expressions. A daughter could be symbolically turned into a son while still expected to marry and bear children as a female (yes, as a wife and mother). As we saw in Chapter 1, a defeated soldier might be taunted that he has been turned into a woman, but everyone involved pretty much understood that he was still a man, especially if they chose to cut off his definitively male penis.

At best, being transgender, especially in the upper classes, provided a person with the prerogatives of a person of the opposite sex, and, as we shall see, this inevitably involved a female adopting male status. For example, a daughter could maintain the family cult in the absence of a brother. Or an Egyptian queen could become pharaoh. But it must be understood that such gender bending was a readily adopted social/legal *fiction*. The relevant societies granted the engendered benefits to the gender-bending individual, but the individual's sex was still understood to align with the biology. At the end of the day, Hatshepsut was still (understood to be) female.

178 *Gender Bending*

What gender bending in the Near East does *not* involve is sexuality. As the next chapter will show, there is evidence for both heterosexuality and homosexuality from the ANE. Neither had any impact on an individual's socially recognized gender identity. As noted by every scholar following Foucault, the pre-modern world did not have our notions of hetero- and homosexuals—people who at least in part self-identify according to their sexual orientation—but rather people who engage in hetero- or homosexual acts. Thus, in Assyria, for example, there is evidence for males engaging in homosexual acts. There is *no* evidence that these males were understood to be either homosexual (anachronistic) or some alternative gender (usually "third"). There is some evidence that they were in a world of trouble, but they were *men* in a world of trouble, nothing more.

It is perhaps best, then, to get out of the way first a number of misunderstandings pertaining to "third" and "fourth" genders in the ANE before moving on to clearly documented cases of gender bending. Because, honestly, there were no third or fourth genders.

Occam's Gender: Some Words on Methodology on Words

When dealing with writing systems as complex as cuneiform and hieroglyphics, orthographies can emerge that can appear to present examples of non-standard, non-binary sexes and genders. However, such instances also produce other potential interpretations that do not involve "troubling" the ancients' sex/gender systems. Consider, as a modern cognate, a list of university personnel as provided by Human Resources. On page 6 one comes across the list of names:

Ms. Mary Smith
Ms. Aisha Jones
Ms. Sara Brown
Ms. Paul Black

"Aha!" cries the gender scholar. "We see here an example of non-binary gender, whereby an individual with a standard masculine name ('Paul') is given a distinctly feminine title ('Ms.'). Furthermore"—might note the gender scholar—"this Paul is listed in context with a group of females (per name and title). We can therefore suggest that Paul Black is a non-binary individual, potentially intersex."[11]

It is also entirely possible to suggest that the feminine title "Ms." before Paul's name is a typo, generated by an overworked administrative assistant after a list of other "Ms.s." It is likely that Paul is simply male. Or, possibly, we are speaking about Ms. Paula Black, and the overworked administrative assistant made a typo in the name itself. In which case Paula is female. Typos (a.k.a. scribal error) happen. A lot, in fact.

Or, we may simply have a case of a woman named "Paul." It is not one of the more currently common bi-gender names, such as Taylor or Robin, but it is certainly a possibility (I once knew a woman named Bruce, who I always assumed was Scottish). The point is, there are numerous very reasonable reasons why the orthography of a person's name might not conform to normal gendering practices within that person's cultural milieu. The first analysis should probably not be to assume "non-standard gender identity" for that individual before considering other options involving omnipresent human error or simple human weirdness ("We named our daughter 'God'!"). And considering that the list up there actually uses the title "Ms." at all rather strongly suggests that it dates to well before the time when anyone even thought in terms of non-binary gender (much less non-binary sex), so the "non-standard gender identity" suggestion, in contrast to the human error/human weirdness suggestions, is anachronistic.

This is a reasonable way to approach the data.

Let us consider a similar scenario, a list of hospital personnel as provided by Human Resources. On page 6 we come across the list of names:

Dr. John Smith
Dr. Samuel Jones
Dr. Leroy Brown
Dr. Paula Black

"Aha!" cries the non-gender-studies-savvy scholar. "We see here an example of scribal error, as we know that medical physicians are male, whereas the name 'Paula' is feminine. Obviously we must be dealing with a physician named 'Paul.' This is also evidenced in the fact that he appears in a list with other exclusively male names."

This is where the rigid, binary-sex ideology that modern gender studies (and feminism) try to address comes in. The title "Dr." is not gendered, so there is technically no discrepancy between "Dr." and "Paula." The problem is that the scholar assumes that physicians cannot be female due to his (I'm assuming this is a male scholar) own understanding of a sex-based division of labor for the society under question. He rationalizes his rejection of evidence that contradicts his assumptions by way of "scribal error" (a.k.a. a typo).

This latter scenario complicates the first one. How do we know when we have an actual typo, and how do we know when we are merely summoning the specter of scribal error to rationalize our own world view?

Ultimately, the answer is context and a *lot* of hard work. One must learn enough about the society in question to determine how they correlated sex with labor practices, including how these correlations changed over time. What other evidence is there for female physicians at this time and place? Is there evidence of women attending medical school? Do other lists of physicians have female names, enough such that "typo" no longer seems to be a viable response? Conversely, how typical are typos? How do they tend to manifest? Especially in an age before auto-correct.

180 *Gender Bending*

Context is the key.

As noted in Chapter 1, all evidence for the ancient Near East indicated that they believed in binary sex—female and male. There is also evidence that they understood gender ("masculinity") to exist (somewhat) independently of biological sex ("man"). Sometimes the gender of one sex was attributed to the other sex ("My conquered foes are women!"). But this kind of gender-bending occurred in very specific contexts (e.g. trash-talking military opponents). Also, it was extremely obvious ("My conquered foes are women!"). If an unexpectedly gendered name appears in a list of workers, and we have no clear evidence (yet) that people of that sex *never* did that job, it is simpler just to accept the sex of the individual as given in the name. And if a name in a long, tedious list has an element that displays a gender irregularity ("Ms. Mary Smith, son of Mr. John Smith"), "typo" is the much more likely scenario than "third gender." Because, to be clear, we have no actual evidence of third gender (or fourth, or fifth) from the ancient Near East as of yet and many, many examples of typos. Typos that we are trying to read 3,000 years later, after corroding in the dirt, such that even the non-typos are pretty damned difficult to read.

Finally, and perhaps most importantly, one must resist the circular reasoning of what I call the Stand Alone Complex. In this process, a piece of evidence is fabricated. This is not necessarily done intentionally or maliciously—there is a lot of human error in research. But someone creates a false datum, a datum that a number of other people, both inside and outside of the academy, want to believe, or are at least willing to believe (e.g. "X is green"). Other researchers now see a precedent and use that precedent to bolster their own findings ("As Dr. Blah has shown in a previous study, X is green[1], so our X is probably/certainly green, too"). It now becomes commonplace to accept that X is green and to interpret all other expressions of X as being green, based on that initial datum. This is what Lester Grabbe refers to as the "Corrupting Consensus."[12] "X" even enters the discipline's lexicon as "green," at which point it is extremely difficult to dislodge it, even when new research based on copious new data—and a reconsideration of the old data—start showing rather conclusively that it is wrong.

This is yet again where the notions of "context" and "hard work" come into play. When trying to determine if X is, in fact, green, one simply has to go back and look at all of the primary sources, independently of what generations of scholars have said about X and how it now appears in the standard references. If one, after going through these primary sources with a hopefully open mind, can find no or minimal attestations of greenness, more likely than not X is not green, and we have to start from scratch.

Most if not all examples of third gender, non-binary sex/gender, and gender bending in the Near Eastern corpora are really Stand Alone Complexes maintained by Corrupting Consensus. Some of these Stand Alone

Complexes emerged because Victorian-age, biblical scholars seem to have been pretty desperate to find sexual perversions in pagan, Canaanite cults, especially anything involving the goddess Ištar. Thus we got GALA and *kurgarrûs* as catamite homosexual transvestites, while *nadītus* and *šamḫatus* became "sacred prostitutes." Some SACs came about in more recent times as we tried to insist that binary sex/gender was a modern, specifically "Western,"[13] construction and came up with utterly modern translations of ancient terms, thus: "*assinnu* (a socially feminine male with feminine essence) and *harimtu* (a socially masculine female with masculine essence)."[14] And, of course, once someone has published such a definition, other researches can simply copy and paste to argue their own interpretations.

In the end, while there is still a lot of work to do on all of these topics, the dictates of Occam's Razor suggest that if in an ancient cuneiform list of palatial personnel we come across "Ms. Paul Black," "Dr. Paula Black," and "Ms. Mary Smith, son of Mr. John Smith," we should accept that Dr. Black is female (they had female physicians in the ANE), Mary Smith is female (scribes did have a habit of leaving the feminizing MUNUS sign off of the DUMU [=son] sign),[15] and Ms. Paul Black is a *bit* more likely than not to be female, because over the course of cuneiform use scribes were more likely to use a masculine determinative before female names than they were to use a female determinative for male names (which they never did). But for Ms. Paul Black, we ultimately just need more data. The likelihood that "they" are non-binary is the least likely solution.

If this sounds a bit facile and jejune, please understand that it is based on an actual Syro-Mesopotamian case study. In a text of 1st-millennium Assyrian prophecies from the Syrian city of Mari (SAA 9.1), one of the (badly) preserved prophecies offered to Esarhaddon was (o ii 40):

> *ša pi-i* Mí.*ba-ia-a* DUMU ^{uru}*arba-ìl*
> Of the mouth of the woman Bayâ, son of Arbela[16]

Here we have an individual who is clearly described as a female—Mí = MUNUS—and who is then called a "son"—DUMU—or citizen (to use a somewhat anachronistic term) of the city of Arbela. A female son. Some Assyriologists have taken this to indicate that Bayâ is of "indeterminate gender." For Simo Parpola in his discussion of the Neo-Assyrian prophets:

> The female determinative preceding the name of the prophet in 1.4 is clear on the tablet and is confirmed by Mí.ba-ia-a listed as a "[servant of] Ištar of Huzirina" in STT 406 r. 10. On the other hand, the prophet is clearly defined as a "son" of Arbela (i.e., male) on the tablet, and there is no way of emending the crucial sign DUMU "son" to DUMU.Mí, "daughter." If oracle 2.2 also originates from Bayâ, the masculine gentilic following the name there would confirm the male sex of the prophet. The

182 *Gender Bending*

female determinative would then imply that the prophet was a "man turned into a woman" through an act of self-castration.[17]

So, for a lack of a Mí sign Bayâ goes from being female to being a specifically *self*-castrated eunuch.[18] Likewise, Martti Nissinen argues, "The gender of the prophet is ambiguous: Bayâ is called a 'son' (DUMU) of Arbela, but the determinative before the PN is feminine: Mí.*ba-ia-a* DUMU. URU.*arbaìl* . . . Bayâ possibly belonged to those with undefinable gender role."[19]

By contrast, Jonathan Stökl considers the well-documented quirks that can plague any scribe and lead to such apparent "irregularities":

> DUMU is occasionally used as an abbreviated spelling of DUMU. MUNUS (which would be read as *mārtu*, "daughter"). Indeed, under the lemma *mārtu*, CAD lists several cases of ^fPN DUMU ^fPN, which suggests that DUMU could describe daughters as well as sons. It is also possible that a grammatically masculine adjective is used for a woman, or the scribe could have heard the name and started writing using the feminine determinative, as he thought that she was probably as woman—as I would when hearing the names Ashley, Carly, and Lindsay. Yet, just as I have met men with these names as well, so the scribe may have been too quick in turning this particular Bayâ into a woman. . . . [I]t is possible that SAA 9 1.4 indicates an "ambiguous" role for Bayâ, but a number of other explanations are also possible.[20]

Bayâ is only one of three prophets recorded in tablet SAA 9.1 who suffers from such gendered irregularities. On the same list we also meet Ilūssa-āmur, who has the feminine determinative before her name but a masculine gentilic: "*ša pî* Mí *Ilūssa-āmur Libbālā[yu]* = Of the mouth of the woman Ilūssa-āmur of the Inner-city (of Aššur)."[21] *Libbālā[yu]* is a masculine form, of which the feminine would be *Libbālītu*. Again, do we have a gender-ambiguous individual or scribal error? And then there is the prophecy *ša pî ʾIssār-lā-tašīyaṭ* DUMU *Arbail*, Of the mouth of Issār-lā-tašīyaṭ, son of Arbela.[22] Here the ? determinative is in place of an apparently ambiguous sign. Some see a Mí (⬡) sign, thus feminine. However, others see a DIŠ (⌐) sign combined with the DIN-GIR (=god) (⮞⊢) sign that would properly precede the form of Ištar in the prophet's name—"Do Not Neglect Ištar!"[23] As the nominal form is masculine, and the DIŠ determinative is also generally masculine, there would appear to be no cause for confusion other than Nissinen's statement, "The masculine determinative of the PN is written over the erased feminine determinative; this either indicated an error of the scribe or his uncertainty about the gender of the prophet."[24] Considering that this seems to be the third possible mistake on a relatively short tablet, maybe the scribe was just having an off day. This is far more likely than that we have three "third gender" prophets, one of whom was self-castrated.

GALA/*Kalû*—KUR.GAR.RA/*Kugarrû*—SAG.UR.SAG/ᴵᵘUR.MUNUS/*Assinnu*

These three titles (Sumerian and Akkadian) belong to male cult functionaries who at some point or another in their very long histories came to serve the goddess Inana/Ištar. This goddess herself is strongly associated with gender bending not only in her own persona (see subsequently) but in a long literary tradition whereby she turns men into women and women into men. Thus, in the Sumerian poem attributed to the *entu* priestess Enheduanna—*Inana, Lady of Largest Heart*—we read in line 120 that:

[NITAḪ] MUNUS-RA MUNUS NITAḪ-RA KU₄-KU₄-DE₃ ᵈINANA ZA-KAM
To turn a man into a woman and a woman into a man are yours, Inana.[25]

In the bilingual (Sumerian-Akkadian) text ASKT no, 21, rev. 43–53, we read of this goddess:

She (Ištar) [changes] the right side into the left side,
she [changes] the left side into the right side,
she [turns] a man into a woman,
she [turns] a woman into a man,
she ador[ns] a man as a woman,
she ador[ns] a woman as a man.[26]

Following up on that notion of adorning a man as a woman, a woman as a man, the 3rd-millennium king Iddin-Dagan hymned the goddess with the words (ll. 60–68):[27]

They adorn their right side with male clothing,
they walk before pure Inana.
To the great lady of heaven, Inana, I would cry "Hail!"
They place female clothing on their left side,
they walk before pure Inana.
To the great lady of heaven, Inana, I would cry "Hail!"
I shall greet the great lady of heaven, Inana!
Competing with ropes of colored cords for her, they parade before her, holy
     Inana
I shall greet the eldest daughter of Suen/the great lady of heaven, Inana!

With such notions in mind, early Assyriologists found copious examples of male cult functionaries whose sex/gender Inana/Ištar had supposedly changed. The three functionaries dealt with here are the most prominent of these, men whom the academy came to understand as, "cultic performers and included in their ranks transvestites, homosexual prostitutes, catamites, castrati, hermaphrodites and the like."[28] As one scholar put it, such terms designated a high-pitched, castrated chanter who was also a male prostitute.[29] For another, "The sphere of possibilities for the meaning of gala can be narrowed down to pederast, homosexual,

184   *Gender Bending*

transvestite, eunuch, or the like."[30] For yet another, the *assinnu* was clearly "the master of ceremonies at the transvestite orgies."[31]

But do the data bear any of this out? Was there in fact any gender (or sexual) ambiguity marking these particular occupations in Mesopotamian history? Were they even transvestites? In reality, the answer is "no," as a survey of the primary sources quickly makes clear.

All three characters appear in related roles in the tale of *Inana's/Ištar's Decent to the Underworld*. The oldest version of this narrative dates to the Old Babylonian period, written in Sumerian. A later version, in Akkadian and found in Aššur, comes from the Middle Assyrian period, while a final Akkadian version found in the library of Aššurbanipal in Nineveh comes from the Neo-Assyrian period. All of them tell how the goddess Inana/Ištar went to visit her sister Ereškigal, Queen of the Underworld, in the Underworld, was stripped of her powers/clothes, and rendered a corpse. In case of just such an eventuality, the goddess first instructed her vizir Ninšubur to go to various deities to get her out again. When Ninšubur went to the wise/wily god Enki/Ea, that deity created beings to send down to rescue the goddess:

Inana's Descent to the Netherworld, 222–225

He removed some dirt from his fingernail and created the *kurgarrû*.
He removed some dirt from another fingernail and created the *galaturra*.
He gave to the *kurgarrû* the plant of life.
He gave to the *galaturra* the water of life.

Inana's Descent to the Netherworld, 263–266

When she [Ereškigal] said, "[Oh], my heart!",
they [said] to her: "Lady of ours, you [are tired!] Oh, your heart!"
When she said, "[Oh], my back!",
they said to her: "Lady of ours, you [are tired!] Oh, your back!"

And in the Neo-Assyrian version:

Ištar's Descent to the Netherworld, 91–92

Ea, in his wise heart, created (what was) called for,
he created Aṣušunamir the *assinnu*.
. . .
"Ereškigal shall see you and rejoice at your presence.
When her heart has calmed and her mind has become cheerful,
have her swear by the great gods.
Lift your head and pay attention to the waterskin (and say:)
"My lady, let them give me the waterskin so that I can drink water from it."

It has been assumed, per the qualities associated with Inana/Ištar previously, that there simply must be something "off" about these characters. They were fashioned from finger-nail dirt: That can't be good. They can go to the Underworld: That must be suspect. And to make matters worse, in the later version when Ereškigal realizes that the *assinnu* tricked Ištar away from her, she cursed him with almost the same curse Enkidu used against Šamḫat in the *Epic of Gilgameš*:

Ištar's Descent to the Netherworld, 103–108

Come, Aṣušunamir, let me curse you with a great curse:
May food of the city plows be your food!
May the city sewers be your drink!
May the shade of the city wall be your standing-place!
May the threshold be your dwelling-place!
May those drunk and the sober slap your cheek!

Obviously, Aṣušunamir the *assinnu* must be a prostitute. It follows logically that he must also be a transvestite. . . . Soon all manner of qualities were accruing to these characters that were not, technically, in the myths at all. For example, in her study of "Inanna-Ishtar as Paradox and Coincidence of Opposites," Rivkah Harris notes of these characters that, "There is no evidence that they were eunuchs or homosexuals. However, in the *Descent of Ishtar* the reference to the *kurgarrû* as neither male nor female may indicate that they were transvestites performing in female apparel."[32] Above and beyond the fact that the *kurgarrû* does not appear in *Ištar's Descent*, but *Inana's*, it must also be observed that there is no reference whatsoever to this character being "neither male nor female." The hypothesis that the *kurgarrû* (et al.) is anything but a guy is fabricated literally out of nothing.

What do we actually see in the myth? In the Sumerian version, it is clear that the *kurgarrû* and the GALATURRA (literally: Junior Gala) are sympathizing with Ereškigal, showing sympathy for her tired heart and her aching back. In the Akkadian version(s), the *assinnu* simply brings joy to the queen's heart. What these males are doing is soothing and bringing joy to the heart of the deity. There is nothing sexual about it, "straight" or otherwise.

All the other data we have regarding these characters bears this out: Their cult functions seem to be to soothe and cheer the hearts of the deities through music and dance.

GALA/**kalû**

The GALA/*kalû* is a musician, most commonly associated with various kinds of drums. His origins in the 3rd millennium (if not earlier; written evidence only goes back so far) show that he was originally a singer of laments, especially in funerary contexts.[33] In the literary texts we see this in *The Curse of Akkad*, dated to the Ur III period. Here lines 196–204 reveal:[34]

The old women who survived those days,
the old men who survived those days,
the GALA-MAḪ who survived those years,

186 *Gender Bending*

for seven days and seven nights,
put in place seven *balag*-instruments, as if they stood at heaven's base, and
together with *ub*, *meze* and *lilis*-drums played for him [Enlil] like Iškur.
The old women did not restrain (the cry) "Alas my city!"
The old men did not restrain (the cry) "Alas its people!"
The GALA did not restrain (the cry) "Alas the Ekur! [temple of Enlil]"

That he was intended to soothe the hearts of the deities appears in another origin
story of the GALA, still at the hands (maybe even fingernails) of Enki. In the narrative *The Fashioning of the Gala* (ll 20–26), we read how Enki made an attempt to
calm down Inana (never a simple task):

Enki heard these words, he troubled himself in the great Earth.
He fashioned for her [Inana] the GALA, him of the heart-soothing laments . . .
He set up for him his *eršaneša*-lament, lamentation and position . . .
He placed in his hand the *ub* and *lilis* drums, and his "alas!"-uttering.
Enki sent him who . . . to holy Inana:
"Oh lady, may your heart be soothed! Seat yourself on your throne!
The GALA has made available to you the lament, the 'alas!'-uttering and the
eršaneša-song."[35]

This role continues well into the 1st millennium. In an inscription from Aššurbanipal,
we still read (ll. 13–14):

Ea's wisdom, the craft of the GALA (NAM-GALA), secret knowledge of the
    experts,
that is suitable to calm the heart of the great gods.[36]

The evidence from non-literary sources reveals the exact same data: The GALA/*kalû*
was a professional lamenter and musician involved with funerals and cult, generally at the highest levels of society.

Galas were important players in economic and religious life. They were
linked to cities as well as temple estates and we know of gala and gala-
mah of deities such as Baba, Nanše, and Ningišzida, and of cities such
as Umma, Zabala, Hurim, and Irisagrig. While they undoubtedly played
an important role in funerals and funerary cults, they also seem to be
linked with all official musical performances in both "cultic" and "royal"
spheres.[37]

Texts from Early Dynastic and Ur III-period Lagaš reveal the GALAS as cult functionaries involved in high-level funerary music. When the lady Baranamtarra,
wife of Lugalanda, died, the pre-Sargonic documents VS 14.180 and 14.137
reveal that 92 GALAS and one GALA.MAH of Girsu were paid in bread and beer for
their performances at her funeral, along with several female workers and a group

of old women, all of whom were identified as "wailers" and "mourners" in the text colophon.[38]

One outstanding GALA (and also GALA.MAḪ!) documented from the Ur III period was Dada, whose presence in the court documents of Kings Šulgi and Šu-Sîn show him to have been the chief GALA.MAḪ of the state. By the time of his death in the 9th year of Šu-Sîn, he was also the NAR.GAL, or "Chief Musician," of the court, suggesting to Piotr Michalowski at least that the two terms may have been synonymous at this period.[39] He was put in charge of other GALAS, various categories of male and female musicians, organized entertainments at royal functions, and was even involved in the creation of musical instruments.[40]

Court documents from Drehem indicate that two of Dada's children (he had children) were also musicians charged with entertaining the king himself and his royal entourage. And as a clear sign of Dada's status in society, a text reveals that his own daughter was married to the royal prince Amur-Šulgi.[41]

Three significant data regarding the GALA's gender come from these texts. First, the fact that he was involved with lamentation possibly put him into a category that was originally occupied by women. As VS 14.137 indicates, the GALAS and NARS performing at Baranamtarra's funeral were accompanied by female mourners, especially those designated as "old women." It is possible, and especially argued by Jerrold Cooper, that the masculine appropriation of this function may have caused the GALA/*kalû* to be seen as feminized in Mesopotamian society, as one who performs the work of women.[42] This, however, is hypothetical. Furthermore, ethnographic evidence indicates that males who take on a female role in a professional contexts are still recognized as male/masculine when they leave work for the day. While even the most adept *onnagata* might set the fashion for what counts as truly *feminine* in Japanese society, he is still (recognized as) a man, with a wife and children.

This leads to a second point: GALAS had children. We see this in the documents related to Dada and his sons and daughters. And he was not unique in this. An Old Akkadian sales receipt (of sorts) (RTC 80, ll 1–10) reveals that:

1 GAL[A] 1 GÉME DÍLI 2 DUMU-MUN[US]-N[I] DAM DUMU-NI-ME^{m}LÚ-TAR^{m}SA-DÚ
ŠEŠ-A-NI-ME LUGAL-UŠUMGAL ÉNSI LAGAŠ^{ki}-KE$_4$ ŠU-Ì-LÍ-ŠU DI-KU$_5$-ŠÈ Ì-NE-ŠI-SA$_{10}$

One [G]ALA, one female servant (and) he[r] two daught[ers]—they are his wife and children—Lutar, Sadu—they are his brothers—Lugal-ušumgal, governor of Lagaš, bought from Šu-ilisu the judge.[43]

Thus a GALA is purchased (hired?) by the governor of Lagaš along with his wife and either "her" or "their" two daughters. It is evident that the GALA could and did marry—women specifically—and that they could and did reproduce. While it is possible that the daughters in the previous text were adopted (thus "her" daughters rather than "their"), the evidence about Dada strongly suggests that the children are the biological offspring of the GALA in question. They were not castrates, nor

188   *Gender Bending*

eunuchs, and it is remarkably unlikely that they were prostitutes (especially considering that we have no evidence for prostitution in Mesopotamia to begin with).

As a result, the third point is that we have no actual evidence that there was anything atypical about the sex or gender of the GALA/*kalû*. There is no cross-dressing. He is not turned into a female. He marries a woman and has children with her. It is his job to make music, especially on drums, originally lamentations to soothe the heart of deity and human alike. When he soothes the heart of the goddess of death herself, he gets Inana as a prize. He is not third gender; he is not a gender bender. He is a musician.

In the end, it must be noted that the primary reason so many scholars have assumed that this character must be sexually suspect is because of his association with Inana/Ištar. This caused scholars to interpret all data associated with this category of individual in the most sexual light. For example, in their study of 3rd-millennium legal and administrative texts, Piotr Steinkeller and J.N. Postgate suggested that the cuneiform signs that make up the word GALA (UŠ + TUŠ) should actually be read GIŠ + DÚR = "penis" + "anus."[44] As the "penis and anus man," the GALA simply had to be some kind of homosexual, right? It is unlikely they would have suggested such a reading if the GALA were associated with, for example, Gula, the goddess of healing.

However, as Ilan Peled has observed, this association with the goddess of love and war was a later aspect of the GALA/*kalû*'s role in Mesopotamian society:

> It seems that in the early periods the gala had no connection whatsoever with this goddess (Ištar). He was a cultic lamenter operating in funerals. He is found in contexts relating to the goddess only in later periods, but not earlier than the Old Babylonian period, from where the narratives, myths and proverbs testifying to the connection between the GALA/*kalû* and Inanna/Ištar stem.[45]

Kurgarrû

If there is no evidence for gender abnormality in the GALA/*kalû*, this is doubly the case with the *kurgarrû*, who not only manifests clear masculine gender but *hegemonic* masculine gender at that. The *kurgarrû* is a cultic warrior, or at least a war-dancer.

As with the GALA previously and the *assinnu* subsequently, the *kurgarrû* was most suspected of gender non-normativity because of his connection with the cult of Inana/Ištar. This connection and its relation to gender bending appeared especially pronounced in the 1st-millennium narrative the *Erra Epic*, wherein the poet claimed (Tablet 4, ll. 52–59):[46]

> As for Uruk, dwelling of Anu and Ištar, city of the *kezrētu*s, *šamḫatu*s, and
> *harimtu*s,
> whom Ištar deprived of husband and delivered into the[ir]/yo[ur] hands;
> The male and female Suteans, who shout "*yarurūt*[*u*]!",
> rose up (in/against) the Eanna; *kurgarrû*s; *assinnu*s,

who, for making the people reverent, Ištar turned their masculinity to f[emininity;]

(*šá ana šup-lu-uḫ*UN.MEŠ ^d**Inana** *zik-ru-su-nu ú-te-ru ana* M[UNUS-*ti*])

The carriers of dagger, carriers of razor, scalpel and flin[t](-blade);

(Those) who, for delighting the mind of Ištar, do regularly . . . .

You have plac[ed] over them a cruel and merciless governor.

That line about how the goddess "turned their masculinity into femininity" spoke strongly for notions of gender bending, for the *kurgarrûs* and the *assinnus*. The problem here, though, is that the word "femininity" is almost entirely restored. Ultimately, we have no idea what Ištar did with their masculinity. What we can read is that these men were carriers of edged weapons: daggers, razors, scalpels, and flints. With these they did . . . something[47] . . . to delight the mind of Ištar.

As discussed, in the Old Babylonian version of *Inana's Descent*, the *kurgarrû* joined the GALA in rescuing the body of Inana from the domain of Ereškigal, primarily by soothing the goddess's heart with compassion and sympathy. Even earlier evidence linking this functionary to Inana/Ištar comes from a Sumerian Hymn (A) of King Iddin-Dagan of Isin, wherein it reads (ll. 76–80):

The ecstatic *kurgarrûs* grasped the *patarru* [weapon],
they walk before pure Inana.
The one who covers the sword with blood, he sprinkles blood,
they walk before pure Inana.
He pours out blood on the dais of the throne-room.[48]

Evidence from Isin-Larsa through Neo-Assyrian times reveals that the *kurgarrûs* were involved in the cult of Inana/Ištar, that they soothed/delighted the mind of this goddess, and that they were associated with weapons, especially edged weapons. Numerous literary texts—*Inana and Enki*, Segment I,19–23; *This City, which Has Been Looted*, Tablet 19,16–19 and 48–59; *Inana and Ebiḫ*, 171–175—all refer to the *patarru* sword/weapon as the distinctive attribute of the *kurgarrû*, just as the latter two describe the drum as the distinctive attribute of the *kalû* (as a matter of fact, in *This City Which Has Been Looted*, the *kalû* uses his *manzû* drum to kill a maidservant who has displeased Inana!).

Later texts, all dating to the Neo-Assyrian period, mention that the *kurgarrû* engaged in some kind of war dance in honor of the goddess. Thus we read that:[49]

CT 15.44, 28'

[^{lú}]KUR-GAR-RA.MEŠ *ša tu-šá-ri i-ma-li-lu mì-il-ḫu i-m*[*al-lu-ḫu*]

The *kurgarrûs* who play war, per[form] *milḫu*.

While K 3438a + K 9912 obv. 9'—11' // K 9923, 15–16 has:

^{lú} KUR-GAR-RA.MEŠ *mi-lu-li‹-i› qab-lu-ú i-za-mu-ru* ^{lú} UR-MUNUS.MEŠ *ia-ru-ru-tú úsaḫ-ḫu-ru mi-il-ḫu i-ma-al-lu-ḫu*

190 *Gender Bending*

The *kurgarrû*s sing: "my play is battle." The *assinnu*s reply: "*yarurūtu*!" and *perform milḫu.*

As Ilona Zsolnay describes it:

> In the festival setting, *kurgarrû* and *assinnū* seem to have reenacted the turmoil of war. A Neo-Assyrian ritual text records that *assinnū* may have sung a song titled "Battle Is My Game, Warfare Is My Game" (*mēlilī qablu mē[lilī] tāḫāzu*), after which the *assinnū* "goes down to battle" and executes the whirl dance (*gūštu*). In a similar ritual *kurgarrû* are said to sing the song titled "Battle Is My Game" (*mēlulī qablu*), and *assinnū* answer with a kind of shout (*yarrurutu*). The *assinnū* are then said to *milḫu imalluḫū*, an opaque phrase that has been understood to mean the wildly differing concepts of "rip and tear themselves" or, more likely, "perform a dance or song."[50]

The idea that the *kurgarrû*s "rip and tear themselves" derives from a belief that these male cult functionaries of Ištar behaved like the *galli* devoted to Phrygian Kybele, and that they self-castrated in a frenzied ritual (although, presumably, not more than once). Kybele is not Ištar, even in the amazingly syncretistic world of the 1st-millennium Mediterranean, and the evidence for *galli* post-date the *kurgarrû* by a millennium at least. So assuming that the *kurgarrû*s were using their knives on themselves is functionally groundless.

Besides, like the GALA, they had children. Thus a Neo-Assyrian legal text (ADD 160) includes as a witness (IGI):

IGI ᵐ*šá-la*-GAŠAN-*man-nu* DUMU ᵐ·ᵈIštar-bàd ˡúKUR-GAR-RA

Witness: Ša-la-Bēlet-mannu, son of Ištar-dūri the *kurgarrû*.[51]

There is far less documentation pertaining to the *kurgarrû* than to either the GALA/*kalû* or the *assinnu*. But what we do have reveals a male cultic performer in the entourage of Ištar. He is associated with bladed weapons and with notions of bloodshed and (mock) warfare. As we saw in Chapter 3, these are the most distinctive hallmarks of masculine gender. Rather than a "third" or "non-normative" gender, the *kurgarrû*'s role in cult seems to have been to play out the idea of hegemonic masculinity, either as an aspect of Ištar herself or as something that the goddess found entertaining. Or both.

SAG.UR.SAG/ˡúUR.MUNUS/Assinnu[52]

This is the most intently scrutinized character in the Mesopotamian repertoire in the search for gender-bending males. A huge part of the issue, other than the association with Ištar, is that the signs that compose the logogram ˡúUR.MUNUS consist of that sign for "person" discussed in Chapter 1 (LÚ); a sign that can mean, among other things,

Gender Bending 191

"man" (UR); and a standard sign for "woman" (MUNUS). "Mr. Man-Woman" is not as bad as, say, "Mr. Penis-Anus," perhaps, but considering the already overwhelming tendency to oversexualize anything associated with Ištar, obviously this was going to be used as evidence for the gender-bending character of this cult functionary.

A few things to keep in mind about this orthography. First, the ^{lú}UR.MUNUS nomenclature only appeared late in the existence of the *assinnu*—in the Neo-Assyrian period. Before this, the logogram used was SAG.UR.SAG. Second, as with most cuneiform signs, multiple readings are possible. As Ilona Zsolnay pithily describes the options:

> lu_2 = the determinative for "person" or "being;" ur = "dog," "lion," "man," "servant," etc.; and SAL, if read sal, = "feminine" or "thin"; or, if read munus, = "woman," or "female." It is even possible that the meaning for ^{lu2}ur.munus could be "servant of women." (The reading "female servant" for ^{lu2}ur.sal is unlikely, as this is regularly rendered geme$_2$ [SAL.KUR].)[53]

Basically, the logograms might also be understood as "lioness," "bitch," "slender man," or "servant of the woman." Considering the fact that Inana/Ištar is often called "the woman" (MUNUS) in Sumerian-language hymns, it would be perfectly reasonable to suggest that the *assinnu* was known as "The servant of the Woman (Inana)" in a cultic context. This is not what we find. We find him called a passive homosexual transvestite hermaphrodite and male cultic prostitute.

There are, to be fair, some good reasons to wonder at the gender identity of the *assinnu* beyond just his association with Ištar. Like the title ^{lú}UR.MUNUS, though, these date mainly to the Neo-Assyrian period, long into the history of this role. The one datum summoned from before this period is the *Hymn of Iddin-Dagan* discussed previously. The relevant lines are (45–68):

> The SAG.UR.SAG comb their hair before her,
> they walk before pure Inana.
> They decorate the napes of their necks with colored bands,
> they walk before pure Inana.
> They place upon their bodies the cloak/skin of divinity,
> they walk before pure Inana.
> The righteous man/king and the first lady, the woman of the great wise women,
> they walk before pure Inana.
> Those who are in charge? of beating? the soothing *balag*,
> they walk before pure Inana.
> They gird themselves with the sword belt, the arm of battle,
> they walk before pure Inana.
> The spear, the arm of battle, they grasp in their hands,
> they walk before pure Inana.
>   *Fourth kirugu*
> **They adorn their right side with male clothing,**
> they walk before pure Inana.

192 *Gender Bending*

To the great lady of heaven, Inana, I would cry "Hail!"
They place female clothing on their left side,
they walk before pure Inana.
To the great lady of heaven, Inana, I would cry "Hail!"[54]

The references to adorning the right side with men's clothing, the left side with women's clothing, suggested ritual transvestitism to pretty much everyone. The SAG.UR.SAG, combing their hair!,[55] are understood to be the subjects, with references to "those who beat the soothing *balag* [drum]" calling to mind the GALA/*kalû*, who must also be involved in this ritual cross-dressing.

Two things should be kept in mind here. First, there are several characters, not all male, between the SAG.UR.SAG and the references to clothing. This includes the man or king (there are variations on different tablets) and the "first lady" (probably the queen), as well as whoever is beating the drum and whoever is taking up the sword belt and the arm of battle. In good Sumerian fashion, none of "them" are gendered, other than the king and queen. Furthermore, we know that Inana/Ištar had female cult functionaries as well as male, and it is wholly feasible that they were involved in this procession. As a result, we need not assume that the reference to male–female clothing pertains specifically to the SAG.UR.SAG, or to any individual in the ritual. We might have here a reference to a procession with male attendants on the right, female to the left.

Corollary: There may well be transvestitism taking place here. Or at least some kind of half-body transvestitism. But, again, this need not pertain exclusively to the SAG.UR.SAG, and it does not indicate that transvestitism was a part of any of the participants' *personal* identities. An *onnagata* dresses as a female for a kabuki performance, but this does not make him a transvestite generally.

Second, there actually isn't that much difference between male and female clothing in the late 3rd–early 2nd millennia (Figure 4.1). Per the statuary of humans, we see men wearing skirts and women wearing skirts with an upper wrap, especially draped over the left shoulder ("They place female clothing on their left side"). However, when in formal wear, males might also have a wrap draped over the left shoulder, as is the typical dress of King Gudea of Lagaš (see Figure 2.23).

To argue for any kind of "transvestitism" in Mesopotamia at all, one would first have to distinguish clearly between male and female garb.

Coming down to the 1st millennium, the most conclusive bit of evidence for a gender-bending aspect of the *assinnu* is list *ḪAR-gud B*, line 133, wherein the scribe wrote:

[ᶫᵘ]UR-MUNUS =   [*a*]*s-sin-nu = sin-niš-* ⌈*a*⌉ -[*nu*]
"man-woman" =   [*a*]*ssinnu* = woman-l[ike][56]

The final word is restored, but likely. So is the second. This is the best, and only, current evidence for the gender bending of the *assinnu*. It isn't much to go on.

Gender Bending 193

Figure 4.1 Early Dynastic Dedicatory Figurines from Tell Asmar, Oriental Institute D32373.
Source: Courtesy of the Oriental Institute of the University of Chicago.

Other data pulled into the fray are far, far more ambiguous. Commonly cited are references to the *assinnu* in sexually explicit omen texts. For example, in the 1st-millennium composition Šumma ālu 104, lines 32–34, we read:

šumma amēlu(NA) a-na as-sin-ni iṭeḫu(TE) dan-na-tu ipaṭṭaršu
šumma amēlu(NA) a-na girseqû iṭeḫu(TE) ka-la šatti 1KÁM
tam-ṭa-a-tum šá šaknā-šú ip-pa-ra-sa
šumma amēlu(NA) ana du-uš-mi-šú iṭeḫu sassu iṣabbassu

If a man has sexual relations with an *assinnu*, hardships will be unleashed from him.
If a man has sexual relations with a *girseqû*, for an entire year the losses that beset him will be kept away.
If a man has sexual relations with a male house-born-slave, hardship will seize him.[57]

It is presented as a good thing for a man (*amēlu*) to have sexual intercourse with an *assinnu* or a *girseqû* (palace personnel) but inauspicious for him to have sex with a household slave. The mere fact that the *assinnu* could be conceived of as the recipient of another man's sexuality cast an aura of (passive) homosexuality upon him. However, this fails to consider the context and ideology of the omen texts generally. The omen texts account for numerous potentialities, both realistic and otherwise ("If a sheep is born with no head . . ."). Furthermore, the Šumma ālu omens present numerous potential sexual partners for a man, both male and

194   *Gender Bending*

female, of varying social classes. Consider, for example, another *Šumma ālu* omen:

> If a man has anal sex with his social peer, that man will become foremost among his brothers and colleagues.[58]

Basically: *Anyone* can be the recipient of sexual advances in the omen series. It is methodologically unsound to single out the *assinnu* as a potential passive homosexual recipient without recognizing that the entire population of Mesopotamia was in the same potential category.

Instead, what becomes a pattern is that if an independent male (*amēlu*) has sex with another male of a free class (i.e. not a slave), that man has prosperity. By contrast, should that *amēlu* have sex with a social inferior (e.g. a slave of his own household), hardships will beset him. One might read this as a condemnation of sexual exploitation, or a suggestion to mingle with one's own kind, rather than seeing it as evidence that the *assinnu* (but not the slave *or* the peer!) is some kind of transvestite homosexual third gender.

A second omen that has been read as indicating the non-normative gender/sexuality of the *assinnu* is *Šumma ālu* Tablet 104, 15

> DIŠ NA *ana zi-ka-ru-ti ina ki-li uš-tak-ti-it-ma u ina* ZI-*e*/*ni-iš na-aq zi-ka-ru-ta ḫu-uš-šu-uḫ-šu i-na pí-qí* ḪUL IGI

Which has been translated as either:

> If a man excited himself to "manhood" in prison, and like an *assinnu* manhood's intercourse is deprived from him, he will experience misfortune in distress.[59]

Or

> If a man excites himself to "manhood" in captivity but, when erect, the rise of the emission (?) of "manhood" is denied him, that man will experience one-time misfortune.[60]

Ann Guinan, the second translator, has argued that the signs reading "*assinnu*" do not compose one word and that this individual is not actually part of the omen.[61] As such, the omen reveals not so much that *assinnu*s are impotent or even castrated but that an erection without orgasm/ejaculation is a signal for bad luck.

So what *was* the *assinnu*? There are actually rather few data, and most effort in the modern scholarship has been directed to his sexuality rather than his function.

An initial understanding was that he was some kind of ecstatic prophet, based on three texts from ancient Mari in which Queen Šibtu sent the prophesies of two *assinnu*s to her husband King Zimri-Lim (ARM 26 197, 198, and 213; ARM 26 212).[62] These men—Šēlebum and Ili-ḫaznaya—delivered divine messages from the goddess Annunītum, a goddess syncretized with Ištar. For a while, then, it was suggested that *assinnu*s were prophets and, of course, transgender prophets at that. However, as Ilona Zsolney has observed, numerous individuals from Mari were recorded has having gone into some kind of trance to deliver oracles to the royal family, including a servant girl (ARM 26 214).[63] These are not professional prophets but people somehow close to the royal family who, one way or another, serve as conduits for divine expression. As such, the *assinnu* cannot be understood as a *professional* oracle or prophet.

Instead, there are data that indicate that, much as with the *kurgarrû*, the *assinnu* was a cultic warrior of some kind, and one relevant for the performance of purification/healing rituals. The warrior function is predicated on the equivalence between Sumerian SAG.UR.SAG and Akkadian *assinnu*, with all due caveats. Already in the Old Babylonian period, the correspondence between these two terms and other words pertaining to heroism were explicit. Thus, in texts *SAG B i 13–14 // SAG A i 8–9*, we read:

| 13//8 SAG UR-SAG | *qar-ra-du* | *qarrādu*/hero |
| 14//9 SAG-UR-SAG | *as-sí-nu* | *assinnu*[64] |

A few Sumerian texts connect the SAG.UR.SAG with notions of heroism and valor. In the *Debate Between Ewe and Grain*, Grain contends:

> Sister, I am your better; I take precedence over you. I am the glory of the lights of the Land. I grant my power to the SAG.UR.SAG—he fills the palace with awe and people spread his fame to the borders of the Land. I am the gift of the Anuna gods. I am central to all princes. After I have conferred my power on the warrior [UR.SAG.RA], when he goes to war he knows no fear, he knows no faltering (?)—I make him leave . . . as if to the playing field.
>
> (ETCSL 5.3.2:71–82)[65]

Likewise, in the Old Babylonian Sumerian hymn to Inana *Uru-Amirabi*, Inana claims to bring NAM.UR.SAG (heroism) for the SAG.UR.SAG (appearing as the Akkadian *assinnu* is a later version of the hymn).[66] So, there is strong evidence that the SAG.UR.SAG at least was similar to the *kurgarrû* in that both were warrior(-like) males associated with the cult of Inana/Ištar. At least some evidence shows the continued equivalence between the Sumerian SAG.UR.SAG and the *assinnu*, and thus that the *assinnu* may have also filled this role.

In the realms of ritual, as opposed to literature, the *assinnu* shows up in contexts together with the *kurgarrû*. Thus in the Neo-Assyrian Akītu festival (New Year's), (K 9876 + K 19534 obv. 10–12):

⌈*i*⌉*-di ana idi ša* ᵈINANA TIN-TIRKI [G]I?-GÍD *as-sin-nu u* LÚKUR-GAR-RA
[*e*]*l-le-e-a*
el-le-e-a-ma

196 *Gender Bending*

Side by side of Ištar-of-Babylon, the [fl]ute(-playing) *assinnu* and *kurgarrû* (sing:) ["*e*]*llea, ellea*", and . . .[67]

Peled suggests that the *assinnu*s and *kurgarrû*s are escorting a statue of Ištar in procession, playing musical instruments.[68]

Other texts show the *assinnu* in rituals pertaining to illness and healing, sometimes associated with the healing goddess Gula rather than Ištar. Thus, in one *Incantation for Ištar*, we read:

May your *assinnu* stand by and extract my illness. May he make the illness which seized me go out the window.[69]

Likewise:

After you have recited this three times, you have the *assinnu* take the *kamānu*-cakes offered to Gula and the scales, and have him leave by the door[70]

Perhaps all we can say is that the *assinnu* is a cult functionary of some sort who works in the cult of Inana/Ištar. His connections to the SAG.UR.SAG on the one hand and the *kurgarrû* on the other, as well as his connection to the martial manifestation of Ištar as Annunnītum in Mari, all strongly suggest that his role had a martial character, either as a warrior, the fife-and-drum band, or both. He is far closer to depictions of hegemonic masculinity than third gender, and it might be a really good time to start focusing on this character as ritualist rather than as a catamite.

These are not all the data pertaining to these male cult functionaries of Inana/Ištar; that would be a monograph-length book, and in fact is a monograph-length book in Ilan Peled's 2016 publication *Masculinities and Third Gender*, which I recommend for those interested in more on these individuals. But what is presented here provides a taste of both the information we have on these individuals and what has been understood about them over the past century or so.

A few significant points reveal themselves. The first is that it is not the data—the primary sources—that caused these men to be seen as effeminate, transvestite, homosexual, intersex, castrated prostitutes, but simply their association with the goddess Inana/Ištar as seen by the 19th- and 20th-century scholars who originally studied them. Unable to deal particularly well with a violent, intensely erotic goddess, these Victorian, biblically trained scholars (and, ironically, their New Age successors) turned her into a paragon of fertility and her male servants into perverted (by Victorian standards) catamites. As Julia Assante deftly put it: "It is scholarship, not Ishtar, who has emasculated them, turning them into passive 'homosexuals', prostitutes, transvestites, eunuchs, hermaphrodites and self-lacerating masochists, circulating like minor moons around a celestial fetish."[71]

Second, it is an interesting fact that it is only the *male* cult functionaries who received this treatment. Somehow, there are no overtly masculinized female cult

Gender Bending 197

functionaries of Inana/Ištar. The gender bending only goes in one direction—from masculine to feminine—even when, as we have seen, there are references to parades in which it could easily be suggested that females are carrying weapons:

The male and female Suteans, who shout "*yarurūt[u]!*",
rose up (in/against) the Eanna . . .

If Inana/Ištar is a gender bender, it should go both ways. It does not. The only other time we see male-to-female gender bending in the ANE corpus is in the insults and curses typically associated with warfare, as discussed in Chapter 1. Either warriors claim that their enemies are women as a form of derision, or those signing treaties are threatened with feminization should they not follow the terms of said treaty. But this is rhetoric, even invective. It is not an expression of lived reality. Remarkably, there are no curses that threaten to turn a woman into a man.[72]

Instead—third point here—what we see in the modern scholarship is that both male and female cult functionaries become *prostitutes*. We have already seen how modern scholars have been far too blithe to identify any female associated with Ištar as a (sacred) prostitute (and several not associated with her at all—the *nadītus*, the *entus*, etc.). Just so have the male cult functionaries been dubbed prostitutes, specifically castrated, homosexual, transvestite prostitutes. I believe the only reason they are not consistently called "sacred" prostitutes in the academic literature is that this would have disrupted the fertility paradigm imagined for female sacred prostitution. Once again to quote Assante:

Either these men are "homosexuals", transvestites, eunuchs, hermaphrodites, temple prostitutes servicing other men, or impotent. In other words, they are travesties of manhood. Although scholars could imagine women being subordinated to "straight" sexual roles, particularly in service to fertility, as "natural", the subordination of men could not be construed as natural, especially under the command of a female deity. Nor could homosexual acts be configured as a fertility rite.[73]

What, then, are we to make of references to the swapping of sexes such as that which began this section:

She (Ištar) [changes] the right side into the left side,
she [changes] the left side into the right side,
she [turns] a man into a woman,
she [turns] a woman into a man . . .

If we were to read, for example, *Inana: Lady of Largest Heart* in more of its totality, we would notice that changing male and female are actually only two examples of switching binary opposites in this poem. Along side lines such as

198   *Gender Bending*

"To turn a man into a woman and a woman into a man are yours, Inana" we also see,

> To shatter earth and to make it firm are yours, Inana.
> To destroy, to build up, to tear out and to settle are yours, Inana.
> Neglect and care, raising and bowing down are yours, Inana.
> To interchange the brute and the strong and the weak and the powerless is yours, Inana.
> To interchange the heights and valleys, and raising up and reducing, is yours, Inana.[74]

To undo reality, to swap binaries, to control the nature of existence are Inana's. It need not be seen simply in terms of sex or gender but in the whole of reality.

> Could make a lady seem a knight;
> The cobwebs on a dungeon wall
> Seem tapestry in lordly hall;
> A nutshell seem a gilded barge,
> A sheeling seem a palace large;
> And youth seem age, and age seem youth;
> All was delusion, naught was truth.
> ("Lay of the Last Minstrel,"
> Sir Walter Scott)

As we shall see, all other references to gender bending in the ancient Near East go female to male. As seen in previous chapters, men were the dominant sex, to one extent or another, in ancient Near Eastern societies, and thus females taking on masculine roles and attributes accorded them a level of power typically denied to regular females.

Violent Goddesses and Heroines

Are warrior goddesses gender benders, or are females more commonly associated with warfare than we give them credit for? The answer is: It depends.

In some societies, females (mortal) are martial. This is especially if somewhat recently being brought to light for cultures such as the Gauls/Celts, Vikings, Scythians, and Sarmatians (the latter two often understood as the basis for the Amazons).[75] Whereas it was once typical to establish the male sex of a grave occupant based on the presence of weapons, the greater use of physical anthropology—examining the bones—has shown that this is simply not always, or even necessarily usually, the case.[76] For some societies, then, having a warrior goddess (Freyja) next to a warrior god (Tyr) appears to reflect the society's own gender constructs of what was (apparently) seen to be acceptable for and/or typical of females and males. Being a warrior deity is perfectly feminine (as well as masculine).

The situation is not so clear cut for other cultures. For example: the ancient Greeks. The Greeks had two primary war deities: Athene and Ares. *Stygeros* ("hateful") Ares represented the baneful aspects of war: violence, terror, destruction. Athene embodied the more noble aspects of strategy and tactics—perfectly reasonable as she was also a goddess of wisdom (and the daughter of a goddess of wisdom).

But apart from some quaint (and late!) tales from Plutarch and Pausanias about women who, when their men were away, took up arms to defeat—specifically—the Spartans,[77] we have no evidence for martial activity on the part of women from ancient Greece. Not even Spartan women were said to take up arms. So, for the ancient Greeks, a female war goddess is, in fact, gender bending, insofar as she is engaged in a distinctly masculine endeavor. Furthermore, this goes along with other aspects of Athene's gender bending. While a warrior goddess (masculine), she is also the goddess of weaving and handicrafts (feminine). After Zeus swallowed her pregnant mother, Athene was born from a male—an exceptionally gender-bending experience, one she shared with her half-brother, the feminine Dionysos, who was born from Zeus' thigh.

The one aspect where Athene's female sex corresponds with her masculine gender in terms of warfare is her virginity. Virginity is absolutely, positively not gendered masculine in Greek society. The one male who fiercely guarded his virginity—Hippolytos—was punished with death by horse trampling at the behest of his own father. *No* Greek god has gone on the record as being a virgin. But four Greek goddesses are extolled for this quality—Hestia, Artemis, Hekate, and, of course, Athene. For Hestia, this quality connotes her stability: the virgin daughter who remains at her father's hearth rather than marrying and moving to her husband's abode.[78] For Artemis, her virginity reflects her perpetual adolescence: the goddess who is always at the brink of womanhood without passing over.[79] What did Athene's virginity mean? That she had not been "breached" by a male in the way that the walls of a conquered city would be breached and the women raped by invading, conquering males. Athene's virginity was a symbol of her unconquered nature as a successful war goddess and the type of protection she provided as citadel goddess.[80]

So, in the end, Athene is a gender-bending goddess, in part because of her role as a martial deity—a masculine association. But at least some aspect of that martial character is dependent on an aspect of her feminine gender—the *virgo intacta*.

What, then, are we to make of the martial qualities of some rather prominent Near Eastern goddesses?

Inana/Ištar

Ištar really should be a gender-bending goddess. Her Semitic name derives from the mixing of Inana (Sumerian) with the Semitic astral-warrior god Aštar (male). So she is male and female combined, with a name that is grammatically masculine, lacking the feminizing –t of the Semitic and Hametic languages. Technically, Ištar should be Ištart, much as her western cognate is Athtart/Aštart, a.k.a. Astarte.

200   Gender Bending

This led to some considerable gender ambiguity/confusion in the Syrian city of Mari, a city located on the upper Euphrates and a natural melting pot between Mesopotamian and west Semitic cultures. Several 3rd-millennium inscriptions from two temples reveal both "male" and "female" Ištars. The first comes from the so-called Ištar temple discovered in 1934, where one of three similar dedications reads:

Lam-gi₄-Ma-eri	Lamgi-Mari
LUGAL *Ma-eri*	King of Mari
ENSÍ.GAL	great governor
ᵈEN.LÍL	of Enlil
ALAM-*su*	his statue
a-na	to
ᵈMÙŠ.UŠ	male Inana
A.MU.RU	dedicated.[81]

The MÙŠ logogram in the second to last line of the inscription is read as the name Inana, while the UŠ sign is a masculine element, as we saw in Chapter 1.[82] As such, it appears that the deity of the temple complex is some manner of "male" Inana, as all three inscribed votives are dedicated to this same deity.

Other inscriptions come from the temple complex to the south of the so-called "Massif Rouge." Here were found small, inscribed statues representing dedicators, as well as an inscribed vase.[83] The two divine names to whom these items were dedicated are MÙŠ.ZA.ZA and the more phonetically construed *(G)iš-dar-ra-at*.[84] Thus a votive from the royal intendant reads:

. . . . . .	
PA. É	Intendant of the "house"
GAL. LÚ	of the king
*In-ha-da*ᵏⁱ	of Inhada
DUL-*su*	his statue
ᵈMÙŠ.ZA.ZA	to female Inana
TUG.SAG.DU	he dedicated.[85]

By contrast, the dedication of Suwada reads:

I-ku-ᵈŠa-ma-gan	Iku-Šamagan
LUGAL *Ma-ri*ᵏⁱ	King of Mari
Su-wa-d[a]	Suwada
QA.ŠU.DU₈	the singer (?)
DUMU.NITA	son
Be-bu-BAD	of Bebu-BAD
RAŠ.GA	the great merchant
ᵈÍD	of the river
ᵈ*(G)eš-dar-ra-at*	to Ešdarrat
SAG.TUG	dedicated.[86]

Gender Bending 201

In some cases it seems that the two names ^{d}MÙŠ.ZA.ZA and ^{d}(G)eš-dar-ra-at were either combined or confused. On an inscription from Dubla, the dedication is made to ^{d}MÙŠ.GIŠ.TIR, while a man identified as "the son of Wananni" dedicated his statue to ^{d}NIN-*darat*.[87] It would appear, then, that rather than two separate goddesses, the names MÙŠ.ZA.ZA and *E/Išdar(r)at* refer to the same deity, one in Sumerian or ideographic form, the other in syllabic form. The ideogram MÙŠ is, once again, taken as an ideogram for the name Inana, and thus what we have at the temple by the Massif Rouge is a cult place of the goddess known either as Ešdar(r)at or as "female" Inana. This is the earliest instance of the divine name Aštar(a)t and the earliest association of this name with the Mesopotamian goddess Inana/Ištar.[88]

It is possible that these deities were understood as the Marian equivalents of Athtar and Aštart, with MÙŠ.UŠ being Athtar, the male Venus deity familiar to the Semitic peoples inhabiting Mari, while MÙŠ.ZA.ZA/Ešdarat might be understood as Ištar/Aštart, the newer, Mesopotamian, female version of this god, who eventually ousted her male counterpart from the pantheon.[89] An alternative opinion, offered by K. Gawlikowska, suggests that rather than a male and female pair of deities, the Marians worshipped one goddess under her male and female names, with the MÙŠ.UŠ not necessarily referring to the sex of the deity but rather the gender of her name. Thus MÙŠ.UŠ would be Ištar (grammatically masculine), while MÙŠ.ZA.ZA is Ašdarat/Aštart, a feminine name.[90]

So, yes, Ištar can be quite a gender-ambivalent character, potentially even for her own worshippers.

To what extent Inana/Ištar breaks gender norms, or was understood to break gender norms, is more difficult to determine. Again, part of the problem comes down to the extent to which we apply *contemporary* gender conventions to her and to what extent we study her through *our own* gender constructs. Thus Rivkah Harris suggested:

> Central to the goddess as paradox is her well-attested psychological and more rarely evidenced physiological androgyny. Inanna-Ishtar is both female and male. Over and over again the texts juxtapose the masculine and feminine traits and behavior of the goddess. She can be at one and the same time compassionate, supportive, and nurturing as well as assertive, aggressive, and strong-willed. In short, she breaks the boundaries between the sexes by embodying both femaleness and maleness.[91]

So, which is which? Obviously we are supposed to assume that compassion and nurturing are feminine attributes, while being assertive and strong-willed are masculine. As we saw in Chapters 2 and 3, this worked for the Mesopotamians to a certain extent, although they would have seen far, far more of the goddess's femininity in her insatiable sex drive. But compassionate, assertive, and strong-willed do not appear to have been gendered one way or another for the Mesopotamians the way they would have been in, say, mid–20th-century America (or now . . .). All kings establishing law codes for their people do so out of benevolence (compassion) and

202   *Gender Bending*

in pious duties to the gods. I doubt they thought of themselves as feminine in those instances.

But belligerence and a martial persona are most certainly gendered masculine, so as a war goddess, an *extremely* martial war goddess, Inana/Ištar must perforce have a masculine element to her character. There is nothing subtle about it: *Exultation of Inana/Inana: Lady of Largest Heart* (ll. 20–33)

> At your battle-cry, my lady, the foreign lands bow low. When humanity comes before you in awed silence at the terrifying radiance and tempest, you grasp the most terrible of all the divine powers. Because of you, the threshold of tears is opened, and people walk along the path of the house of great lamentations. In the van of battle, all is struck down before you. With your strength, my lady, teeth can crush flint. You charge forward like a charging storm. You roar with the roaring storm, you continually thunder with Iškur. You spread exhaustion with the stormwinds, while your own feet remain tireless. With the lamenting BALAĜ drum a lament is struck up.[92]

Inana vs. Ebih (ll. 1–9)

> Goddess of the fearsome divine powers, clad in terror, riding on the great divine powers, Inana, made perfect by the holy A-AN-KAR weapon, drenched in blood, rushing around in great battles, with shield resting on the ground (?), covered in storm and flood, great lady Inana, knowing well how to plan conflicts, you destroy mighty lands with arrow and strength and overpower lands.
>
> In heaven and on earth you roar like a lion and devastate the people. Like a huge wild bull you triumph over lands which are hostile. Like a fearsome lion you pacify the insubordinate and unsubmissive with your gall.[93]

Thus too of Akkadian Ištar:

> I rain battle down like flames in the fighting,
> I make heaven and earth shake (?) with my cries,
> I . . ., I make my feet . . .
> I, Ištar, am queen of heaven and (?) earth.
> I am the queen, . . .
> I constantly traverse heaven, then (?) I trample the earth,
> I destroy what remains of the inhabited world,
> I devastate (?) the lands hostile to Šamaš.
> I am the most heroic of the gods,
> she who slays the inhabited world,
> I draw back on its bridle (?), he who slays . . .
> The [Mo]on-god begot me, I abound in terror![94]

In spite of this intensely martial character complementing her intensely erotic character, there is relatively little that is pointedly transgender about the goddess.

She remains, for the most part, resolutely female/feminine. Apart from martial characteristics, her masculine aspects are few in number.

Perhaps most masculine is the fact that she occasionally, rarely, has a beard. This appears in a single 1st-millennium bilingual hymn to the goddess once she had syncretized with the goddess Nanâ/Nanaya. It begins (ll. 2–4):

> Wise daughter of Sîn, beloved sister of Šamaš, I am powerful in Borsippa,
> I am a *ḫarīmtu* in Uruk, I have heavy breasts in Daduni,
> I have a beard in Babylon, still I am Nanaya.[95]

Equally masculinizing in appearance is the fact that she is the only goddess to be portrayed with her feet separated in the glyptic iconography. Typically, females (women and goddesses) when shown standing are still with their feet together. They are stationary, one could even argue "passive." By contrast, Ištar appears to be striding, active, much as male divine beings. Thus, on an Akkadian-period cylinder seal, we see an active, armed Ištar dominating a lion while a more static Lamma goddess stands before her (Figure 4.2):

Finally, there is the fact that every once and a while the goddess refers to herself as male. In the same hymn where she claims to be a "loving *ḫarīmtu* who knows the penis" she also claims:

É KAŠ-A-KA TUŠ-A-[ĜU₁₀-NE] NU-NUS-ĜENŠUL GIRI₁₇-ZAL-LA ME-E-ĜEN-[NA]

When I sit in the alehouse, I am a woman, and I am an exuberant young man.[96]

In a Hellenistic-period bilingual hymn we read:

[NU.NUN]UZ.MÈN GURUŠ KA.ZAL ME.E ŠI.IN.GA.MÈN
Sinnišāku eṭlu mu-tál-lum anāku[ma]
Though I am a woman, I am a noble young man.[97]

It is clear that Inana/Ištar is at her most masculine when in martial guise. The attribute is a dominant sign of masculinity throughout the ANE, and she wields

Figure 4.2 Akkadian Seal Depicting Ištar, Oriental Institute A27903.
Source: Drawing by Paul C. Butler. Used with kind permission.

204   *Gender Bending*

it with a passion. When portrayed with weapons, she is also shown striding, even dominating, in a posture that is far more typical of males than females in the iconographic history of Mesopotamia. In this she is also masculine. But her masculinity need not restrict itself to contexts of violence: She is an exuberant young man at the tavern and bearded in Babylon. She is at her most masculine right when she is also claiming to be a woman, and thus we see once again her tendency to play with binary opposites. But she is never called by a masculine title in the Mesopotamian texts, and more often than not she refers to herself as a MUNUS ("woman"). Just as she can be the most feminine of women, she can also be the most masculine of women. But she is usually a woman.

Šauška

Inana/Ištar had numerous syncretic forms throughout the ANE; in Anatolia, her main cognate was the Hurrian goddess Šauška.[98] This is actually a bit of a simplification. By the mid-2nd millennium there were various geographic versions of Ištar (e.g. of Nineveh, of Arbela, etc.), and there were likewise different geographic manifestations of Šauška (e.g. of Hatti, of Lawazanta, etc.). Different "types" of Ištar were more or less similar to different "types" of Šauška. This will be relevant.

As with Ištar, the Hurrian goddess's apparent gender bending came about because of her martial persona. Certain conceptions of Šauška were absolutely martial. In the inscribed words of the great military king Hattušili III:

> And there, too, belonged to me the grace of Ištar,[99] my mistress. But the weapon that I wielded there, I seized it and handed it to my goddess, my mistress.

In ritual texts we read of the queen herself performing in honor of the armed goddess (KUB XLV 32 III 7'–10'):

> Then the priest gives her (the queen) an axe. The queen bowed. She takes the axe and dances in front of God (Šauška). Then she gives the axe and the cloth belt back to the priest, he cleans them with water and places them in front of the deity.

Some texts strongly remind us of the roles of the GALA and *kurgarrû* (IBoT III, 115, ll. 5–8):

> Then the priest ties red wool to the axe
> And he strikes the musical instrument and he dances
> He purifies them and places them before the deity (Šauška).[100]

Weapons, sometimes of gold, were given to the goddess as votive offerings.[101] However, her significant role in the realms of the erotic likewise induced worshippers to present her with offerings of golden breasts, while her powers to seduce were recorded in the epics. Thus, in *The Song of Hedammu*, we read (fragments 11 and 16):

> When Teššub finished speaking he went away, but Šauška went to the bath house. She went there to wash herself. She washed herself. She . . . She anointed herself with fine perfumed oil. She adorned herself. And . . . love ran after her like puppies.
>
> . . .
>
> Šauška holds out her naked members towards Hedammu. Hedammu sees the beautiful goddess and his penis springs forth . . .[102]

This gender complementarity resulted in Hurrian Šauška having both female and male identities in the Hurro-Hittite pantheon. In offering list KUB XXVII both Šauška of the Field and Ištar of the Heavens appear in the list of *male* deities receiving offerings, while Šauška of Hattarina, Tameninga, and Lawazantiya (among others) received offerings together with the female deities later in the list.[103] She could be dressed either as a male or as a female. At the 13th-century rock sanctuary of Yazılıkaya where the deities are shown in procession—the gods processing behind Teššub, the goddesses behind Ḫebat—Šauška is depicted twice—once in *each* category.[104] It is evident that the Bronze Age Anatolians saw this being as simultaneously female and male. Or, at least, that certain manifestations of her were feminine, while others were masculine.

Nevertheless, as Ilse Wegner observed, she was never both at once ("Zwar ist die Gottheit entweder als Mann *oder* als Frau gekleidet und mit den entsprechenden Attributen versehen, *nie aber mit beiden gemeinsam.*")[105] Furthermore, while she never refers to herself in the texts as male, she does refer to herself as female and specifically not a man. Thus, in *The Song of Ullikummi*, when Šauška goes to join her brothers to defeat eponymous rock monster, she states (§33) "If I were a . . . man, you would be . . ."[106] She then attempts to confront Ullikummi not with weapons, but with music and song (unfortunately for her, he turned out to be literally stone deaf . . .). Rather than an androgyne *per se*, argues Wegner, it might be better to see Šauška as a female deity with masculinizing elements.

And even then it depends on which version of the goddess one is studying. For cross-dressing, it is most likely to be Šauška of Lawazantiya. For martial qualities, Šauška of Šamuha is the way to go. When dealing with Šauška of Nineveh, however, one is far more likely to encounter the goddess not as martial but as a seductress,[107] while a more indigenous version of the goddess associated less with Mesopotamian Ištart than Anatolian Anzili is the goddess invoked in magic rituals.[108]

As with Ištar, Šauška is a gender bender primarily because of her martial qualities, qualities that caused her Anatolian worshippers to recognize her in part as masculine. Rather than seeing the goddess herself as non-binary, transgender, or hermaphroditic, though, she was *subdivided*, with different aspects of her persona attributed to different manifestations of the goddess. While she was never

206 *Gender Bending*

male, she could be more or less masculine depending on which version was being invoked.

Female Sex–Masculine Gender: Anat and Pughat

Anat

Ugaritic Anat is an interesting reflection on the goddess Inana/Ištar. With Inana, we have a goddess who is deemed confusing and "paradoxical" because she combines the feminine qualities of intense eroticism with the distinctly masculine attributes of the warrior ("Make love *and* war" was apparently a catch phrase of ancient Mesopotamia). Anat, by contrast, is a goddess who displays none of the feminine erotic aspect in her martial identity. Nonetheless, modern scholarship has rather insisted on *making* her erotic. The tendency, discussed in Chapter 2, of making all ANE goddesses "fertility" deities completely warped the early portrayal of this goddess. Comparing her to Ištar, early scholars claimed that, "Like Ishtar, Anath is beautiful and sexy; that she is also a ferocious warrior is the most obvious part of her character."[109] Neal Walls remarked in his monograph-length study of this goddess that previous scholars went to exorbitant lengths to imbue texts pertaining to Anat with the most lascivious translations possible. Thus,

> Such a motivation is certainly apparent to Gray . . ., who translates Anat's actions at first sighting Aqhat (1.17 vi 15), *larṣ kst tšm*, as "She raises her skirts from the earth." The better reading is clearly *larṣ kst tšpmk [l'pr]*. ". . . to the ground, she spilled her cup [in the dust]." In a particular and most fanciful interpretation, Margalit . . . understands KTU 1.18 I 22–7 as an explicit love scene between Anat and Aqhat.[110]

Basically, Anat is understood as a stereotypical "goddess of love and war."[111] This melding of masculine and feminine aspects is not without moral condemnation in the study of Anat. While modern scholars might be a tad nonplussed by Ištar, Anat as a Canaanite goddess, anathema to the people of the Bible (then and now), receives much harsher interpretations. As Peggy Day remarked:

> [Anat] is typically described as a fertility goddess and given the status of Baal's "consort," a word that can denote partnership outside of marriage. Thus her alleged sexual relationship with him is not quite legitimate. She is further alleged to act like a hooker, both to entice Baal in particular and in her general conduct.[112]

All this in spite of the fact that, as we shall see, her feminine attributes in Ugarit are minimal at best. Perhaps this is part of the problem. We can happily shake our heads in confusion at a goddess who is masculine and feminine, but a goddess who utterly defies our gender expectations in her pure masculinity is simply

Gender Bending 207

unendurable. Anyway, to be clear, Inana/Ištar is weird because she combines masculine and feminine attributes. Anat is weird because she has primarily masculine attributes. Goddesses really can't get a break.

In the texts from Ugarit, Anat is most assuredly marked by extreme violence both as a warrior and a hunter. Her hunting persona appears briefly, yet clearly, in the *Baal Cycle*, where (KTU 1.5 VI, ll. 25–28):

> Then Anat goes about hunting
> In every mountain in the heart of the earth,
> In every hill in the heart of the fields.[113]

Likewise, in text KTU 1.114, l. 23, Anat is mentioned hunting with the goddess Athtart.

Her warrior aspect comes across clearly when we first meet her in the *Baal Cycle*, where (KTU 1.3, II, ll. 4–16):

> She meets youths (*ǵlmm*) at the base of the mountain
> And lo! Anat fights in the valley,
> Battles between the two towns
> She fights the people of the coast,
> Strikes the people of the rising sun [east].
> Under her, heads are like balls,
> Above her—hands like locusts,
> Like locusts are heaps of warrior (*mhr*) hands.
> She fixes the heads to her back,
> Clasps the hands to her belt.
> Knee-deep she wades in soldiers' blood,
> Neck-deep in the gore of warriors.
> With a club she drives off captives,
> Wither her bow, the enemy.

Later, at the death of her dear friend Baal at the hands of Môt (Death) (KTU 1.6, II, ll. 30–35):

> She seizes divine Môt
> She cleaves him with a sword,
> She winnows him with a sieve,
> With fire she burns him,
> With mill stones she grinds him,
> In a field she sows him.

She boasts of the monsters and deities she has slain (CAT 1.3 III, ll. 38–42)

> Surely I fought Yamm (Sea), the beloved of El
> Surely I finished off River, the Great God,

208　*Gender Bending*

> Surely I bound Tunnan and destroyed him.
> I fought the Twisty Serpent,
> The powerful one of seven heads.[114]

And even when dealing with her own elderly father, she exhibits something less than true filial piety (CAT 1.3, V, ll. 23–25; see also CAT 1.18, Tablet 2, I, ll. 11–12)

> I will smash your head!
> I will make your beard run with blood!
> The grey hair of your beard with gore!

So, Anat is indeed a bit impetuous, without much respect for the elderly. It should be noted, though, that if one were, in fact, to argue that Anat is some kind of fertility deity, her killing of Môt—Death—to bring back Baal—giver or fertilizing rains—did have a beneficial impact on the land.

The goddess shows equally antisocial—and potentially masculine—behavior in the *Tale of Aqhat* (CAT 1.17–19), wherein she orchestrates the slaughter of the eponymous hero Aqhat—the son of Danel—when he refuses to give Anat his bow and arrows. If the refusal were not enough, it came with an insult to the goddess's perceived gender: (Colum VI, ll. 39–41):

> Bows are [weapons] of warriors;
> Will womankind now be hunting?[115]

Unlike the case of Môt, though, Anat does not kill Aqhat herself. Rather, she gets a mortal man named Yatpan to slaughter the boy when he is hunting. In *The Tale of Aqhat*, Anat is violent in spirit, but we do not see her enact violence herself.

Is the Ugaritic war goddess Anat acting in masculine fashion when she combats Môt to avenge and restore Baal, or demands Aqhat's bow, and eventually his life, from the young hero? Or is such behavior considered feminine according to the dictates of Bronze Age Ugaritic gender constructs? Is it possible that extremes of passion, irrationality, and concomitant violence are understood to be markers of out-of-control, adolescent females, thus feminine gender? Or are the violence and bloodshed as masculine for the residents of ancient Ugarit as they might be here and now?

The answer, based on the Ugaritic texts themselves, is that Anat is behaving in masculine fashion. This first and most obviously comes across in Aqhat's disdainful comment, when he asks if womankind might now be hunting. For him, clearly, this is not a normal state of affairs: Women do not hunt, are not warriors, and thus have no need for bows and arrows. Anat's desire, then, skews masculine.[116] Likewise, in the *Baal Cycle*, Anat never fights with other females. She threatens Father El, annihilates male Môt, and fights both with and against specifically male warriors (*ǵlmm, mhrm*) in her first appearance. This last passage pointedly suggests that martial violence is a masculine trait, a fact supported by non-fictional texts from the Bronze Age Levant which consistently list male names and categories as serving in martial contexts. Anat—consistently called *btlt*, adolescent girl—is a rare exception to this, an exception both divine and, ultimately, fictional.

Anat's epithet calls to mind another aspect in which the goddess does not display female gender, and this is her lack of expressed maturity and maternity. Anat does not grow up, marry, and bear children. As Neal Walls put it in his study of the goddess:

> Anat's role as life-taker demonstrates a masculine aspect of her character which directly contrasts with the feminine role of natural procreation. These contradictions between her female sex and her masculine actions result in a definite gender ambiguity from the ancient androcentric perspective; Anat causes men to bleed in death without herself bleeding in procreative sex and childbirth. . . . Significantly, Anat does not bestow life through the female process of childbirth, but through the masculine act of depriving her male enemy of his life.[117]

There is one aspect of her persona where Anat acts in a manner concordant with ANE conceptions of feminine gender: She functions as an intermediary.[118] In the *Baal Cycle*, when Baal wants a house (read: temple) of his own, he must seek the permission of the head of the pantheon for it—El. Rather than approaching El himself, Baal sends Anat to speak on his behalf (considering how that turned out, one simply must wonder at Baal's understanding of baseline diplomacy). The two together also approach El's wife Athirat to speak on their behalf, and when El accedes to his wife's request, it is Anat who brings the news to Baal (*CAT* 1.4 V, ll. 20–27). When Baal is killed by Môt, it is Anat who fetches and returns his corpse (*KTU* 1.6 I, ll. 1–18).

ANAT IN EGYPT

So, in the Levant Anat is masculine. The goddess displays far more gender ambiguity in her cult in Egypt, when she and several other Levantine deities come to be worshipped there in the New Kingdom. For the Egyptians, Anat was simultaneously a warrior goddess and consummately maternal.

Her warrior persona is clear in her iconography. As she appears on the base of the 19th Dynasty Stele of Qeh (Figure 4.3), Anat, named by inscription, is seated, wearing the long gown typical of elite Egyptian females. She bears a spear above her head, holds another spear and a shield in her other hand, and bears an *atef* crown on her head.[119] This iconography, both seated and standing, is standard for the goddess in Egypt.[120]

Likewise, on a relief inscription dating to the reign of Ramses III and located in Medinet Habu, the praise of the pharaoh boasts that "Montu and Seth are with him in every fray, Anat and Astarte are a shield for him, while Amun distinguishes his speech."[121]

210 *Gender Bending*

However, Anat was apparently favorite of Ramses II, who styled himself her child.[122] Twice in official inscriptions he calls himself the "nursling of Anat."[123] And she, apparently, was his mother. Thus a statue of Ramses II and Anat (Louvre AF 2576) has inscribed on one of its columns: "[Spoken by] Anat 'O Lord of the Two Lands, Usermaatra Setepenra, Lord of Crowns, Rameses, I am your mother Anat'."[124] A further statue of the pair (Cairo JE 6336) has Anat claiming, "I am your mother, beneficial in her love."[125]

It appears that kings were not the only ones able to suckle at the breasts of Anat. A 19th–20th-Dynasty incantation from Memphis calls on such a rapport with the goddess:

> Don't you know me, O *smn*? Behold, it is *Mri* who knows me, that I belong to the people of *'Irtḳn*, those who converse with the snakes, those who kill the [snakes], those who have made an end of the breath of their mother Qety. Behold, I have sucked at the breasts of Anat, the great cow of Seth.[126]

An actual example of Anat's *androgyny* in Egypt comes from a magical spell on pChester Beatty VII, verso 1.5–2.4. After she is raped (*'mk*) by Seth:

> Then came Anat the divine, she the victorious, a woman (*s.t-ḥm.t*) acting as a warrior (*'ḥꜣwty*), clad as men (*tꜣy.w*) and girt/adorned as women (*ḥm.wt*), to Pre her father. And he said to her: "What is the matter with you, Anat the divine, you the victorious, woman acting as a warrior, clad as men and girt/adorned as women?"[127]

Not a warrior *or* a mother, Anat is in this one instance simultaneously depicted as crossing the gender divide.

Anat, then, is an example of fluid gender. Her sex is definitively female—she is consistently referred to as *btlt* "adolescent girl," *ilt* "goddess," *aḫt* "sister" (of Baal), and *bt* "daughter" (of El). Her refusal to take on the roles of wife and

Figure 4.3 Stela of Qeh, Bottom Detail, British Museum EA191.

Source: © The Trustees of the British Museum.

mother removes her from the realm of normal femininity for mortal women in the Bronze Age Levant, and her proclivity for violence is specifically presented as masculine per the terminology and expectations presented within the works themselves.[128] In Egypt, the goddess can be presented as both utterly militaristic *and* maternal—although not in the same texts. In Ugarit, Anat is a "tomboy," female of sex but masculine of gender; in Egypt, she is both feminine and masculine. In either event, she bends normal gender paradigms to the breaking point.

Those scholars who see Anat as an adolescent tomboy rather than a "goddess of love and war" generally agree that it is the goddess's perpetually liminal age that leads to her perpetually liminal gender. That is: Anat is masculine because she never grows up to become a feminine woman. For Peggy Day, "Anat as perpetual *btlt* is suspended, as it were, at this crucial point in time where male and female are becoming differentiated . . . she is caught in the liminality of adolescence, where male and female are not yet fully distinct."[129] For Walls, "Anat's liminal identity in Ugaritic myth is made clearer by understanding her as an unrestrained, adolescent female with an unresolved self-identity."[130]

This lack of maturity is complemented by her outright refusal to submit to patriarchal authority, either that of a father in her (perpetual) youth or to an eventual husband. Thus Smith, "She is a young female, unattached to any male; therefore, her social position is unresolved. She is not fully under the control of patriarchal authority, as she may defy El and she is not beholden to a husband. Moreover, her passion and intensity cannot be controlled."[131] While Walls concludes:

> [W]hile Anat is a female character, her gender is ambiguous. The adolescent Anat refuses to submit to the patriarchal institutions of marriage and the social expectations of feminine behavior. Disdaining feminine social roles and domestic responsibility, Anat engages in the masculine activities of hunting, warfare, and politics. This rejection of the normative social position as wife and mother forces Anat into a liminal position within the ancient gender and social ideology. Anat's liminal identity is a source of discord and strife within the pantheon: she threatens the patriarchal authority with physical abuse, destroys the royal heir, and defies normative gender roles.[132]

Ultimately, Anat's masculinity is seen negatively.

Pughat

One of the most blatant examples of gender bending, what might be called transgenderism, in the ANE manifests in the literary character of Pughat in the Ugaritic *Tale of Aqhat*. Aqhat is the young prince (?) who refused to give his bow to Anat, adding insult to injury by scorning the idea that any female would have use of such a masculine item (see previously: Anat). Anat has him killed. After the burial of and mourning for the young male hero, Aqhat's sister Pughat (literally "Girl") seeks vengeance for her brother's death, a duty normally ascribed to male kin.

212 *Gender Bending*

It is typically this fact alone that has caused scholars to recognize an element of gender bending in the Ugaritic heroine: that she avenges her brother. However, there are actually numerous elements to the tale that emphasize Pughat's masculine identity. Foremost is her adoption of the filial duties narrated so emphatically and repeatedly earlier in the text, the duties that the deities themselves make clear belong to a son specifically (CAT 1.17, Column II, 26–33):

> To set up a stela for his divine ancestor,
> A votive marker for his clan in the sanctuary;
> To send his incense up from the earth,
> The song of his burial place from the dust;
> To shut the jaws of his abusers,
> To drive off his oppressors;
> To hold his hand when he is drunk,
> To support him when he is full of wine;
> To eat his grain-offering in the temple of Baal,
> His portion in the temple of El;
> To patch his roof when it gets muddy,
> To wash his clothes when they get dirty.[133]

Pughat assumes several of these in the narrative. Because the preserved text does not deal with the period after her father Danel's death, we cannot determine how the duties performed on behalf of a dead father would pertain to her (although see subsequently on this). However, Pughat's role as avenger of crimes against her family immediately places her within the context of "driving off oppressors."[134] As Danel is too old and Aqhat dead, Pughat becomes the source of justice for her family.

We do not see Danel drunk in the extant text. However, we do see him in grief and sorrow, another context in which the body is rendered infirm and in need of assistance. It is Pughat who is present to assist her ailing father, notably in 1.19 Column II, ll. 5–11:

> Pughat attends, the bearer of water,
> Collector of dew from the fleece,
> Who knows the course of the stars.
> Weeping she leads the donkey,
> Weeping, she ropes the ass.
> Weeping, she lifts up her father
> Onto the back of the donkey,
> The shapely back of the ass.[135]

Later, in Column IV, what remains of the text suggests that Pughat is present at Danel's ritual that ends the mourning for Aqhat. In lines 20–22, he dismisses the mourners; in lines 22–25, he sets up a meal and incense for the deities. Although lines 25–27 are awkward, Pughat's presence is established (as well as her role as avenger) in her own words to her father in lines 29–35:

My father presented a meal for the gods,
Into the heavens sent incense,
[To the] stars the Harnemites' incense.
Bless me—I would go blessed!
Empower me—I'd go empowered!
I would slay the slayer of my sibling,
Finish [who] finished my brother.[136]

Pughat's presence at her father's rite, including the reference to the burning of incense, places her within the context of "eat[ing] his grain-offering." Pughat, like a dutiful son, performs the sacred acts alongside her father.

Several aspects of Pughat's presence in the narrative link her with the final, rather mundane tasks at the end of the filial duties list. We have already seen how Pughat fetches a donkey and assists her father in mounting it. More significant is the girl's epithet, the longest by far in *Aqhat*. Pughat is (*CAT* 1.19, Column II, 5–7):

She who carries water,
Who collects dew on her hair,
Who knows the course of the stars.

Thus the dutiful daughter brings water from the stream or well for the household, attending to her duties as the evening or morning dew falls. It is not difficult to suppose that her "aquatic" chores extend into matters of cleaning and laundry, just as is mentioned in the filial duties list.

In contrast to such mundane tasks, it is also important to note the last line of her epithet—*who knows the course of the stars*. This would suggest that Pughat is acquainted with the combined disciplines of astronomy/astrology and thus the ability to read the state of the world through natural phenomena. An identical conclusion might be drawn from her first introduction in the *Aqhat* narrative, at the start of the drought, when the girl sees the vultures circling over her father's house, foretelling both the drought and the soon-to-be-revealed death of Aqhat. Pughat went into mourning ("Pughat weeps in her liver, sheds tears in her heart") before Danel or his torn clothing is even mentioned. Both astrology and the reading of bird omens were prevalent in Bronze Age Mesopotamia, Syria, and Anatolia,[137] suggesting that in the cultural milieu of Ugarit, Pughat's talents would qualify her as a kind of soothsayer/wise-woman, even if an extremely young one. Significantly, such "learned" forms of prophesy were more commonly associated with men (e.g. the *barû*), whereas women mainly prophesied via a kind of divine revelation (ecstasy or dreams), the medium literally being physically infused by the divinity. Pughat, then, was not only capable of prophesy but did so in a pointedly masculine way.[138]

214   *Gender Bending*

Most important in the analysis of Pughat's gender is, of course, her role as avenger of her brother's death. Lines 41–46 of Column IV delineate her preparations, starting with a bath, the application of rouge, and the donning of clothing. Concerning the latter, Pughat (Colum IV, ll. 44–46):

t[]/tlbš npṣ ġzr
tšt.ḫl[pm b]/nšgh.
ḥrb.tšt bt'r[th]/
w'l.tlbš.npṣ att.

[P]uts on a hero's outfit [below?],
Places a knife in her belt,
In her [scabbard] places a sword,
A woman's outfit on top.[139]

Here Pughat is deliberately rendered androgynous, a female with the weapons and garb of a male warrior (*ġzr*), all underneath the dress of a woman (*att*).

As has been noted by numerous scholars, there is nothing specifically engendered in her first two acts, either the bathing or the application of rouge. Such actions typify Anat in the *Baal Cycle* (CAT 1.3, Columns II–III), just as they were taken by Kirta in both ritual and military contexts in the *Kirta Epic* (CAT 1.14, Column III, 52–54).[140] Her clothing, however, is significant. As Mark Smith observed, "Her exceptional dress signals her exception to her gender and anticipates her exceptional execution."[141] Ilimilku, the scribe of the tale, was clearly emphasizing the simultaneous male and female nature of Pughat's revenge apparel. The girl is deliberately rendered androgynous.

Furthermore, this androgyny is manifest not only in her clothing, but in her adoption of her father's and brother's title *ġzr*, "hero/warrior." According to Mark Smith:

When Danil enters into the formal acts of mourning, Aqhat the Hero is the one he laments (1.19 IV 11–12, 15–16), and at this point the father too is again called the Hero (1.19 IV 19). With the father mourning the son, the two are linked in this title: the elderly hero weeps for his son, the young slain hero. The final use of the title is deployed for neither father nor son, but for Danil's daughter, Aqhat's sister Pughat. In the final, extant scene of the text, it is this female figure who takes on the clothing of the hero (1.19 IV 43). Clothing marks her identity in this scene, to avenge the death of her brother, the Hero, and the honor of her father, the Hero.[142]

Obviously, Pughat is a fascinating character in the study of ANE gender. Perhaps one of the more interesting aspects of her impact on the discipline is how her ambivalent gender has been understood in the modern scholarship, especially in comparison with Anat. Much of the scholarship on Anat has been negative, as seen previously—condemning her for being too masculine, too sexual, and ultimately of an "unresolved self-identity." Pughat gets none of that. Pughat gets praise. And this is likely because Pughat is understood to be defying gender expectations only for a brief period and for a good cause. Unlike Anat the defiant, perpetual adolescent, it is accepted that Pughat:

> serves as the archetype of the obedient female who actively supports patriarchal structures. . . . In avenging her brother's murder Pughat *temporarily* takes on the masculine warrior characteristics of Anat. . . . Once her quest is completed, Pughat *surely returns to her normative feminine role*.[143]

Missing the end of the narrative, we have no idea what Pughat went on to do, or even if she succeeded in her vengeance for her brother. But it is notable that a female who challenges the gender binary is praised for doing so in defense of the patriarchy, while the "tomboy" who openly and consistently defies the patriarchy is seen as immature, incomplete, and occasionally even a whore.

A Word on Names

A final word is needed on these female-sex, masculine-gender goddesses, and that pertains to naming practices in the ANE. Names were often theophoric, meaning that they were constructed around the name of a deity. Thus Aššur-uballit means "[the god] Aššur causes to live," while Meryre means "Beloved of [the god] Re" and Samuel "He hears [the god] El." It was often the case that a person, male or female, received a name that indicated that a deity, male or female, was that person's parent. Remarkably, neither the sex of the deity nor that deity's parental status had any bearing on whether s/he was rendered a mother or a father in the prosopography. Thus, next to the attested name Ištar-abî ("Ištar is my father"), we have Bellet-akkad-ummî[144] ("The Mistress of Akkad [Ištar] is my mother"). From the city of Mari in Syria, we meet Ummi-Ḥanat ("Anat is my Mother"), just as in Ugarit, we meet Anati-umme ("Anat is my Mother"). Even so, in Ugarit, we also find the name Il'nt ("My God (m.) is Anat").[145] Whether a deity was presented as a nominal "parent" in the naming practices of the ANE has nothing to do with that deity's sex, gender, or sexual/reproductive status. When it came to names, it seems neither sex nor gender were all that important.

The Female Kings of Egypt

Ancient Egypt had a long history of queens, women who were the wife-mother-sister-consort-regent of the king/pharaoh. There were appreciably fewer female kings, women who ruled in their own right as head monarch-king-pharaoh. When they did, they masculinized themselves.

There were good reasons for this. According to the dictates of Egyptian religio-political ideology, the king is the living embodiment of the god (male) Horus, just as the dead king assimilated with the netherworld god (male) Osiris. The king, then, had to be male to take on the appropriate symbolism and embodiments. Isis

216 *Gender Bending*

might be the wife of Osiris and the mother of Horus, but somehow she was never a ruler in her own right, merely regent for the young Horus until he came of age (again, we are dealing with patriarchal societies here).

Two queens are notable for reigning independently as female kings: The 12th-Dynasty King Sobekneferu (r.c. 1777–1773 BCE) and the 18th-Dynasty King Hatshepsut (r.c. 1479–1458). The former ruled independently during her very brief reign, while the latter served first as regent, then co-pharaoh with her step-son Thutmosis III. Both used a variety of techniques to masculinize themselves so as to fulfill the gender dictates of the ancient Egyptian ideology of rulership.

Sobekneferu

A deliberate mixing of masculine and feminine attributes is clear in the royal propaganda of Sobekneferu, apparent in her names and her iconography. Egyptian kings had a specific series of five names consisting of a Horus Name, a *Nbty* Name, a Golden Horus Name, a First Cartouche Name (also known as *Prenomen*), and an actual Birth Name (*Nomen*) (the one we generally use when talking about them). For Sobekneferu these were:

> Horus name: *myrt R'* (She who is beloved (f.) of Re)
> *Nbty* name: *s3t shm-nbt t3wy* (Daughter of power, Lady of the Two Lands)
> Horus of Gold name: *ddt h'* (She whose appearance is stable)
> Prenomen: *sbk k3 R'* (The one of Sobek, the *ka* of Re)
> Nomen: *sbk nfrw* (The Beauties of Sobek)[146]

A blue glazed cylinder seal now in the British Museum (BM 16581) reveals a similar address for this female king, "She who is beloved of Sobek of Shedet, King of Upper and Lower Egypt Sokekneferu-Shedety, may she live, the Two Ladies, Daughter of Power, Lady of the Two Lands, She whose appearance is stable, the Female Horus, she who is beloved of Re."[147]

In both instances, Sobekneferu is not shy about revealing her female sex: She is the feminine "beloved" of Re, the "Daughter" of Power, the "Lady" of the Two Lands. At the same time, she is also the "King" of Upper and Lower Egypt, and she nominally binds herself not to a goddess such as Hathor or Mut, but the quite masculine crocodile god Sobek.

This tendency towards gender-mixing exists side by side with an effort to present herself, at least nominally, as wholly male: A cylinder seal in the Cairo Museum (JE 72663) provides an exclusively masculine form of her name, with the title "Son of Re" and the word "beloved" written without the feminizing "–t."[148] Sobekneferu could thus be either the gender-bending monarch or the masculine-while-female king.

Her iconography is also a mixture of feminine and masculine, perhaps best revealed in a quartzite statue in the Louvre (Figure 4.4), of which now only the torso remains. Here, over a high-waisted shift dress (feminine), Sobekneferu added the kingly wrap-around, lion-tailed kilt with a triangular panel in the front

Figure 4.4 Statue of Sobekneferu, Louvre E 27135.

Source: Drawing by Paul C. Butler. Used with kind permission.

(masculine). However, whereas men wore their belts below the navel, Sobekneferu has her belt set above the midriff (feminine). She wears a leather chest pouch pendant similar to that worn by her earlier predecessor Senwosret III (c. 1838) (masculine) and remnants of a *nemes* headdress can be seen on her shoulders (also masculine). Beneath the headdress are small breasts (feminine).[149] This mixing of genders is also visible on the remains of a seated statue of Sobekneferu (now lost) from Tell el-Dab'a showing her feet upon an image of the Nine Bows—representative of the traditional enemies of Egypt. By placing these enemies literally under the feet of the king, the iconography reveals the king as a military protector of the Land of Egypt and an upholder of *ma'at* (masculine). However, unlike in more standard masculine iconography, where the king's feet (e.g. Ramesses II) appear

218   *Gender Bending*

one before the other, Sobekneferu's feet appear side by side in "proper" feminine fashion.[150] Again, a mixing of masculine and feminine attributes.

Hatshepsut

Hatshepsut is to ancient Egypt what the *assinnu* was to Mesopotamia—a focus of study which tends to say a lot more about the gender *zeitgeist* of modern scholars than anything actually apparent in the ancient sources. It is easy to see how this happened (far easier than in the case of the *assinnu*s, really . . .). Hatshepsut was the daughter of the 18th-Dynasty Pharaoh Thutmose I and sister-wife of her father's heir Thutmose II. When Thutmose II became Pharaoh, Hatshepsut became his formal consort (he had several wives) and as was customary took on the titles and functions of Great King's Wife and God's Wife of Amun.[151] When her husband died he left behind a very young son—Thutmose III, born of a lesser wife named Isis—as his heir, and Hatshepsut took on the role of regent until the young prince came of age. However, something apparently occurred seven years after Thutmose II's death that caused Hatshepsut to take on the role of pharaoh herself. It has been suggested (reasonably) that the young prince became life-threateningly ill before he could produce an heir himself, thus threatening the royal lineage and potentially leaving Egypt with no rightful king.[152] Or, possibly, there was the threat of a coup d'état during the reign of an underaged prince. Or, maybe, Hatshepsut was really ambitious. In any event, Hatshepsut stepped up and filled the apparent void in leadership by having herself proclaimed king.

It should, at this point, be made perfectly clear that Egyptian kingship had certain unique features. One was, as noted, that the king was understood to be the earthly embodiment of the god Horus, just as the (most recently) deceased king was understood to merge with the Underworld god Osiris. This means that in addition to the general patriarchy that marked all ANE civilizations, Egyptian kingship was specifically gendered masculine due to the conflation of king–Horus. Second was the fact that once one became a god (i.e. Horus), there was no mechanism or mentality that allowed one to stop being a god. That is: Once one became king of Egypt, there was no way to abdicate. So, once Hatshepsut became king, she was in it for life, regardless of the presence of Thutmose III. She ruled from 1479–1458, most of that time side by side with her stepson.

As an official female king of Egypt, Hatshepsut took a page from her female king predecessor—Sobekneferu—and altered her iconography to adopt male portraiture. Hatshepsut, then, has *strongly* gender-bending personal imagery, with images of herself in various media ranging from completely feminine—following Egyptian conventions for the portrayal of women—to quite masculine—following Egyptian conventions for the portrayal of the king specifically—and a mishmash between these two poles.

As discussed by Dmitri Laboury, the successive stages in Hatsepsut's "masculinization" can be clearly observed at the southern temple of Buhen in lower Nubia, begun just after Hatshepsut's accession to kingship. Four stages are discernable:

Gender Bending 219

First: At least one scene testifies that the cutting of the reliefs started with the . . . model of a female pharaoh, represented with her queenly gown and, according to the tradition of ancient Egyptian art, with her feet set close together.

Second: On two reliefs of the nearby inner sanctuary, the reigning queen was originally still depicted garbed in a feminine dress but with an unusually elongated stride, between the one of women and the one of men.

Third: Two other scenes clearly portrayed the female sovereign with the same posture but this time wearing royal kilt, on a slender—androgynous—anatomy, that was later enlarged and further masculinized.

Fourth: Finally, some reliefs showed from the beginning—it seems—the reigning queen in a fully masculine guise, while all her previously carved figures were, probably at the same time, altered to display the same image of a virile pharaoh, with larger stride and stature.[153]

Following this chronology, dating to early in her reign is a graffito from the granite quarries of Aswan at el-Mahatta of Hatshepsut as queen standing opposite her attendant Senenmut (Figure 4.5).

Here Hatshepsut wears the traditional long, clingy dress typical of upper-class Egyptian women of the 18th Dynasty and the double plume crown of queenship and carries the *ankh* symbol and "a mace that could fit for a god's wife of Amun as well as for a king."[154] She is completely feminine.

By slight contrast, very early in her reign as king, a low relief portrayal of Hatshepsut from Karnak, Thebes (Figure 4.6), shows her wearing, once again, the

Figure 4.5 Graffito of Hatshepsut and Senenmut from the Granite Quarries of Aswan at el-Mahatta.

Source: From Laboury 2014: 71.

220 *Gender Bending*

Figure 4.6 Hatshepsut in the Chapelle Rouge at Karnak, Thebes.

sheath robe but wearing a double-plumed crown with ram's horns (masculine). Her cartouches are preceded by the inscription "the *King* (m.) of Upper and Lower Egypt, the *Mistress* (f.) of the rites, Maatkara,[155] may she live."[156]

In three-dimensional representations, the most feminine (by Egyptian conventional standards) is MMA 30.3.3, a black diorite seated sculpture of Hatshepsut from Deir el-Bahri (Figure 4.7).

She again wears the feminine, clingy, full-length gown that reveals breasts and, in this instance, navel. On her head she wears the *khat* headdress, which could be worn by both female and male members of the royal family, as well as by goddesses[157]—thus crossing both gender and mortal–immortal divides. Underneath her feet is a representation of the Nine Bows, symbolic of the traditional enemies of Egypt; thus, like her predecessor Sobekneferu, even in her most feminine portrayal, Hatshepsut is already depicted as a defender of the land and of *ma'at*.[158]

A somewhat more masculine seated statue also comes from Deir el-Bahri, MMA 29.3.2 (Figure 4.8). Again she wears the feminine long dress, but upon her head she wears the *nemes* headdress with uraeus that is emblematic of Egyptian kingship, normally a masculine marker. Even so, her "clean-shaven" face, distinctive breasts, and feet rendered together are all markers of female sex, and thus this statue might truly be called the depiction of a "female king."

Contrast this with her statue from Djeser-djeseru (Figure 4.9), Hatshepsut's mortuary temple, commissioned after she became king (and moved her burial spot from an original location at Wadi Sikkat Taqa el-Zeid to the Valley of the Kings).[159] Here she appears as fully masculine. The king wears the full *nemes* headdress with prominent uraeus, a beard, and the *shendyt* kilt, and her feet are

Gender Bending 221

Figure 4.7 Diorite Statue of Hatshepsut, Metropolitan Museum of Art 30.3.3.

Figure 4.8 Statue of Hatshepsut from Deir el-Bahri, Metropolitan Museum of Art 29.3.2.

222 *Gender Bending*

Figure 4.9 Statue of Hatshepsut from Djeser-djeseru, Metropolitan Museum of Art 28.2.18.

shown in an active, striding stance. In all aspects Hatshepsut is portrayed as a fully male/masculine king, even including the musculature of her arms.

If there were ever a time when one might reasonably use the term "transvestite" in antiquity, this is it. But even "transvestite" does not fully capture the phenomenon, for the gender bending was not limited to clothing. Not only did Hatshepsut reveal (masculine) muscular arms (and something less than feminine pectorals), but even her skin tone changed color. While some of her sculptures reveal the king with pale, yellowish skin—feminine in Egyptian iconography, at least for the upper classes—Hatshepsut's statuary also reveals her with the reddish-brown skin of upper-class males.[160]

What is of particular interest is the fact that this full change in iconography took place in a remarkably short period of time. It began when Hatshepsut became king in the seventh year of the reign of Thutmose III. It was completed by no later than the end of his eighth year, meaning the full metamorphosis occurred in about a year's time.[161]

This masculinized self-portrayal also occurred when Hatshepsut showed herself alongside her co-pharaoh Thutmosis III. The two were presented side by side over the course of the 15 or so years of their rule together, and in all cases 1) Hatshepsut was portrayed as male, and 2) she was the dominant male in the composition, shown standing in front of Thutmose.[162] Thus on a wall relief of the aforementioned Chapelle Rouge at Karnak, Thebes (Figure 4.10), the dual pharaohs are represented as identical figures, Hatshepsut (identified by her cartouche) striding before the "junior" pharaoh.[163]

Gender Bending 223

Figure 4.10 Relief of Hatshepsut and Thutmosis III at the Chapelle Rouge at Karnak, Thebes.

And yet, while Hatshepsut's *iconographic* identity displayed a range of gender manifestations, her *written* identity did not. In the texts, she is almost always female, using feminine forms whenever it was feasible to do so. That is to say: As there was no feminine form of "Pharaoh," she used the masculine form to refer to herself. Where there was a feminine form, however, she quite consistently used it. In the texts, Hatshepsut always presents herself as female.

This is first and foremost evident in her royal names (on the five royal names, see previously under Sobekneferu). Hatshepsut's were:

Horus Name: *wsrt-k3w* = "Powerful (f.) of *kas*"
Nbty Name: *w3dt-rnpwt* = "Flourishing (f.) of Years"
Golden Horus Name: *nṯrt-ḫʿw* = "Divine (f.) of Appearance"
Prenomen: *m3ʿt-k3-rʿ* = "True one (f.)/Ma'at of the *ka* of Ra"
Nomen: *ḥ3t-špswt* = "Foremost (f.) of Noblewomen"[164]

In every instance the feminizing –t is present, rendering all the participial forms (e.g. Powerful, Flourishing) feminine in gender. Hatshepsut's female sex is also evident in her birth name, which makes her the feminine *Foremost* of *Noblewomen*.

But feminine gender is expressed even beyond the grammatical endings. As Gay Robins observes of the king's Horus Name (*wsrt-k3w* = "Powerful (f.) of *kas*"):

> Thutmose I, II, and III all used the epithet *k3 nḫt*, "strong bull", as the first element in their Horus names, which subsequently became standard for all

224 *Gender Bending*

New Kingdom kings. Hatshepsut does not customarily include *kꜣ nḫt* in her Horus name, probably because the bull was a symbol of male strength and potency, and would neither have been particularly appropriate for a women, nor easily feminized. . . . Finally, *kꜣw* also means "nourishment", and might have been chosen as a reference to Hatshepsut's duty as king to ensure the nourishment of Egypt.[165]

As Robins further notes, the feminine form of her *Prenomen* (*mꜣ'̣t-kꜣ-r'*) allowed for a very politically useful pun. A phonetic orthography for the name rendered the king the "True one" (f.) to the *ka* of Re," thus associating the monarch with the solar deity.[166] However, Hatshepsut had the name written with the hieroglyph of the homonymous goddess Ma'at.

> Hatshepsut's writing of her first cartouche name with the image of the goddess ensured that everywhere her name appeared an image of Maat was displayed, thus presenting Hatshepsut as the legitimate champion of Maat. In addition, Maat was one of the goddesses identified as the daughter of Ra. As a female king, Hatshepsut too bore the title "daughter of Ra", so she may also have been claiming obliquely to be a manifestation of the goddess.[167]

So Hatshepsut made use of specifically feminine names, even as she portrayed herself in art with *nemes*, *uraeus*, beard, biceps, and *shendyts*. And not just her names but her epithets were also presented in feminine gender. Attached to her birth name when she became king was the epithet *hnm.t-jmn* = "United/Imbued (f.) with Amun."[168] No longer "God's Wife of Amun" (she gave that title to her daughter Neferure),[169] Hatshepsut instead became *ḥrt*, "female Horus"; *nṯrt nfrt*, "perfect goddess"; and *sꜣt r'*, "daughter of Ra," all feminine forms of traditional kingly titles.[170]

What, then, one might ask, was Hatshepsut doing with her gender? And, for that matter, what are *we* doing with her gender? The apparent contrast between her masculine-feminine-androgynous iconography and her consistently feminine nomenclature has been explained in a number of not mutually exclusive ways. For Gay Robins, it was simply a matter of having feminine word forms readily available while there was simply no feminine iconography for kingship:

> One answer might be that the female image would not have immediately told viewers that they were looking at a king, and presumably the unequivocal identity of the figure as king was more important than the reality of Hatshepsut's biological sex. She was playing a male gender role and for the role to be recognized, it had to be given its traditional male form. . . . Further, the change in texts from masculine to feminine grammatical gender was far less radical than the replacement of the typical male image of a king by an image with female dress and physique, especially as more people would be aware of the visual impact of the images than would have occasion to read the texts even if literate. It seems unlikely, then, that Hatshepsut was trying to disguise

her biological sex, but rather that she was making clear her identity as king, for which role only male iconography existed.[171]

Kelly-Anne Diamond concurred, noting especially how iconography would have far more of an impact on a society that was, ultimately, not especially literate:

> As most of her citizens were illiterate, her visual images were more powerful than the written word. Her audience responded positively to her masculinized appearance throughout her twenty-year rule even though her inscriptions maintained her feminine identity.[172]

To this Cathleen Keller added the notion of Egyptian decorum and idealized forms, thus suggesting that the image of the Egyptian king did not technically reflect reality anyway, and thus the depicted gender of the king bore little relationship to the actual person of the king:

> Hatshepsut's female identity had been an appropriate aspect of her representation as the chief queen of Thutmose II and wife of Amun. However, it was not, ultimately, considered adequate if she was to appear as a king with the status equivalent to that of her male co-regent. In Egyptian art, facial features and bodies were translated into ideal forms, and it was according to a similar process of transformation that Hatshepsut's female nature was altered. In ancient Egypt kingship had its own idealized graphic and textual vocabulary, with an icon of kingship that was male. If Hatshepsut desired to achieve the status and power of an Egyptian king, it was necessary that she conform to that idealized icon. Her royal titular was clearly female, and there was never an attempt to pretend that as an individual she was anything other than female. Yet in the imagery of the statues that presented her as king she of necessity portrayed herself as male: King Maatkare. The Son of Re, Hatshepsut, united with Amun, may (s)he live![173]

More recently, more postmodernist theories have come to the fore, coating the legacy of Hatshepsut in a patina of Judith Butler. This is most clearly expressed in Kelly-Ann Diamond's 2020 article "Hatshepsut: Transcending Gender in Ancient Egypt." Here Diamond theorized that:

> Hatshepsut challenged the contemporary form of hegemonic masculinity and destabilized Egypt's hetero-patriarchal culture. [She] demonstrated . . . that the manipulation of gender was an accepted method to achieving and maintaining power and that female masculinity was an effective tool to secure authority. . . . Our view of Hatshepsut originated in a nineteenth-century context that followed contemporary gender constructs and was not reflective of the ancient Egyptian gender spectrum.[174]

because, apparently, "gender trouble was flourishing in ancient Egypt."[175]

226 *Gender Bending*

Kristen Gaylord had similar musings about Hatshepsut's personal gendered identity:

> Did she see herself as a woman resisting the preferred state of affairs, ruling Egypt for years while a male heir waited in the wings? Or did *he* see *himself* as a king. . . . Or, in true Egyptian fashion, was it a combination?[176]

It might be (and is) argued that we interpret Hatshepsut's gender based on our own, contemporary models, or at least the contemporary models of the 19th century (see subsequently). And yet our most recent revisitings of this topic simply swap out Victorian hypotheses with those of the late 20th century CE. Hatshepsut "destabilized Egypt's hetero-patriarchal culture"? What did she do that affected ancient Egyptian heteronormativity? Did she openly have a lesbian affair while king? Did she not have a daughter named Neferure and foster her stepson in properly feminine maternal fashion? Could one not argue that she *reinforced* the patriarchal norms by showing, as did Sobekneferu before her, that one must be masculine to be king? If "gender trouble" truly were "flourishing" in ancient Egypt, why did no female kings take up the crown (or *nemes*) after Hatshepsut? Why do we not see the rise of an independent, feminine portrayal of the monarch? Both Diamond and Gaylord refer to a "gender spectrum," and yet when confronted with the consistently feminine gender of Hatshepsut's titulary, Diamond must address the utterly binary nature of Egyptian language (and ability to theorize human concepts therein) in observing: "Hatshepsut had only two choices when selecting her titles and gender endings for public display: male or female. *The Egyptian system supported the gender binary* and thus limited Hatshepsut's choices."[177]

On a more positive note, recent examinations of Hatshepsut and her admittedly atypical reign have given a far more positive spin on the female king and her rapport with Thutmosis III. As might be easily imagined, when Hatshepsut and her reign first came to light in the early years of Egyptology, her "usurpation" was understood entirely in light of her "weaker" sex. She was either some kind of demonic, fairy-talesque, evil stepmother; a conniving *femme fatale*; or the puppet-lover of a devious male instigator—probably Senenmut, whose archaeological artifacts were not destroyed like those of his "lover" and thus were subject to earlier analysis. Thus early 20th-century conceptions of the female king, as explained by Cathleen Keller:

> But how could one explain the extraordinary fact that a woman had occupied the throne during the early expansion of the empire, when Egypt was becoming a world power? Surely Hatshepsut could not have accomplished such a feat alone; the actual maneuvering must have been done by powerful male courtiers who used the female king as a figurehead. Leading this supposed "palace camarilla," . . . was Senenmut, administrator in charge of the Amun temple at Karnak, tutor to Hatshepsut's daughter, Neferure, and steward of the king's own household. Only this "canny politician and brilliant

administrator" could have been the "evil genius" behind her reign. Indeed, if Senenmut was actually what he claimed to be, "an intimate" of Hatshepsut, he must also have been her lover.[178]

Thankfully, gender studies have progressed to the point that we can actually conceive of a powerful female who is powerful in her own right, with the intelligence and political savvy to rule and even rule well. Additional data presented over the years of other female Egyptian rulers, such as Sobekneferu previously or the 6th-Dynasty queen Neith-Iquerti or Queen Ahmose-Nefertari at the dawn of the 18th Dynasty, have provided predecessors for Hatshepsut that allow modern scholars to understand how unique this female king was (or wasn't). We have gotten to the point that we can accept that the Egyptians could accept a female king. We now just have to remind ourselves that the king they were accepting was actually female.

MUNUS *ù* NITAḪ

Certain regions of the Mesopotamian cultural landscape had a practice whereby females could legally be turned into males. This was done for both legal and religious reasons, often when a household had daughters but no sons upon the death of the family patriarch, or said patriarch wanted to guarantee economic privileges for his female kin. By turning wives into both mothers *and* fathers, and by making daughters sons, the household's womenfolk could inherit as males and perform the religious duties of an eldest son. In the meantime, such "sons" were usually expected to marry men and bear children, and the future marriages of "fathers" were dealt with. This category of gender bending was purely theoretical.

In the following, there are eight examples of such legal gender-bending from the Hurro-Mesopotamian cultural orbit (for a complete list of such documents, see Yamada 2014 and 2016). The oldest one (an outlier) comes from Karum Kaneš, ancient Kültepe, Turkey, an Old Assyrian trading colony; the other seven come from the cities of Emar (Tell Meskene, northern Syria) and Nuzi (Yorghan Tepe and Kirkurk, Kurdistan) and date to the late Bronze Age. Seven are last wills and testaments of the *pater familias*, and one is a record of adoption. Each presents an example of females being given male gender/status, either by having a wife or daughter declared to be "father and mother," "female and male," or having a daughter adopted as a son.

Karum Kaneš, 20th Century BCE

Kt o/k 196c, last will and testament of Agua:[179]

> Agua's testament is thus: "The house in Aššur is that of my wife. Concerning the silver, she will share it with my children. Concerning the silver, her portion of the inheritance, **she is father and mother (*abat ù ummat*)**. The house and the silver, her inheritance, and also all that she owns will then belong to

228 *Gender Bending*

Šu-Belum. The house in Aššur belongs to Šu-Belum. My sons will reimburse my creditors, and whatever silver remains, Ab-šalim will begin with 1/3 a mina of gold, 1 mina of silver, and a servant."[180]

Emar, c. 13th Century

RA 71/1: Last will and testament of Zikri-Dagan, son of Ibni-Dagan:

From this day Zikri-Dagan, son of Ibni-Dagan, in good health has gathered his brothers. He spoke thus:

I have here established my daughter Unara as a woman and a man (*Unara* DUMU.MUNUS-*ia ana* MUNUS *ù* NITAH *aškunši*). May she invoke my gods and my ancestors. May my three sons—Adda the eldest, Dagan-Bali, and Ba'l-limi—support their mother Unara.[181] Whoever among my three sons does not support their mother, he will have no right to his part of the inheritance.

While their mother lives the inheritance will not be claimed. Whoever claims his inheritance will have no right to the inheritance: May he pay seventy shekels of silver, the wife's *terhatu*, and may he go where he will.

When their mother dies, then my three sons will acquire my house, fields, all my property, all my goods, and may they share the house that belongs to both as brothers.[182]

HANE/M 2 57, Last will and testament of Iddi-ma:

From this day Iddi-ma, son of Zu-Ašdi, has gathered his brothers, has set the fate of his household and of his daughter the *qadištu*.

"Baliya, **my daughter, the *qadištu* , is father and mother of my household (**DUMU.MUNUS-*ia* < NU>.GIG *a-bu ù um-mu ša* É-*ia ši-it*). I have given to my daughter Baliya, the *qadištu*, these objects: a bed and its covers, a bronze vessel of 400 (shekels') weight, a shekel of silver, an *asallu* vessel of 300 (shekels') weight, a three-year-old cow. And I declare that Baliya will give these goods to her daughter Ete; Ete's brothers will not make a claim (against her) concerning these goods. . . . While Baliya lives, they will have no rights to the inheritance."[183]

Emar 6 31, last will and testament of Haya, son of Ipqi-Dagan:

[Bef]ore Šahurunuwa, son of Šarri-Kušuh, king of Ka[rkemi]š, Haya, son of Ipqi-Dagan, has created this contract regarding his household. **He has established his daughter Dada,[184] the *harīmtu* , to fatherhood and motherhood (*ana abbūti u ummūti*) of the household.**

(So speaks Haya): "I have bestowed upon my daughter Dada a bed with its sheets, . . . and a bronze headboard that covered the top (of the bed); these objects as well as two slaves, Au-milki y Ašti-. . .

I have adopted as sons my two daughters Dagan-niwari and Abi-qiri (anuma 2 DUMU.MUNUS-*ia* Dagan-niwari ù Abi-qiri *ana* DUMU.utti-*ia* *epuššunu*). I have given Dagan-niwari as wife to Alal-abu. If [Dagan-niwari does not bear offspring], Alal-abu shall take another wife.

May my daughters honor **their father and mother Dada**. If anyone of my daughters decides not to honor **Dada, their father and mother**, [she will not have the right] to her portion of the inheritance. May she take her clothing from the chair and go wherever she wishes. If they honor their father and mother, when (Dada) di[es] my two daughters will acquire my property and divide up the household and all my possessions equally."[185]

HCCT-E 37, Last will and testament of Muzzazu, son of Šamanu:

From this day, Muzzazu, son of Šamanu, willingly has fixed the destiny of his house. He speaks thus:

My wife Ḫepate is father and mother of my household. I have established my daughter Al-ḫati as woman and man (Al-ḫati DUMU. MUNUS-*ia ana* MUNUS *ù* NITAḪ *aškunši*). May she invoke my gods and my ancestors. I have bequeathed all my goods, all that I have to my daughter Al-ḫati.

If my wife Ḫepate leaves the house for that of another (man), may she leave her clothes on the stool and go where she will.

If my daughter Al-ḫati dies with no offspring, then may her husband Aḫu-yaqaru take another wife; the sons that she bears—before and after—will be my sons. And if Al-ḫati and Aḫu-yaqaru die without progeny, then Al-ummi and Patil will inherit.[186]

TBR 74, adoption contract of Ba'al-wapi, son of Abbanu:

Thus has said Ba'al-wapi, son of Abbanu, son of Ella:

"I have adopted Tae, son of Ili-Da, [as] my son, and **made my eldest daughter Šamaš-la'i my son (**DUMU.MUNUS-*ia* GAL *ana* DUMU.NITA-*ia etepušši*), and given her to him [as] wife. As long as his father Ba'al-wapi and his mother Aštar-kimi live, Tae shall honor us. If he honors us, whenever we die . . . [Šamaš-la'i] has no progeny; all [the children] she bears shall share my goods and property among themselves. Concerning Šamaš-la'i: The gods belong to the main household.

. . . .

As long as his wife Šamaš-la'i lives, Tae shall not take [another] wife; if he does, this document shall prevail. And if Šamaš-la'i dies, may Tae take whomever of my remaining daughters."[187]

Nuzi, c. 13th Century

IM 6818, last will and testament of Unap-tae, son of Taya:

230   *Gender Bending*

Testament of Unap-Tae, son of Taya. I have established a testament in favor of my daughter Šilwaturi. Thus Unap-tae:

I have adopted my daughter Šilwaturi as a son/into sonship (DUMU-SAL-*ia mî Šilwaturi ana mārūti* DÙ^{uš}). All my fields, my houses, all my earning, my acquisitions, my slaves . . . my inheritance, all in Alsa and the cities of Anzukalli, Unzuri, Takurrampe, or in Matiḫa . . . to Šilwaturi, **my daughter whom I have made as a son**, I have given.[188]

YBC 5142, last will and testament of Pui-tae, son of Wullu:

[Will of Pui-tae s]on of W[ullu]. He made a will in favor of Watilla, of . . . (f.), of Uriš-elli, and in favor of Ašte, daughter of . . . Thus declared Pui-tae:

These [my] **three d[aughters] I have given the status of sons (3** [DUMU.MUNUS.MEŠ-*ia*] *ana mārūti epēšu*). All my fields, buildings, miscellaneous property, I have given to these my daughters.

. . .

Thus further declared Pui-tae:

If Ašte dies, then whoever among my daughters is holding fields, my buildings, and is remaining in my house, shall serve the gods and my spirits.[189]

As noted by Masamichi Yamada, the designation "father and mother" is generally used when the *pater familias* designates his wife (occasionally daughter, as was the case with Dada) as the head of household upon his death. The "woman and man" clause, by contrast, appears when the father makes a daughter his primary heir,[190] and "*ana mārūti epēšu*" appears when the father designates one or more daughters as heirs. In this final usage, one can argue that the daughters are given a new gender, as they are made to be "sons." In the other instances, the woman involved now has both genders: She is either "female *and* male" or "father *and* mother." It is likely that the daughters-turned-sons were similar and were understood to be both daughters and sons simultaneously.

In *all* cases, the gender adjustment is enacted by a male authority figure—a (dying) father or husband. The purpose of the adjustment appears to be two-fold: to allow wives and daughters to enjoy the inheritance rights of males, and to permit women to take over the ancestral cult. In RA 71/1 and HANE/M 2 57, it is stated at the outset that the testator has brought the matter before his brothers. By endowing a daughter with masculine gender, the father keeps the paternal uncles from claiming the paternal estate from her. In RA 71/1, Zikri-Dagan also pushes three sons behind his daughter Unara, who may be the mother of the boys. In this way, the estate neither falls back to the uncles nor skips Unara. The desire for a female inheritor appears whether there are potential male inheritors or not. Thus, Unara as noted, as well as the wife of Agua, who inherits before her sons, and Šamaš-la'i, who inherits along with her adopted brother-*cum*-husband Tae. In other cases, it appears that the testator is dying with no male heirs and thus makes some, as is clearly the case with Dada the *ḫarīmtu*, who is father and mother to her younger sisters, who are made sons. A similar dynamic appears with the daughters of Pui-tae.Ašte seems to be the oldest of three or four sisters-turned-sons; when she dies, another of the sisters will take over the family property and the ancestral cult. Šilwaturi appears to be an only child.

Four documents make it clear that the daughter will take over the ancestral cult, a privilege/responsibility normally accorded to the oldest son: RA 71/1, where Zikri-Dagan has Unara invoke his gods and ancestor; HCCT-E 37, where Muzzazu has his daughter Al-ḫati do the same; TBR 74, where it appears that Ba'al-wapi places his daughter Šilwaturi in charge of the household cult; and YBC 5147, where Pui-tae declares that whichever daughter should succeed Ašte will also "serve the gods and my spirits." The gender adjustment, then, gives the females under consideration legal, economic, and religious rights recognizable within the community.

This apparent fluidity of gender, though, has no impact upon the women's sex. With two exceptions, Baliya the *qadištu* and Dada the *ḫarīmtu*, it is written into several wills that the daughters-tuned-sons will marry and have children. A *qadištu* is a ritual specialist, and her status seems to provide certain privileges in marriage. It is unknown why Dada is a *ḫarīmtu*, a woman with neither father nor husband. Her *ḫarīmtu* status may come from the fact that the father in question is dying (thus a will) and that there appears to be no intention to marry her off. By contrast, Ḫaya clearly states that his daughter (and son) Dagan-niwari is already betrothed, and it is possible that the youngest sister is also expected to marry. Otherwise, Al-ḫati is already married per the will, and Šamaš-la'i is actively engaged to her adopted brother in the contract.

As is typical for widows ("fathers" and otherwise), the wills complicate their ability to remarry (and thus potentially remove property from the paternal line). Even though Muzzazu has made Ḫepate father and mother of the household, he leaves his inheritance to their daughter while proclaiming, "If my wife Ḫepate leaves the house for that of another (man), may she leave her clothes on the stool and go where she will." The wife of Agua is also father and mother of the household, but control over the property is still handed over to Šu-Belum and, after, their sons. Masculine gender does not give wives any individual right to their husbands' property, and the inheritance tends to be regulated to the third generation, to the potential sons of the sonly daughters (who, again, are expected to marry men and bear children).

It is ultimately impossible to know how the women involved experienced or performed this adjustment to their gender. The ability to care for the family cult would have probably given a sense of agency denied to "normal" women, as would, to some extent, the economic rights acquired and responsibility over (younger) siblings. But their female sex is never disputed—the women have occupations and designations reserved exclusively for women (*qadištu*, *ḫarīmtu*), and they are expected to marry and become mothers. And there is no evidence whatsoever that such women are expected to take on any other aspects of masculine gender (e.g. dress, masculine name, a female wife).

Iconography

The quest for various genders does not stop with the examination of texts: Iconography is also brought into the fray. This requires its own set of methodologies. Two paths are typically followed when seeking out gendered identity in the portrayal of humans in ancient art: How the (naked) body itself is rendered and the stereotypical poses and actions adopted by the individual portrayed. The former is basically an examination of primary and secondary sexual characteristics: Does the individual have a penis and beard? It's probably a man. Does the individual have breasts and a vulva? Probably female.

Confusion emerges because we do not always "read" these attributes the way the ancients did. For example, both human females and males have pectorals and nipples. The difference is mostly a matter of scale, and some males actually have larger pectoral than some women. An accurate representation of a male will have pectorals and nipples, and it is left to the viewer to decide if those are pectorals (male) or breasts (female). A figurine with "breasts" and a penis might thus be a hermaphrodite, or simply a guy with pecs.

The same goes for beards.[191] Clearly rendered facial hair and locks can generally be accepted as a beard and thus male. A pointy or jutting chin, however, might simply be a chin. It is up to the (modern) viewer to determine if a beard is at issue. As such, an individual with breasts (???) and a beard (???) might be a hermaphrodite, a female (breasts and prominent chin), or a male (beard and pectorals). The safest bet is to go with genitalia, if available. And they aren't always.

Additional problems emerge in the sexing of human depictions. Getting back to that beard, it is clear that in later Mesopotamian history hegemonic males (like the king) had elaborate beards, at least in their portrayals, and this tendency goes back even into Sumerian times, although inconsistently (see Gudea). However, certain groups of males, especially cult functionaries, were clean shaven, perhaps as a marker of purity. And eunuchs were certainly beardless. Thus, while one can use the presence of a beard as a sex marker (male), one cannot use its absence as a sex marker. Men come in both categories. Except in Egypt, where both males and females are typically beardless, unless it's a king being shown with a clearly tie-on ceremonial beard, matching the clearly ceremonial tie-on tail. Also worn by female kings.

Generally much more consistent are actions and postures: Certain culturally specific poses or actions are consistently associated with males or females. In Sumer, for example, male votive figurines carry sheep to the deities. In Egypt, females embrace their husbands in funerary wall paintings. With the exception of Senenmut in 18th-Dynasty Egypt, only women carry babies. *In general*, males are depicted as relatively more active than females, especially when the imagery is meant to be idealizing rather than realistic.

Nevertheless, various three-dimensional images of individual humans have been used as evidence of alternative sexes/genders in the ancient world, often because of the ambiguity involving the use and identification of secondary sex characteristics. Two case studies are presented here.

Cypriot "Hermaphrodites"

In the Early Bronze Age in Cyprus (EC) a new and prevalent style of figurine arose on the island, the simplest style of which were called plank figurines (see Figure 2.3). As with perhaps far too many images from the ancient world, the plank figurines were early on identified as female (some seem to display breasts) and based on that sex further categorized as either goddess/fertility figurines or possible *ushabti* images (ersatz wives/concubines for the dead).[192] Thus Vassos Karageorghis recognized the EC III plank figurines either as cult functionaries or, especially in the case of the multi-headed varieties, as deities,[193] while the transitional MC I versions of the plank figurines (discussed subsequently) "illustrate the persistence of the fertility goddess or mother goddess type which we see first in the Chalcolithic period."[194] By contrast, Orphanides has argued that, "The female figures may represent the wife (wives) or female servant(s) of the dead," although he also suggests that "We cannot exclude the possibility that some of our figurines represent goddesses with a kind of sexual purpose."[195] Desmond Morris admits his "bias favouring the fertility charm interpretation of prehistoric Cypriot figurines," but later he asks, "Could they after all be substitute figures—effigies of widows placed in their husbands' graves to accompany them in death?"[196] (The reader should be having very vivid flashbacks to Chapter 2 right about now).

Other scholars maintained the female identity of the images but came to less "fertile" (or "dead") theories regarding their meaning(s). Marcia Mogelonsky, for example, in her 1988 study of Early and Middle Bronze Age Cypriot figurines, saw the figurines as female but offered a fuller range of meanings based on the theories of Peter Ucko and Mary Voigt.[197] Anna L. a Campo, in her 1994 analysis of Early Cypriot anthropomorphic figurines, argued that, "the primary meaning of plank-figures seems to be the representation of individual, human women in role as wife and mother, within their 'lineage'."[198]

Starting in the 1980s a new approach was taken, suggesting that not only was it methodologically unsound to identify these images as specifically female but that, in the absence of any sex markers on approximately 2/3 of the extant examples, sex ambiguity might actually be a critical aspect of the interpretation of the plank figurines.[199] Notions of ambiguity were not merely revealed in the absence of distinct sexual traits such as breasts, genitals, or even facial hair on the majority of such figurines, but concepts of hermaphroditism seemed implied on a small number of figurines that portrayed multiple sexual characteristics, such as breasts and a penis, or possibly breasts and a beard. Thus Tracy Cullen and Lauren Talalay concluded that,

> The imposition of gendered identity on Cypriot plank figures seems to us to impose a specificity of interpretation that is rarely warranted and to overlook a sexual ambiguity that may well have been intended by the artist and of complex social significance and efficacy within a ritual context.[200]

By contrast, Naomi Hamilton suggested that,

If sex is not indicated on figurines, it is reasonable to suppose that it was not considered relevant—perhaps because the users of the figures knew what sex was indicated, because they were meant to be sexless, or children, or because sex was not perceived to be important.[201]

To categorize the plank figurines as "female," then, was to overlook other possible identifications and to deny a concept of sex and gender different from that prevalent in the modern West. The intermingling of the sexes was a long-enduring artistic motif in Cyprus dating from the Neolithic,[202] and thus hermaphroditism might be playing an important role here in the terracotta repertoire. Likewise, as Eleanor Ribeiro pointed out in her article "Altering the Body: Representations of Pre-Pubescent Gender Groups on Early and Middle Cypriot 'Scenic Compositions'," the absence of sexual identifiers may indicate not sex but age.[203] To assign a sex to these figurines would be to overlook possible age distinctions and concepts of childhood in the archaeological and artistic record.

This trend in ungendering (or regendering) the figurines intensified in light of four or so examples that are seen to be "clearly" intersex (Figures 4.11–4.14).

The first two examples appear to have both breasts and a penis. The third has no penis but a beard, while the fourth has breasts (one actively lactating) but what appears to be a phallic bulge. Thus: Intersex.

Nevertheless, a few ideas must be kept in mind here. First, and this goes for any study of art: One cannot assume that all examples of an art or craft were done

Figure 4.11 Early Cypriot Anthropomorphic Terracotta Figurine, Glasgow Art Gallery and Museum.

Source: Drawing by Paul C. Butler. Used with kind permission.

Gender Bending 235

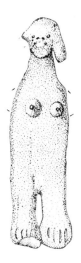

Figure 4.12 Terracotta Figurine, possibly from Paphos, Berlin Museum Antiquarium T.C. 6683.

Source: From V. Karageorghis 1991: 178, fig. 137.

Figure 4.13 Early Cypriot White Painted Figurine from Ayia Paraskevi, Cyprus Museum, Nicosia, CS2028/I.

Source: Drawing by Paul C. Butler. Used with kind permission.

236 *Gender Bending*

Figure 4.14 Middle Cypriot Red Figure Kourotrophos, Oriental Institute X.1611.

Source: Drawing by Paul C. Butler. Used with kind permission.

by competent adult professionals. We must always keep in mind that in addition to the painting by Botticelli we might also find the painting done by Botticelli's four-year-old niece. Figure 4.12 up there certainly seems to fall into this category: a sheep rendered by a child trying to express both udders and a tail—not a human at all.[204]

Then we have the matter of ambivalent secondary sexual characteristics, as noted. Figure 4.13 may have a beard or may simply have a jutting, awkwardly rendered chin, a longish face. Or, conversely, the chin may be a beard, which was considered sufficient to express the concept of "male," a male who might be understood as clothed, and thus no genitalia were deemed necessary or relevant. Likewise with Figure 4.11: Are those breasts and a penis, pectorals and a penis, or breasts and a really awkwardly rendered vulva?

Finally, there is the matter of gendered action, in this case the kourotrophos. As discussed in Chapter 1, all kourotrophoi outside of 18th-Dynasty Egypt are female, so to make this example intersex would be to acknowledge its extreme exceptionalism. Or we might instead look at the "phallic" portrusion and identify it as a navel, considering the location, with its protruding nature coming from the recently parturiant nature of the female depcited (she does have a baby there). A phallic bulge would be more likely at the top of the legs, which is flat, and even appears to have a slit, possibly to indicate a vulva.

Is there a final answer regarding the sex or gender of these Cypriot figurines? It is difficult to say. While indeed 2/3 of them are without clear sex markers, the 1/3 that have them appear to show breasts; none but the one or two (sheep?) shown here actually have anything akin to phalloi; a few are in fact kourotrophic; and they appear in a series of figurines that eventually evolve to be exclusively female, with very obvious breasts and pubic triangles (Figures 4.15–4.17).

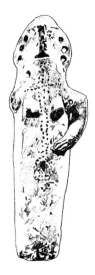

Figure 4.15 Middle Cypriot Terracotta Figurine, K. Severis Collection, Nicosia, 1539.
Source: Drawing by Paul C. Butler. Used with kind permission.

Figure 4.16 Middle Cypriot Dark Ware Figurine, Metropolitan Museum of Art 74.51.1537.
Source: Drawing by Paul C. Butler. Used with kind permission.

Figure 4.17 Late Cypriot Bird Face Figurine from Hala Sultan Teke, Larnaca District Museum 1021.

Source: Drawing by Paul C. Butler. Used with kind permission.

In the past I saw these all as female; now I am not quite as certain. But the weight of the evidence is much stronger for "usually" female with an occasional atypical male thrown into the mix than for the deliberate rendering of intersex for which we have no other, and certainly no clear or unambiguous, evidence.

Ur-Nanše

Ur-Nanše was a chief singer (NAR.MAḪ) in the 3rd-millennium Syrian city of Mari. His[205] personal statue has been the subject of considerable debate regarding Ur-Nanše's sex/gender.[206] On the one hand, the singer wears clothing typical of Sumerian males: a flounced skirt with no upper-body apparel (see Figure 4.1). On the other hand, he has no beard, has long hair, and what appear to be female breasts. Male? Female? Eunuch? Intersex? Unlike the case with some of our Cypriot figurines, we cannot here argue that an incompetent artist (or an artist's niece) is responsible.

Nevertheless, as Julia Asher-Greve observed, Ur-Nanše's iconography actually does fit in well with contemporary iconographic gendering practices. The clothing, to begin, is standard for males. Sumerian females can appear in the nude, especially in cultic contexts, just as males do.[207] When they are clothed, however, the upper torso is consistently covered, either by a wrap covering at least the

Figure 4.18 Statue of Ur-Nanše, National Museum of Damascus S 2071.

breasts and left shoulder (again, see Figure 4.1) or a top covering the chest and both shoulders, although still with more cloth on the left shoulder. In this respect, then, Ur-Nanše is in standard male raiment.

Beards are hardly obligatory for Sumerian males. Even a (presumably) hegemonic male such as King Gudea of Lagaš (see Figure 2.23) is clean shaven. What is atypical in the case of Ur-Nanše is that, normally, the clean-shaven face is accompanied by a clean-shaven head: Beardless men are also portrayed bald. This is not the case with Ur-Nanše, who has no facial hair but head hair descending down the back. This attribute especially has suggested to some an identity as a eunuch, who—at least in much later iconography (Neo-Assyrian)—are typified by a lack of facial hair but elaborate coiffures (see Chapter 3). Ur-Nanše is not described in his inscription as a *ša rēši*, and it is not possible to suggest that Neo-Assyrian iconographies applied a millennium earlier, anyway. What is relevant, however, is, eunuch or not, Ur-Nanše's hair is at least compatible with masculine identity.

Finally, the breasts/pectorals. The Mesopotamians in general, throughout their long history, were never as focused on breasts as either sex markers or signs of eroticism as in modern times.[208] As with the signing of their names, female sex was always more linked to the vulva, just as the vulva was the focus of female eroticism (see Chapter 2). While depictions of nude females showed both breasts and vulva, clothed females revealed neither. As males, by contrast, could be shown clothed but topless, their pectorals were visible, and could be portrayed as

240 *Gender Bending*

three-dimensionally as in reality. In other words, prominent pectorals need not be breasts and need not be markers of female sex.

If Ur-Nanše does not conform to our own, modern conceptions of what *should* have been the depiction of masculinity in 3rd-millennium Mesopotamia, that's on us. Maybe he just wasn't hegemonic. It doesn't mean he wasn't male.

Conclusion

There are clearly a number of places where the "standard" or "normative" constructions of gender in the ANE were set on their heads—warrior goddesses, female kings, daughters as sons, and so on. But a couple of points must be brought to the fore. First, there is not as much gender bending in the ANE as is commonly presented in current academic debates. The so-called effeminate, catamite, transvestite, third-gender, and so on, and so on male prostitutes of Inana/Ištar discussed previously clearly weren't. The female sons of Nuzi were still recognized as feminine females, expected to carry out the traditional female roles of wife and mother (unless they were *ḫarimātu*!). Deities are not mortals, and they follow different rules.

Second, *positive* gender bending goes feminine to masculine, very consistently. It would seem that the primary purpose of gender bending in the ANE is to provide females (mortal or divine) with the prerogatives of males. Thus goddesses can hunt, women can be kings, and daughters can inherit and take over the family cult. As noted by Egyptologist Mark Depauw in his work on "Transgressing Gender Boundaries" in ancient Egypt, "Willingly behaving like the opposite sex may be rare and alien for goddesses, but seems to be *entirely unattested* for male gods. None of them wears typically feminine clothes or is apparently ever said to behave like a woman."[209]

Third, when the gender bending goes masculine to feminine, we have either been mistaken (e.g. the *assinnu*), or it is some manner of insult or curse, as with the feminization of enemy warriors discussed in previous chapters. As Julia Assante observed, no *curse* ever goes the other way, threatening to turn women into men.[210]

What we see of gender bending, then, really supports the patriarchal tendencies in ANE civilizations. Men are the first sex with dominance in politics, law, economics, and to a certain extent even religion. When women take a stand in these fields, they masculinize. When men try to kick other men out of these arenas, they feminize each other.

Notes

1 One must also keep in mind that any society's notions of gender are extremely time and context dependent. For example, in the United States (*inter alia*) in the 20th century, cooking was seen as woman's work. Unless, of course, we are talking about professional chefs, in which case the vast majority were men. In such a case, it is not so much the action itself—cooking—that is gendered but the private/public dichotomy: Women cook in the home for their families; men cook for a paying public. But there

are even further subtleties. Housecleaning is, again, associated with women, especially but not exclusively housewives. However, being a professional housecleaner/maid/cleaning woman is a commonly accepted form of female professional labor outside the home, thus bypassing the private/public gendered divide. And yet, while we easily envision female cleaners in a domestic (just not her own) context; males are more likely to be *janitors* or *custodians* in non-domestic contexts such as office buildings. Thus the feminine/masculine divide is split here between domestic/industrial. The feminine is still associated with the domestic, even if not her own. Furthermore, we envision these women with a scrub brush (light), and males with industrial-grade floor-polishers (heavy), reinforcing (subconscious) notions of weak females and strong males. And, of course, there is the ongoing issue that even when men and women do have comparable occupations, house- and child-care are still gendered feminine, as complained about by numerous women forced to choose family over career during the COVID-19 crisis (which I am really hoping is over by now). See, inter alia: www.nytimes.com/2020/05/06/upshot/pandemic-chores-homeschooling-gender.html (Accessed 14 April 2021).

2 Lambert 1987: 126.
3 *Ibid.*
4 See especially Michel 2020.
5 See, for example, Ebeling and Homan 2008.
6 See Hedenstierna-Jonson et al. 2017; Price et al. 2019.
7 See especially Budin 2021.
8 Julia Asher-Greve referred to it as an "exemplary androcentric masterpiece" (2000: 2).
9 The use of the independent term as an aspect of gender identity theory did not exist before the 21st century and thus is neither relevant to antiquity nor most of our scholarship on antiquity.
10 It must be noted, however, that these women continue to be understood as women in spite of all this adoption of masculine identity. Neighbors used mixed grammatical genders when speaking about them; they are denied certain burial honors reserved exclusively for "men," and, of course, they are denied sex and children in a way that "real" men most assuredly are not. For more on this, see Grémaux 1994; Young 2000.
11 If this strikes you as absurd, then you have clearly done very little reading on modern studies of ancient gender.
12 Grabbe 2011.
13 For those who insist on thinking that binary sex is a "Western" construction, I invite you to read the *Kojiki*.
14 McCaffrey 2017: 79. No citations are given for these definitions.
15 Stökl 2013: 75.
16 http://oracc.museum.upenn.edu/saao/corpus
17 Parpola 1997: IL. (Yes, roman numerals for page numbers)
18 I cannot quite fathom where this detail came from.
19 Nissinen 2003: 105, n. f.
20 Stökl 2013: 75.
21 Nissinen 2003: 106.
22 Ibid: 103.
23 Parpola 1997: L.
24 Nissinen 2003: 103, n. f.
25 https://etcsl.orinst.ox.ac.uk/cgi-bin/etcsl.cgi?text=t.4.07.3&display=Crit&charenc=j&lineid=t4073.p13#t4073.p13
26 Sjöberg 1975: 225.
27 https://etcsl.orinst.ox.ac.uk/cgi-bin/etcsl.cgi?text=c.2.5.3.1&display=Crit&charenc=gcirc#
28 George 2003: 175.

242　*Gender Bending*

29　Al-Rawi 1992: 183, n. 22.
30　Gelb, quoted in Peled 2016: 139.
31　Lambert 1999: 276.
32　Harris 2000: 170.
33　Peled 2016: 88 and 108. Michalowski 2006: *passim*.
34　https://etcsl.orinst.ox.ac.uk/cgi-bin/etcsl.cgi?text=c.2.1.5&display=Crit&charenc=gc irc&lineid=c215.1.120#c215.1.120
35　Peled 2016: 63.
36　Ibid: 93: *Aššurbanipal Inscription O*, 13–16.
37　Michalowski 2006: 49.
38　Peled 2016: 98.
39　Michalowski 2006: 50.
40　*Ibid.*
41　*Ibid.* See also Peled 2016: 105.
42　Cooper 2006. See also Peled 2016: 92.
43　Peled 2016: 102.
44　Steinkeller and Postgate 1992: 37.
45　Peled 2016: 282.
46　Ibid: 80.
47　Translators typically restore "[forbidden things]," almost certainly sexual!
48　https://etcsl.orinst.ox.ac.uk/cgi-bin/etcsl.cgi?text=c.2.5.3.1&display=Crit&charenc= gcirc#
49　Peled 2016: 182.
50　Zsolnay 2013: 93–4
51　Peled 2016: 168.
52　There is continued debate as to whether the SAG.UR.SAG is the Sumerian equivalent of the Akkadian *assinnu*. For both Henshaw and Peled, the SAG.UR.SAG was associated with a variety of cult functionaries throughout the Bronze Age, only one of whom was the *assinnu*. For Zsolnay, the one-to-one correspondence goes back to Sumerian times. Henshaw 1994: 284; Peled 2016: 257–259; Zsolnay 2013: *passim*. Here I follow Zsolnay.
53　Zsolnay 2013: 85, n. 16.
54　Peled 2016: 263.
55　Such attention to one's appearance is assumed to be a feminine trait, utterly ignoring the fact that the consummately macho Spartans combed their hair before going into battle: Herodotos 7.208.
56　Peled 2016: 156.
57　Guinan 1998: 50. See also Chapter 5 on this text.
58　Guinan 1998: 45.
59　Lambert 1992: 151.
60　Guinan 1998: 50.
61　In Peled 2016: 193–194.
62　Stökl 2013: 69.
63　Zsolnay 2013: 95, n. 57.
64　Peled 2016: 159. Peled himself believes that the SAG UR.SAG and SAG.UR.SAG in this list are separate and distinct individuals, one being the heroic *qarrādu*, the other the sexually penetrated *assinnu*.
65　Zsolnay 2013: 87.
66　Ibid: 88.
67　Henshaw 1994: 284–285; Peled 2016: 185.
68　Peled 2016: 185.
69　Ibid: 197.
70　Ibid.

Gender Bending 243

71 Assante 2009: 24.
72 Ibid: 47.
73 Ibid: 34.
74 https://etcsl.orinst.ox.ac.uk/cgi-bin/etcsl.cgi?text=t.4.07.3#
75 Mayor 2016.
76 Hedenstierna-Jonson et al. 2017, Price et al. 2019.
77 Plutarch, *On the Bravery of Women*, §4 "The Women of Argos"; Pausanias 8.48. 4–5.
78 Vernant 1969.
79 Budin 2016: 40.
80 *Ibid*: 39.
81 Thureau-Dangin 1934: 140, #174.
82 Lambert 1985: 537.
83 Dossin in Parrot et al. 1967: *intra*.
84 *Ibid*, and Lambert 1985: 537.
85 Dossin in Parrot et al. 1967: 316, #9 (M 2268 + 2283 + 2413).
86 *Ibid*: 329, M 2241.
87 *Ibid*: 319–20. M 2278 and M 2447 respectively.
88 Bonnet, in her monograph on Ashtart, argues that the earliest attestation of the goddesses name appears in 3rd-millennium Ebla, where the name aš-dar is given as the equivalent of ^{d}Inana (Bonnet 1996: 136–137). However, this form of the name lacks the feminizing "t," which specifically distinguishes feminine Aštart from her male companion and progenitor Athtar, as well as from her eastern cognate Ištar. The Eblaic name is clearly feminine, being seen as the equivalent of Inana, but the orthography does not yet distinguish between Ašdar/Ishtar and Aštart *per se*. As such, I am inclined to see the Marian material as a more definitive representation of this goddess's name.
89 Lambert 1985: 537. See also Bordreuil 1985: 547.
90 Gawlikowska 1980: 28.
91 Harris 2000: 163.
92 https://etcsl.orinst.ox.ac.uk/cgi-bin/etcsl.cgi?text=t.4.07.2&charenc=j#
93 https://etcsl.orinst.ox.ac.uk/cgi-bin/etcsl.cgi?text=t.1.3.2&charenc=j#
94 Foster 1993: 77.
95 Reiner 1974: 233.
96 https://etcsl.orinst.ox.ac.uk/cgi-bin/etcsl.cgi?text=c.4.07.9&display=Crit&charenc=j& lineid=c4079.A.16#c4079.A.16
97 CAD *muttallu*.
98 Wegner 1981: 21–23. See also Beckman 1998; Archi 2013: 12; and Bachvarova 2013: 24 *sqq*. Also written "Šawuška."
99 The name is translated as "Ištar" when written logographically and as "Šauška" when written syllabically. See Beckman 1998: 3.
100 All three texts translated into German by Wegner (1981: 53). My translations from the German.
101 Wegner 1981: 47 and 51.
102 Hoffner 1998: 54–55, adapted.
103 Wegner 1981: 46.
104 Archi 2013: 10.
105 Wegner 1981: 47. My emphases.
106 Hoffner 1998: 60.
107 Beckman 1998: 7.
108 Bachvarova 2013.
109 Hillers 1973: 74. For more on such personifications of Anat, see Day 1991; Walls 1992; and Smith 2001: 56–57.

244 *Gender Bending*

110 Walls 1992: 193, n. 32. For more on Margalit and his issues with Anat, see Budin 2018: 63.
111 Hillers 1973: 74.
112 Day 1991: 141–142.
113 Smith in Parker 1997: 150.
114 All Smith in Parker 1997.
115 Parker 1997: 62.
116 Walls 1992: 203.
117 Ibid: 221–222, excerpted.
118 Ibid: 180 and 186.
119 Tazawa 2009: 72–73.
120 Cornelius 2004: 85.
121 Tazawa 2009: 77.
122 Cornelius 2004: 85.
123 Tazawa 2009: 76–77.
124 Ibid: 74
125 Ibid.
126 Ibid: 80.
127 Ibid: 78, adapted. See also Depauw 2003: 56.
128 I get the feeling in modern times people would argue that Anat was assigned the wrong gender at birth . . .
129 Day 1991: 145.
130 Walls 1992: 218.
131 Smith 2001: 56.
132 Walls 1992: 217.
133 Coogan and Smith 2012: 35–36.
134 Wright 2001: 61–62 and 68.
135 Parker 1997: 68.
136 Ibid: 76–77.
137 On bird-omens in Anatolia, see Bryce 2002: 151–152.
138 See especially Henshaw 1994: Chapter Three.
139 Parker 1997: 77.
140 Wright 2001: 206–209.
141 Smith 2014: 136.
142 Ibid: 129.
143 Walls 1992: 209, excerpted. My emphases.
144 This is a *great* name for a cat.
145 On Anat in personal names, see Lloyd 1994: 21–33.
146 Diamond 2020: 8.
147 Diamond 2021: 275.
148 Diamond 2020: 9.
149 Ibid: 5, 2021: 278.
150 Diamond 2021: 276.
151 Dorman 2005: 87.
152 Robins 1999a: 110–111, n. 55.
153 Laboury 2014: 76, excerpted.
154 Ibid: 70.
155 Hatsepsut's royal *Prenomen*: see subsequently.
156 Laboury 2014: 72; Dorman 2005: 88.
157 Robins 1999: 67.
158 Diamond 2020a: 179; Laboury 2014: 72.
159 Diamond 2020a: 178; Laboury 2014: 66, n. 40.
160 Diamond 2020a: 180.

161 Laboury 2014: 85.
162 Gaylord 2015: 50; Laboury 2014: 52; Diamond 2020a: 177.
163 Gaylord 2015: 50.
164 Robins 1999a.
165 Ibid: 104.
166 Ibid: 105.
167 Ibid: 106.
168 *Ibid*: 107; Laboury 2014: 71.
169 Gaylord 2015: 56.
170 Robins 1999a: 103.
171 Ibid: 111, excerpted.
172 Diamond 2020a: 181. Granted, we don't actually know how her "audience" "responded."
173 Keller 2005: 162–163.
174 Diamond 2020a: 170, excerpted.
175 *Ibid*: 171.
176 Gaylord 2015: 56, emphases in original.
177 Diamond 2020a: 170. My emphasis.
178 Keller 2005a: 295, excerpted.
179 Michel 2000: 2–3.
180 Trans. Michel. My translation from the French.
181 Either Zikri-Dagan has formally made Unara the guardian of the three boys, thus their "mother," or Zikri-Dagan is actually their grandfather but is treating them like sons.
182 Justel 2008: 264, my translation from the Spanish. See also Ben-Barak 1988: 94.
183 Justel 2014: 129–130. My translation from the Spanish.
184 Not to be confused with Dada the GALA-MAḤ!
185 Justel 2014: 131. My translation from the Spanish.
186 *Ibid*: 131–132, with citations. My translation from the Spanish. See also Ben-Barak 1988: 93 for additional text.
187 Justel 2014a: 70.
188 Lion 2009: 10; Ben-Barak 1988: 91–92; Paradise 1980:189. See also Justel 2014: 132–133 for additional clauses of the will.
189 Paradise 1987: 203–204. See also Lion 2009: 10; Ben-Barak 1988: 92.
190 Yamada 2016: 136.
191 See especially López-Bertran and Garcia-Ventura 2016.
192 Frankel and Tamvaki 1973: 41. Karageorghis 1991: 52, toning down his earlier theories, nevertheless insists that the plank figurines "all have basic connections with fertility." On ushabti notions, Åström 1972: 254. Merrillees 1980: 184 is more circumspect, seeing the figurines as symbols of "the continuity of human existence through procreation and life after death."
193 Karageorghis 1977: 58–60.
194 Karageorghis 1975: 62.
195 Orphanides 1983: 46.
196 Morris 1985: 162.
197 Mogelonsky 1988: 236 ff.
198 A Campo 1994: 169.
199 Merrillees 1980: 173–174; Knapp and Meskell 1997: 197–198.
200 Talalay and Cullen 2002: 190.
201 Hamilton 2000: 23.
202 See Knapp and Meskell 1997: Figs. 2 and 3.
203 Ribeiro 2002: *passim*.
204 Obviously I cannot prove this, but it would take considerable argumentation to convince me otherwise.

246 *Gender Bending*

205 We'll get to this.
206 For full bibliography, see Asher-Greve 1998: 33, n. 37.
207 Budin 2022.
208 Asher-Greve 1998: 14.
209 Depauw 2003: 57. My emphasis.
210 Assante 2009: 47.

5 Sexuality

Heteronormativity

The inhabitants of the ancient Near East were heteronormative. This fact has nothing to do with matters of desire or sexual orientation or gender identity. It has to do with the structure of ANE society, which was based on the family. Families need children to function (labor) and to continue in existence, and the only way to create children was and is via heterosexual intercourse, to wit: sexual reproduction (i.e. the reason sex exists in the first place).

There is no evidence that the ancients thought of themselves as heteronormative, just as they did not think of themselves as pagan. To do so would have required some other category, which they did not recognize, at least not as presented in their texts and images. Rather, heteronormativity expresses in the repeated references to heterosexual relationships in all genres of literature and art, and the extreme paucity of references to homosexuality (see subsequently). All the law codes, the wisdom literature, the love songs, the literature are filled with the expression and regulation of heterosexual relationships: engagement and dowries and marriage and adultery and what makes a good wife and how to be a good husband; families with mothers and fathers and how they pass on inheritance to their children and others; what constitutes adultery and what rape and how do we distinguish between the two;[1] the curing of sexual dysfunction with sexual partners of consistently the opposite sex;[2] hymns to a beloved who is quite consistently a member of the opposite sex;[3] funerary reliefs depicting married couples—husband and wife—with or without their children;[4] lists of workers with families and assorted dependents, most showing men and women in heterosexual marriages and families, a few showing unmarried men and women, none showing same-sex couples;[5] and so on. What R.B. Parkinson describes for Egypt pretty much applies to the ANE in general:

> Marriage is, of course, no evidence for a lack of "homosexual" activities or inclinations, but it is an indication of the prevailing social attitudes. Egyptian ideology gave prominence to the family . . . and marriage. In a society where state concerns and values are formulated in terms of kinship, one can hypothesise that any sexual relationships which deviated from the family

DOI: 10.4324/9780429318177-5

248 *Sexuality*

norm would provoke a hostile attitude. The same is true of attitudes towards inherently infertile sexual acts in a society where . . . sex and fertility were inseparable, and where begetting a son was of great importance. Art and texts show clearly distinct gender roles; there is no tradition of any "indeterminate sex" as having an established role in human society; androgyny in representations is limited to divine or royal figures who are demiurges.[6]

We have already seen much of this in the preceding chapters.

By contrast, references to homosexuality are absurdly scarce, far more so than one would guess from how much hullabaloo people make of it in modern legal systems. As we shall see, the ancients just don't seem to have given all that much thought to homosexuality, certainly less than we do. It certainly existed in the ANE: There are enough data to indicate that they knew of it. It just didn't come up all that often—one or two laws over the entire course of Mesopotamian legal history, a few references in three millennia's worth of Egyptian literary history, a passing reference from Anatolia. (Probably needless to say, all our data pertain to men; we have nothing on lesbianism.) To put it simply, when it comes to sex, we have far, far more data pertaining to incest and bestiality than we do to homosexuality.[7]

At best, the ancients had some concept of what in modern times we might call "Bromance": extremely close, emotional relationships between men, usually of a warrior/hero class. These never pass into the sexual. While in recent times there is a tendency to see these relationships (Gilgameš and Enkidu, David and Jonathan) as expressions of homoeroticism (see subsequently), it is equally valid to consider them in light of the intense relationships formed by males in martial settings, like what we see in the works of Jonathan Shay and J.R.R. Tolkien.

Homosexuality

To judge from the evidence—what there is of it—the denizens of the ancient Near East were not all that concerned about what we now call homosexual intercourse: copulation between two members of the same sex. As is typical of the ancient world generally, there is virtually nothing on female same-sex eroticism, that is, lesbianism. So we are left with the scant evidence available for male homoeroticism. As is the case with the study of ancient women and men generally, study thereof comes with a lot of academic baggage. We can blame the Greco-Roman Classicists.

What the Literal Fuck Has Athens to Do With Jerusalem???

Classicists tend to get to theoretical things before Assyriologists and Egyptologists, things like feminist studies, gender studies, and queer studies. As a result, there is a tendency in ANE studies to look at what the Greco-Romanists have done in a new field as a starting point, applying their hypotheses and theories to new data. Problems emerge when there is insufficient recognition of the fact that very different cultures and data sets are being considered, not to mention insufficient consideration of whether what the Classicists said was correct in the first place. This is a monumental issue in the study of ANE homosexuality because ANE scholars adopted whole cloth the Classicist idea that penetrative sex is all about domination: the one who penetrates—who puts his penis into another—is the dominant, active partner, while the one who is penetrated is the subordinate, passive, innately "feminine/effeminate" partner. In Classics the paradigm was first canonized by Kenneth Dover, the father of Greek homosexuality studies in his seminal book *Greek Homosexuality*, published in 1978. Here, in a chapter section on "Dominant and Subordinate Roles," after a section on the humiliation of apparent prostitutes in vase painting, he turns to relations between males.

> There seems little doubt that in Greek eyes the male who breaks the "rules" of legitimate eros detaches himself from the ranks of male citizenry and classifies himself with women and foreigners. . . . It is not only by assimilating himself to a woman in the sexual act that the submissive male rejects his role as a male citizen, but also by deliberately choosing to be the victim of what would be, if the victim were unwilling, hubris. . . . To choose to be treated as an object at the disposal of another was to resign one's own standing as a citizen . . . it should become so when we recall circumstances in which homosexual anal penetration is treated neither as an expression of love nor as a response to the stimulus of beauty, *but as an aggressive act demonstrating the superiority of the active to the passive partner.*[8]

This construct became the norm in the academy. In one of the most-cited works for the study of ancient homosexuality (not specifically Greco-Roman: *ancient*), David Halperin takes up this torch in his work *One Hundred Years of Homosexuality*, published in 1988 (and republished in 1990), with not a little flavoring from Foucault thrown in for good measure.

> Scholars sometimes describe the cultural formation underlying this apparent refusal by Greek males to discriminate categorically among sexual objects on the basis of anatomical sex as a bisexuality of penetration or—even more intriguingly—as a heterosexuality indifferent to its object, but I think it would be advisable not to speak of it as a sexuality at all but to describe it, rather, as *a more generalized ethos of penetration and domination*, a socio-sexual discourse structured by the presence or absence of its central term: the phallus.[9]

Also in 1988, David Greenberg, in his extensive work, *The Construction of Homosexuality*, picked up on this theme:

> As in Greece, the Romans tended to consider the passive or receptive role incompatible with the honor and dignity of a free citizen, especially when it continued into adulthood. Sexual submission to a powerful patron was, seemingly, a familiar way of building a career, but it left the client vulnerable to potentially

250   *Sexuality*

ruinous denunciation. A man's failure to live up to the standard of masculinity expected of someone in his rank was especially disturbing in a society that was attempting the systematic subjugation of the entire known world.[10]

This Roman construction is most clearly laid out in Jonathan Walter's 1997 essay "Invading the Roman Body: Manliness and Impenetrability in Roman Thought":

> In Latin, when a male was sexually penetrated by another, a standard way of describing this was to use the expression *muliebria pati*; that is, he was defined as "having a woman's experience." Clearly, what happened to the sexually passive man is conceived of as being the same as what happens to a woman. . . . This usage is congruent with the characterization, widespread in the public discourses of the Greco-Roman world, that sex is a one-way street, something one person does to another. . . .
>
> This also places emphasis on the pleasure experienced by the "active," penetrating partner in the sexual act, and the sense that the other participant is primarily there for the use of the penetrating man. Sexual activity is routinely conceptualized in Roman public discourse as penetrative, sexual pleasure (particularly in the male homosexual context) as accruing to the penetrator, and the penetrator-penetrated relationship as "naturally" involving a more powerful individual wielding power over a less powerful one. . . . [T]he passive partner in the sexual act is described as something other than a "man," whether a woman or a boy. This is in accordance with Roman (and classical Greek) sexual protocols, which view the sexually "active" role as the only appropriate one for an adult male citizen, the homosexually "passive" role being appropriate for *pueri*, a term that covers both male children and male slaves of any age.[11]

This penetrator = dominant = masculine vs. penetrated = passive = feminine paradigm[12] was not seen to be a problem when discussing heterosexual intercourse: Throughout the ages it was understood as "natural" that women, the penetrated, were innately passive and subordinate anyway, at least from the perspective of those tracing their cultural lineage back to the Greeks and Romans (as we saw in Chapter 2, this was hardly the case for actively erotic ANE females). But once male homosexuality came under scrutiny in ancient Near Eastern studies, the entire discourse became dominated by the "who's on top" question, and all approaches to the evidence for male homoeroticism in the ANE became a study of how male homoeroticism is problematic because of the way it creates unstable hierarchies among men by causing effeminacy and sub/dom dynamics. Thus:

Mesopotamia

> One could further consider the wider viewpoint of social differentiation and power-relations, a perspective according to which the sexual act may be regarded as reflection of power relations between **penetrator** and **penetrated**. In academic discourse this topic is frequently discussed in the term 'the active-passive model'. . . . This perspective regards the active partner as the stronger party,

possessing power in the sexual relations. The passive partner is then regarded as the weak party, from which power is denied.[13]

Does homosexuality produce effeminacy? Does it result from effeminacy? Is the receptive party effeminate? One thing can be said with certainty: the receptive party in homosexual relations did not conform to ancient Near Eastern features of hegemonic masculinity. . . . Mesopotamian society viewed both third gender figures and males who were sexually penetrated as individuals who defied the common conventions of proper sexual and gender conduct. A man who was sexually penetrated assumed the sexual role reserved for women, and therefore undermined the gender boundaries between men and women.[14]

Just as every man can be a penetrator, he can also be penetrated. The binary structures of gender asymmetry are located on the same male body. A male equal who chooses to be penetrated makes the somatic contradiction inherent in the logic of gender asymmetry all too close to becoming visible. His act threatens the logic of binary gender and undermines the terms of gender hierarchy on which social organization is predicated. Sex between male equals, which opens the possibility of reversible positions and the symmetrical deployment of the body, is a double annihilation of hierarchy.[15]

An inexorable, almost geometric logic governs Mesopotamian imaginings of sex between male social equals. Any possibility of mutuality and eroticism instantly is collapsed into positionality, and reinscribed with hierarchy and power. . . . Somebody has to go in front, by this Mesopotamian logic, and somebody has to go behind.[16]

Insertive sex, a "real man's" prerogative indeed, but one to which he was limited, was the very definition of sexual activity, and phallic penetration the only truly performable act. By contrast, the other group, made up of women, children, foreigners and slaves, that is, everyone who was not an adult male citizen, was characterized as having feminine traits, as submissive and receptive rather than active. As mere recipients of phallic action, those in this group had no sexual autonomy; they did not "do" sex, but rather sex was done to them.[17]

Hebrew Bible

A sexual contact between two men mirrored the male and female roles: it was the former from the active partner's point of view and the latter from that of the passive partner. Since these expressions, in practical terms, hardly can indicate anything else but penetration or being penetrated, the concrete point of reference in Leviticus 18:22 and 20:13 seems to be male anal intercourse, which caused the other partner to acquiesce in a female role. . . . Sexual contact between two men was prohibited because the passive party assumed the role of a woman and his manly honor was thus disgraced.[18]

Egypt

The only references to same gender sexual activities in the artefacts and non-literary texts of the Middle Kingdom present the act as one of denigrating the passive partner, and a sign of the mastery of the active partner, who does not step outside his gender role.[19]

252 *Sexuality*

And so forth. . . . There is no actual evidence for this top/bottom construct from the ANE data themselves. We have put it there.

In reality, there are very few references to male-male sexual intercourse from the ANE (and nothing on women . . .). Some are prohibitions, some seem to be beneficial, and some deal with matters that don't actually pertain to homosexuality at all; they just got caught up in the fray of discourses. Let us here consider the data regionally. But first:

A Few Words on Verbs

It is difficult to discuss sex in English. The problem is vocabulary. As is lamented, English provides only one word for two distinct concepts: "sex" (the biological role an individual plays in reproduction as expressed in genes, anatomy, and gamete size—see Chapter 1) and "sex" (genital friction, generally between two or more individuals, a.k.a. intercourse). There is also the problem in English that we have no non-obscene verbs that convey the action of sexual intercourse in a Subject-Verb-Direct Object construction whereby one person (Subject) Xs the other person (Direct Object). In English, most verbs for discussing sexual intercourse have the sex act itself as the direct object, with the non-subject person presented as an indirect object. Thus, "Bob (subject) has sex (direct object) with Bill (indirect object)." Or "Bob (subject) makes love (direct object) to Bill (indirect object)." And so forth. To express the Subject-Verb-Direct Object construction we see in the ANE texts, more profane verbs are necessary: "Bob fucks Bill," "Bob schtups Bill."[20] But in English use of such verbs makes the act sound harsher than is necessarily intended. Other means of expressing the Subject-Verb-Direct Object construction have implication in English that are not necessarily present in the original texts, for example, "Bob sodomizes Bill," which inevitably brings up the matters of dominance and feminization mentioned previously. In what follows I have attempted to get as close as possible to the original meaning of the verbs used, which, remarkably, are often non-sexual except for context.

Anatolia

The Hittites were far, far more concerned with incest and bestiality than homosexuality of any kind. The only reference to male–male sexual intercourse appears in §189 of the *Hittite Laws*, in the midst of several sections (§§187–200) pertaining to the regulation of sexual relations:

> §189: tá-ku LÚ-aš a-pé-e-el-pát an-na-aš-ša-aš kat-ta wa-aš-ta-i ḫu-ur-ki-il
> tá-ku LÚ-aš DUMU.MUNUS-aš-ša kat-ta wa-aš-ta-i ḫu-ur-ki-il
> tá-ku LÚ-aš DUMU.NITA-aš kat-ta wa-aš-ta-i ḫu-ur-ki-il[21]

> §189: If a man with (*katta*) his own mother commits a (sexual) offence (*waštai*),[22] it is an unpermitted sexual pairing (*ḫūrkil*).[23]

If a man with (his own) daughter commits a (sexual) offence, it is an unpermitted sexual pairing.

If a man with (his own) son commits a (sexual) offence, it is an unpermitted sexual pairing.

Harry A. Hoffner and others take the legal term *ḫūrkil/ḫūrkel* as a reference to a combination of incest and bestiality—a specifically sexual liaison that is not permissible according to Hittite law or morality.[24] In §189 the ban is clearly on close-family incest, not homosexuality. To quote Hoffner, "Homosexuality as such is not termed *ḫurkil*. A man who sodomizes his son is guilty of *ḫurkil* because his partner is his son, not because they are of the same sex."[25]

Mesopotamia

There are six references to male homosexuality from Mesopotamia, two laws from the *Middle Assyrian Laws* (MAL) dating to the late second millennium, and four omens dating to the first. Only one of the laws treats the topic of homosexuality *per se* as the subject of the law; the other is about sexual slander. Of the four omens, three have positive outcomes, while the fourth seems to have more to do with sexual exploitation than homosexuality.

The primary passage in the MAL is §20:

§20: *šumma a 'īlu tappâšu inīk ubta 'eruš ukta 'inuš inikkuš ana ša rēšēn utarruš.*[26]

§20: If a man fucks (*inīk*) his peer (*tappâšu*) (and) they prove the charges against him and find him guilty, they will fuck him (*inikkuš*) and turn him into/over to a/the *ša rēšēn*.

The verb I have translated here as "to fuck" is *nâku/niāku*, which means "to fornicate, to have illicit intercourse." (I used the translation "to fuck" to preserve the Subject-Verb-Direct Object structure of the original, and because the verb generally has a cast of disapproval in the original as well.) It is the verb used to describe sexual intercourse in cases of adultery as well and thus is not reserved for cases of homosexuality. As such, the translation:

If a man sodomizes his comrade and they prove the charges against him and find him guilty, they shall sodomize him and turn him into a eunuch.

has allusions that are not entirely present in the original text.[27] *Nâku* need not have the overtones of sodomy *per se*. Of course, it seems a rather appropriate translation for the punishment, where the original man appears to be gang-raped by whoever "they" are.

The latter part of the punishment is open to debate. The standard understanding is that the man is castrated: turned into a *ša rēši*, translated as "eunuch." This is possible. However, as discussed in Chapter 3, there are good reasons

254 Sexuality

to question this translation of *ša rēši*, and an alternative translation, offered by Stephanie Dalley, is that they turn the man *over to* a *ša rēši*, that is, a high-ranking administrator.[28]

As noted by Martti Nissinen, Ann Guinan and Peter Morris, the law pertains exclusively to sex with a *tappâ'u*, a man equal in status to the man committing the crime.[29] Thus it is not male–male sexual intercourse that is under consideration but specifically sex between male peers. Furthermore, it is only the man committing the *nâku* who is punished, not both partners (contra Leviticus 20:13, see subsequently).

As is typical, this law is generally understood in terms of the dominant masculine vs. passive feminine/effeminate paradigm. For Nissinen, "Penetrating a *tappā'u* was tantamount to rape and deliberate disgrace, because the penetrating partner effects a change in the other partner's role from active (male) to passive (female)."[30] For Guinan and Morris,

> Either by word or by deed, one close associate has subordinated another—it is an infringement of masculine position or agency in a community of men who share the prerogatives of power. It is not hard to detect a sense of masculinity under threat in these legal texts.[31]

For Julia Assante on the eventual punishment:

> This violent feminization of the *awīlu* offender clearly casts him forever out of his peer group and asserts a radical gender hierarchy between *awīlu* and criminal. The offender's altered position as the "other," a viable object of male predation, one who can never again penetrate, recovered and exaggerates the lost masculine status of the violated *awīlu*.[32]

However, it must be observed that there is no reference to force being used by the first man.[33] The word *emūqamma*—"forcibly"—appears in the laws pertaining to adultery to distinguish between sex as adultery and sex as rape ("forcibly"). This word does not appear in §20, and thus it appears that rape is *not* at issue. So whatever punishment accrues to the *nâku*-ing subject, it is not because of rape. Furthermore, there is no indication of who brings the matter to court (so to speak): That is, it is not stated that the *object* of the *nâku*-ing is prosecuting the man who fucked him. This may also argue against the rape hypothesis, as there is no male accusing another male of violence. Finally, it must be recalled that this is not a law about homosexual sex *per se* but homosexual sex specifically between social peers. There is no mention of homosexual intercourse between members of different classes, and thus we might at best suggest that this law pertains not to homosexuality or rape so much as the regulation of class relations.

Ultimately, §20 is unique in the Mesopotamian corpus, not just in the MAL but the *entire* corpus of Mesopotamian jurisprudence. In the absence of any comparable laws, it is impossible to hypothesize what it meant to the Assyrians

Sexuality 255

who formulated it and possibly enforced it. But its uniqueness and narrow focus (*tappâ'u*) indicate quite a limited interest in homosexuality in the Mesopotamian laws.

Immediately preceding §20 is §19,[34] which is also often taken as evidence for homosexuality in Mesopotamia. It reads:

> §19: If a man (*a'īlu*) furtively spreads rumors about his comrade (*tappā'išu*), saying "Everyone fucks (*ittinikkuš*) him," or in a quarrel in a public place says to him, "Everyone fucks (*ittinikkuka*) you," and further, "I can prove the charges against you," but he is unable to prove the charges and does not prove the charges, they shall strike that (first) man 50 blows with rods; he shall perform the king's service for one full month; they shall cut off his hair; moreover, he shall pay 3,600 shekels of lead.

This law itself is preceded by a similar law:

> §18: If a man says to his comrade, either in private or in public quarrel, "Everyone fucks your wife: I can prove the charges," but he is unable to prove the charges and does not prove the charges, they shall strike him 40 blows with rods; they shall cut off his hair and he shall pay 3,600 shekels of lead.

Two linguistic points must be considered. In both laws, the Gtn form of the verb *nâku* is used, referring to continuous and ongoing action. Thus, it is not a matter of a single illicit schtup, but a regular practice of illicit sex. Second, the *nâku*-verb is presented in the third person masculine plural: "They (males) fuck." This form may, however, refer to males and females combined. Granted, females are more likely to be the subjects of the passive construction of *nâku* (CAD *nâku*, IV and V), so the active form in use in the laws would more likely be understood as referring to male subjects. But it remains a possibility that both male and female subjects can be understood.

Both laws pertain to *slander*. In both §§18 and 19, either a married woman or a man of a certain social standing (*a'īlu*) is accused of having a lot of sex with people they are not supposed to have sex with. So while the slander is of a sexual variety, what is being prosecuted and punished is not any kind of sexual behavior but slander. It is the *slanderer* who is under consideration and potentially punished—NOT the individual being libeled.

For §18 this is eminently reasonable, considering the penalties for adultery pronounced immediately previously in the MAL—§§13–16. Here are laid out the punishments for an adulterous wife and her lover, depending on whether the lover knew the woman was married and whether force (rape) was involved. In most instances, the penalty is death, either for the wife, the lover, or both. §§14–16 allow the cuckolded husband to decide the fate of the wife. As we saw in Chapter 3, §15 allowed the husband to kill or disfigure both the wife and the adulterer. So there are some serious consequences to the slander discussed and regulated

256 *Sexuality*

by §18. So much so that the laws permitted various avenues of approach when dealing with the issue: The slander of §18 was only truly pronounced after other avenues had been exhausted. For example, §17 states:

> If a man should say to a man, "Everyone always fucks your wife" but there are no witnesses, they shall draw up a binding agreement, they shall undergo the River Ordeal.[35]

One could quite reasonably argue that adultery was important to the Assyrians, with several laws pertaining to the regulation of sex within and outside of a marriage.

By contrast, there is no follow-up to law §19. That is: What happens if it *is* proven that everyone fucks a particular man? Unlike the accusation of adultery, there is no consequence present in the laws. There is no law against a man *being* fucked. At best, we might argue that the follow-up law is §20, and that if it were in fact proven that a man was routinely fucked by men who turned out to be his *tappâ'u*s, then the next step would be to go prosecute *them* for *nâku*-ing a peer. At which point it seems that the slander is less against the man who got *nâku*ed than against the men who (repeatedly) *ittinikku*ed him.

At best, we might argue that what we seem to have here is the antithesis of the Greco-Roman discourse. In the Greco-Roman materials, it is shameful to be the *penetrated* male (unless one is already outside of the standard adult citizen male category, as with boys). Such is the position of women and slaves and prostitutes. By contrast, in MAL, there appear to be no (stated) repercussions for being the penetratee, only for being the penetrator of a peer. In which case, the punishment is to be repeatedly penetrated and then, depending on one's take on the expression *ana ša rēšēn utarruš*, to be castrated or turned over to the appropriate authorities. For a Middle Assyrian man, it is illegal to be the man on top when dealing with one's peers. But there are no indications—other than pure speculation mostly derived from a later, foreign culture—as to why this is the case.

The omens provide a different point of view entirely. These appear in the *Šumma ālu* omens, codified around the middle of the 7th century BCE. According to one omen (CT 39 44:13):

> DIŠ NA *a-na* GU.DU *me-eḫ-ri-šu₂* TE, NA.BI *ina* ŠEŠ.ME[-*šu₂*] *u₃ ki-na-ti-šu₂ a-ša₂-re-du-tam* DU-*ak*.

> If a man (NA=*awīlum*) penetrates (TE=*sahālu*) his social peer (*meḫru*) via the buttocks/anus (*ana* GU.DU), that man will become foremost among his brothers and colleagues.

Farther along, three additional omens deal with a similar subject, although with slightly less anatomical specificity:

> (CT 39 45:32) DIŠ NA *a-na as-sin-ni* TE, *da-na-tu* DU₈-*šu*.[36]

> If a man penetrates an *assinnu*, hardships will be unleashed from him

Sexuality   257

(CT 39 45:33) DIŠ NA *a-na* GIR₃.SI₃.GA TE, *ka-la* MU.1.KAM₂ *tam-t·a-a-tum ša₂* GAR.MEŠ-*šu₂ ip-pa-ra-sa.*

If a man penetrates a *girseqû*, for an entire year the deprivations which beset him will be kept away.

(CT 39 45:34) DIŠ NA *a-na du-uš-mi-šu₂* TE, KI.KAL.DIB-*šu.*

If a man penetrates a male house[-born] slave, hardship will seize him.

Four omens pertaining to a man "penetrating" other men. In the first, as was the case with the MAL laws, it is a peer (*meḥru*) who is penetrated, specifically via the buttocks/anus. Thus, anal sex with a peer. In the other three, penetration (without reference to the body-part entailed) occurs with an *assinnu*—a cult functionary of Ištar (see Chapter 4), a *girseqû*—a palace official, or a household slave. In the first three, the apodosis is beneficial: The penetrating man gets status, or at least dodges hardships. It is only the final apodosis that is negative: The man who penetrates a household male slave is beset with hardships.

Ann Guinan noted the punning logic driving the meaning of the first omen:

> The term *meḥru* (peer) refers to parity of status. The omen turns on the switch of positions from "behind" to "in front" [*maḥru* = "before"] and on the paronomastic relationship between the words *qinnatu* ("anus") and *kinātu* ("colleagues"). Thus, one can put oneself ahead of one's peers in the community by penetrating one of them from behind. The possibility that collegiate relations could also be sexual is underscored by the telling pun.[37]

In any event, the action is positive: There is no echo of the punishment facing a man who "penetrates" a peer as seen in the earlier MAL §20.

It is perhaps the lack of pun on *kinātu*/colleagues that accounts for the lack of the reference to the *ana* GU.DU in the other three omens. Or, possibly, the authors chose to leave open and optional the receptive bodily orifice. What is clear, though, is that for a man to penetrate either an *assinnu* or a *girseqû* was positive. In both instances, it is not necessarily a peer with whom the man is having sex but what might a dubbed a respectable functionary in the religious and royal hierarchies of the city, respectively. That is: free men with agency and status. By contrast, misfortune attends on the man who penetrates a slave of his own household. For Guinen, this sexual encounter does not lead to a beneficial outcome because it does not occur in the public arena: Dominance over a member of one's own household is a private affair that does not entail repercussions in society at large.[38] However, this does not account for the *negative* nature of the apodosis. Based on the contrast with the other three, positive omens, one might suggest that sex with one not merely a social inferior but one with no status or agency (a slave) is a form of rape, of what the Greeks would have called hubris. A man who commits hubris in his own household is potentially in for a world of trouble.

All in all, the Mesopotamian data give a mixed view of male homosexuality. One or two laws dating to late 2nd-millennium Assyria suggest that sexual

258 *Sexuality*

relations between male peers, specifically, were problematic, either if one were a habitual penetratee or so much as a one-time penetrator. To be the penetrator was illegal, to be the penetratee was . . .? In direct contrast, three omens dating to the 1st millennium indicate that sex between relatively equal males was beneficial, at least for the penetrator. By contrast, to penetrate a man with no agency brought misfortune. Overshadowing this handful of data is the immense silence about homosexuality throughout the entire rest of the Mesopotamian corpora—thousands of years and texts, including several law codes, that have nothing to say whatsoever about sex between men (or women). Relatively speaking, homosexuality was not a concern in Mesopotamia.

Hebrew Bible

Remarkably, the same can be said for the Hebrew Bible. There are only four references to homosexuality in that text, two *pairs* that appear to be variations on each other. As such, two references both written two ways.

Leviticus

The more obvious references appear in the book of Leviticus, regulations that date to c. 550, during the Babylonian Captivity:[39]

> Leviticus 18:22: *wĕ'et zākār lō'tiškab miškĕbê 'iššâ tô'ēbâ hî'*.
>
> And with a male you shall not lie the lying down of a woman; it is *tô'ēbâ*.[40]
>
> Leviticus 20:13: *wĕ'îš 'ăšer yiškab 'et zākār miškĕbê 'iššâ tô'ēbâ'āsû šĕnĕhem môt yûmātû dĕmêhem bām*.
>
> And as for the man who lies with a male the lying down of a woman, they— the two of them—have committed a *tô'ēbâ*; they shall certainly be put to death; their blood is upon them.[41]

Saul Olyan, in his study of these laws, presents three critical points. First, the expression *miškĕbê 'iššâ*—the "lying down of a woman"—is a *hapax legomenon*, appearing exclusively in these two phrases. Second, "[t]hey are the only such laws in the Hebrew Bible: there is absolutely nothing analogous to them in the other Israelite collections mediated to us."[42] As with the MAL laws, then, we are working in a vacuum when attempting to understand these statutes.

Third, 20:13 appears to be a later editorial reworking of the original 18:22. In both 18:22 and the opening portion of 20:13, only the male penetrator is addressed, either directly in the second person singular (18:22), or indirectly in the third person masculine singular (20:13). However, the latter portion of 20:13 changes the focus to include *both* males—"the two of them"—and *they* (third person masculine plural) will be put to death. A comparable change of focus can be seen in the adultery law 20:10, where the initial reference is to the man who commits adultery with the wife of his neighbor and is to be put to death (*môt yûmat*—third person masculine singular), and then an awkward "both of them" is tacked on at the end to include the woman who is not present in the formation of any actual verb in the clause. Just so, Leviticus 18:22 refers exclusively to the male penetrator, who is again the focus at the beginning of Leviticus 20:13, which then switches to a masculine plural to round out the consequences for both parties. It is possible, then, that 18:22 and 20:13 are variations on a single original law, an earlier version of which penalized only the penetrator and a later edition that included both partners in the punishment (as the adulterous wife came to join her lover in death in 20:10).[43] If this reconstruction be the case—and it is speculative—then what we have in Leviticus is not two laws against male homosexuality but one at slightly different points in time, with slightly different foci.

What is exceptionally clear is that this reference to male–male sexual intercourse is unique and atypical. It appears in the midst of numerous laws prohibiting, repeatedly, every possible manifestation of incest imaginable, including (Leviticus 18:6–18) one's own mother, one's own father, one's step-mother, one's sister or step-sister, one's niece, one's granddaughter, one's aunt, one's sister-in-law, one's mother-in-law, one's daughter-in-law, or one's third cousin twice removed on the father's or mother's side.[44] On the off-chance none of that was specific enough, Leviticus 18:20 reiterates, "You shall not have sexual relations with your kinsman's wife." If that is not enough, it all gets repeated in Leviticus 20, another clue that 18:22 and 20:13 are repeats of each other, just as 18 and 20 are mostly repeats. Furthermore, sex with animals is right out (e.g. Lev. 18:23), repeatedly, as is sex with any woman who is menstruating (e.g. Lev. 20:18). Leviticus is quite clear that menstrual blood is defiling, as is semen, repeatedly (Leviticus 15).

In contrast to all this, male–male sexual intercourse is quite the outlier. It appears almost as an afterthought and provides no comparanda with which to understand its meaning in the Holiness Code. We are left to speculate, and only speculate. Some have speculated on the wasting of "seed," especially in a community concerned with population growth in the face of empires such as the Babylonians and Persians. The idea of a common theme throughout the Holiness Code of sex with any individual who will not generate a child with a clear place in the social hierarchy may strengthen this suggestion. Others have considered a "double-impurity" aspect, whereby impure semen gets combined with other impure materials (e.g. feces, menstrual blood) creating a full-blown *tô'ēbâ*.[45]

Two hypotheses are of particular interest: 1) the concern with gender transgression—the penetrator/penetratee aspect, and 2) the idea that these purity regulations help to distinguish between the Israelites and their "pagan" neighbors. The former hypothesis, the most popular in the current discourse, seems the least likely here, because the one thing that seems even less important to the biblical authors and editors than homosexuality was gender transgression. Only one regulation pertains to it, and that not even in Leviticus but Deuteronomy. Deut. 22:5 states that "[For] a woman shall not be the implements (*kelî*) of a man/warrior (*geber*) and [for] a man not to wear the clothing (*simlat*) of a woman, for whoever does these things is *tô'abât* to the LORD your God." This regulation comes

260   *Sexuality*

between the commandment to help your neighbor's donkey or ox if you see it injured on the road and the injunction against hurting a mother bird when stealing her eggs. The biblical authors were not unclear communicators; if something was important to them (apostasy, incest, purity), they were very good at expressing the idea *ad nauseum*. Gender transgression was clearly not one of those concerns.

The matter of differentiating the (post-)Captivity Israelites from their neighbors is an interesting speculation in light of the codes of the surrounding peoples, who maintain *similar* sex laws as those presented in Leviticus. The same focus on adultery appears in MAL, *inter alia*, while similar prohibitions on bestiality appear in the Hittite Laws (e.g. §§187–188).[46] In point of fact, the closest cognate to Lev. 18:22 and 20:13 is MAL §20, a law that, to judge from the *Šumma ālu* series, was no longer in effect at the time of the Captivity. The only peoples from whom the Israelites would specifically be differentiating themselves with their sex prohibitions are, in fact, the Greeks, who practiced pederasty; "incest" in terms of close-relation marriage, especially as concerns the marriage of *epikleroi* (girls with no brothers who marry the closest male relative on the father's side); and where bestiality formed a substantial element in the mythology if not daily practice (that I know of).

In the end, I suggest that there are simply not enough data to interpret Lev. 18:22 and 20:13. They are unique among the Biblical laws and were clearly of far less concern than matters of incest and adultery. We cannot know what their author was thinking in the absence of any comparanda. What does appear to be clear, though, is that the Greco-Roman concern with gender "integrity" and power dynamics has no supporting evidence in this instance. Again to quote Olyan:

> Did Israelites abhor male couplings, as has been generally assumed up to the present? Certainly the evidence of the Hebrew Bible is insufficient to support this view. Such a generalization is more easily defended for adultery, incest, and human-animal couplings, all of which are prohibited in legal materials outside of the Holiness Source. But intercourse between males is mentioned in no other Israelite legal setting.[47]

Rape

There are two places in the Bible where men threaten other men with rape. The first, and more (in)famous, is the tale of Sodom presented in Genesis 19. In this narrative, while Lot is living in Sodom, two angels in disguise come to visit the city and Lot offered them hospitality for the night. Later, the men of the city came to Lot's house and demanded that he send out the visitors so that they might "know" them. In attempting to defend the visitors he offers to send out instead his virgin daughters. This offer was rejected, leading the men of Sodom to threaten Lot—a foreign resident—with violence in addition to the two visitors. In the end, the angels blinded the male aggressors and eventually God destroyed the town.

The cognate tale is narrated in Judges 19. Here an anonymous man of Ephraim travels south to Bethlehem in Judah to recover his secondary wife/concubine. After staying several days with his father-in-law, he and the secondary wife

Sexuality 261

traveled until they reached Gibeah in Benjaminite territory, where they were eventually taken in by a man also from Ephraim now residing in Gibeah. As was the case in Sodom, at night the men of the town came to the man's house demanding that he hand over the visitor so that they might "know" him. Again, the man offered instead his virgin daughter and the man's secondary wife. Again, the men refused. But when the husband threw the secondary wife out to them, the men gang-raped her until she died. This was then used as an excuse for the men of the north to unite and fight a war against the Benjaminites.

Both tales relate how one or more male entities (man, angels) were threatened with rape when visiting a (non-Israelite) town. In both instances, their host, also a foreigner in the town, attempted to protect the guests by offering one or more virgin daughters to the gang of rapists, who declined. In the latter narrative, nevertheless, it is in the end a woman who is cast out, raped, and killed.

It is the former tale—the story of Sodom (and Gomorrah)—that is the better known and the one more commonly turned to when considering the Biblical take on homosexuality. Obviously, we get the word "sodomite" from it. Along with the laws of Leviticus 18:22 and 20:13, the tale of the Sodomites is marshalled as evidence that the Hebrew Bible disapproves of and demonizes male–male homosexual intercourse. However, three points must be considered in this regard.

First, what is presented in both Genesis 19 and Judges 19 is not intercourse, but (threatened) rape. Rape is its own category of sexuality and cannot be used as evidence for the social acceptability or morality of consensual forms of sexuality. Rape is independent of both homosexuality and heterosexuality.

Furthermore, the close parallels between both narratives highlight the *formulaic* quality of the tales in question, where a set of "pre-scripted" actions leads to a "justifiable" war against, and even extermination of, a predetermined category of villains. Both tales present travelers (angels, man, and concubine) being offered hospitality by another man who is a resident foreigner in a land not known for hospitality. To emphasize this fact, the native men of the town show up, banging on the door, demanding "to know" (have sex with) the men under the protection of the host. In both cases, (a) virgin daughter(s) is offered as a substitute but declined. In the end, the natives are destroyed either directly through God's wrath or through warfare.

Related rape narratives occur elsewhere in the Bible, with similar outcomes. In Genesis 34, we read of Dinah, a daughter of Jacob and Leah, who was raped by Shechem son of Havor. In the end, her brothers Simeon and Levi (Gen. 34:25–29) "came upon the city unmolested and slew all the males. . . . The other sons of Jacob came upon the slain and plundered the town." All their possessions, including their wives and children, were taken as booty. Rape leads to carnage.[48] In 2 Samuel 13, it is the rape of Tamar by her half-brother Amnon that led to the death of the latter at the hands of his brother Absalom and the initiation of Absalom's attempted coup d'état against his own father King David. Rape leads to carnage. It is likely, then, that the matter of threatened rape in Genesis 19 and Judges 19 pertains to a literary trope whereby rape leads to the destruction of the perpetrators. The variation here is that the originally threatened victims are male. And,

262 *Sexuality*

to repeat: threatened. No male–male sexual intercourse actually occurs in either Genesis 19 or Judges 19: both males and females (the daughters and concubine) are threatened, but it is *only* a female who is ever actually raped in any of the rape narratives.[49] But even with the male variation, the same formulaic results manifest.

Second, the common theme of rape is presented as merely one aspect of the overarching sin of bad hospitality as displayed by the Sodomites and Benjaminites. In *both* towns, no one offers the travelers a place to stay for the evening except for a foreigner living among the natives (Lot, the man of Ephraim). In *both* narratives, they appear *en masse* to harass both the host and his guests. The threat of rape is part and parcel of a greater issue pertaining to what the Greeks would call a total lack of *xenia*.

This explains the third point: that neither the Biblical authors nor the Talmudic scholars thought of the Sodom narrative as pertaining to homosexuality or rape. Rather, the sin of the Sodomites was greed and a lack of charity.[50] This is most clearly expressed in Ezekiel 16:48–50:

> As I live, says the Lord GOD, your sister Sodom and her daughters have not done as you and your daughters have done. This was the guilt of your sister Sodom: She and her daughters had **pride, excess of food, and prosperous ease, but did not aid the poor and needy. They were haughty, and did abominable things** before me; therefore I removed them when I saw it.

Likewise, in Jeremiah 23:14, the poet compares the evil prophets of the now-destroyed Jerusalem with their forebears in Sodom and Gomorrah:

> But in the prophets of Jerusalem
>   I have seen a more shocking thing:
> **they commit adultery and walk in lies;**
>   **they strengthen the hands of evildoers**,
>   so that no one turns from wickedness;
> all of them have become like Sodom to me,
>   and its inhabitants like Gomorrah.

In the Babylonian Talmud: Sanhedrin 109b a recorded number of (admittedly humorous) anecdotes about the sins of Sodom (all pertaining to greed) culminates with:

> There was a young woman who would take bread out to the poor people in a pitcher so the people of Sodom would not see it. The matter was revealed, and they smeared her with honey and positioned her on the wall of the city, and the hornets came and consumed her. And that is the meaning of that which is written: "And the Lord said: Because the cry of Sodom and Gomorrah is great [*rabba*]". And Rav Yehuda says that Rav says: *Rabba* is an allusion to the matter of the young woman [*riva*] who was killed for her act of kindness. **It is due to that sin that the fate of the people of Sodom was sealed**.

Again, there was a *lot* less homosexuality—and its condemnation—attested in the Hebrew Bible than people tend to think.

Egypt

As noted previously, gender and queer studies came relatively late to Egyptology. As if to compensate, queer theory has now been raging through the discipline, see(k)ing homoerotic relationships throughout the literary and art historical corpora. This is a good thing: It is always important to consider old data in new ways. On the flip side, one must take care not to become so overzealous that *all* data are forced into a new, trendy paradigm. In the following, a handful of case studies are considered that are now in the midst of various debates about homosexuality/homoeroticism in ancient Egypt, whether it exists in plain sight and we have refused (or been heretofore unable) to see it or are over-pushing an agenda. How any of these references were understood in their ancient contexts is still a matter of considerable debate in Egyptology, and thus all the interpretations here should be understood as extremely provisional.

Horus and Seth

The narrative that is perhaps easiest for a modern audience to understand, the one that most conforms to the "Classical Paradigm," is the tale of Horus and Seth, wherein both protagonists succeed to one extent or another at penetrating each other. The dynamics, however, change over the course of Egyptian history. A version from the Pyramid Text of Pepy I from the 6th Dynasty (Old Kingdom) indicates that there was complete reciprocity in the sexual encounter(s) between Horus and Seth, thus:

> Horus has insinuated (*n'*) his semen into the backside (*'rt*) of Seth;
> Seth has insinuated his semen into the backside of Horus.[51]

Such reciprocity conforms to the general balance between these two deities as presented in the Old Kingdom Memphite Theology, wherein:

> [Geb, lord of the gods, commanded] that the Nine Gods gather to him. He judged between Horus and Seth; he ended their quarrel. He made Seth king of Upper Egypt in the land of Upper Egypt, up to the place in which he was born, which is Su. And Geb made Horus king of Lower Egypt in the land of Lower Egypt, up to the place in which his father was drowned which is "Division-of-the-Two-Lands." Thus Horus stood over one region, and Seth stood over one region. They made peace over the Two Lands at Ayan. That was the division of the Two Lands.[52]

Rather than a narrative aspect, John Baines sees this confrontation as conforming to the conventions of early Egyptian magic: "The reciprocity of the action has more to do with the structure of magical spells than with a narrative, where an

264 *Sexuality*

asymmetrical outcome would be normal; in later versions, Seth fails to conquer Horus homosexually."[53]

From the Middle Kingdom, a 12th-Dynasty text from Lahun reveals a somewhat different take on this encounter. In this piece of literature we read what appears to be a bit of comedy, wherein Seth uses an ancient Egyptian "pick-up line" on his young relative:

> And then the Person of Seth said to the Person of Horus: "How lovely is your backside (*nfr.wj.phwj* = *kj*)! Broad (*wsh*) are [your] thighs [. . .]"[54]

For Parkinson, the humor of the piece lies in its skewing of more traditional forms of greeting:

> The "chat-up line" (*nfr.wj.phwj* = *kj*) is apparently a parody of *nfr.wj-hr* = *k*, "How fair is your face!", attested as a ritual greeting, and this probably marks the overture as ridiculous and irregular by replacing "face" with "backside." The second verse of Seth's speech is of uncertain reading; it may be a parody of the autobiographical epithet "broad of strides" (*wsh-nmtwt*).[55]

The best-known version of this confrontation between Horus and Seth appears in the New Kingdom tale *The Contendings of Horus and Seth*, where Seth attempts to sodomize Horus as a means of defeating his young opponent in court.

> Now afterward, at evening time, bed was prepared for them, and they both lay down. But during the night Seth caused his phallus to become stiff and inserted it between Horus's thighs. Then Horus placed his hands between his thighs and received Seth's semen. Horus went to tell his mother Isis: "Help me, Isis, my mother, come and see what Seth has done to me." And he opened his hand and let her see Seth's semen. She let out a loud shriek, seized her copper knife, and cut off his hand.[56] . . . Then she fetched some fragrant ointment and applied it to Horus's phallus. She caused it to become stiff and inserted it into a pot, and he caused his semen to flow down into it.
>
> Isis at morning time went carrying the semen of Horus to the garden of Seth and said to Seth's gardener: "What sort of vegetable is it that Seth eats here in your company?" So, the gardener told her: "He doesn't eat any vegetable here in my company except lettuce." And Isis added the semen of Horus onto it. Seth returned according to his daily habit and ate the lettuce, which he regularly ate. Thereupon he became pregnant with the semen of Horus.
>
> They both went to the tribunal and stood in the presence of the Great Ennead. . . . Said Seth: "Let me be offered the office of Ruler, for as to Horus . . . I have performed the work of a man against him." The Ennead let out a loud cry and spat on Horus's face.[57]

At this point Horus laughs at Seth and calls upon both of their units of semen to be called forth. Seth's is in the marsh, whereas that of Horus is in Seth, whereupon

Seth gives birth to the solar disk—offspring of Horus—out of his head. Horus is proclaimed victor, and Seth shrieks.

This is the clearest ANE portrayal of the penetrator=dominator=masculine vs. penetrated=submissive=effeminate paradigm. Seth specifically refers to his act as "performing the work of a man" against Horus. However, it is noteworthy that even though Horus emerges as the victor, he does not actually reciprocate Seth's actions. Horus does not attempt to sodomize Seth; rather, it is Isis who gathers Horus's semen and tricks Seth into *eating* it—no phallic penetration. The gender reversal is thus not defined by penetration *per se* but by infiltration and role reversal. To quote Greenberg:

> Since gender roles are defined only by contrast, Seth's announcement that he played the "male role" implies that Horus's role was "female." Although both Seth and Horus are morphologically male, the myth defines their gender not by their anatomy but by the roles they played.[58]

In the end, "Seth not only fails to 'do the deed of a man' to Horus, he is forced to play the feminine role in giving birth to Horus's offspring."[59] Furthermore, it is this very act of "masculine" domination that grants Horus victory over Seth in a court determining who will receive kingship in the wake of Osiris's death. Even though Horus does not technically penetrate Seth phallically, by effeminizing Seth via male pregnancy, Horus becomes the hegemonic male. Through the efforts of his mother Isis . . .

Niankhkhnum and Khnumhotep

To date, *no* topic in Egyptology has generated the amount of debate over queer readings than the iconography of the 5th-Dynasty mastaba of the men Niankhkhnum and Khnumhotep, identified as "Chief manicurists," "Overseer of the Manicurists of the Palace," "King's Acquaintances," and "Royal Confidants."[60] Contrary to standard practice throughout Egyptian history, in this mastaba two men are consistently shown together in a relationship of closeness and intimacy, a relationship that in other cases can only be compared to the closeness and intimacy of husband and wife (see Figure 5.1)

Several walls also show them in the presence of their families: Both men were married, and both had children who are shown as family members throughout the tomb. However, as often observed of the pair, the closer one gets to the heart of the tomb, the less frequently other family members appear and the more closely Niankhkhnum and Khnumhotep appear in intimate contact with each other.[61] Furthermore, in the tomb's banquet scene, Khnumhotep is shown in the absence of any wife, while Niankhkhnum's wife Khentikaus was deliberately erased from the composition.[62] All the iconographic evidence from the tomb focuses on the relationship the two men had with each other, almost to the deliberate exclusion of other family members.

Of course, there isn't a single hieroglyph preserved that actually says what their relationship was—whether they are brothers, lovers, or extremely close friends.

266 *Sexuality*

Figure 5.1 Scene from Mastaba of Niankhkhnum and Khnumhotep.
Source: Sailingstone Travel/Alamy Stock Photo.

When first discovered, and up to the dawn of the 21st century, the standard interpretation of the relationship depicted was that of brothers, probably even twins. This hypothesis was primarily proposed by John Baines in 1985, wherein he argued:

> The tomb is exceptional in many ways. It gives equal space throughout to the two men, and contains groups of them embracing and holding hands; their titles are almost identical and their names closely similar; a series of figures probably constituting a family scene gives them a special treatment. . . . Their kinship, if any, is never stated, which is not surprising, because Old Kingdom tombs are relatively sparing in the genealogical information they give. The point is therefore insignificant for their proposed status as twins, except in that it makes it unprovable.[63]

In 1995, though, Nadine Cherpion completed a study of conjugal depictions in Old Kingdom tomb iconography, and she noted that the postures adopted by Niankhkhnum and Khnumhotep could best be compared to those depicted between husbands and wives. That is, in spite of the unique nature of the tomb's iconography, the closest parallels could be found between married couples. This opened the possibility that rather than being entirely unique, Niankhkhnum and Khnumhotep's tomb simply portrayed the men as an intimate couple, comparable to such scenes between men and women.

Building on this notion, Greg Reeder furthered this analysis by noting not only that Niankhkhnum and Khnumhotep were depicted as a "married" couple, but that

Niankhkhnum was consistently shown as the "husband" and Khnumhotep consistently appeared as the "wife." Throughout the mastaba, Niankhkhnum appears to the right of Khnumhotep, who fills the position usually held by the wife in depictions of married couples. On the southern wall of the entrance hall the two men walk together: Niankhkhnum leads Khnumhotep by the hand, again as is typical in husband–wife depictions. When shown seated before their offering table, Niankhkhnum sits to the right, while Khnumhotep opposite him holds a lotus to his nose, a gesture that was typically reserved for women in the Old Kingdom. To quote Reeder, "I can only speculate that the designers of this tomb recognized that Khnumhotep was in some special way occupying the space normally reserved for the wife."[64]

So, two men with no reference to family relationship between them who repeatedly eschew depictions of their wives while appearing in close proximity to each other that in any other context would be accepted as marital intimacy. Even in 1986 Cherpion suggested that it was the "inseparable" relationship between Niankhkhnum and Khnumhotep that accounted for the minimal representation of their wives in the tomb.[65] Do we, in fact, have here what in modern times would be considered a homosexual couple?

As with twinship, the matter is impossible to prove. While the postures of the two men have their closest cognates in married couples, they are not the only cognates, and not all cognates are necessarily (sexually) intimate. As noted by Baines:

> Since the embracing and hand-holding scenes are unique in private tombs, little can be said about their meaning beyond the fact that they express publicly the close involvement of the two men. Elsewhere the motifs do not have a sexual meaning, as opposed to displaying socially and emotionally linked roles, and such a meaning should not be sought here. The lack of sexual associations can perhaps be seen most easily in cases where several figures in a group have their arms round one another, more or less regardless of sex or relative age. Embraces normally symbolise protection or close identification and reciprocity, of which the latter is relevant here.[66]

Likewise, the minimizing of the display of the wives, including the complete erasure of Khentikaus in the banquet scene, might be related to changing trends in tomb decoration observed at this period. Wives only came to appear in their husband's tomb paintings in the 4th Dynasty, a trend which continued into the 5th. But by the end of the 5th Dynasty, the presence of wives again began to decrease in the tomb decoration, such that by the reigns of Kings Izezi and Unas wives are absent from 77% of husbands' tombs, even when other family members such as children are present and labeled.[67] As the tomb of Niankhkhnum and Khnumhotep is roughly contemporary with the reign of Unas, it appears right when it is becoming increasingly trendy *not* to feature wives in tomb paintings.

So, are Niankhkhnum and Khnumhotep lovers, fashionistas, or both? At the moment, it is impossible to say. There is little more vexing in the study of antiquity than something that is unique. All the comparanda are provisional; no paradigms

268 *Sexuality*

quite fit. In spite of a wealth of evidence, one has to start from scratch. Is there much to argue for the reading as twins? Yes. Should the hypothesis of lovers be jettisoned because it is unique? No. If every new discovery is rejected because it is different from whatever is considered the norm, then there is never a body of evidence to turn to when more of what is different is found. Niankhkhnum and Khnumhotep may not be brothers, and they may not be lovers, but it is only by continuously pushing the questions and seeking creatively for answers that any resolution has any hope of being found. Stay tuned.

King Neferkare and General Sasenet

Perhaps the least ambiguous reference to male homoeroticism comes from the New Kingdom narrative *The Tale of King Neferkare and General Sasenet*, composed in the 19th Dynasty but pertaining to the final king of the Old Kingdom Pepy II (here called by the name Neferkare).[68] After making it clear in the opening portion of the text that General Sasenet/Sisene *jw-nn-wn-st-ḥmt m* [. . .] "had no wife [with him]"[69] the later text reveals that:

> He (the king) arrived at General Sasenet's house. He tossed a brick, he stomped his foot, at which point a [ladder] was tossed down to him. He climbed. . . . After His Majesty had done what he desired with him (the general) (*jrj-mr(t) f-ḥr f*), he went to his palace. . . . Then, His Majesty went to the house of General Sasenet, while four hours passed in the night. He spent four additional hours in the house of General Sasenet. And (then) he returned to the Great Domicile, where he remained four hours until dawn.[70]

Basically, the king makes a nighttime booty call to the general. The expression "did what he desired with," as both Posener and Parkinson observe, appears in an 18th-Dynasty reference to sex between god and queen and clearly seems to refer to sexual intercourse.[71] So, a homosexual liaison between the king and his general.

What this meant in the contemporary society—New Kingdom Egypt—is more difficult to determine. Pepy II, who reigned for close to a century, was the final king of the Old Kingdom, and there is a strong sense that his weaknesses as king led to the First Intermediate Period in Egyptian history. He was not necessarily highly regarded by later generations. Furthermore, the story of Neferkare and Sasenet itself appears to be a work of comedy, with much of the humor predicated on the bad actions of the king during his reign (e.g. having a plaintiff drowned out in court by excessive music, in contrast to the king's duty to provide justice/*ma'at* in the land). As such, the fact that the king has a sexual relationship with his bachelor general may be understood as one more cause for mockery. The baseline approach to the narrative has been one of basic disapproval. For Posener, publishing the *editio princeps* of the text in 1957, "le récit se présente comme une satire des moeurs qui montre la decomposition de l'Ancien Empire à la veille de sa chute" (The tale appears as a satire of customs that demonstrate the breakdown of the Old Kingdom just before its fall).[72] For Parkinson, "The tone of the tale . . . does imply that a sexual relationship between men was scandalous, although it was not 'unspeakable', even when it concerned the very centre of society, the king."[73]

The Book of the Dead

Another datum that offers utterly ambiguous evidence about ancient Egyptian views of homosexuality comes from the 18th-Dynasty *Book of the Dead*, Chapter 125, §27, wherein the heart of the deceased swears that: *n nk.i nkk*, "I did not *nk* a *nkk(w)*"[74] The verb *nk* is sexual in meaning and has what C.J. Eyre calls "the same sense and range of meaning as the standard English transitive four-letter word."[75] So, basically, the deceased swears that he "did not fuck a fucked man." He does not swear that he did not fuck men *in general*, and later he swears that he also did not fuck a *ḥmt-tꜣj*—a married women (i.e. commit adultery). Whatever the specific nature of the "sin" denied was, there are insufficient data to determine how this testimony may or may not relate to homosexuality.

The Teaching of the Vizier Ptahhotep

Perhaps the most baffling text (possibly) pertaining to homosexuality from ancient Egypt is the 32nd maxim of the *Teaching of the Vizier Ptahhotep*. In her translation of this important piece of didactic literature, Miriam Lichtheim says of this passage: *"This maxim is an injunction against illicit sexual intercourse. It is very obscure and has been omitted here."*[76] The text as translated by Parkinson reads:

> May you not have sex (*nk*) with a woman-boy (*ḥmt-hrd*), for you know that what is opposed will be water upon his breast.
> There is no coolness/relief for what is in his belly/appetite.
> Let him not spend the night doing what is opposed;
> He shall be cool after renouncing his desire.[77]

One of the most problematic aspects of the text is the definition of *ḥmt-hrd*. *Ḥmt* is "woman." *Hrd* is "child." When P. Prisse first translated the passage, he took the term as "femme (qui est encore) enfant," and it appeared that the passage was an admonition against raping/seducing a female child.[78] However, as noted by Parkinson *inter alia*, the gendered suffixes of the remaining text indicate that the object of the *nk*-action is masculine, thus leading to translations such as "woman-boy" or even "vulva-boy."[79] Furthermore, the problem with *nk*-ing this individual does not appear to have to do with his (her?) age but the fact that this individual is apparently insatiable—"There is no relief for what is in his belly." Rather than being a matter of homosexuality or pederasty, both Hans Goedicke and Parkinson suggests that this passage seems to pertain to having continual sex with someone who is unrestrained and cannot be fulfilled by sex. Rather than seeking satisfaction in sex, it would behoove the *ḥmt-hrd* instead to forsake his desire/libido. Until

270   *Sexuality*

a clearer understanding of the meaning is *ḥmt-hrd* is achieved, the passage will remain as Lichtheim describes it.

ḤM

The datum currently appearing in Egyptological gender studies that probably has the least to say about homosexuality in ancient Egypt is the word *ḥm* (⬭🦉─⬭), also rendered *ḥmtý* or *ḥmjw* depending on date and context.[80] The word derives from the verb *ḥmi*—"to retreat" (⬭🦉△)—and because it features an ejaculating penis, it has come to be understood as having a sexual component, thus rendering a translation as "back-turner" with an innate understanding of one who offers his buttocks. Thus for Parkinson, "Presumably to 'turn the back' is tantamount to allowing oneself to be buggered."[81]

The word first appears in Old Kingdom tomb scenes of daily life, wherein male harvesters—called *ṯȝj* = male/lad—abusively call those not in their group *ḥmjw*. Because the word combines the verb "to retreat" with a homophone for the word "woman" (*ḥmt*—⬭🪶—and because the word is used in opposition to *ṯȝj*/male, it appears that the term is an insult to both the masculinity and the bravery of the one insulted. In the Middle Kingdom, the word—again as *ḥmjw*—appears on the boundary stelae of Senwosret III at Semna and Uronarti, wherein the Egyptian king proclaims (Berlin ÄM 1157 and Khartum Nr. 3, ll. 8–9):[82]

> Aggression is bravery;
> Retreat is vile.
> He who is driven from this boundary is a true *ḥmjw*.[83]

In the New Kingdom, after the Battle of Qadesh, Pharaoh Ramesses II asks:

> What are these *ḥm.w* to you, for millions of whom I care nothing?"[84]

The word is clearly an insult, pertains to running away and thus cowardly behavior, and appears to have a gender component manifest both in the phallus hieroglyph and the similarity in sound to the word for "woman." Translations reveal the extent to which modern translators engender the word. At the most basic, and common, it is simply taken as "coward."[85] Mark Depauw, giving an effeminate edge to the notion, offers instead "sissy."[86] Perhaps the most vicious translation comes from Robert Delia, who translates "fag."[87] A personal favorite is "effeminate poltroon."[88] As an insult, it can provide some sense of ancient Egyptian ideology on what constitutes a "good" man, insofar as he is not a coward, not a "back-turner," not one who runs away. It can be argued that the word stands in contradistinction to terms pertaining to maleness—*ṯȝj*—and sounds like "woman," and thus there may be a gendered aspect to the insult. But there is nothing innate to the term or its orthography that indicates that it has anything to do with homosexuality. If a

Sexuality 271

coward turns his back, he probably runs rather than inviting penetration. Cowards are not specifically homosexual, or vice versa.

Bromance

"Bromance" is a modern slang term for an intensely intimate relationship between two males that apparently teeters on, but never passes over, the dividing line into eroticism. When presented in the arts (e.g. Anne Proulx's "Brokeback Mountain" and the eventual film with Heath Ledger and Jake Gyllenhaal), it is interpreted as a closeted homoerotic/homosexual relationship. In modern academia, we take the same approach to ancient examples of such intense male–male relationships and see them as examples of homosexual relationships in antiquity. The most common exemplars of such ancient bromances are Gilgameš and Enkidu from the Mesopotamian *Gilgameš Epic* and David and Jonathan in the Hebrew Bible.

Before delving into the evidence on these relationships, one important caveat must be considered: The expression of physical affection is relative throughout different cultures. That is, what are deemed acceptable—even typical—physical expressions of emotional states between people vary from one society to the next. In a more openly emotive society, it may be completely permissible and quite expected to hug and kiss a close friend or family member of either sex as a means of greeting or bidding farewell, and tears may be involved. In a more restrained society, shaking hands may be the norm, or even bowing in a society that frowns upon bodily contact. Anyone fond of British murder mysteries may marvel at the emotional restraint of members of the upper classes upon being told that a beloved family member has been killed (there may be a single tear). Even within individual cultures, what is deemed acceptable contact or open displays of affection can vary between females and males: Females are generally permitted more openly affectionate behavior (hugging and kissing each other as a greeting); in America at least, males may only hug if it's followed up by manly slaps on the back.[89] By contrast, in Russia, for example, males are permitted and expected to be more demonstrative. Thus the anecdote in Hedrick Smith's book *The Russians*, wherein he related how, at a special viewing of the movie *Doctor Zhivago*, the audience burst out laughing at the scene where Yuri greets his family on the train platform with subdued handshakes, like proper Englishmen. *Real* Russians would be smothering each other in bear hugs and crying copiously.[90]

All of this must be kept in mind when considering the evidence for Gilgameš, Enkidu, David, and Jonathan, because the data mined for evidence of their homoerotic relationships mainly boil down to expressions of love and references to crying or caressing, without any evidence for actual sexual actions or even necessarily attraction.

Gilgameš and Enkidu

In her book *When Heroes Love: The Ambiguity of Eros in the Stories of Gilgamesh and David*, Susan Ackerman points to eleven data points that imply a homoerotic

272 *Sexuality*

relationship between Gilgameš and Enkidu. These include the eroticized language of Gilgameš's dreams foretelling his meeting with Enkidu, potential puns pertaining to characters thought at the time to be genderqueer (e.g. the *assinnu*), references to the equality and even brotherhood of these two heroes, the lack of interest either displays in women after meeting each other—including Gilgameš's rejection of Ištar's marriage offer, and the simile of Gilgameš's veiling the dead Enkidu "like a bride" upon the latter's death.[91] The gender identity of individuals such as the *assinnu* were dealt with in the previous chapter and probably, in the end, do not constitute good evidence for the topic at hand. Instead, we might consider the terminology used in the dream interpretation scenes, and the expression—or lack thereof—of heterosexual desire from our heroes.

Heterosexuality?

Beginning with the latter, as noted by Neal Walls, neither hero displayed any interest in the opposite sex once they met each other.[92] For Enkidu, this might be contrasted with an earlier scene where the wild man:

> For six days and seven nights
> Enkidu was erect, as he had sex with Šamhat.

This is most assuredly an expression of heterosexual desire. Once Enkidu meets Gilgameš, however, he is somewhat distracted: He forms a friendship with the king of Uruk, they go off to kill the monster of the Cedar Forest, they kill the Bull of Heaven, and then Enkidu dies. There is not a point in this later narrative where Enkidu's sexuality comes into play again before his death. It is not really feasible to discuss his sexuality at this point.

This leaves Gilgameš himself. His own sexuality is more difficult to determine. At the start of the epic, the people of Uruk are complaining to the deities because (Tablet 1, ll. 83–4 and 91)

> His companions are kept on their feet by his contests,
> [the young men of Uruk] he harries without warrant . . .
> Gilgameš lets no girl go free to her bridegroom.[93]

It is generally assumed (but only assumed), that the latter line refers to Gilgameš having frequent sex with the young women of Uruk. What the data make clear is only that Gilgameš is being a non-stop nuisance to the people of Uruk, not letting them get about their own business: There is no clear reference to sexual exploitation. So, from the beginning, we have no actual data pertaining to Gilgameš's sexuality.

The next significant event in this regard is Gilgameš's rejection of Ištar's proposal of marriage in Tablet VI. The encounter between Ištar and Gilgameš is blatantly sexual—it occurs in the context of a bath, the goddess pointedly requests the hero's "fruit," and a proposal of marriage is directly stated. Gilgameš counters

Sexuality 273

that the goddess is being deceitful: All of her past lovers/husbands have died and/or been transformed into beasts. Not wishing to share their fate, Gilgameš impolitely declines the goddess's offer.

While debate continues regarding who, really, is in the wrong in this exchange, I believe that Vanstiphout (1990) and Walls (2001) came closest to the mark when they noted that Gilgameš's refusal of Ištar was a rejection of his royal duties. Since Sumerian times Inana/Ištar was understood to be a kingmaker, the goddess who legitimated the king's right to rule and whose good graces were required for stability and prosperity.[94] Ištar's "seduction" or "proposal" was a mark of her favor, that she accepted Gilgameš as a legitimate king of Uruk and offered to bless his reign with prosperity.

However, to be a responsible king also implied adulthood, a stage of life in which Gilgameš had very little interest. To be king required responsibility, listening to the town elders, marriage, and the production of an heir. None of these pertained to Gilgameš until the very end of the epic, when Enkidu was forcefully taken from him and immortality denied him—the hero was forced to grow up. In Tablet VI, Gilgameš was still a young man, low in wisdom, impetuous, and irresponsible. And Gilgameš wishes to stay the headstrong, irresponsible, adventuring dude that he is, having adventures with his best bro' Enkidu. What Ištar offers is antithetical to his current desires, and thus his vehement rejection of her. As Neal Walls put it:

> Gilgamesh here represents the selfish hero at the height of his arrogance rather than the good shepherd who would sacrifice himself for his flock. . . . Ishtar's proposal of marriage thus presents Gilgamesh with a choice between the hero's homosocial adventures with Enkidu and a royal existence as the goddess's spouse.[95]

Again, this narrative need not reflect Gilgameš's sexuality.[96]

The final exchange summoned in the study of Gilgameš's sexuality is the advice offered either by Siduri or Ut-Napištum (depending on the version of the epic), that is: to marry and have children. Gilgameš does not seem thrilled with the notion, and he continues to seek immortality not through great works or offspring but by not dying. He fails in this as well. In the end, he returns to Uruk with a new male friend—Ur-Šanabi—and his narrative ends. As Gilgameš is not listed as the last king of Uruk, we might assume he went on to marry and sire children, as a king must.

The absence of heterosexual encounters in the epic once the two heroes meet need not be seen as an expression of homoeroticism. The *Epic of Gilgameš* is the first "Buddy Tale" in the Western tradition, and the focus is ultimately on the exploits of a pair of young male friends, not on their individual relationships outside of that friendship. Other than the civilizing of Enkidu at the hands (and other body parts) of Šamhat, we do not see these heroes closely engaging with people other than each other until after the death of Enkidu. Heteroeroticism is simply not part of the narrative.

274   *Sexuality*

Word Play

Some of the terminology in the epic casts an erotic air over the relationship between Gilgameš and Enkidu, specifically the wording used in the premonition dreams Gilgameš has prior to his confrontation with the wild man. In the first, as Gilgameš recounts it to his mother, he sees a meteor (SBV, Tablet 1, ll. 247–258, excerpted):

> The stars of heaven appeared to me;
> [Something] like a meteor of Anu kept falling on me.
> I tried to lift it, but it was too heavy for me;
> I tried to turn it over, but I was unable to move it.
> . . .
> The young warriors were mobbed around it;
> They were kissing its feet like a baby.
> [I loved (*arāmšu*) it] like a wife (*kî aššate*), I caressed (*aḫbub*) it.
> [I lifted it,] I laid it at your feet
> [And you made it] equal to me.[97]

In the next dream, Gilgameš sees an axe (*haṣṣinnum*[98]) in the center square of Uruk (OBV, Tablet 1, 34):

> I saw it and rejoiced,
> I loved (*arāmšuma*) it and caressed (*aḫabbub*) it
> Like a wife (*kīma aššatim*).
> I took it and placed it at my side (*ana aḫīya*)[99]

The words/expressions of relevance are *râmu* (to love), *ḫabābu* (to carress), *kīma aššatim*, and, to a lesser extent, *ana aḫīya*. Gilgameš *loves* and *caresses* the meteor or axe *like a wife* (or "woman"—*aššatu* can mean both). In the end, Gilgameš places the axe at his side (*ana aḫīya*), which can also mean "as a brother." Thus, they become equals. As Ackerman and Walls note, the verbs *râmu* and *ḫabābu* appear just after these same verbs are used to describe Enkidu's sexual encounter with Šamḫat, lending a general sense of eroticism to the dream description.[100] In his premonitions about Enkidu, there is clearly a portrayal of intense love and affection.

However, very little of this translates over to Enkidu himself. Once we are dealing with the man, not an axe, the erotic imagery and vocabulary cease. While Gilgameš does love Enkidu like a brother, the closest we come to physical/erotic affection between the two is when they first become friends, "They kissed each other and formed a friendship."[101] Whether kissing can be seen as a homoerotic gesture is based on the surrounding cultural matrix, both of the tale and of the reader. An Englishman will no doubt read this differently than a Russian . . .

In spite of a long hike on the way to confront Humbaba in the Cedar Forest, there are no additional references to love or caresses between the heroes. No additional words of potential homoerotic affection appear until after the death of Enkidu, when (SBV, Tablet 8, ll. 58–60):

> He covered the face of his friend like a bride (*kî kallati*)
> Like an eagle he circles around him,
> Like a lioness deprived of her cubs.[102]

That Gilgameš treats the body of Enkidu "like a bride" is taken as further evidence of the erotic relationship between the two.[103] I would point out, though, that the bridegroom *uncovers, unveils* the bride; it is the bride's parent who veils her for the wedding. This fact, combined with the imagery of the bereft lioness, suggests that Gilgameš is not playing the role of the widowed husband quite so much as the mourning parent, one about to bury the "brother" who first appeared in dreams where the people of Uruk kissed his feet as those "of a baby."

Special Comrades

The *ana aḫīya* reference in the axe dream and a later scene in the epic where Gilgameš's mother Ninsun makes Enkidu the equal of Gilgameš make it clear that Enkidu was regarded as the peer of the king of Uruk, often referred to as his "brother." As neatly summarized by Mark Smith:

> The corresponding companionship of the two heroes [Gilgameš and Enkidu] is cast in terms of brotherhood. . . . After they butcher the Bull of Heaven, "the two brothers sat down" (SBV VI.150). Later their *ibru* [companion]-relationship is qualified by brotherhood. Shamash tells Enkidu when the council of the gods has pronounces judgment on his life: "Now Gilgamesh, your friend and brother (**talīmu*)/[will] lay you out on a great bed" (SBV VII.139–40). Here the word *talīmu* stands in construct to and qualifies *ibru*; literally, Gilgamesh is . . . "friend who is your brother."[104]

But I do not agree with Ackerman's assessment that Gilgameš and Enkidu *could not* have been lovers *because they were equals*.[105] A few ideas should be kept in mind in this respect. First, as discussed previously, there is no reason to assume that the Mesopotamians (or any denizen of the ANE) thought in the penetrator/dominator vs. penetrated/submissive paradigm presumed for the Greeks. This ideology does not apply to the cultural matrix of the *Epic of Gilgameš*.

Furthermore, as Walls observes, there is no reason to assume that their relationship affected the gender of either hero, especially as Enkidu—who had long tresses "like a woman" (SBV Tablet 1, l. 106)—is occasionally identified in modern scholarship as the feminine/effeminate counterpart to über-masculine Gilgameš:[106]

> Neither hero demonstrates signs of feminine gender, although some feminine images are applied to each of them. The attempt to force one of the heroes

276 *Sexuality*

into a feminine role is reminiscent of the homophobic question concerning a gay couple: "Which one wears the dress?"[107]

Finally, the intense emotional attachment shared between Gilgameš and Enkidu and their expressed sense of brotherhood might instead reflect the emotional bonding seen in combat veterans, men[108] who have depended on each other for life and limb in the unbearably harrowing circumstances of war. Granted, as noted in Chapter 3, neither Gilgameš nor Enkidu were technically warriors, as they do not experience war *per se* in the epic. Nevertheless, the core of their relationship in the epic consists of battles, first against Humbaba and then against the Bull of Heaven, soon after which Enkidu dies. So we can say that their friendship was spent in martial pursuits, pursuits which they shared with each other almost exclusively. As observed by Jonathan Shay, who worked extensively with Vietnam veterans suffering from severe, long-term PTSD, "Combat calls forth a passion of care among men who fight beside each other that is comparable to the earliest and most deeply felt family relationships."[109] Quoting a veteran who attempted to explain this martial intimacy:

> It's a closeness you never had before. It's closer than your mother and father, closest than your brother or sister, or whoever you're closest with in your family. It was . . . y'know, you'd take a shit, and he'd be right there covering you. And if I take a shit, he'd be covering me. . . . We needed each other to survive.[110]

As Shay interpreted this relationship:

> The kin relationship, brother, seems to be the most accessible and commonly spoken symbol of the bond between combat soldiers who are closest comrades. Modern American English makes soldiers' love for special comrades into a problem, because the word *love* evokes sexual and romantic associations. But *friendship* seems too bland for the passion of care that arises between soldiers in combat.[111]

And furthermore, "Many combat veterans are denied compassionate understanding by civilians, because so many people cannot comprehend a love between men that is rich and passionate but not necessarily sexual."[112]

David and Jonathan

The martial relationship between David and Jonathan is the inverse of that between Gilgameš and Enkidu. While the latter never are shown fighting in actual warfare, they do fight together, side by side. By contrast, both David and Jonathan are traditional warriors, having fought in numerous battles (Philistines, Amalekites, etc.). However, the Bible does not preserve records of the two of them fighting alongside each other. They are warriors, but not brothers-in-arms.

Sexuality 277

Even so, there is now a tradition in academia that these two men were lovers, a paradigm even for (male) homoeroticism in the Hebrew Bible. This has been most clearly and fervently endorsed by Silvia Schroer and Thomas Staubli in their 2000 article "Saul, David and Jonathan—The Story of a Triangle? A Contribution to the Issue of Homosexuality in the First Testament" which begins with the statement:

> David and Jonathan shared a homoerotic and, more than likely, a homosexual relationship. The books of Samuel recount the love of the two men with utter frankness. In his song mourning the death of the beloved, David explicitly ranks the love of men he experienced with Jonathan above the love of women (2 Sam. 1.26).[113]

The evidence on which the nature of this relationship is predicated is the terminology used in the narrative of Jonathan's relationship with his father Saul's rival David, who ultimately replaces the line of Saul as ruler of Israel (as well as Judah). In most instances, this is a reference to the love (*ahavah*) that Jonathan felt for David. Thus:

> 1 Samuel 18:1–4: When David had finished speaking to Saul, the soul of Jonathan loved him as his own soul. Saul took him [David] that day and would not let him return to his father's house. Then Jonathan made a covenant with David, because he loved him as his own soul. Jonathan then stripped himself of the robe that he was wearing and gave it to David, and his armor, and even his sword and his bow and his belt.
>
> 1 Samuel 20:14–17: Jonathan said to David "If I am still alive, show me the faithful love of the LORD, but if I die, never cut off your faithful love from my house, even if the LORD were to cut off every one of the enemies of David from the face of the earth." Thus Jonathan made a covenant with the house of David, saying, "May the LORD seek out the enemies of David." Jonathan made David swear again by his love for him; for he loved him as he loved his own life.

A variation on this expression of love appears in 1 Samuel 19:1, where instead we read that, "But Saul's son Jonathan took great delight (*haphetz*) in David."[114]

What is rather consistent is that the expression of affection is entirely one sided: It is *always* Jonathan who loves David, never vice versa.[115] As Mark Smith has noted:

> Yet David seems hardly to reciprocate on the affective level. Even with Jonathan, the affection of David is hardly symmetrical. This can be seen in two important details. According to the longer recension in 1 Sam 18:1–4, even as the text tells us that the two loved each other dearly, it is Jonathan who is said to love David as himself (see also 20:17). It is also Jonathan who gives to David his clothing and weapons.[116]

278 *Sexuality*

The only variation on this appears in 1 Samuel 20, when David is banished from Saul's kingdom and presence. As he goes into hiding, Jonathan, in defiance of his father, assists David. When they have a final meeting (1 Sam 20:41):

> As soon as the boy had gone, David rose from behind the stone heap and prostrated himself with his face to the ground. He bowed three times, and they kissed each other and wept with each other; David wept the more.

When David is completely down on his luck, then, and only then, does he have a mutual display of affection with Jonathan. One might debate as to why he was weeping . . .

In contrast to David's relative reticence while Jonathan was alive, once both he and Saul are dead in battle, then, and only then, does David extoll the feelings his brother-in-law[117] had for him (please note the very deliberate wording there). In 2 Samuel 25–26, in his lament over Saul and Jonathan, David intones:

> Jonathan slain upon your heights!
> I am in pain over you, my brother (*aḥî*);
> O Jonathan, you were so desirable to me.
> Wondrous was your love for me (*ahavatka lî*)/For me, your love was wonderful,[118]
> Greater than the love of women (*ahavat našim*).[119]

It is very much that last line: "Greater than the love of women," that has induced many a modern academic to suggest that David and Jonathan shared a homoerotic relationship, one that was specifically preferable to a romantic/sexual relationship with women. Putting together all of these data, Ackerman has suggested that, "Jonathan's offering of his bow in 1 Sam 18:4, his shooting of arrows in 1 Sam 20:36, and David's subsequent lauding of Jonathan's prowess as an archer in 2 Sam. 1:22 might therefore all be read in terms of homoerotic innuendo: a sexual proposition, followed by coitus, and then a fulfilled lover's words of gratitude."[120]

This is probably an inaccurate reading. To begin, let us consider the matter of *love* (*ahavah*). As noted by numerous scholars of the Hebrew Bible and ANE generally, the word "love" can refer not only to the bond between, say, parent and child, deity and people, and husband and wife, but is also prominent in the vocabulary of *covenant*. That is, "love" is the bond that binds two parties which make a covenant—an oath—with each other, be it Yahweh and the people of Israel, kings and vassals in the Amarna archives,[121] or, in this instance, Jonathan and David. With the exception of 1 Sam. 19:1, where Jonathan takes "delight" in David, every reference to Jonathan's love of David takes place in a context of *karat berit*—cutting a covenant. In addition to those previous examples (1 Sam. 18 and 20), we might also consider 1 Samuel 23: 16–18:

> Saul's son Jonathan set out and came to David at Horesh; there he strengthened his hand through the LORD. He said to him, "Do not be afraid; for the

Sexuality 279

hand of my father Saul shall not find you; you shall be king over Israel, and I shall be second to you; my father Saul knows this is so." Then the two of them made a covenant before the LORD.

As Saul Olyan put it:

> The mention of "cutting a covenant" (*karat berit*), "doing covenant loyalty" (*asah hesed*), and the swearing of an oath in the David/Jonathan narratives suggests clearly that the love that accompanies these actions, and even prompts them, is covenant love. Similarly, the use of the terms *servant* in 1 Sam. 20:7–8 and *brother* in 2 Sam. 1:26 also suggests a covenant setting, though the texts apparently disagree on the nature of the treaty relationship between Jonathan and David, with 1 Sam. 20:7–8 casting David as the subordinate partner, and 2 Sam. 1:26 suggesting a treaty of equals.[122]

One might argue that *all* expressions of Jonathan's (unrequited) love for David are expressed in the context of such covenants, putting the weight of evidence squarely in the field of political loyalty rather than homoerotic expression. As Olyan expressed, even the terminology typically read in favor of the homoerotic reading, words such as "brother," finds parallels in the loyalty oaths of the highly international Amarna Age: A "brother" is one's political equal (king to king, for example), whereas a "servant" is one's subordinate (e.g. governor to king).

All of this must be considered in light of the realpolitik facing the authors of David's biography in the books of Samuel: David is a usurper. Saul is the (divinely) appointed and anointed king, and he has several sons to follow him, the eldest of whom is Jonathan, his rightful heir. Over the course of the books of Samuel, David claims this birthright, even after the death of Jonathan, when Saul's son Ishbaal becomes, temporarily, the king of Israel. To justify the (illicit) reign of David over Israel, the authors of 1 and 2 Samuel have several tricks up their sleeves. The first, and most clearly and repeatedly stated, is that Jonathan willingly cedes his birthright to David: "'you shall be king over Israel, and I shall be second to you; my father Saul knows this is so.' Then the two of them made a covenant before the LORD." Cheryl Exum notes a similar dynamic in 1 Sam. 18, where Jonathan hands over to David the royal symbols of robe, armor, sword, bow, and belt.[123] Thus, David is Saul's legitimate heir because—like Jacob and Esau—the rightful son grants his birthright to the usurper.

Strengthening his claim to the throne, David also marries Saul's daughter Michal. As a son-in-law to the king, David acquires the role of adopted son, thus also making him a potential heir to the throne of Israel. The problem here is that, at the death of Saul, David is no longer married to Michal, who has been taken by her father and given in remarriage to Palti, son of Laish (1 Sam. 25:44). Meanwhile, David himself acquired not a few extra wives of his own. According to 2 Samuel 3:2–5, David had sons with Ahinoam, Abigail, Maacah, Haggith, Abital, and Eglah. Even so, in a move that strengthened his claim to the Israelite throne, David demands of both Abner and Ishbaal that they return to him "my

280   *Sexuality*

wife Michal, to whom I became engaged at the price of one hundred foreskins of the Philistines" (2 Sam. 3:14). His first wife was returned to him, "But her husband went with her, weeping as he walked behind her all the way to Bahurim." By 2 Samuel it becomes clear that the crush Michal had on David in 1 Samuel has long faded. The tenor of their relationship is made explicit in 2 Samuel 6, where (2 Sam. 6:16): "As the ark of the LORD came into the city of David, Michal daughter of Saul looked out of the window and saw King David leaping and dancing before the LORD; and she despised him in her heart." Furthermore (2 Sam. 6:21–23):

> David said to Michal, "It was before the LORD who chose me in place of your father and all his household, to appoint me as prince over Israel, the people of the LORD, that I have danced before the LORD. I shall make myself more contemptable than this, and I shall be abased in my own eyes; but by the maids of whom you have spoken, by them I shall be held in honor." And Michal the daughter of Saul had no child to the day of her death.

Again, we see David (or his biographers) emphasizing David's right to take kingship from the line of Saul, both because he was chosen by the LORD but also because Michal herself does not mother an heir for David. By claiming Michal as his wife but having no son with her (or daughter, for that matter), David contributes to the extermination of Saul's line, and with it a rival claimant to the throne of Israel.

With these political realia in mind, we might reconsider David's lament over Jonathan and Saul in 2 Sam. 1. To be clear, the lament is sung over *both* heroes— Jonathan *and* Saul. So this is no love letter to Jonathan specifically. Second, we might consider the conundrum mentioned by Olyan regarding the covenant terminology that appeared between Jonathan and David—*servant* vs. *brother*. In 1 Sam. 20:7–8, David says to Jonathan, "Therefore deal kindly with your servant, for you have brought your servant into a sacred covenant with you." David clearly takes the subordinate role in covenant terminology. However, *once Jonathan is dead*, the son of Saul becomes the *brother*, the equal, of David. Or, more accurately, David can pronounce himself the equal of Jonathan. Third, because Jonathan is now dead, the covenant he cut with David cannot be undone: David has for perpetuity the birthright granted to him, repeatedly, by Saul's rightful heir. Granted because of their love; specifically, the love Jonathan had for David (*ahavatka lî*) (and not necessarily vice versa). This simply cannot be stressed enough. It is a love that cannot die because the one bearing it has himself died. The claim to the birthright is permanent.

Contrast this with the love of Michal. As we see in 2 Samuel, David's first bride—and claim to the throne of Israel—comes to despise her husband once she is rendered merely one in a harem, and without a son to boost her status. Her love is not an expression of loyalty (*hesed*), not a permanent means to a royal end. At best, by failing to bear a son, Michal serves David by extinguishing a rival line. It becomes easy to see how Jonathan's love served David better, was better than the love of women/wives.

Sexuality 281

If David and Jonathan were a homoerotic couple, they desperately needed therapy. It was a wholly unbalanced, non-reciprocating relationship where David clearly exploited Jonathan and his family to the fullest extent possible. I really hope this is not held up as a model for gay relationships.

"Curing" Men of "Something"

In part of the ongoing trend to cure ANE scholarship from the ravages of heteronormativity, two Hittite texts pertaining to men's health and sexual function have been reinterpreted in light of the current Greco-Roman discourse on homosexuality. That is, rituals that appear to deal with matters of impotence or infertility are instead presented as curing men of submissive, passive, effeminate homosexuality.

Paskuwatti's Ritual (CTH 406)

The more prominent of these is the Hittite text known as *Paskuwatti's Ritual to the Goddess Uliliyassi*, composed in the Middle Hittite period but known from a single tablet dating to the 13th century BCE.[124] Based on the textual data, the purpose of this ritual performed by the woman Paskuwatti of Arzawa before the goddess Uliliyassi is to deal with a man who "has no reproductive power or is not a man vis-à-vis a woman."[125] This is accomplished by invoking the goddess in the steppe with bread rituals while removing the patient's femininity and replacing it with masculinity. The relevant portions of the text are:

1) Thus Paskuwatti, the Arzawa woman, who lives in Parassa. If some man has no reproductive power or is not a man vis-à-vis a woman. (*ma-a-an* LU₂-*ni ku-e-da-ni ha-aš-ša-tar*/NU.GAL₂ *na-aš-ma-aš* SAL-*ni me-na-aḫ-ḫa-an-da* Ú-UL LU₂ [. . .]-*aš*.
2) I make offerings to Uliliyassi on his behalf and entreat her for three days . . .
4) I tie them (gates of reeds)[126] together with red and white wool. I place a spindle and a distaff in the patient's [hand], and he comes under the gates. When he steps forward through the gates, I take the spindle and distaff away from him. I give him a bow (and) arrows, and say to him all the while: "I have just taken femininity away from you and given you masculinity in return. You have cast off the behavior expected [of women]; [you have taken] to yourself the behavior expected of men . . . .
8) (Speaking to the goddess) "Come to this man! You are his 'wife of children' for him! So look after him! Turn to him [in favor] and speak to him! Turn your maidservant (the man's wife) over to him, and he will become a yoke. Let him take his wife and produce for himself sons and daughters![127]

The evidence from the text itself reveals that procreation is what is at issue, as the rite begins with a references to a man with no reproductive power and continues and ends with a repeated reference to that man taking his wife and producing for himself sons and daughters. One way or another, reproduction is at issue.

282   *Sexuality*

The ongoing question is what it is—exactly—about this man that keeps him from reproducing. For Hoffner, the problem was one of impotence:

> [The] 13th century tablet deals with the very important subject of male impotence. It is clear from the language of the ritual ("this mortal can only defecate and urinate," . . . i.e. he cannot ejaculate) that the patient's complaint was that he was unable to sustain an erection and consummate the act of intercourse. His problem, then, was not infertility (insufficient sperm), but impotence.[128]

But nothing in the text actually makes this fact explicit; we only know that he is incapable of siring offspring. Furthermore, there is the problematic reference in the ritual to the symbolic removal of femininity (in the form of distaff and spindle) and replacement with symbols of masculinity (bow and arrows—see Chapter 3). Whatever Paskuwatti is doing, it involves somehow changing or manipulating the man's *gender*.

This has brought queer theory into the debate. Predicated on the discourse discussed previously—based in the Greco-Roman Classics—that sexual intercourse must inevitably be a hierarchical relationship with an active, dominating penetrator and a passive, subjugated penetratee, *Paskuwatti's Ritual* has come to be seen as a cure for a male homosexual "bottom." As Jared Miller has argued:

> The ability to sustain an erection is hardly a feminine trait to be taken away from the patient. No, the taking away of the patient's feminine inclinations likely refers to something else. The passage seems considerably more sensible when viewed in light of the possibility that the ritual aims at curbing the patient's passive homosexual inclination. He is to cast off what is generally viewed in traditional cultures as the expected sexually passive behavior of women, i.e. allowing oneself to be penetrated by a man, and to assume the active or aggressive role of the proper, dominant man, who is supposed to be the penetrator.[129]

Problematic in this interpretation is that it assumes that the currently hegemonic discourse about Greco-Roman sexuality is not only accurate but applicable to societies vastly removed in time and place from 5th-century Athens, as the Hittites most assuredly were. As we have seen throughout this book, the idea that females are sexually passive (see Chapter 2) does not apply to the ANE, nor do we have any evidence that the penetrator=dominator=real man vs. penetratee=submissive=effeminate paradigm applies to any of the cultures of the ANE (see previously). To argue that curing effeminacy is a cure for homosexuality is anachronistic in this instance.

Furthermore, there is no reason that a man who prefers the receptive role in intercourse with another man would not be able to sire children with his wife. Unless that man scored a 7 on the Kinsey Scale, he is still fertile and capable of impregnation. There would be no reason for the language of reproduction to emerge in curing him of "effeminacy."

Instead, it might be better to consider the fact that, throughout the ANE, an important aspect of masculine identity was fertility (see Chapters 1 and 3). A man who is insufficiently fertile is a man who is insufficiently masculine. To cure this, the antithesis of masculinity—femininity—needed to be removed and replaced with its opposite. It would, of course, help to know what the Hittites believed the "behavior expected of men" or women actually was, but it should probably be noted that the word "woman" in the text is entirely restored.

Anniwiyani's Ritual (CTH 393/VBoT 24)

This Hittite ritual is less explicit than Paskuwatti's. There is no statement as to what it is intended to accomplish, merely how to enact the ritual itself. It begins:

> UM-MA ᶠA-an-ni-ú-i-ya-ni AMA ᵐA-ar-ma-ti ˡúMUŠEN.DÙ
> ARAD ᵐḪu-u-ur-lu-u ma-a-an ᵈLAMMA lu-li-mi-ya-aš
> SÌSKUR i-ya-mi nu ki-i da-aḫ-ḫi

> Thus (speaks) Anniwiyani, mother of Armati, the Augur,
> Servant of Ḫurlu: When I perform the ritual of ᵈLAMMA lulimi,
> Then I take . . .[130]

. . . with references to variously colored wool strands, beer, and so on. What is clear from the *incepit* is that the ritual pertains specifically to the goddess Lamma with the epithet *lulimi*—the name with epithet appears in the text three times. The lines of the ritual taken to be relevant to gender are 28–29:

> nu DUMU.MUNUS hal-za-a-i pa-ra-a-wa-kán e-hu ᵈLAMMA lu-li-mi-[eš]
> an-sa-wa-kán ᵈLAMMA in-na-ra-u-wa-an-za ú-iz-zi.

> The girl cries out: "Come out, Lamma *lulimi*!
> Lamma *innarawanza* will come in!"[131]

Ilan Peled takes the epithet *innarawant-* to translate as "masculine" and the epithet *lulimi* to be its antonym, thus "feminine" or even "the effeminate."[132] As such, the invocation would appear to be: "Come out, feminine Lamma, and come in, masculine Lamma!", reflecting the call in Paskuwatti's ritual to drive out femininity and to replace it with masculinity. That is, as with Paskuwatti's ritual, a changing of gender, specifically the removal of the feminine and replacement with the masculine. From here the standard academic path leads to the queer interpretation, "The appearance of the 'effeminate' deity in the paragraph opening the ritual and explaining its purpose can now be understood as subtle wording indicating that the ritual is aimed at dealing with the 'problem' of passive homosexuality, represented by this deity."[133]

However, in her analysis of *Anniwiyani's Ritual*, Daliah Bawanypeck discusses the fact that the meaning of neither *lulimi* nor *innarawant* is known ("Die Bedeutung des adjektivischen Epithetons *lulimi* ist unbekannt").[134] Hypotheses

284 *Sexuality*

regarding *lulimi* tend to involve positive implications, such as prosperity and fertility, or even simply "deer."[135] The epithet *innarawant-* is a hapax, with comparative linguistics suggesting a meaning pertaining to vivacity or vigor.[136] There is no reason to assume that either word pertains to gender.

This idea is strengthened by the noun to which both adjectives are attached: ᵈLAMMA. As discussed in Chapter 2, the Lamma deity is an intervening goddess, quite consistently female. Unlike Ištar, she does not manifest both feminine and masculine components.[137] While I am admittedly arguing Hittite culture from a Mesopotamian perspective, it might in this instance be better to consider the potential adjectives as something more in line with the persona of the Lamma deity herself and the various ways she may assist her mortal beneficiaries. This seems more likely than postulating that there is a goddess of passive homosexuality in the Hittite pantheon.

In the end, there can be little doubt that ancient people experienced same-sex desire just as often as happens in modern times. Same-sex desire has been a part of humanity since before we came down from the trees: Both of humankind's closest simian ancestors/relatives—chimpanzees and bonobos (*especially bonobos!*)—display homoerotic pairings of males and females, as do other mammals and birds (notably penguins).[138] What differs historically and culturally is how the surrounding social matrix accepts such sexuality, and thus, the degree to which it can be (openly) expressed and what kinds of information are presented about it. Whether we, in modern times, can *recognize* presentations of homoeroticism in ancient data is debatable. Some say that heteronormative tendencies blind us to the evidence. I would argue, rather, that heteronormative tendencies cause us to skew the evidence. The modern bias against homosexuality—to the point that we once debated whether it was a sin, illegal, or simply a form of mental illness— gets its rationale from "antiquity," especially the Bible. But when we look at the evidence from the Bible and its surrounding cultures, we actually find very little, and not all of it negative. Heteronormativity does not keep us from seeing ancient homosexuality; it causes us to see too much, all mixed up with independent issues such as rape, through anachronistic lenses, with an unwarranted negative patina.

Caveat Lector

It is incontestable how important women's studies and feminist, gender, and queer theories are to the study of the world, ancient and modern. The rise of these new ways of looking at the data have provided critical new approaches to our understanding of antiquity, especially concerning the role of women (and also men) and the nature of human eroticism. It is critical that these approaches remain flexible and reasonable as we attempt to see a world as it was rather than how we wish it to be (which is incredibly difficult and why we need theory). On the one hand, it is to be desired that all of these theories will become part and parcel of standard studies of the ancient world, not ghettoized as liminal to "real" history, archaeology, and so on. On the other hand, balance is absolutely needed. We must not inflict upon antiquity our own desires and political agendas for the modern world. On that note I end this work with two quotations calling for open-mindedness in the study of antiquity, one by an Egyptologist in the vanguard of queer studies in that field and one by one of the first great feminist archaeologists. Words to the wise.

> A search for subaltern history need not insist on interpretations that place essentially "queers" and other subalterns in a central and normative position as accepted members of an elite culture (as with some readings of the mastaba of Niankhkhnum and Khnumhotep). Although such positive interpretations can provide politically beneficial positive images for contemporary society, they also run the risk of simply creating another sort of binary normative history. Instead, we can perhaps try to read between the lines about the diverse and nuanced ways in which masculinity was presented; we can thus consider the contingent nature of all cultures, including our own, and in doing so begin to explore readings and histories that are multiple rather than monolithic.
>
> (R.B. Parkinson)[139]

> Attitudes towards sexuality and gender (closely connected in our society at least) are changing rapidly; moreover, both gender and sexuality are considered major components of personal identity and therefore of great interest to everyone. It is surely not by chance that changing attitudes in our own times should coincide with challenges to traditional categories in interpretations of the past. In this respect, the search for multiple genders and gender transgression in prehistory is just as ethnocentric as the binary male/female dichotomy that is criticized (referring simply to different phases of our own recent history). It is arguable, at least, that concentration on the individual and issues of personal identity represents a peculiarly contemporary concern and may not be very relevant to prehistoric societies.
>
> (Ruth D. Whitehouse)[140]

Notes

1 See usefully on these issues M. Roth 2014: *passim*.
2 On the ŠÀ.ZI.GA texts and the curing of erectile dysfunction in Mesopotamia, see Biggs 2002 and, more recently and completely, Zisa 2021.
3 See Leick 1994.
4 For example: "The funerary record shows a lack of unmarried people. Whale's survey of 93 cases from the New Kingdom provides only three examples of men whose tombs contain no evidence for a wife." Parkinson 1995: 60, with citations.
5 For example, McDowell 1999: 51–52.
6 Parkinson 1995: 61, excerpted.
7 Perhaps, being without issue to be concerned about, the ancients simply felt that such relationships were none of their business.
8 Dover 1978: 103–104, excerpted. My emphasis.
9 Halperin 1990: 34–35. My emphasis.
10 Greenberg 1988: 158.
11 Walters 1997: 30–31, excerpted.

286 *Sexuality*

12 This paradigm tracing its lineage back to Dover is now actually receding in Classical studies. As Konstantinos Kapparis put it, "Dover reached some absurd conclusions, which essentially removed any form of love, pleasure, or self-respect from Greek homosexual relations" (2019: 197). For more on the backlash against the Dover-Foucault model, see Ibid 187–209, with further bibliography on page 188.
13 Peled 2010: 626 (bold in original).
14 Peled 2016: 290–291, excerpted.
15 Guinan 1997: 471.
16 Guinan and Morris 2017: 168, excerpted.
17 Assante 2017: 49.
18 Nissinen 1998: 44 (excerpted).
19 Parkinson 1995: 67.
20 Thank heavens for Yiddish!
21 Hoffner 1997: 149.
22 Hoffner 1997: 306 defines *wašta* + *katta* as, "to sin with, commit a sexual offence with." In general, the word refers to an offence or, perhaps more religiously, to commit a sin. It is the context of the word plus the use of the genitive marker *katta* that leads to the sexual nuance in the translation.
23 On this term, see Hoffner 1973: 83–84.
24 "There is not case to my knowledge in published Hittite texts where *ḫurkel* describes a crime which does not involve a sexual combination which is condemned by social mores" Hoffner 1973: 83.
25 Ibid: 83.
26 Guinan and Morris: 2017: 169.
27 Roth 1997: 192. This fact is acknowledged by Roth herself.
28 Dalley 2001: 200. See here Chapter 3, "Eunuchs," on this debate.
29 Nissinen 1998: 25–26; Guinan and Morris 2017: 151.
30 Nissinen 1998: 26.
31 Guinan and Morris 2017: 152.
32 Assante 2017: 48. *Awīlu* is the more standard form of *a'īlu*.
33 *Contra* Greenberg 1988: 126.
34 You probably already guessed that.
35 Roth 2014: 161, slightly adapted.
36 Transliterations from Guinan 1997: 479.
37 Ibid: 469.
38 Ibid: 469.
39 Crompton 2003: 32.
40 On *tô'ēbâ*. See Olyan 1994: 180, n. 3. The usual translation is "abomination," but one might also take it as "a sin highly offensive to a particular deity." The Greeks might say οὐ θέμις.
41 Transliterations and translation from Olyan 1994: 180. On the distinction between *'iš* (man) and *zākār* (male) see Chapter 1.
42 Olyan 1994: 181.
43 Ibid: 187–188.
44 Yes, that last one is a bit of a joke but not atypical of Leviticus's prohibitions.
45 On the various interpretations and understandings of these laws in Leviticus, see Olyan 1994: 197–204; Nissinen 1998: Chapter Three.
46 An exception—§200a—permits sex with a horse or a mule, which really makes me wonder about those Hittites.
47 Olyan 1994: 205.
48 It is worth noting that Dinah is not listed among the children of Jacob originally, and she ceases to exist after the conquest. She exists exclusively as an *aition* for the destruction of the men of Havor.
49 I find it somewhat horrific that for centuries we have disdained and condemned "Sodomites" for a threatened but never actually enacted homosexual rape but have never

had a problem with "Benjaminites" in spite of the equally threatened homosexual rape compounded by the actual heterosexual rape and eventual, institutionalized mass heterosexual rape. Do we condone the potential homosexual, violent behavior of the Benjaminites because they "proved" their heterosexuality in the end? Or is it that, as one of the twelve tribes of Israel, we condone their behavior because they are one of "us"?

50 Crompton 2003: 36–39; Greenberg 1988: 136.
51 Parkinson 1995: 65.
52 Lichtheim 2006, Vol I: 52.
53 Baines 1991: 95.
54 Parkinson 1995: 70. It's not like he could ask "What's your sign?"
55 Ibid: 70–71.
56 Which she later heals and replaces.
57 Simpson 1972: 120–121, excerpted.
58 Greenberg 1988: 131.
59 Walls 2001: 115.
60 Reeder 2008: 146.
61 Reeder 2000: *passim*; Baines 1985: 466–467.
62 Reeder 2000: 200.
63 Baines 1985: 463–464.
64 Reeder 2008: 147.
65 Cherpion 1986: 67
66 Baines 1985: 467.
67 Roth 1999: 39–40.
68 Montet 1957: 2.
69 Posener 1957: 124.
70 Ibid: 130–131. My translation from the French.
71 Parkinson 1995: 72; Posener 1957: 130–131, n. 9.
72 Posener 1957: 137.
73 Parkinson 1995: 74, excerpted.
74 Seriously unhelpful translation by Parkinson 1995: 61.
75 Eyre 1984: 93.
76 Lichtheim 2006, vol. I: 72. Needless to say, there is only so far I plan on getting with it . . .
77 Parkinson 1995: 68.
78 Goedicke 1967: 97.
79 Ibid: 100.
80 Matić 2021: 114–115; Depauw 2003: 50; Parkinson 1995: 66; Faulkner 1962: 169.
81 Parkinson 1995: 66.
82 Matić 2021: 114.
83 Parkinson 1995: 66.
84 Matić 2021: 115, adapted.
85 Faulkner 1962: 169.
86 Depauw 2003: 50.
87 Cited in Matić 2021: 115.
88 Greenberg 1988: 133.
89 One might recall the scene in "Bill and Ted's Excellent Adventure" where the two friends give each other a joyful hug, pull back, wipe away the contact, and simultaneously call each other "Fag!"
90 Smith 1984: 136–137.
91 Ackerman 2005: 50–51.
92 Walls 2001: 59.
93 George 1999: 4.
94 See especially Cooper 1993.
95 Walls 2001: 44 and 46.

288 *Sexuality*

96 In modern times we call this "fear of commitment."
97 Ackerman 2005: 52, adapted.
98 Likened to "assinnu" by Ackerman.
99 Ackerman 2005: 48, adapted.
100 Ibid: 54; Walls 2001: 54.
101 George 1999: 17, OB Yale, Tablet 1, ll. 19–20.
102 George 1999: 65.
103 E.g. Ackerman 2005: 71–72.
104 Smith 2014: 53–54, excerpted.
105 Ackerman 2005: 78–80.
106 E.g. Smith 2014: 86.
107 Walls 2001: 56.
108 To date much of the research has been conducted on Vietnam veterans, and thus the exclusively male pronoun. As this work continues, I have no doubt female veterans will become implicated as well.
109 Shay 1994: 39.
110 Ibid: 40.
111 Ibid.
112 Ibid: 42–43.
113 Schroer and Staubli 2000: 22.
114 Concerning the use of this word in this line Schroer and Staubli (2000: 28) make the observations that, "The expression 'to delight in' (. . .ב חפצ) has sexual connotations both in Gen. 34.19, which tells of Shechem's delight in Dinah, and Deut. 21.14, which is about the appropriate ordering of the relations between free Israelite men and women prisoners of war." They do not seem to consider the fact that both instances refer to rape.
115 Exum 1992: 80.
116 Smith 2014: 66.
117 David was married to Jonathan's sister Michal, more on her subsequently.
118 The Hebrew allows for both variations equally.
119 Smith 2014: 268.
120 Ackerman 2005: 184.
121 Olyan 2006: 9.
122 Ibid: 8.
123 Exum 1992: 78. See also Ackerman 2005: 188.
124 Hoffner 1987: 280.
125 Ibid: 277.
126 These are mentioned in the preceding paragraph.
127 Hoffner 1987: 277–278. The final line about producing sons and daughters is repeated in section 14.
128 Ibid: 287.
129 Miller 2010: 85.
130 Bawanypeck 2005: 52–53.
131 Peled 2010: 70; Bawanypeck 2005: 54–55.
132 Peled 2010: 70; 74–75.
133 Ibid: 76.
134 Bawanypeck 2005: 184.
135 Ibid: 184–185, with citations.
136 *Ibid*: 185, with citations.
137 On feminine and masculine Ištar/Aštart, see Budin 2004 and Chapter 4 here.
138 See especially de Waal 2022: Chapter 12.
139 Parkinson 2008: 133.
140 Whitehouse 2007: 31.

Bibliography

Abrahami, Philippe (2011) "Masculine and Feminine Personal Determinatives before Women's Names at Nuzi: A Gender Indicator of Social or Economic Independence?" *Cuneiform Digital Library Bulletin*, 2011.1, 1–3.

A Campo, Anna Letitia (1994) *Anthropomorphic Representations in Prehistoric Cyprus: A Formal and Symbolic Analysis of Figurines, c. 3500–1800 B.C.* Paul Åströms Förlag, Jonsered.

Ackerman, Susan (2005) *When Heroes Love: The Ambiguities of Eros in the Stories of Gilgamesh and David.* Columbia University Press, New York, NY.

Allen, James P. (2003) "From Pyramid Texts Spell 527 (1.3)." In W. M. Hallo and K. L. Younger, Jr. (eds.) *The Context of Scripture*, vol. 3. Brill, Leiden.

———. (2001) *Middle Egyptian: An Introduction to the Language and Culture of Hieroglyphs.* Cambridge University Press, Cambridge, UK.

Al-Rawi, F.N.H. (1992) "Two Old Akkadian Letters Concerning the Offices of *kala'um* and *nārum*." *Zeitscrift für Assyriologie*, 82, 180–185.

Archi, Alfonso (2013) "The West Hurrian Pantheon and Its Background." In B.J. Collins and P. Michalowski (eds.) *Beyond Hatti: A Tribute to Gary Beckman.* Lockwood Press, Atlanta, GA, 1–22.

Ashby, Solange (2019) "Milk Libations for Osiris: Nubian Piety at Philae." *Near Eastern Archaeology*, 82, 200–209.

Asher-Greve, Julia (2018) "From La Femme to Multiple Sex/Gender." In S. Svärd and A. Garcia Ventura (eds.) *Studying Gender in the Ancient Near East.* Eisenbrauns, University Park, PA, 15–50.

———. (2002) "Decisive Sex, Essential Gender." In Simo Parpola and Robert M. Whiting (eds.) *Sex and Gender in the Ancient Near East.* Neo-Assyrian Text Corpus Project, Helsinki, 41–81.

———. (2000) "Stepping into the Maelstrom: Women, Gender and Ancient Near Eastern Scholarship." *NIN*, 1, 1–22.

———. (1998) "The Essential Body: Mesopotamian Conceptions of the Gendered Body." In M. Wyke (ed.) *Gender and the Body in the Ancient Mediterranean.* Blackwell Publishers, Oxford, UK, 8–37.

Asher-Greve, Julia and Deborah Sweeney (2006) "On Nakedness, Nudity, and Gender in Egyptian and Mesopotamian Art." In S. Schroer (ed.) *Images and Gender: Contributions to the Hermeneutics of Reading Ancient Art.* Academic Press Fribourg, Vandenhoeck & Ruprecht, Göttingen, 125–176.

290 Bibliography

Asher-Greve, Julia and Joan Goodnick Westenholz (2013) *Goddesses in Context: On Divine Powers, Roles, Relationships and Gender in Mesopotamian Textual and Visual Sources*. Academic Press Fribourg, Vandenhoeck & Ruprecht, Göttingen.

Assante, Julia (2017) "Men Looking at Men: The Homoerotics of Power in the State Arts of Assyria." In I. Zsolnay (ed.) *Being a Man: Negotiating Ancient Constructs of Masculinity*. Routledge, London, UK, 42–82.

———. (2009) "Bad Girls and Kinky Boys? The Modern Prostituting of Ishtar, Her Clergy and Her Cults." In T.S. Scheer and M. Linder (eds.) *Tempelprostitution im Altertum*. VerlagAntike, Berlin, 23–54.

Assmann, Jan (2005) *Death and Salvation in Ancient Egypt*. Cornell University Press, Ithaca, NY.

———. (1978) "Eine Traumoffenbarung der Göttin Hathor: Zeugnisse <<Persönlicher Frömmigkeit>> in thebanischen Privatgräbern der Ramessidenzeit." *Revue d'égyptologie*, 30, 22–50.

Åström, Paul (1972) *The Swedish Cyprus Expedition: Vol. IV, Part 1B: The Middle Cypriot Bronze Age*. The Swedish Cyprus Expedition, Lund.

Baadsgaard, Aubrey (2008) "A Taste of Women's Sociality: Cooking as Cooperative Labor in Iron Age Syro-Palestine." In Beth Alpert Nakhai (ed.) *The World of Women in the Ancient and Classical Near East*. Cambridge Scholars Publishing, Newcastle upon Tyne, UK, 13–44.

Bachvarova, Mary R. (2017) "Wisdom of Former Days: The Manly Hittite King and Foolish Kumarbi, Father of the Gods." In I. Zsolnay (ed.) *Being a Man: Negotiating Ancient Constructs of Masculinity*. Routledge, London, UK, 83–111.

———. (2013) "Adapting Mesopotamian Myth in Hurro-Hittite Rituals at Hattuša: IŠTAR, the Underworld, and the Legendary Kings." In B.J. Collins and P. Michalowski (eds.) *Beyond Hatti: A Tribute to Gary Beckman*. Lockwood Press, Atlanta, GA, 23–44.

Bailey, Douglas W. (2013) "Figurines, Corporality, and the Origins of the Gendered Body." In Diane Bolger (ed.) *A Companion to Gender Prehistory*. Wiley-Blackwell, Oxford, 244–264.

Baines, John (1995) "Origins of Kingship." In D. O'Connor and D.P. Silverman (eds.) *Ancient Egyptian Kingship*. E.J. Brill, Leiden, 95–156.

———. (1991) "Egyptian Myth and Discourse: Myth, Gods, and the Early Written and Iconographic Record." *Journal of Near Eastern Studies*, 50.2, 81–105.

———. (1985) "Egyptian Twins." *Orientalia*, Nova Series, 54.4, 461–482.

Barjamovic, Gojko (2011) "Pride, Pomp and Circumstance: Palace, Court and Household in Assyria 879–612 BCE." In J. Duindam, T. Artan, and M. Kunt (eds.) *Royal Courts in Dynastic States and Empires*. Brill, Leiden, 25–61.

Barry, Dave (1998) *Dave Barry Turns 50*. Crown Publishers, Inc., New York, NY.

Bawanypeck, Daliah (2005) *Die Rituale der Auguren*. Universitätsverlag, Heidelberg.

Beckman, Gary (1998) "Ištar of Nineveh Reconsidered." *Journal of Cuneiform Studies*, 50, 1–10.

Ben-Barak, Zafira (1988) "The Legal Status of the Daughter as Heir in Nuzi and Emar." In M. Heltzer and E. Lipiński (eds.) *Society and Economy in the Eastern Mediterranean (c. 1500–1000 B.C.)*. Peeters Publishers, Leuven, 87–97.

Biggs, Robert D. (2002) "The Babylonian Sexual Potency Texts." In S. Parpola and R.M. Whiting (eds.) *Sex and Gender in the Ancient Near East*. Neo-Assyrian Text Corpus Project, Helsinki, 71–78.

Black, J., G. Cunningham, E. Robeson, and G. Zólyomi (2004) *The Literature of Ancient Sumer*. Oxford University Press, Oxford, UK.

Bibliography 291

Blackless, Melanie et al. (2000) "How Sexually Dimorphic Are We? Review and Synthesis." *American Journal of Human Biology*, 12, 151–166.

Bolen, K.M. (1992) "Prehistoric Construction of Mothering." In C. Claassen (ed.) *Exploring Gender Through Archaeology*. Prehistory Press, Madison, WI, 49–62.

Bolger, Diane (ed.) (2013) *A Companion to Gender Prehistory*. Wiley-Blackwell, Malden, MA.

Bonnet, Corinne (1996) *Astarté: dossier documentaire et perspectives historiques*. Consiglio Nazionale delle Ricerche, Roma.

Bordreuil, Pierre (1985) "Ashtart de Mari et les Dieux d'Ougarit." *M.A.R.I.*, 4, 545–548.

Brettler, Marc (2017) "Happy Is the Man Who Fills His Quiver with Them (Ps. 127:5): Constructions of Masculinities in the Psalms." In I. Zsolnay (ed.) *Being a Man: Negotiating Ancient Constructs of Masculinity*. Routledge, London, UK, 198–220.

Brinkman, John A. (2007) "Masculine or Feminine? The Case of Conflicting Gender Determinatives for Middle Babylonian Personal Names." In M.T. Roth (ed.) *Studies Presented to Robert D. Biggs*. Oriental Institute of Chicago, Chicago, IL, 1–10.

Bryce, Trevor (2003) *Letters of the Great Kings of the Ancient Near East: The Royal Correspondence of the Late Bronze Age*. Routledge, London, UK.

———. (2002) *Life and Society in the Hittite World*. Oxford University Press, Oxford, UK.

———. (1998) *The Kingdom of the Hittites*. Oxford University Press, Oxford, UK.

Buccellati, G. and Marilyn Kelly-Buccellati (2002) "Tar'am-Agade, Daughter of Naram-Sin, at Urkesh." In L. al-Gailani Werr (ed.) *Of Pots and Plans: Papers Presented to David Oates*. Nabu Publications, London, 11–31.

———. (1995–1996) "The Royal Storehouse of Urkesh: The Glyptic Evidence from the Southwestern Wing." *Archiv für Orientforschung*, 42/43, 1–32.

Budin, Stephanie Lynn (2022) "Nude Awakenings: Early Dynastic Nude Female Iconography." *Near Eastern Archaeology* 85.1, 34–43.

———. (2021) *Freewomen, Patriarchal Authority, and the Accusation of Prostitution*. Routledge, New York, NY.

———. (2019) "Jar Handles, Nudity, and the Female." In M. Cifarelli, S.L. Budin, A. Garcia-Ventura, and A. Millet Albá (eds.) *Gender, Methodology and the Ancient Near East: Proceedings of the Second Workshop Held in Barcelona, February 1–3 2017*. Barcino. Monographica Orientalia, IPOA (Institut del Pròxim Orient Antic) y Universitat de Barcelona Edicions, Barcelona, 179–198.

———. (2018) "Gender in the Tale of Aqhat." In S. Svärd and A. Garcia-Ventura (eds.) *Studying Gender in the Ancient Near East*. Eisenbrauns, University Park, PA, 51–72.

———. (2016) *Artemis*. Routledge, London, UK,

———. (2011) *Images of Woman and Child from the Bronze Age: Reconsidering Fertility, Maternity, and Gender in the Ancient World*. Cambridge University Press, Cambridge, UK.

———. (2004) "A Reconsideration of the Aphrodite-Ashtart Syncretism." *Numen*, 51.2, 95–145.

———. (2002) "Creating a Goddess of Sex." In D. Bolger and N. Serwint (eds.) *Engendering Aphrodite: Women and Society in Ancient Cyprus*. ASOR Archaeological Reports, Boston, MA, 315–324.

Butler, Judith (1993) *Bodies that Matter: On the Discursive Limits of "Sex"*. Routledge, New York, NY.

———. (1990) *Gender Trouble*. Routledge, New York, NY.

Catling, H. (1971) "A Cypriot Bronze Statuette in the Bomford Collection." In C. Schaeffer (ed.) *Alasia: Mission Archéologique d'Alasia*, vol. 4. Brill, Paris, 15–32.

292   *Bibliography*

Cherpion, Nadine (1986) "Deux manicures royaux de la Ve dynastie." In A. Théodoridès, P. Naster, and J. Ries (eds.) *Archéologie et philologie dans l'étude des civilizations orientales*. Peeters Publishers, Leuven, 65–71.

Chodorow, Nancy (1978) *The Reproduction of Mothering: Psychoanalysis and the Sociology of Gender*. University of California Press, Berkeley.

Clark, Kenneth (1959) *The Nude: A Study in Ideal Form*. Doubleday Anchor Books, New York, NY.

Collon, Dominique (1987) *First Impressions: Cylinder Seals in the Ancient Near East*. The University of Chicago Press, Chicago, IL.

Connell, Raewyn and Rebecca Pearse (2015) *Gender: In World Perspective* (Third Edition). Polity Press, Cambridge, UK.

Coogan, M.D. and Mark S. Smith (2012) *Stories from Ancient Canaan* (Second Edition). Westminster John Knox Press, Louisville, KY.

Cooper, Jerrold S. (2017) "Female Trouble and Troubled Males: Roiled Seas, Decadent Royals, and Mesopotamian Masculinities in Myth and Practice." In I. Zsolnay (ed.) *Being a Man: Negotiating Ancient Constructs of Masculinity*. Routledge, London, UK, 112–124.

———. (2006) "Genre, Gender, and the Sumerian Lamentation." *Journal of Cuneiform Studies*, 58, 39–47.

———. (1997) "Gendered Sexuality in Sumerian Love Poetry." In I.L. Finkel and M.J. Geller (eds.) *Sumerian Gods and Their Representations*. Styx Publications, Groningen, 85–97.

———. (1993) Sacred Marriage and Popular Cult in Early Mesopotamia. In E. Matushima (ed.) *Official Cult and Popular Religion in the Ancient Near East*. Universitätsverlag C. Winter, Heidelberg, 81–96.

Cornelius, Izak (2004) *The Many Faces of the Goddess*. OBO 204. Academic Press Fribourg, Göttingen.

Couto-Ferreira, M. Erica (2016) "Being Mothers or Acting (Like) Mothers? Constructing motherhood in ancient Mesopotamia." In S.L. Budin and J. MacIntosh Turfa (eds.) *Women in Antiquity: Real Women across the Ancient World*. Routledge, London, UK, 25–34.

Couturaud, Barbara (2021) "Kings or Soldiers? Representations of Fighting Heroes at the End of the Early Bronze Age." In E. Wagner-Durand and Julia Linke (eds.) *Tales of Royalty: Notions of Kingship in Visual and Textual Narration in the Ancient Near East*. De Gruyter, Berlin, 109–138.

Crompton, Louis (2003) *Homosexuality & Civilization*. Harvard University Press, Cambridge, MA.

Curtis, J.E. and J.E. Reade (eds.) (1995) *Art and Empire: Treasures from Assyria in the British Museum*. Metropolitan Museum of Art, New York, NY.

Dales Jr., George F. (1960) *Mesopotamian and Related Female Figurines: Their Chronology, Diffusion, and Cultural Functions*. Ph.D. Dissertation, University of Pennsylvania, Philadelphia, PA.

Dalley, Stephanie (2001) Review of R. Mattila's *The King's Magnates* (SAAS XI), published in *Bibliotheca Orientalis*, 58.1–2, 197–206

———. (1989) *Myths from Mesopotamia*. Oxford University Press, Oxford, UK.

David, Arlette (2014) "Identification in Ancient Egypt from the Old Kingdom to the End of the New Kingdom (2650–1100 BCE)." In Mark Depauw and Sandra Coussement (eds.) *Identifiers and Identification Methods in the Ancient World: Legal Documents in Ancient Societies III*. Peeters Publishers, Leuven, 57–74.

Day, Peggy L. (1991) "Why Is Anat a Warrior and Hunter?" In D. Jobling, P.L. Day, and G.T. Shepherd (eds.) *The Bible and the Politics of Exegesis: Essays in Honor of Norman K. Gottwald on His Sixty-Fifth Birthday*. Pilgrim Press, Cleveland, OH, 141–146 and 329–332.

De Graef, Katrien (2018) "Puppets on a String? On Female Agency in Old Babylonian Economy" In S. Svärd and A. Garcia-Ventura (eds.) *Studying Gender in the Ancient Near East*. Eisenbrauns, University Park, PA, 133–156.

Depauw, Mark (2003) "Notes on Transgressing Gender Boundaries in Ancient Egypt." *Zeitschrift für Ägyptische Sprache und Altertumskunde*, 130, 49–59.

Depla, Annette (1994) "Women in Ancient Egyptian Wisdom Literature." In L.J. Archer, S. Fischler, and M. Wyke (eds.) *Women in Ancient Societies: An Illusion of the Night*. MacMillan Press, London, UK.

De Waal, Frans (2022) *Different: Gender through the Eyes of a Primatologist*. W.N. Norton & Co., New York, NY.

———. (2007) *Chimpanzee Politics: Power and Sex among Apes* (25th Anniversary Edition). Johns Hopkins University Press, Baltimore, MD.

Diamond, Kelly-Anne (2021) "Gender, Deities, and the Public Image of Sobekneferu." *Near Eastern Archaeology*, 84.4, 272–280.

———. (2020) "The Reign of King Sobekneferu and Her Performance of Gender." *Birmingham Egyptology Journal*, 7, 1–18.

———. (2020a) "Hatshepsut: Transcending Gender in Ancient Egypt." *Gender & History*, 32.1, 168–188.

Dieleman, Jacco (1998) "Fear of Women? Representations of Women in Demotic Wisdom Texts." *Studien zur Altägyptishen Kultur*, 25, 7–46.

Dijkstra, M. (1994) "The Myth of Astarte, the Huntress (KTU 1.92): New Fragments." *Ugarit Forschungen*, 26, 113–126.

Dorman, Peter F. (2005) "Hatshepsut: Princess to Queen to Co-Ruler." In C.H. Roehrig (ed.) *Hatshepsut: From Queen to Pharaoh*. The Metropolitan Museum of Art, New York, NY, 87–89.

Dover, Kenneth (1978/1989) *Greek Homosexuality*. Harvard University Press, Cambridge, MA.

Dowson, Thomas A. (2008) "Queering Sex and Gender in Ancient Egypt." In C. Graves-Brown (ed.) *Sex and Gender in Ancient Egypt: 'Don Your Wig for a Joyful Hour'*. The Classical Press of Wales, Swansea, Wales, 27–46.

Dunham, Dows and M.F. Laming Macadam (1949) "Names and Relationships of the Royal Family of Napata." *Journal of Egyptian Archaeology*, 35, 139–149.

Ebeling, Jennie (2016) "Engendering the Israelite Harvests." *Near Eastern Archaeology*, 79.3, 186–194.

Ebeling, Jennie R. and Michael M. Homan (2008) "Baking and Brewing Beer in the Israelite Household: A Study of Women's Cooking Technology." In Beth Alpert Nakhai (ed.) *The World of Women in the Ancient and Classical Near East*. Cambridge Scholars Publishing, Newcastle upon Tyne, UK, 45–62.

Exum, J. Cheryl (1992) *Tragedy and Biblical Narrative: Arrows of the Almighty*. Cambridge University Press, Cambridge, UK.

Eyre, C.J. (1984) "Crime and Adultery in Ancient Egypt." *The Journal of Egyptian Archaeology*, 70, 92–105.

Fairservis Jr., W.A. (1991) "A Revised View of the Na'rmr Palette." *Journal of the American Research Center in Egypt*, 28, 1–20.

Faulkner, Raymond O. (2007) *The Ancient Egyptian Pyramid Texts*. Digireads.com Publishing, Stilwell, KS.

294   *Bibliography*

———. (1962) *A Concise Dictionary of Middle Egyptian.* Griffith Institute, Oxford, UK.

Fausto-Sterling, Anne (2000) *Sexing the Body: Gender Politics and the Construction of Sexuality* (Revised Edition). Basic Books, New York, NY.

———. (1993) "The Five Sexes: Why Male and Female Are Not Enough." *The Sciences,* March/April, 20–25.

FHN = Fontes Historiae Nubiorum (1998) *Textual Sources for the History of the Middle Nile Region Between the Eighth Century BCE and the Sixth Century AD,* volume 1. University of Bergen, Norway.

Fischer, Henry George (2000) *Egyptian Women of the Old Kingdom and of the Heracleopolitan Period* (Second Edition). Metropolitan Museum of Art, New York, NY.

———. (1989) "Women in the Old Kingdom and the Heracleopolitan Period." In B.S. Lesko (ed.) *Women's Earliest Records from Ancient Egypt and Western Asia.* Scholars Press, Atlanta, GA, 5–30.

Foster, Benjamin R. (1993) *Before the Muses: An Anthology of Akkadian Literature.* CDL Press, Bethesda, MD.

Foster, John L. (1974) *Love Songs of the New Kingdom.* Charles Scribner's Sons, New York, NY.

Frankel, David and Angela Tamvaki (1973) "Cypriot Shrine Models and Decorated Tombs." *Australian Journal of Biblical Archaeology,* 2, 39–44.

Frayne, Douglas R. (1998) *The Royal Inscriptions of Mesopotamia Early Periods/Volume 1: Presargonic Period (2700–2350 BC).* University of Toronto Press, Toronto, CA.

Frymer-Kensky, Tikva (1992) *In the Wake of the Goddesses: Women, Culture, and the Biblical Transformation of Pagan Myth.* Fawcett Columbine, New York, NY.

Gatens, M. 1996. *Imaginary Bodies: Ethic, Power and Corporeality.* Routledge Press, New York, NY.

Gawlikowska, K. (1980) "Eshtar et Ishtar à Mari au IIIè millenaire." *Rocznik Orientalistyczny* 41.2, 25–28.

Gaylord, Kristen (2015) "A Royal Queer: Hatshepsut and Gender Construction in Ancient Egypt." *Shift,* 8, 49–59.

George, Andrew R. (2003) *The Babylonian Gilgamesh Epic: Introduction, Critical Edition and Cuneiform Texts.* Oxford University Press, Oxford, UK.

———. (1999) *The Epic of Gilgamesh: The Babylonian Epic Poem and Other Texts in Akkadian and Sumerian.* Penguin Books, London, UK.

Goedicke, Hans (1967) "Unrecognized Sportings." *Journal of the American Research Center in Egypt,* 6, 97–102.

Grabbe, Lester L. (2011) "The Case of the Corrupting Consensus." In B. Becking and L.L. Grabbe (eds.) *Between Evidence and Ideology: Essays on the History of Ancient Israel Read at the Joint Meeting of the Society for Old Testament Study and the Oud Testamentisch Werkgezelschap, Lincoln, July 2009,* OTS 59. Brill, Leiden, 83–92.

Graves-Brown, Carolyn (ed.) (2008) *Sex and Gender in Ancient Egypt: 'Don Your Wig for a Joyful Hour.'* The Classical Press of Wales, Swansea.

Grayson, A. Kirk (1995) "Eunuchs in Power: Their Role in the Assyrian Bureaucracy." In M. Dietrich and O. Loretz (eds.) *Vom Alten Orient zum Alten Testament: Festschrift fur Wolfram Freihern von Soden zum 85. Geburtstag am 19. Juni 1993.* AOAT 240, Neukirchener Verlag, Neukirchen-Vluyn, 85–98.

Greenberg, David F. (1988) *The Construction of Homosexuality.* University of Chicago Press, Chicago, IL.

Grémaux, René (1994) "Woman Becomes Man in the Balkans." In Gilbert Herdt (ed.) *Beyond Sexual Dimorphism in Culture and History.* Zone Books, New York, NY, 241–281.

Groß, Melanie and Reinhard Pirngruber (2014) "On Courtiers in the Neo-Assyrian Empire: *ša-rēši* and *mazzāa pāni*." *Altorientalische Forschungen*, 41.2, 161–175.

Grosz, E. 1994. *Volatile Bodies: Towards a Corporeal Feminism.* Indiana University Press, Bloomington, IN.

Guinan, Ann K. (1998/1997) "Auguries of Hegemony: The Sex Omens of Mesopotamia." In M. Wyke (ed.) *Gender and the Body in the Ancient Mediterranean.* Blackwell Publishers, Oxford, UK, 38–55. (Reprint of 1997 publication in *Gender & History* 9.3, 462–479.)

Guinan, Ann K. and Peter Morris (2017) Mesopotamia before and after Sodom: Colleagues, Crack Troops, Comrades-in-Arms." In I. Zsolnay (ed.) *Being a Man: Negotiating Ancient Constructs of Masculinity.* Routledge, London, UK, 150–175.

Hackett, Jo Ann (1989) "Can a Sexist Model Liberate Us? Ancient Near Eastern 'Fertility' Goddesses." *Journal of Feminist Studies in Religion,* 5.1, 65–76.

Hadjicosti, Maria (2002) "Evidence of Gender and Family Relations in a Tomb of the Cypro-Archaic I Period." In D. Bolger and N. Serwint (eds.) *Engendering Aphrodite: Women and Society in Ancient Cyprus,* CAARI monograph vol. 3. ASOR, Boston, MA, 133–142.

Halperin, David M (1990) *One Hundred Years of Homosexuality.* Routledge, London, UK.

Hamilton, Naomi (2000) "Ungendering Archaeology: Concepts of Sex and Gender in Figurine Studies in Prehistory." In M. Donald and L. Hurcombe (eds.) *Representations of Gender from Prehistory to the Present.* St. Martin's Press, Inc., New York, NY, 17–30.

Handy, Lowell K. (1994) *Among the Host of Heaven: The Syro-Palestinian Pantheon as Bureaucracy.* Eisenbrauns, Winona Lake, IN.

Harris, Rivkah (2000) *Gender and Aging in Mesopotamia: The* Gilgamesh Epic *and Other Ancient Literature.* University of Oklahoma Press, Norman, OK.

Hays, Harold M. (2012) *The Organization of the Pyramid Texts.* Brill Publishers, Leiden.

Hedenstierna-Jonson, Charlotte *et al.* (2017) "A Female Viking Warrior Confirmed by Genomics." *American Journal of Physical Anthropology,* 164, 853–860.

Henshaw, Richard A. (1994) *Female and Male: The Cultic Personnel: The Bible and the Rest of the Ancient Near East.* Princeton Theological Monograph Series. Pickwick Publications, Princeton, NJ.

Hillers, Delbert R. (1973) "The Bow of Aqhat: The Meaning of a Mythological Theme." In H.A. Hoffner (ed.) *Orient and Occident: Essays Presented to C.H. Gordon.* AOAT 22. Neudirchen-Vluyn, Neukirchener, 71–80.

Hoffner, Harry A. Jr. (1998) *Hittite Myths* (Second Edition). Scholars Press, Atlanta.

———. (1997) *The Laws of the Hittites: A Critical Edition.* Brill, Leiden.

———. (1987) "Paskuwatti's Ritual against Sexual Impotence (CTH 406)." *Aula Orientalis,* 5, 271–287.

———. (1973) "Incest, Sodomy and Bestiality in the Ancient Near East." In H.A. Hoffner (ed.) *Orient and Occident: Essays Presented to C.H. Gordon.* AOAT 22. Neudirchen-Vluyn, Neukirchener, 81–90.

———. (1966) "Symbols for Masculinity and Femininity: Their Use in Ancient Near Eastern Sympathetic Magic Rituals. *Journal of Biblical Literature,* 85.3, 326–334.

Hollis, Susan Tower (1990) *The Ancient Egyptian "Tale of Two Brothers": The Oldest Fairy Tale in the World.* University of Oklahoma Press, Norman, OK.

Hutton, Ronald (2019) *The Triumph of the Moon* (New Edition). Oxford University Press, Oxford, UK.

Hyde, Janet Shibley (2005) "The Gender Similarities Hypothesis." *American Psychologist,* 60.6, 581–592.

296 Bibliography

Jacobsen, Thorkild (1987) *The Harps That Once . . .: Sumerian Poetry in Translation*. Yale University Press, New Haven, CT.

Jones, Philip (2003) "Embracing Inana: Legitimation and Mediation in the Ancient Mesopotamian Sacred Marriage Hymn Iddin-Dagan A." *Journal of the American Oriental Society*, 123.2, 291–302.

Justel, Josué J. (2016) "Women, Gender and Law at the Dawn of History." In S.L. Budin and J. MacIntosh Turfa (eds.) *Women in Antiquity: Real Women Across the Ancient World*. Routledge, London, 77–100.

———. (2014) *Mujeres y derecho en el Próximo Oriente Antiguo: La presencia de mujeres en los textos jurídocos cuneiformes del segundo y primer milenios a.C.* Libros Pórtico, Zaragoza.

———. (2014a) "Women and Family in the Legal Documentation of Emar (With Additional Data from Other Late Bronze Age Syrian Archives)." *KASKAL*, 11, 57–84.

———. (2008) *La Posicíon jurídica de la mujer en Siria durante el Bronce Final: Estudios de las estratagias familiars y de la mujer como sujeto y objeto de derecho*. Instituto de Estudios Islámicos y del Oriente Próximo, Zaragoza.

Kapparis, Konstantinos (2019) *Prostitution in the Ancient Greek World*. De Gruyter, Berlin.

Karageorghis, Jacqueline (1992) "On Some Aspects of Chalcolithic Religion in Cyprus." *Report. Department of Antiquities of Cyprus*, 1992, 17–27.

———. (1977) *La grande déesse de Chypre et son Culte à travers l'iconographie de l'époque néolithique au VIème s. a.C.* Maison de l'Orient Mediterranéen Ancien, Lyons.

Karageorghis, Vassos (2000) *Ancient Art from Cyprus: The Cesnola Collection in the Metropolitan Museum of Art*. The Metropolitan Museum of Art, New York, NY.

———. (1991) *The Coroplastic Art of Ancient Cyprus, Volume I. Chalcoloithic – Late Cypriote I*. A.G. Leventis Foundation, Nicosia.

———. (1975) "Kypriaka II: A. Five terracotta figurines in the K. Severis Collection." *Report. Department of Antiquities of Cyprus*, 58–62.

Keel, Othmar and Christophe Uehlinger (1998) *Gods, Goddesses, and Images of God in Ancient Israel*. Fortress Press, Minneapolis, MN.

Keller, Cathleen A. (2005) "The Statuary of Hatshepsut." In C.H. Roehrig (ed.) *Hatshepsut: From Queen to Pharaoh*. The Metropolitan Museum of Art, New York, NY, 158–164.

———. (2005a) "Hatshepsut's Reputation in History." In C.H. Roehrig (ed.) *Hatshepsut: From Queen to Pharaoh*. The Metropolitan Museum of Art, New York, NY, 294–297.

Kelly-Buccellati, Marilyn (2010) "Uqnitum and Tar'um-Agade: Patronage and Portraiture at Urkesh." In J.C. Finke (ed.) *Festschrift für Gernot Wilhelm anläßlich seines 65. Geburtstages am 28. Januar 2010*. ISLET, Dresden, 185–202.

———. (1998) "The Workshops of Urkesh." In G. Buccellati and M. Kelly-Buccellati (eds.) *Urkesh and the Hurrians: Studies in Honor of Lloyd Cotsen*. Udena Publications, Malibu, 35–50.

Kemp, Barry J. (2006) *Ancient Egypt: Anatomy of a Civilization* (Second Edition). Routledge, New York.

King, Helen (2016) *The One-Sex Body on Trial: The Classical and Early Modern Evidence*. Routledge, London, UK.

———. (1983) "Bound to Bleed: Artemis and Greek Women." In A. Cameron and A. Kuhrt (eds.) *Images of Women in Antiquity*. Wayne State University Press, Detroit, 109–127.

Kirova, Milena (2020) *Performing Masculinity in the Hebrew Bible*. Sheffield Phoenix Press, Sheffield, UK.

Klein, Jacob (1981) "The Royal Hymns of Shulgi King of Ur: Man's Quest for Immortal Fame." *Transactions of the American Philosophical Society*, 71.7, 1–48.

Knapp, A. Bernard and Lynn Meskell (1997) "Bodies of Evidence on Prehistoric Cyprus." *Cambridge Archaeological Journal*, 7:2, 183–204.

Kramer, Samuel N. (1985) "BM 23631: Bread for Enlil, Sex for Inanna." *Orientalia*, Nova Series, 54.1/2, 117–132.

Laboury, Dimitri (2014) "How and Why Did Hatshepsut Invent the Image of Her Royal Power?" In J.M. Galán, B.M Bryan, and P.F. Dorman (eds.) *Creativity and Innovation in the Reign of Hatshepsut*. Oriental Institute of Chicago, Chicago, IL, 49–91.

Lambert, W.G. (1999) Review of "Groneberg, B.R.M. *Lob der Ištar. Gebet und Ritual an die altbabylonische Venusgöttin. Tanatti Ištar.* (Cuneiform Monographs 8)." *Archiv für Orientforschung*, 46–47, 274–277.

———. (1996) *Babylonian Wisdom Literature*. Eisenbrauns, Winona Lake, IN.

———. (1992) "Prostitution." *Xenia*, 32, 127–157.

———. (1987) "Goddesses in the Pantheon: A Reflection of Women in Society?" In J.-M. Durand (ed.) *Compte Rendu de la XXXIIIe Rencontre Assyriologique Internationale.* Editions Recherche sur les Civilisations, Paris, 125–130.

———. (1985) "The Pantheon of Mari." *M.A.R.I.*, 4, 525–540.

Langlois, Anne-Isabelle (2016) "The Female Tavern-Keeper in Mesopotamia." In S.L. Budin and J. MacIntosh Turfa (eds.) *Women in Antiquity: Real Women across the Ancient World*. Routledge, London, UK, 113–125.

Laqueur, Thomas (1992) *Making Sex: Body and Gender from the Greeks to Freud*. Harvard University Press, Cambridge, MA.

Leick, Gwendolyn (1994) *Sex and Eroticism in Mesopotamian Literature*. Routledge, London, UK.

Lemke-Santangelo, Gretchen (2009) *Daughters of Aquarius: Women of the Sixties Counterculture*. University Press of Kansas, Lawrence, KS.

Lesko, Barbara S. (1999) *The Great Goddesses of Egypt*. University of Oklahoma Press, Norman, OK.

Levine, Baruch (2002) "'Seed' versus 'Womb': Expressions of Male Dominance in Biblical Israel." In S. Parpola and R.M. Whiting (eds.) *Sex and Gender in the Ancient Near East*. Neo-Assyrian Text Corpus Project, Helsinki, 337–344.

Li, Jean (2017) *Women, Gender and Identity in Third Intermediate Period Egypt: The Theban Case Study*. Routledge, London, UK.

Lichtheim, Miriam (2006) *Ancient Egyptian Literature*, vols. 1–3. University of California Press, Berkeley.

Lion, Brigitte (2011) "Literacy and Gender." In K. Radner and E. Robson (eds.) *The Oxford Handbook of Cuneiform Culture*. Oxford University Press, Oxford, UK, 90–112.

———. (2009) "Sexe et Genre (1)." *Topoi*, Supplement 10, 9–25.

Lion, Brigitte and Cécile Michel (eds.) (2016) *The Role of Women in Work and Society in the Ancient Near East*. De Gruyter, Berlin.

Lipka, Hilary (2017) "Shaved Beards and Bared Buttocks: Shame and the Undermining of Masculine Performance in Biblical Texts." In I. Zsolnay (ed.) *Being a Man: Negotiating Ancient Constructs of Masculinity*. Routledge, London, UK, 176–197.

Lloyd, Jeffrey B. (1994) *The Goddess Anat: An Examination of the Textual and Iconographic Evidence from the Second Millennium B.C.* Ph.D. Dissertation, University of Edinburgh, Edinburgh.

Lohwasser, Angelika (2021) "The Role and Status of Royal Women of Kush." In Elizabeth Carney and Sabine Müller (eds.) *The Routledge Companion to Women and Monarchy*. Routledge, London, UK, 61–72.

298   *Bibliography*

———. (2001) "Queenship in Kush: Status, Role, and Ideology of Royal Women." *JARCE*, 38, 61–76.

López-Bertran, Mireia and Agnès Garcia-Ventura (2016) "The Use of Facial Characteristics as Engendering Strategies in Phoenician-Punic Studies." *Near Eastern Archaeology*, 79.3, 206–213.

Maccoby, Eleanor Emmons and Carol Nagy Jacklin (1974) *The Psychology of Sex Differences*. Stanford University Press, Stanford, CA.

Masson, O. (1973) "Remarques sur les Cultes Chypriotes à l'Époque du Bronze Recent." In *Acts of the International Archaeological Symposium "The Mycenaeans in the Eastern Mediterranean"*. Nicosia 27th March—2nd April 1972. Dept. of Antiquities, Cyprus, Nicosia, 110–121.

Masterson, Mark, Nancy Sorkin Rabinowitz, James Robson, and Lloyd Llewellyn-Jones (2015) "Introduction." In Mark Masterson, Nancy Sorkin Rabinowitz, and James Robson (eds.) *Sex in Antiquity*. Routledge Press, New York, NY, 1–12.

Matić, Uroš (2021) *Violence and Gender in Ancient Egypt*. Routledge, London, UK.

Matuszak, Jana (2018) "Assessing Misogyny in Sumerian Disputations and Diatribes." In S.L. Budin, M. Cifarelli, A. Garcia-Ventura, and A. Millet Albà (eds.) *Gender and Methodology in the Ancient Near East: Approaches from Assyriology and Beyond*. Universitat de Barcelona, Barcelona, 259–272.

———. (2016) "'She Is Not Fit for Womanhood': The Ideal Housewife According to Sumerian Literary Texts." In B. Lion and C. Michel (eds.) *The Role of Women in Work and Society in the Ancient Near East*. Walter de Gruyter, Berlin, 228–254.

Mayor, Adrienne (2016) "Warrior Women: The Archaeology of Amazons." In S.L. Budin and J. MacIntosh Turfa (eds.) *Women in Antiquity: Real Women across the Ancient World*. Routledge, London, UK, 969–985.

McCaffrey, Kathleen (2017) "Gendering for Fortune and Misfortune: Ritual Gender Assignment in the Ancient Near East." In O. Drewnowska and M. Sandowicz (eds.) *Fortune and Misfortune in the Ancient Near East*. Eisenbrauns, Winona Lake, IN, 75–96.

———. (2002) "Reconsidering Gender Ambiguity in Mesopotamia: Is a Beard Just a Beard?" In S. Parpola and R.M. Whiting (eds.) *Sex and Gender in the Ancient Near East*. Neo-Assyrian Text Corpus Project, Helsinki, 379–392.

McDowell, A.G. (1999) *Village Life in Ancient Egypt: Laundry Lists and Love Songs*. Oxford University Press, Oxford, UK.

Meier, Samuel A. (2000) "Diplomacy and International Marriages." In Raymond Cohen and Raymond Westbrook (eds.) *Amarna Diplomacy: The Beginnings of International Relations*. Johns Hopkins University Press, Baltimore, MD, 165–173.

Merrillees, R.S. (1980) "Representations of the Human Form in Prehistoric Cyprus." *Opuscula Atheniensia*, 13, 171–184.

Meskell, Lynn and Rosemary Joyce (2003) *Embodied Lives: Figuring Ancient Maya and Egyptian Experience*. Routledge, New York, NY.

Meyers, Carol (2013) *Rediscovering Eve: Ancient Israelite Women in Context*. Oxford University Press, Oxford, UK.

———. (2003) "Material Remains and Social Relations: Women's Culture in Agrarian Households of the Iron Age." In William G. Dever and Seymour Gitin (eds.) *Symbiosis, Symbolism, and the Power of the Past: Canaan, Ancient Israel, and Their Neighbors from the Late Bronze Age Through Roman Palestine*. Eisenbrauns, Winona Lake, IN, 425–444.

Michalowski, Piotr (2006) "Love or Death? Observations on the Role of the Gala in Ur III Ceremonial Life." *Journal of Cuneiform Studies*, 58, 49–61.

Bibliography 299

Michel, Cécile (2020) *Women of Assur and Kanesh: Texts from the Archives of Assyrian Merchants*. SBL Press, Atlanta, GA.

———. (2016) "Women Work, Men are Professional in the Old Assyrian Archives." In Lion and Michel (eds.) *The Role of Women in Work and Society in the Ancient Near East*. Walter de Gruyter, Berlin, 193–208.

———. (2001) *Correspondance des marchands de Kanish*. LAPO 19. Éditions du Cerf, Paris.

———. (2000) "À propos d'un testament paleo-assyrien" Une femme de marchand <<père et mère>> des capitaux." *Revue d'Assyriologie et d'Archéologie orientale*, 94, 1–10.

Miller, Jared L. (2010) "Paskuwatti's Ritual: Remedy for Impotence or Antidote to Homosexuality?" *Journal of Ancient Near Eastern Religions*, 10.1, 83–89.

Minas Belmont, Ann (1993) *Gender Basics: Feminist Perspectives on Women and Men*. Wadsworth, Belmost, CA.

Mogelonsky, Marcia K. (1988) *Early and Middle Cypriot Terracotta Figurines*. Ph.D. Dissertation, Cornell University, New York.

Money, John, Joan G. Hampson, and John L. Hampson (1957) "Imprinting and the Establishment of Gender Role." In *A.M.A. Archives of Neurology and Psychiatry*, 333–336.

Montet, Pierre (1957) "Le Pharaon et le Général: CONTE." *Revue de l'histoire des religions*, 152.1, 1–7.

Moore, Celia L. (2000) "Review Work: Sexing the Body: Gender Politics and the Construction of Sexuality by Anne Fausto-Sterling." *American Scientist*, 88.6, 554–555.

Moorey, P.R.S. (2001) *Ancient Near Eastern Terracottas: With a Catalogue of the Collection in the Ashmolean Museum, Oxford*. Ashmolean Museum, Oxford, UK.

Morris, Desmond (1985) *The Art of Ancient Cyprus*. Phaidon Press, Oxford.

Morris, Ellen (2013) "Propaganda and Performance at the Dawn of the State." In J.A. Hill, P. Jones, and A.J. Morales (eds.) *Experiencing Power, Generating Authority: Cosmos, Politics, and the Ideology of Kingship in Ancient Egypt and Mesopotamia*. University of Pennsylvania Museum of Archaeology and Anthropology, Philadelphia, PA, 33–64.

Muller, Virginie (2016) "Women and their Activities in Divinatory Texts." In B. Lion and C. Michel (eds.) *The Role of Women in Work and Society in the Ancient Near East*. Walter de Gruyter, Berlin, 429–446.

Niederreiter, Zoltán (2015) "Cylinder Seals of Eleven Eunuchs (*Ša Rēši* Officials): A Study on Glyptics Dated to the Reign of Adad-Nērārī III." In N.N. May and S. Svärd (eds.) *State Archives of Assyria Bulletin* 21. S.A.R.G.O.N. Editrice e Libreria, Padua, 117–156.

Nissinen, Martti (2003) *Prophet and Prophecy in the Ancient Near East*. Society of Biblical Literature, Atlanta, GA.

———. (2001) "Akkadian Rituals and Poetry of Divine Love." In R.M. Whiting (ed.) *Melammu Symposia* 2. The Neo-Assyrian Text Project, Helsinki, 93–136.

———. (1998) *Homoeroticism in the Biblical World: A Historical Perspective*. Fortress Press, Minneapolis, MN.

Nissinen, Martti and Risto Uro (2008) *Sacred Marriages: The Divine-Human Sexual Metaphor from Sumer to Early Christianity*. Eisenbrauns, Winona Lake, IN.

Nordbladh, Jarl and Tim Yates (1991) "This Perfect Body, This Virgin Text: Between Sex and Gender in Archaeology." In Ian Bapty and Tim Yates (ed.) *Archaeology After Structuralism: Post-Structuralism and the Practice of Archaeology*. Routledge Press, London, 222–239.

N'Shea, Omar (2018) "Empire of the Surveilling Gaze: The Masculinity of King Sennacherib." In S. Svärd and A. Garcia-Ventura (eds.) *Studying Gender in the Ancient Near East*. Eisenbrauns, University Park, PA, 315–335.

300 Bibliography

———. (2016) "Royal Eunuchs and Elite Masculinity in the Neo-Assyrian Empire." *Near Eastern Archaeology*, 79.3, 214–221.

Oakley, Ann (1972) *Sex, Gender, and Society*. Ashgate Publishing, London.

Olyan, Saul M. (2006) "'Surpassing the Love of Women': Another Look at 2 Samuel 1:26 and the Relationship of David and Jonathan." In M.D. Jordan, M.T. Sweeney, and D.M. Mellott (eds.) *Authorizing Marriage? Canon, Tradition, and Critique in the Blessing of Same-Sex Unions*. Princeton University Press, Princeton, NJ, 7–16.

———. (1994) "'And with a Male You Shall Not Lie the Lying down of a Woman': On the Meaning and Significance of Leviticus 18:22 and 20:13." *Journal of the History of Sexuality*, 5.2, 179–206.

Orphanides, A.G. (1983) *Bronze Age Anthropomorphic Figurines in the Cesnola Collection at the Metropolitan Museum of Art*. Paul Åströms Förlag, Göteborg.

Orriols-Llonch, Marc (forthcoming) "External Male Genitalia Semograms (D52, D53) in the Pyramid Texts." In J. Cervelló Autuori and M. Orriols-Llonch (eds.) *Signs, Language, and Culture. The Semograms of the Pyramid Texts Between Iconicity and Referential Reality* (Harvard Egyptological Studies). Brill, Leiden/Boston.

Ortner, Sherry B. (1974) "Is Female to Male as Nature Is to Culture?" In M.Z. Rosaldo and L. Lamphere (eds.) *Woman, Culture, and Society*. Stanford University Press, Stanford, CA, 67–88.

Paradise, Jonathan (1987) "Daughters as 'Sons' at Nuzi." In D.I. Owen and M.A. Morrison (eds.) *Studies on the Civilization and Culture of Nuzi and the Hurrians*, vol. 2. Eisenbrauns, Winona Lake, IN, 203–213.

———. (1980) "A Daughter and Her Father's Property at Nuzi." *Journal of Cuneiform Studies*, 32.4, 189–207.

Parker, Simon (ed.) (1997) *Ugaritic Narrative Poetry*. Scholars Press, Atlanta, GA.

Parkinson, R.B. (2008) "Boasting about Hardness: Constructions of Middle Kingdom Masculinity." In C. Graves-Brown (ed.) *Sex and Gender in Ancient Egypt: 'Don Your Wig for a Joyful Hour'*. The Classical Press of Wales, Swansea, Wales, 115–142.

———. (1995) "'Homosexual' Desire and Middle Kingdom Literature." *The Journal of Egyptian Archaeology*, 81, 57–76.

Parpola, Simo (1997) *Assyrian Prophecies*. Helsinki University Press, Helsinki.

Parrot, André *et al.* (1967) *Mission Archéologique de Mari, Vol. III: Les Temples d'Ishtarat et de Ninni-Zaza*. Librarie Orientaliste Paul Geutner, Paris.

Paul, S.M. 2002. "The Shared Legacy of Sexual Metaphors and Euphemisms in Mesopotamian and Biblical Literature." In S. Parpola and R.M. Whiting (eds.) *Sex and Gender in the Ancient Near East*. Neo-Assyrian Text Corpus Project, Helsinki, 489–498.

Peled, Ilan (2016) *Masculinities and Third Gender: The Origins and Nature of an Institutionalized Gender Otherness in the Ancient Near East*. Ugarit-Verlag, Münster.

———. (2010) "Expelling the Demon of Effeminacy: Anniwiyani's Ritual and the Question of Homosexuality in Hittite Thought." *Journal of Ancient Near Eastern Religions*, 10.1, 69–81.

Pinch, Geraldine (1983) "Childbirth and Female Figurines at Deir el-Medina and el-'Amarna." *Orientalia*, 52, 405–414 and Pl. V—VI.

Pongratz-Leisten, Beate (2008) "Sacred Marriage and the Transfer to Divine Knowledge: Alliances between the Gods and the King in Ancient Mesopotamia." In M. Nissinen and R. Uro (eds.) *Sacred Marriages: The Divine-Human Sexual Metaphor from Sumer to Early Christianity*. Eisenbrauns, Winona Lake, IN, 43–73.

Posener, Georges (1957) "Le Conte de Néferkarè et du Général Siséné." *Revue d'égyptologie*, 11, 119–137.

Bibliography 301

Price, Neil et al. (2019) "Viking Warrior Women? Reassessing Birka Chamber Grave Bj.581." *Antiquity*, 93, 181–198.

Puhvel, Jan (2002) "*Genus* and *Sexus* in Hittite." In S. Parpola and R.M. Whiting (eds.) *Sex and Gender in the Ancient Near East*. Neo-Assyrian Text Corpus Project, Helsinki, 547–550.

Reade, Julian E. (1995) "Reliefs and Sculptures: Reign of Ashurbanipal." In J.E. Curtis and J.E. Reade (eds.) *Art and Empire: Treasures from Assyria in the British Museum*. Metropolitan Museum of Art, New York, NY, 72–91.

Reeder, Greg (2008) "Queer Egyptologies of Niankhkhnum and Khnumhotep." In C. Graves-Brown (ed.) *Sex and Gender in Ancient Egypt: 'Don Your Wig for a Joyful Hour'*. The Classical Press of Wales, Swansea, Wales, 143–156.

———. (2000) "Same-Sex Desire, Conjugal Constructs, and the Tomb of Niankhkhnum and Khnumhotep." *World Archaeology*, 32.2, 193–208.

Reiner, Erica (1974) "A Sumero-Akkadian Hymn of Nanâ." *Journal of Near Eastern Studies*, 33.2, 221–236.

Ribeiro, Eleanor C. (2002) "Altering the Body: Representations of Pre-Pubescent Gender Groups on Early and Middle Cypriot 'Scenic Compositions'." In D. Bolger and N. Serwint (eds.) *Engendering Aphrodite: Women and Society in Ancient Cyprus*. ASOR Archaeological Reports, Boston, MA, 197–210.

Robins, Gay (2008) "Male Bodies and the Construction of Masculinity in New Kingdom Egyptian Art." In S.H. D'Auria (ed.) *Servant of Mut: Studies in Honor of Richard A. Fazzini*. Brill, Leiden, 208–215.

———. (1999) "Hair and the Construction of Identity in Ancient Egypt, c. 1480–1350 B.C." *Journal of the American Research Center in Egypt*, 36, 55–69.

———. (1999a) "The Names of Hatshepsut as King." *The Journal of Egyptian Archaeology*, 85, 103–112.

———. (1996) "Dress, Undress, and the Representation of Fertility and Potency in New Kingdom Egyptian Art." In N.B. Kampen (ed.) *Sexuality in Ancient Art*. Cambridge University Press, Cambridge, UK, 27–40.

———. (1993) *Women in Ancient Egypt*. Harvard University Press, Cambridge, MA.

Rodden Robinson, Tara (2010) *Genetics for Dummies* (Second Edition). Wiley Publishing, Inc., Hoboken, NJ.

Rorabaugh, W.J. (2015) *American Hippies*. Cambridge University Press, Cambridge, UK.

Roth, Ann Macy (2006) "Little Women: Gender and Hierarchic Proportion in Old Kingdom Mastaba Chapels." In Miroslav Bárta (ed.) *The Old Kingdom Art and Archaeology: Proceedings of the Conference held in Prague, May 31–June 4, 2004*. Publishing House of the Academy of Sciences of the Czech Republic, Prague, 281–296.

———. (2005) "Gender Roles in Ancient Egypt". In Daniel C. Snell (ed.) *A Companion to the Ancient Near East*. Blackwell Publishing, Oxford, UK, 211–218.

———. (2000) "Father Earth, Mother Sky: Ancient Egyptian Beliefs about Conception and Fertility." In A. E. Rautman (ed.) *Reading the Body: Representations and Remains in the Archaeological Record*. University of Pennsylvania Press, Philadelphia, PA, 187–201.

———. (1999) "The Absent Spouse: Patterns and Taboos in Egyptian Tomb Decoration." *Journal of the American Research Center in Egypt*, 36, 37–53.

Roth, Martha T. (2014) "Women and Law." In M.W. Chavalas (ed.) *Women in the Ancient Near East: A Sourcebook*. Routledge, London, 144–174.

———. (1997) *Law Collections from Mesopotamia and Asia Minor*. Scholar's Press, Atlanta, GA.

Sax, Leonard (2002) "How Common Is Intersex? A Response to Anne Fausto-Sterling." *The Journal of Sex Research*, 39.3, 174–178.

302   *Bibliography*

Schroer, Silvia and Thomas Staubli (2000) "Saul, David and Jonathan—The Story of a Triangle? A Contribution to the Issue of Homosexuality in the First Testament." In A. Brenner (ed.) *A Feminist Companion to the Bible*. Sheffield Academic Press, Sheffield, UK, 22–36.

Sefati, Yitzhak (1998) *Love Songs in Sumerian Literature: Critical Edition of the Dumuzi-Inanna Songs*. Bar-Lina University Press, Ramat-Gan, Israel.

Shay, Jonathan (1994) *Achilles in Vietnam: Combat Trauma and the Undoing of Character*. Scribner, New York.

Siddall, Luis R. (2007) "A Re-Examination of the Title *Ša Reši* in the Neo-Assyrian Period." In J. Azize and N. Weeks (eds.) *Gilgameš and the World of Assyria*. Peeters, Leuven, 225–240.

Simpson, William K. (1973) *The Literature of Ancient Egypt*. Yale University Press, New Haven, CT.

Sjöberg, Åke W. (1975) "in-nin šà-gur₄-ra. A Hymn to the Goddess Inanna by the en-Pristess Enḫeduanna." *Zeitschrift für Assyriologie*, 65, 161–253.

Smith, Hedrick (1984) *The Russians*. Ballantine Books, New York, NY.

Smith, Mark S. (2014) *Poetic Heroes: Literary Commemorations of Warriors and Warrior Culture in the Early Biblical World*. William B. Eerdmans Publishing, Grand Rapids, MI.

———. (2002) *The Early History of God: Yahweh and the Other Deities in Ancient Israel*. William B. Eerdmans Publishing, Grand Rapids, MI.

———. (2001) *The Origins of Biblical Monotheism: Israel's Polytheistic Background and the Ugaritic Texts*. Oxford University Press, Oxford, UK.

Sofaer, Joanna (2013) "Bioarchaeological Approaches to the Gendered Body." In D. Bolger (ed.) *A Companion to Gender Prehistory*. Wiley-Blackwell, Malden, MA, 226–243.

Steinkeller, Peter and J.N. Postgate (1992) *Third-Millennium Legal and Administrative Texts in the Iraq Museum, Baghdad*. Eisenbrauns, Winona Lake, IN.

Stock, Kathleen (2021) *Material Girls: Why Reality Matters for Feminism*. Fleet Publishers, London, UK.

Stökl, Jonathan (2013) "Gender 'Ambiguity' in Ancient Near Eastern Prophecy? A Reassessment of the Data behind a Popular Theory." In J. Stökl and C.L. Carvalho (eds.) *Prophets Male and Female: Gender and Prophecy in the Hebrew Bible, the Eastern Mediterranean, and the Ancient Near East*. Society of Biblical Literature, Atlanta, GA, 59–80.

Stol, Marten (2000) *Birth in Babylonia and the Bible: Its Mediterranean Setting*. Styx Publications, Groningen.

Suter, Claudia E. (2000) *Gudea's Temple Building: The Representation of an Early Mesopotamian Ruler in Text and Image*. Styx Publications, Groningen.

Svärd, Saana (2012) *Power and Women in the Neo-Assyrian Palaces*. Ph.D. Dissertation, University of Helsinki, Helsinki.

Svärd, Saana and Agnès Garcia-Ventura (eds.) (2018) *Studying Gender in the Ancient Near East*. Eisenbrauns, University Park, PA.

Sweeney, Deborah (2016) "Women at Deir El-Medîna." In S.L. Budin and J. MacIntosh Turfa (eds.) *Women in Antiquity: Real Women across the Ancient World*. Routledge, London, UK, 243–254.

Talalay, Lauren (2005) "The Gendered Sea: Iconography, Gender, and Mediterranean Prehistory." In E. Blake and A.B. Knapp (eds.) *The Archaeology of Mediterranean Prehistory*. Blackwell Publishing, Oxford, 130–155.

———. (2000) "Archaeological Ms. conceptions: Contemplating Gender and the Greek Neolithic." In L. Hurcombe and M. Dobald (eds.) *Representations of Gender from Prehistory to the Present*. Palgrave MacMillan, London, UK, 3–16.

Bibliography 303

Talalay, Lauren E. and Tracey Cullen (2002) "Sexual Ambiguity in Plank Figures from Bronze Age Cyprus." In D. Bolger and N. Serwint (eds.) *Engendering Aphrodite: Women and Society in Ancient Cyprus*. ASOR Archaeological Reports, Boston, MA, 181–195.

Tatton-Brown, Veronica (1997) *Ancient Cyprus*. British Museum Publications. London, UK.

Tazawa, Keiko (2009) *Syro-Palestinian Deities in New Kingdom Egypt*. BAR International Series 1965. Archaeopress, Oxford, UK.

Thureau-Dangin, F. (1934) "Inscriptions Votives sur des Statuettes de Ma'eri." *RAA*, 31, 137–144.

Troy, Lana (1986) *Patterns of Queenship in Ancient Egyptian Myth and History*. University of California Press, Berkeley, CA.

Tuana, Nancy (1996) "Fleshing Gender, Sexing the Body: Refiguring the Sex/Gender Distinction." *The Southern Journal of Philosophy*, 35. Supplement, 53–71.

Van Dijk, J. (1964) "Le motif cosmique dans la pensée sumérienne." *Acta Orientalia*, 28, 1–59.

Vanstiphout, H.L.J. (1990) "The Craftmanship of Sîn-Leqi-unninni." *Orientalia Louvaniensa Periodica*, 21, 45–79.

Veldhuis, Niek (2018) "Gender Studies and Assyriology: Expectations of an Outsider." In S. Svärd and A. García-Ventura (eds.) *Studying Gender in the Ancient Near East*. Eisenbrauns, University Park, PA, 447–459.

Vernant, Jean-Pierre (1969) "Hestia-Hermes: The Religious Expression of Space and Movement among the Greeks." *Social Science Information*, 8.4, 131–168.

Von Soden, Wolfram and Joachim Oelsner (1991) "Ein spät-altbabylonisches pārum-Preislied für Ištar." *Orientalia*, Nova Series, 60.4, 339–343.

Walker, Phillip L. and Della Collins Cook (1998) "Brief Communication: Gender and Sex: Vive la Difference." *American Journal of Physical Anthropology*, 106, 255–259.

Walls, Neal H. (2001) *Desire, Discord and Death: Approaches to Ancient Near Eastern Myth*. American Schools of Oriental Research, Boston, MA.

———. (1992) *The Goddess Anat in Ugaritic Myth*. Scholars Press, Atlanta, GA.

Walters, Jonathan (1997) "Invading the Roman Body: Manliness and Impenetrability in Roman Thought." In J.P Hallett and M.B. Skinner (eds.) *Roman Sexualities*. Princeton University Press, Princeton, NJ, 29–43.

Ward, William A. (1989) "Non-Royal Women and their Occupations in the Middle Kingdom." In B.S. Lesko (ed.) *Women's Earliest Records from Ancient Egypt and Western Asia*. Scholars Press, Atlanta, GA, 33–46.

Wegner, Ilse (1981) *Gestalt und Kult der Ištar-Šawuška in Kleinasien*. Verlag Butzon & Bercker Kevelaer, Neukirchen-Vluyn.

Westenholz, Joan Goodnick (1987) "A Forgotten Love Song." In F. Rochberg-Halton (ed.) *Language, Literature, and History: Philological and Historical Studies Presented to Erica Reiner*. American Oriental Society, New Haven, CT, 415–425.

Westenholz, Joan Goodnick and Ilona Zsolnay (2017) "Categorizing Men and Masculinity in Sumer." In I. Zsolnay (ed.) *Being a Man: Negotiating Ancient Constructs of Masculinity*. Routledge Press, New York, NY, 12–41.

Wheelwright, Julie (1989) *Amazons and Military Maids: Women Who Dressed as Men in the Pursuit of Life, Liberty and Happiness*. Pandora, London, UK.

Whitehouse, Ruth D. (2007) "Gender Archaeology and Archaeology of Women: Do We Need Both?" In S. Hamilton, R.D. Whitehouse, and K.I. Wright (eds.) *Archaeology and Women: Ancient and Modern Issues*. Left Coast Press, Walnut Creek, CA, 27–40.

WHO (2014) World Health Organization "Genomic Resource Centre." www.who.int/genomics/gender/en/

304   Bibliography

Wiener, John S. (1999) "Insights into Causes of Sexual Ambiguity." *Current Opinion in Urology*, 9.6, 507–511 (n.p. in online version)

Wiggermann, Frans A.M. (2010) "Sexualität (sexuality), A: Mesopotamia." *Reallexikon der Assyriologie*, 12, 410–426.

Wilkinson, Toby A.H. (2000) "What a King Is This: Narmer and the Concept of the Ruler." *Journal of Egyptian Archaeology*, 86, 23–32.

Winter, Irene J. (1997) "Art in Empire: The Royal Image and the Visual Dimensions of Assyrian Ideology." In S. Parpola and R.M. Whiting (eds.) *Assyria 1995: Proceedings of the 10th Anniversary Symposium of the Neo-Assyrian Text Corpus Project*. University of Helsinki, Helsinki, 359–381.

———. (1985) "After the Battle Is Over: The 'Stele of the Vultures' and the Beginning of Historical Narrative in the Ancient Near East." In H. Kessler and M.S. Simpson (eds.) *Pictorial Narrative in Antiquity to the Middle Ages*. National Gallery, Washington, DC, 11–32.

Wolkstein, Diane and Samuel Noah Kramer (1983) *Inanna: Queen of Heaven and Earth: Her Stories and Hymns from Sumer*. Harper & Row Publishers, New York.

Wright, D.P. (2001) *Ritual in Narrative: The Dynamics of Feasting, Mourning, and Retaliation Rites in the Ugaritic Tale of Aqhat*. Eisenbrauns, Winona Lake, IN.

Wright, Jacob L. and Michael J. Chan (2012) "King and Eunuch: Isaiah 56:1–8 in Light of Honorific Royal Burial Practices." *Journal of Biblical Literature*, 131.1, 99–119.

Yamada, Masamichi (2016) "How to Designate Women as Having Both Genders: A Note on the Scribal Traditions in the Land of Aštata." In S. Yamada and D. Shibata (eds.) *Cultures and Societies in the Middle Euphrates and Habur Areas in the Second Millennium BC., Vol 1, Scribal Education and Scribal Traditions*. Harrassowitz Verlag, Wiesbaden, 133–143.

———. (2014) "The Women Designated 'Man and Woman' in Emar and Ekalte." In *REFEMA*. (n.p.).

Young, Antonia (2000) *Women Who Become Men: Albanian Sworn Virgins*. Berg, Oxford.

Zisa, Gioele (2021) *The Loss of Male Sexual Desire in Ancient Mesopotamia*. De Gruyter, Berlin.

Zsolnay, Ilona (2018) "Analyzing Constructs: A Selection of Perils, Pitfalls, and Progressions in Interrogating Ancient Near Eastern Gender." In S. Svärd and A. Garcia-Ventura (eds.) *Studying Gender in the Ancient Near East*. Eisenbrauns, University Park, PA, 461–479.

———. (ed.) (2017) *Being a Man: Negotiating Ancient Constructs of Masculinity*. Routledge, London, UK.

———. (2014) "Gender and Sexuality: Ancient Near East." In J. O'Brien (ed.) *The Oxford Encyclopedia of the Bible and Gender Studies*. Oxford University Press, Oxford, UK, 273–287.

———. (2013) "The Misconstrued Role of the *Assinnu* in Ancient Near Eastern Prophecy." In J. Stökl and C.L. Carvalho (eds.) *Prophets Male and Female: Gender and Prophecy in the Hebrew Bible, the Eastern Mediterranean, and the Ancient Near East*. Society of Biblical Literature, Atlanta, GA, 81–100.

Index

Abimelech 136
active/passive 60, 65–67, 193, 203, 249–252, 254, 282
Adad 147
Admonitions of Ipuwer 33
adrenogenital syndrome (AGS) *see* congenital adrenal hyperplasia (CAH)
adultery 71–72, 247, 253, 254, 255–256, 258–259, 260, 262, 269
aggression *see* violence
ahavah 277, 278, 280
Amun(-Re) 94–96, 146, 209, 225
ana martūti epešu 175, 177, 227–231, 240
Anat 51, 77, 104, 124, 135, 142, 206–211, 215, 243n109, 244n110, 244n128, 244n145
androgyny 201, 205, 210, 214, 219, 224, 248
aneuploidy 6–8
Anniwiyani's Ritual 283–284
Aqhat 147–148, 206, 208, 211
Aqhat Epic (*Tale of Aqhat*) 122, 147–148, 206, 208, 211–215
Asherah 33, 71; *see also* Athirat
Aspelta 94–96
Assinnu (SAG.UR.SAG, ^{lú}UR.MUNUS) 181, 183, 184–185, 188, 190–198, 240, 242n52, 242n64, 256–257, 272
Aššurbanipal 82, 98, 136–137, 160–161, 168
Athirat 31, 33, 71, 72–73, 77–78, 104, 124, 209; *see also* Asherah
Athtart (Aštart, Astarte) 49, 67, 72, 176, 199–201, 207, 209, 243n88, 288n137
Athtart the Huntress 67
Atrahasis 30, 32, 147, 150
Atum 30, 67, 144, 146, 149
Aya 79–80, 82, 112n69

Baal 33, 51, 67, 71, 72, 73, 76–79, 104, 123–125, 147–148, 206, 207, 208, 209, 210, 212
Baal Cycle 72–73, 76–79, 104, 123–125, 142, 147, 207, 208, 209, 214
bath 60, 65–67, 272
Bathsheba 67
beard 23, 43n110, 117, 127, 130, 160–169, 174n182, 203–204, 220, 224, 232–239
beauty 24, 54–76, 116; *see also* eroticism
biological essentialism 115
birth *see* childbirth (parturition)
Birth of the Gracious Gods 31
Book of the Dead 269
breastfeeding *see* lactation
Bromance 248, 271–281
btlt 209, 210, 211
Butler, Judith 11, 115, 225

castration 163–170, 182, 190, 196, 197, 253, 256
childbirth (parturition) 29, 34, 36, 37, 120, 149, 209
childcare 29, 34–39, 105
chromosomes 2, 37
Coffin Texts 144
complete androgen insensitivity syndrome (CAIS) 6–7
congenital adrenal hyperplasia (CAH) 7
Connell, Raewyn 9, 10, 14, 115, 118
Contendings of Horus and Seth 145, 148, 264
cosmogony 144–148
Counsels of Wisdom 153–160
cuneiform 14–16; DINGIR 182; DIŠ 16, 182; DUMU 181, 182; DUMU.MÍ 181, 182; ĜURUŠ 15–16, 23, 120, 133; KI-SIKIL 16; LÚ/LU$_2$ 15, 16, 17, 18, 24, 97, 152, 190; SAG 14–15, 16; SAL/MUNUS/MÍ 15, 16, 18,

306   *Index*

42n86, 97, 152, 181, 182, 191, 204; UR
191; UŠ/NITA/NITAḪ 15, 120, 200
Curse of Akkad 185–186

Daily Prayer to Telipinu 143
David 67, 117, 119, 148, 166, 248, 261,
271, 276–281
death 86–88
Debate between Ewe and Grain 195
Deborah 135
Deir el-Medina 89, 92, 108, 119, 151–152
Dinah 261, 286n48, 288n114
Disappearance of Telipinu 99–100
Disputation between Wood and Reed
67–68
domesticity 100–106, 135, 140, 211,
240–241n1
Dumuzi 68, 74

Eannatum 128–130
Egyptian Love Songs 66, 69–70, 74
El 31, 71, 72–73, 76–79, 104, 147, 208,
209, 210, 211, 212, 215; Ugaritic, for
Israelite (*see* God)
emotional labor 98, 100
Enki (Ea) 24, 30–31, 67, 72, 73, 74, 146,
147, 148–149, 184, 186
Enki and Ninhursag 149
Enki and Ninmah 30, 31, 144
Enki and the World Order 30, 146
Enkidu 53, 54–55, 79, 98–99, 122–123,
185, 248, 271–276
Enlil 24, 65, 67, 81, 83, 111n33, 130, 132,
146, 150
Enlil and Ninlil 65, 146
Enuma Eliš 142
Ereškigal 65–66, 73, 75, 184–185, 189
eroticism 24, 53–76, 140, 201, 202,
204, 206, 239, 251, 271, 284; sexual
enjoyment 67–71; *see also* beauty
Erra Epic 120, 188
eunuch (*ša rēši*/LÚ.SAG) 160–170, 182,
183–184, 185, 187–188, 232, 238, 239,
253–254
Eve 107, 150

Fashioning of the GALA 186
Fausto-Sterling, Anne 4, 5, 13n17
fertility 29–30, 33, 45–53, 55, 75, 76,
96, 119, 120, 121, 143, 144–150,
196, 197, 206, 208, 233, 245n192, 248,
284
fluidity (gender) 10, 11–14, 115, 118,
175–177, 210, 226, 231

GALA/*kalû* 181, 183, 184, 185–188, 189,
190, 192, 204
Geb 67, 87, 144–145, 263
generosity 155–156, 158
genetics 2
Gilgameš 79–80, 122–123, 131–132,
171n28, 248, 271–276
Gilgameš and Agga 17
Gilgameš, Enkidu, and the Netherworld 24
Gilgameš, Epic of 53, 54–55, 79–80,
98–99, 122–123, 185, 271–276
God (Israelite/Judean El, Elôhîm, LORD,
YHWH) 32–33, 142, 146–147, 149–150, 154,
156, 159, 259–263, 277, 278, 279, 280
Gudea 85–86, 192, 232, 239

Ḫannaḫanna 73, 99
ḫarīmtu 26, 28, 54–55, 98, 113n120, 120,
163, 169, 181, 188, 203, 228, 231, 240
Hathor 72, 73, 88, 100, 126, 176
Hatshepsut 29, 175, 177, 216, 218–227
Hattušili III 89, 204
Ḫebat 104, 205
Hedammu 205
hegemonic gender 29, 115–116, 117–119,
121, 138, 166, 170n14, 188, 190, 196,
225, 232, 239, 240, 251, 265
hermaphroditism *see* intersex
heteronormativity 118, 225–226, 247–248,
281, 284
heterosexuality 118, 261, 272–273, 287n49
hieroglyphs 18–20; A1 18, 20; A17 20;
A17a 20; A18 20; B1 18, 20, 270; D52
19; D53 19, 270; D280 19; N41 19, 270;
X1 19, 270
Hieros Gamos see Sacred Marriage
Hittite Laws 252–253, 260
ḫm 270–271
homosexual/ity 183, 185, 188, 193–194,
196, 197, 247–285
horus 33, 73, 87, 93, 148, 215–216, 218,
224, 263–265
ḫūrkil/ḫūrkel 252–253, 286n24
Hymn of Iddin-Dagan 189, 191
Hymn to the Aton 34

Illuyanka 99
Inana 24, 46, 50, 51, 52, 54, 68–69, 72, 73,
74, 75, 80–81, 83, 89, 120, 175, 183, 184,
186, 188, 189, 191, 192, 195, 196, 197,
198, 199–204, 206–207, 273; *see also* Ištar
Inana and Ebiḫ 189, 201
Inana Lady of Largest Heart (*Exultation of
Inana*) 183, 197, 202

Inana's Descent to the Underworld see Ištar's Descent to the Underworld
Inara 99
Instruction for Amenemope 153–160
Instruction of King Amenemhet/ Ammenemes 122, 134
Instruction of Ptahhotep 107, 153–160, 269–270
Instructions of Any 97, 153–160
Instruction of Šimâ Milkī 153–160
Instructions of Šurrupak/Šurrupag 24, 138, 153–160
intermediary 76–96, 209
intersectionality 10, 29
intersex (hermaphroditism) 4–6, 7, 8, 41n63, 178, 183, 196, 205, 232, 233–238
'iš 21, 286n41
Isis 33, 73, 87, 93, 97, 148, 215–216, 264, 265
'iššah 21
Ištar 25, 26, 46, 68–69, 72, 81, 98, 120, 135, 141, 175, 177, 181, 182, 183, 184–185, 188, 189, 190, 191, 192, 195, 197, 199–204, 205, 206–207, 215, 272, 273, 284n137; *see also* Inana
Ištar's Descent to the Underworld 184–185, 189

Jael 135, 142
Jonathan 142, 148, 248, 271, 276–281
Judges 19 260–263

kalû see GALA/*kalû*
Kamrusepa 99–100
Karum Kaneš 100, 101, 102, 105, 119, 176, 227–228
Khnumhotep 118, 265–268, 285
KI NAM-NITAH-KA 138, 142
King Cheops and the Magicians 72
Klinefelter syndrome 6
kourotrophos 34–39, 97
Kumarbi 149
Kurgarrû 181, 183, 184, 185, 188–190, 195, 196, 204

lactation 29, 36–37, 210; *see also* wet-nurse
Lament for the City of Unug 83
Lamma 83–86, 203, 283–284
Leviticus 258–260
Lion Hunt Stele 127–128
LÚ.AZLAG₂ A 152
LÚ.GAL 127, 130
LÚ.SAG *see* Eunuch

Ma'at (*maat*) 87, 133, 217, 219, 224, 268
Marduk 142
marriage 72, 88–90, 91, 141, 206, 247, 272, 273
masturbation 144, 145
maternity 55, 72, 73, 97, 100, 102, 116, 120, 139, 140, 209, 210, 211, 240
Maxims of Ptahhotep see Instruction of Ptahhotep
Medinet Habu 27, 209
Middle Assyrian Laws (MAL) 163–164, 165–166, 253–256, 258, 260
militarism (martial) 24–28, 119, 128–130, 198–199, 202, 203, 204, 205, 206, 217, 248, 276
Min 145, 146
Money, John 4, 5, 7, 41n63
motherhood *see* maternity
Mursili 131
mutual support groups 91, 105

nâku 253–256
NAM.MUNUS 23
NAM.NITAH 23, 24
Nanaya 82, 203
Narmer Palette 125–127
Nasala 94–96
nbt pr 103, 113n136
Neith 86, 100, 143, 176
neqebah 20–21
Nergal and Ereškigal 65–66
Niankhkhnum 118, 265–268, 285
Nikkal 82
Ningirsu 128–130
Ninhursag 129, 130, 149
Ninlil 65, 111n33
Ninsun 79–80, 275
Nintu 30
Nisaba 175
nk 19, 269
nourishment 76, 224; *see also* nurturing
Nubia 27, 93–96, 218; Nuri Cemetery 93–94
nurturing 96–100, 201
Nut 86, 87, 144–145

Osiris 33, 87, 146, 215–216, 218, 265

Papyrus Ashmolean 1945 108
Papyrus Bremmer-Rhind 144
Papyrus Chester Beatty VII 210
Papyrus Jumilhac 145
Papyrus Lansing 138–139, 151
parturition *see* childbirth

308   *Index*

*Paskuwatti's Ritual to the Goddess
   Ululiyassi* 25–26, 281–283
performance (gender) 10, 28, 115, 116,
   117–119, 121, 166, 170n14
phenotype 2–3
pišnātar (LU₂-*nātar*) 24, 97
pregnancy 29, 34, 37, 75, 86, 148–150,
   264, 265
professionalism 101, 119, 120, 121,
   150–153, 240–241n1
*Propitiation Ritual for the King's Sister
   Ziplandawiya* 143
prostitution/prostitute 26, 53–54, 72,
   74, 111n20, 113n120, 169, 175, 183,
   185, 188, 196, 197, 206, 256; sacred
   prostitution 46, 47, 53, 74, 181, 191,
   197, 240
Proto-Lu₂ 17
Proverbs, Book of 103–104, 154–160
Puduḫepa 89–90
Pughat 206, 211–215
Pyramid Texts 20, 33, 97, 144, 263

Qedešet 145–146
Qeh, Stele of 60, 209–210

Rameses II 89–90, 210, 270
rape 65, 111n33, 148, 149, 210, 247, 254,
   255, 257, 260–263, 269, 284, 286n49,
   288n114
reproduction *see* sexual reproduction

Sacred Marriage (*Hieros Gamos*) 50, 80–82
Šalmanezer III 162
Šamaš 155, 168, 202, 203, 275; *see also*
   Utu
Šamḫat 28, 53, 54–55, 98–99, 122, 185,
   272, 273, 274
Samsî-Addu 119, 120, 134, 167
ša rēši see Eunuch
Sargon II 165
Satire on the Trades 151
Saul 135, 142, 148, 278, 279, 280
Šauška 66, 72, 73, 104, 204–206
ša ziqni 160–162, 167
seduction 65, 205, 269, 273
self-control 119, 120, 121, 138, 153–159
semen 29–30, 130, 148, 162, 167, 259,
   264, 282
Seth 67, 148, 209, 210
sex 1–8, 14–21; biological (*see* eroticism)
Sex-determining Region Y (SRY) 3, 7
sexual reproduction 1, 29–34, 247, 252,
   273, 281

Shay, Jonathan 248, 276
Shu 30, 87, 144–145
sinnišūtu(m) 23
Sisera 135
śnt njśwt 93–95
Sobekneferu 29, 175, 177, 216–218, 226,
   227
Sodom 260–263
Song of Hedammu 66, 104, 205
Song of Kumarbi 149
Song of Songs 70–71, 74
Song of Ullikummi 205
spindle 25–26, 104, 136, 141, 281, 282
Stele of the Vultures 128–130
Šulgi 81, 82, 131–133
Šulgi O 131–132
Šulgi X 81
Šumma ālu 193–194, 256–258, 260
Sun God, the Cow, and the Fisherman 107

Tale of Aqhat see Aqhat Epic
Tale of Neferkare and General Sasenet
   268–269
Tale of Two Brothers 33, 71–72
Tamar 261
Tar'am Agade 110
Tašmetu 82
Teaching for Merikare 133–134, 153
Teaching for the Vizier Kagemni 153–160
*Teaching of the Vizier Ptahhotep see
   Instruction of Ptahhotep*
Tefnut 30, 87, 144
Telipinu 99–100, 147
Teššub 104, 205
Teumman 136–137
textiles 25, 102–103, 105, 114n139, 151;
   see also spindle
third gender 118, 169, 178, 180, 182, 190,
   196, 240, 251
Thutmosis III 216, 218, 222–224, 226
Tiamat 142
transgender 14, 176–178, 195, 202–203,
   205, 211–215
transsexual 176
transvestite 176–178, 183–184, 185,
   192, 196, 197, 205, 210, 222, 240,
   259
tukul 143
Turner's syndrome 6
Tutankhamun 137–138

Uqnitum 108–110
Ur-Nanše 238–240
Utu 24, 54, 130, 132, 138; *see also* Šamaš

violence 9, 121, 122–141, 199, 201, 204, 207, 208, 211, 282; kings and 131–136
voice: female 74, 108–110; male 28

warfare 72, 122, 211, 276
warrior 99, 120, 140, 195, 196, 198–199, 206, 207, 208, 209, 210, 214, 215, 240, 248, 259, 274, 276; *see also* militarism
weapons 55, 99, 120, 122, 123, 124, 127, 132–133, 136, 140, 141–143, 162, 165, 168, 189, 191, 198, 202, 204, 208, 211, 214, 277, 278, 279, 281, 282; *see also* TUKUL
wet-nurse 105; *see also* lactation

X Inactive-Specific Transcript (XIST) 2, 6, 40n26

Yasmah-Addu 119, 134, 167

zakar 20–21, 286n41
zikrūtu(m) 23

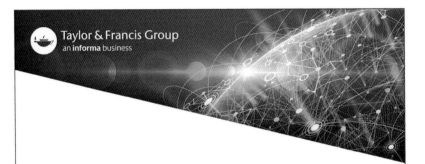